OPINIONS

ON

VARIOUS SUBJECTS

DEDICATED TO THE

INDUSTRIOUS PRODUCERS

BY

WILLIAM MACLURE

THREE VOLUMES
VOLUME II
[1837]

REPRINTS OF ECONOMIC CLASSICS

Augustus M. Kelley · Publishers
NEW YORK 1971

First Edition 1837

(New Harmony, Indiana: *Printed at the School Press*, 1837)

Reprinted 1971 by
AUGUSTUS M. KELLEY · PUBLISHERS
REPRINTS OF ECONOMIC CLASSICS
New York   New York   10001

I S B N   0 678 00712 8
L C N   68 18220

PRINTED IN THE UNITED STATES OF AMERICA
by SENTRY PRESS, NEW YORK, N. Y. 10019

Reprints of Economic Classics

OPINIONS ON VARIOUS SUBJECTS

THREE VOLUMES
VOLUME II

OPINIONS

ON VARIOUS SUBJECTS,

DEDICATED

TO THE

INDUSTRIOUS PRODUCERS.

BY

WILLIAM MACLURE.

VOL. II.

NEW-HARMONY, INDIANA.
Printed at the School press.

ADVERTISEMENT

DURING the greater part of the time these letters have been composing, the author has resided in a foreign country; they have been transmitted at irregular intervals, and generally published soon after their arrival in the Disseminator.

The publisher requests, therefore, the indulgence of the reader towards some discrepancies in the dates, and consequent inaccuracies in the connection, which the personal attendance of the author would no doubt have prevented. The same cause also will excuse a few verbal repetitions, and a return to the same subjects, as they revolve to notice, on the surface of the moral and political horizon.

June, 1837.

INDEX

	PAGE
Age of Majority	1
Advantages of Direct Taxation	6
Abuses of Government, Remedy for	3
Aristocracy, Deceptions of	268
Advantages of Equality to the Arts	294
Armies, how best to raise	315
Advantages of Small Political Associations	549, 451, 433
Armies, standing	446
raised by Conscription the best	472

B

Banking, Abuses of	51
Banks and Bank Notes	89
Efforts of, to Destroy Freedom	258
Injustice and oppression of	281
Few Chartered in Europe	307
Proper System of	319
British reform of little use to the Millions	386, 482

C

Circulating Medium, Improvement in	10
Confederate Governments, advantages of	21
Canals and Rail Roads	69
Corruption and Bribery	174
Conscription	178
Church and State	186
Statistics of	477
Civilization, progress of	253
different ideas of	272
inquires concerning the effects of	277
Charters, oppression of	281
Caricatures, utility of	378
Cheap food and drink the most useful	382
Church and State religion	467
Centralism	509
Correct Ideas, difficulty of acquiring	541

D

Disadvantages of a crowded population	2
Division of Property favorable to Freedom	14
Despotism proportioned to extent of territory	342
Difficulties of acquiring correct ideas	541

E

Errors, correction of	74
Education, National	25
Republican	145
Practical	198
Necessity of changing	210
Parental, superiority of	290
in Prussia and France	504
Equality, how to restore	549
Elective and hereditary power	402
Executive patronage	455

INDEX.

F
Freedom of the Press 37
    Progress of 45, 429, 120
Fear a concomitant of slavery 84
    destructive of freedom ib.
Few, the tyranny of 160
Fiction of Church and State 285
Impossibility of arresting the
    progress of 350
Faith, quarrels about 358
Force of public opinion 472

G
Governments, the effects of
    climate on 442

H
High salaries injurious 144
Holy Alliance 333
History, deceptions of 525

I
Interests of the Working Men 3
Inequality, Mischiefs of 29
Improvement, opposition to 60
    effected by the
    producers 95
Imprisonment for debt 103
Increase of crime, the cause of 117
Internal policy of the States 333

J
Jewish Government 128

K
Knowledge indispensible to
    Freedom 29
    Hostile to the govern-
    ments of the Few 124, 437
    in proportion to Civilization 442
    will be soon Universal 499

L
Labor the basis of wealth 114
Legislation, errors of 202
Labor, the division of 433
Learning, ostentation of 537
Language, the perversion of 227
Literary flattery 227

M
Millions, the, without sufficient
    Knowledge to govern them-
    selves 91

Monopolies prohibited 194
    of Banks 407
March of Freedom 528

N
Napoleon Code 33
National Debt, oppressions of 328
Nations behind individuals in
    change of Opinions 397
National Debt 495

O
Over-population, evils of 88
Oppression productive of free-
    dom 105
Oratory, delusive effects of 358

P
Physical improvements great-
    er than moral 1
Producers and consumers 17, 523
    ought to be the distri-
    buters of wealth 29
    Apathy of 56
    Neglect of the comfort of ib.
Power, the abuse of 169
Presidential Election 174
Paper Money 235, 240, 244, 248
    Abuse of 289
Public Lands 64
Power, intoxicating effects of
    Hereditary and elective 354
Political Economy 390
Power, division of 420
People their own Police 218

Q
Quakers, policy of 464

R
Reform, the consequences of 142
    Objects of 190
    Tardy progress of 214
Respect due to office 145
Revolutions, progress of 182
Representations to the Eye,
    advantages of 378
Ricardo and Malthus, systems
    of 491

S
Swiss Federation 51
Self-interest Political 78
Standing armies 105

INDEX.

Schools, suggestions concerning 133, 139
Suffrage, rights of 366
    Obstacles to 366
    Universal 444
Sugar tax, what for 370
Slave-holders, advice to 370
Steam facilitates Civilization 415
Selfishness the motive to action 425
Speech-making 446

T
Talents, great, not necessary to office 40
Taxation, abuses of 51
    Britain compelled to modify 67
    Indirect, expense of 67
Taxation, the proportions of 165
Temptations of Power 394
Trades' Unions 411
Trade, Free, useful to all 459
Taxation, inequality of 487

U
Uuniversal Suffrage 554

V
Veto 15, 694

W
Working Men, their true interests 227, 307
    Encroachments on 324
    Oppression of 328
    Progress of 222

MISCELLANEOUS.

AGE OF MAJORITY.—PHYSICAL IMPROVEMENTS GREATER THAN MORAL IMPROVEMENTS.

February 2, 1830.

PHYSICAL force is the first that domineers in the beginning of civilization, and continues by habit long after mankind think they have relinquished all barbarous practices. The old continue to tyrannize over the young in all countries, in proportion to the arbitary power by which they are governed. In Spain, the age at which they arrive at majority is twenty-five years; in Britain, twenty-one; but in the pure democracies of the four little Cantons of Switzerland they are admitted to all the rights of citizens at sixteen years of age. The jealousy of the old, of aspiring qualities of the young, seems to have fixed the gradation corresponding to the degree of arbitary power with which the whole are oppressed. In our country, we have copied Britain in that, as in many other customs, laws, and regulations, and fixed the age of majority at twenty-one years. Since children have escaped from the arbitary discipline of their parents and relations sooner than formerly, by the introduction of infant schools, and the adoption of systems free from punishment or coercion, whereby they acquire as much useful knowledge before they are twelve years old as they used to do at eighteen, it might perhaps be useful to follow the knowledge of the day in introducing the youth into the world earlier, and fix the age of majority nearer the age of puberty. In the savage life, the physical power is almost exhausted before the moral begins, because they benefit less by the acquirements of those who precede them. As we advance in civilization, we ought to recede from the habits and customs of the savage, and make the physical yield to the moral, whenever the latter, by early instructions, is capable to direct the former. That the corporeal has had such an undue influence over the moral, that in all our wars, pastimes and pleasures, there still remains so much of savage barbarity, must in part depend on the usurped authority of the few over the many. For, if those who assume the power to make war were obliged to fight and risk their own lives in the contest, they would be more mild, and less cruel and barbarous; as it cannot possibly be the interest of the millions, in any country, to conquer, oppress and tyrannize over the millions in any other country. All wars must be to gratify the caprice, passions, and appetites of the rulers, and must of course cease when the millions acquire a knowledge of their interest.

A CROWDED POPULATION DISADVANTAGEOUS.

February 4, 1830.

Multiply and replenish the earth, with misery and wretchedness as in China! Of all evils that torment — an over population is the most horrible in its effects. What purpose can it subserve? for whose benefit is it? to whose happiness does it add? Not to that of the millions who are crushed together so as scarcely to have the benefit of freely breathing wholesome air; half-fed, half-clothed, and worse lodged, they linger out a miserable existence; pinched of the necessaries of life, they die before half their natural life is spent. Their superiors, masters, rulers, and governors, think they gain by the number of their subjects or slaves they control and coerce. Like a farmer who pockets more money by the greater number of cattle he can bring to market; with this difference, however, that the farmer, if he over-stock his farm, loses by the poverty and death of his stock. Whereas the masters or rulers of men lose nothing. Our uninhabited, unowned, and uncultivated lands, are the patrimony of the industrious producers; but for the immense quantity of it, the stock, land, and bank speculations, would have monopolized them, and retailed them out to the poor at as high prices as they sell for in most parts of Europe; until they are all owned and cultivated, the industrious laborers cannot be poor and oppressed. It is therefore their interest to retain them in a state of nature as long as possible, however contrary it may be to the interest of the land or other speculators.

INTERESTS OF THE WORKING MEN:—THEIR POVERTY THE CONSEQUENCE OF THEIR WANT OF EDUCATION. REMEDY FOR THE ABUSES OF GOVERNMENT.

February 24, 1830.

For nearly half a century have the industrious producing classes, through the medium of universal suffrage, had the legal right and privilege of electing a vast majority of both legislators and executives, to enact laws and put into execution all that their necessities, wants or wishes required. For nearly half a century have they imprudently, indolently, and ignorantly permitted the consuming classes, who live on the produce of their labor, to legislate for the interest of their own class, by granting exclusive charters, corporations, and monopolies, heaping and fixing wealth on the already rich at the expense of the industrious laborers, endowing universities, colleges and seminaries, for the education of the children of the rich with the people's money, and neglecting to establish free schools for the instruction of the millions. It is only now that the accumulating consequence of so long and so patiently suffered injustice has brought on the pinching of poverty and starvation, that they begin to claim their long neglected rights and legal privileges of freedom and equality.

It may be a query, whether a legislature, elected to authority for a certain fixed time, have any right to make grants by privileges, by charters, or otherwise, for a period extending beyond the time they are authorized to legislate, and whether one legislature has any legal right to bind their successors by any law. Monopolies of all kinds being prohibited by the freedom and equality secured to the people by all the constitutions, all exclusive privileges ought to be considered unconstitutional in elective governments of universal suffrage, as an assumption of the powers and prerogatives of the hereditary aristocracies of Europe.

All impartial observers must have been astonished that the great class of industrious producers has permitted the consumers for so long a time to have the sole control and distribution of the wealth created by the working classes. Such long undisturbed possession as forty years, seems to have emboldened the aristocracy to claim it as an inheritance, if we may judge by the speeches of their orators, and the calumnies of their hired presses, presuming to transfer the liberties of a nation like the soil under their feet. So exactly do they copy the hereditary aristocracy of Europe, that they make use of the same abusive language in reviling their fellow-citizens, members of the same freedom and equality, with which the arbitary rulers of Europe insult their subjects. The adoption of their arbitary laws and customs, which have retained in subjection to absolute power the inhabitants of the other side of the Atlantic, would as certainly produce the same effect on this side, if continued, as that when you sow in the spring you reap in the autumn. It is high time to check the growing abuses of a monied aristocracy, and if, for want of union, (the only thing that can possibly prevent complete success,) the first attempt should fail, their future situation will be deplorable, inasmuch as the fear of reaction will force the few that have assumed the power to crush every means of opposition far below the par that hereditary aristocracy may consider their safety requires; and the situation of our laborers will hence become more miserably dependent than the wretched paupers in Europe, and with this additional sting of conscience, that it is their own fault, as they are possessed of the power of legally doing themselves justice, which a shameful ignorance of their vital interest has prevented them from putting in execution.

Where there is a great inequality of property, labor saving machinery gives additional advantages to the possessor of capital over the laborer, by affording the articles so much cheaper, that the greatest part of the profit gained by the use of machinery, is paid to the capitalist for the use of his money. This is an advantage attached to property in all situations where it can be substituted for manual labor, and the only cure in a popular government is the removing of the causes, and drying up the source of this great inequality, which originates generally either in force or fraud. Labor and industry are the only legitimate means of accumulating property. But the activity and industry of any class of men over the rest is not sufficient to create any great inequality. The power of the sword has enabled the conqueror to seize on the produce of the labor of the millions, and divide it amongst his few friends and companions. This is the origin of the great inequalities in the old world. In our country, a very small part may be owing to industry, and therefore legitimate; but nine-tenths of the inequality is owing to the injustice of those in power, granting exclusive monopolies to stock, land, and bank speculations, the profits of which enrich the few at the expense of the many. This inequality is continually augmented by the indirect taxation on consumption, burdening the great working classes with the greatest part of public expenses, which ought in justice to be borne by every one in proportion to the property protected by the government; as the greatest part of the public expenditure, is to secure the rich against the encroachments of the poor.

The stock and land speculations, have had their effects in creating an artificial inequality of property, counteracted, however, by the propensity of nature to equalize property. Three abuses still weigh heavily on the working classes; *the exclusive privileges granted to banks to stamp a piece of paper not intrinsically worth one cent, to pass current for many thousand dollars* for the benefit of the rich; *complicated, litigious,* and *expensive laws,* equally for the benefit of the rich, by placing the poor at their mercy; and *indirect taxation on consumption,* throwing the public burdens on the laborers. The *remedy for the first* would be the abolishing of bank charters, and perhaps the substituting a national bank, as recommended by President Jackson, which, if it were possible to have honestly and righteously administered, the profit on the business of the Union would pay all the expenses both of the United States and State governments. The *second abuse would be cured,* by a simple, plain, well defined code, like the code of Napoleon, which has benefited all classes in every country where it has been adopted, so as to leave no doubt of its great advantages, to all people who are wise enough to choose it for their legal guide. The *third abuse may be corrected* by a direct tax on all kinds of property; the only tax suited to the continuance of freedom and equality. All the above reforms might be made in one session, if the industrious producers would unite their suffrage at the polls *to exclude all those from the legislatures who live or benefit by the abuses.*

NECESSITY OF ECONOMY IN A REPUBLIC.—GREAT ADVANTAGE TO THE PEOPLE OF A DIRECT TAX.—MANUFACTORIES.

March 4, 1830.

The Federation of Switzerland, which has continued for five hundred years to promote and cherish the comfort and happiness of those who live under its mild sway, owes its durability, and its peaceably fulfilling all that could be expected of it, entirely to its great simplicity, and still greater economy. The Ladamman, or president of the federation, has five hundred louis d'ors or two thousand dollars per annum, and is assisted by an aid-de-camp, who has two hundred louis d'ors, or eight hundred dollars per annum, with which he performs all the duties of receiving foreign ambassadors, sending agents to foreign courts, presiding over the Diet, etc. The members of the Diet are paid by the Cantons they represent, and board and lodge in the principal families of the towns, where the Diet is alternately held, at small expense. There are no troops belonging to the federation. Every man in Switzerland is disciplined in the militia, where every citizen is a soldier and every soldier a citizen. They do duty by rotation, at all posts, strong places or fortifications. There is no indirect taxation, no customs or excise to obstruct the free circulation of either knowledge or property. They once tried the experiment of indirect tax on consumables, but found it to encourage smuggling and crime, tending to demoralize the citizens and infringe on their freedom and equality. For a law-breaker can be neither free nor independent, but must be the slave of those who hold the scourge of the law over him. The public expenses are raised by a direct tax on all species of real and personal property in every Canton, and paid into the treasury of the federation, as their exigency requires. Every thing is regulated by the strictest economy. There is no wasteful expenditure, nor extravagant show of wealth by the servants of the people at their expense; no mortifying contrasts of luxury and poverty, so irritating to the industrious producers; which accounts for the peace, order, and contentment that have so long prevailed amongst the honest and industrious inhabitants of Switzerland, whose federation unites in the bonds of friendship and strict amity all the different religions and sects, as well as the political associations of pure democracy and hereditary aristocracy.

The key stones of the federation in Switzerland are, economy, prudence and moderation; without which the federal arch, in all countries, risks the breaking down and crushing those it was intended to protect. The hereditary rulers in arbitary governments have the monopoly of pillaging and plundering the people's money as one of their most profitable privileges; but when in a popular government of universal suffrage they copy the laws, habits, or customs of hereditary aristocracy, the right of pillaging the people's money, like all other vices or virtues, pervades all classes to the smallest ramification of society, without being stopped by any dike or barrier of distinction of rank. It is the chiefs only in hereditary aristocracy that retain the perquisites of plunder. But when corruption is permitted, by the apathy of public opinion, in popular governments, the subaltern officers, as low as corporal, come in for their share; which causes all public works to cost dear, and ought to deter all free people from allowing their rulers to interfere in the improvement of roads, bridges and canals.

The only possible excuse for an indirect tax on consumption in any country, is the protection of infant manufactories from the competition of populous countries, farther advanced in the useful arts. If the small over-peopled territory of Switzerland can dispense with such a tax, certainly every other country on the globe may; because, from the poverty of their soil and climate, every inch of ground cultivated cannot support the crowded population, and manufactories are the only resource for those who cannot be maintained by the produce of the soil. Great part of their food being supplied by the surrounding and more abundant nations, makes the expense of living, and of course the price of labor, higher; necessitating a countervailing duty on foreign manufactures to enable the home fabrics to meet them on equal terms. But, say the friends of indirect taxation on this side the Atlantic, the superior knowledge, activity, and industry of the Swiss Cantons enable them to undersell their neighbors in certain manufactures, in spite of the dear living and high wages; as the inhabitants of Newfchattel, where living is still higher, are enabled to furnish the greatest part of the globe with watch movements. What can be the cause of this physical and moral superiority? Is there any other cause than the long enjoyment of more freedom than their surrounding neighbors? If so, can we, the most enlightened nation and the freest on earth, plead either ignorance or tyranny as a reason for risking the demoralization of our citizens by encouraging fraud, deception, and smuggling by an indirect tax on consumption? If there was nothing against such an unjust tax but the moral depreciation of our free citizens, it ought to be detested and abhorred by every friend to the freedom and happiness of our country. But besides the moral desolation and temptation to crime offered as a premium for breaking the laws of our free country, the consequence of the physical injustice of burdening the industrious workmen with the greatest part of public expenses is to plunge them into the gulph of poverty and ignorance; like their forefathers in Britain who, twenty years ago, did not foresee the wretchedness and misery that was to accrue from the wasteful and extravagant expenditure of the public money, the cause of the enormous taxation that now crushes the millions into starvation and despair. The effects of those causes are too slow to be perceived by the short-sighted egotist, and yet are equally certain as the accomplishment of any of nature's laws, though the distance seems so far oft as to sanction the egotism of the common saying, "it wont happen in my time, and I have no interest in any thing after I am dead."

The over-stocked population of the greatest part of the nations in Europe, where the land is so monopolized by the rich and influential, that the poor cannot own a foot. and scarcely their length and breadth at the end of their fatigue and constant toil, is a great additional reason why all classes should strive to protect manufactories, as the only means either of maintaining or employing a surplus population; but it ought to have no influence on either the governors or the governed of a country where the two-hundredth part of their rich land is neither cultivated nor inhabited, nor is like to be for many centuries to come. It is a source of nourishment and independence for the rapid increase of population of our country for many ages, relieving them from the necessity of being packed, like herring in a barrel, in the confined, unhealthy atmosphere of cotton mills, and other depositories of weakness and wickedness, which ignorance alone of their real interest could induce them to depend on for a precarious living, subject to the whims and caprices of others, whilst a vast territory is at their disposal, by universal suffrage, where they may live independent of all but their own exertions: where they may enjoy the unbounded freedom of the savage, with many of the advantages of civilization; out of the reach of many of the humiliating mortifications imposed on the laborer by the artificial craft and combinations of populous societies, where the monopoly of the few leaves little to the many. The looking up to Europe for precedent and example, is in favor of the power of the few, and as certainly against the independence of the many. The capitalist who gains cent per cent by his money invested in machinery, cares very little about hundreds of thousands who finish a life of toil and trouble by premature death, in consequence of laboring in an unhealthy trade; and whilst that class of the monied interest can obtain the majority of votes in the ballot boxes, the interest of the millions must be sacrificed to the interest of money.

IMPROVEMENT IN THE CIRCULATING MEDIUM.
March 18, 1830.

Circulating paper, while judiciously managed, is like the four wheels to a carriage; it lessens the friction of transfers and business; but when over-done, is like putting forty wheels to the carriage, which increase the friction and risk of breaking down. There are two evils to be gaurded against in circulating bank notes, or any substitute for them; first, to limit the quantity to what is necessary to transfer real sales and deliveries; and, secondly, to prevent forgeries. This can be done by adopting the mode of the Spanish rulers, by making the paper payable *to order*, in place of to bearer. Every one who passes it must indorse it and become responsible for its validity, that is, for its not being a forgery. The rogue who forged it, not having credit to pass it, the circulation would be stopped in the hands of the criminal who made it. None might be issued under fifty dollars, and all under that filled by specie. Bank post bills might be used to facilitate remittance as in Britain. This would secure the legal proprietor as well as the bank; it would take away all temptation to robbing mails, and give a security to the transfer of money that cannot possibly be obtained under the present system of notes payable to bearer.

How to prevent, by taking away the temptation, the issuing more paper than is necessary to transfer bona fide sales and deliveries, is much more difficult. The present system of chartered banks offers an immense premium to force all concerned in the management to issue as much paper as the confidence of the public will permit them. Irresponsible directors, debtors to the bank, which they repay in case of failure at an advancement of from thirty to seventy per cent, according to the depreciation of the notes, makes them gainers by the loss of the banks; whilst their only advantage, as long as it is solvent, is the amount of discounts they can divide amongst their friends, which is in proportion to the quantity of notes they can put in circulation. They are therefore forced by their interest to extend the circulation of the paper they have the distribution of as far and wide as possible. The deplorable state of a society in which there are five hundred manufactories of rag money can be easier conceived than described. Temporary remedies there are many: such as, giving no charters, and allowing the trade of the banker to be as free as any other trade; only constituting a protested note for non-payment an execution on the property, real and personal, of every one who has at any time received any part of the profits of the bank by a dividend; they might be required to give real security for the amount of notes they issued, into the hands of the governor, who would countersign these notes to that amount, and no notes to circulate without such signatures: they might be prohibited under certain penalties from discounting all fabricated paper, or wind paper as it is called in Britain, and be restricted rigorously to the discounting of notes given for property sold and delivered, as is the general regulation with all bankers in Britain.

Unless some way could be contrived to make directors of a chartered bank personally responsible for the losses that accrue by their mismanagement, there is no possibility of preventing the evils inseparable from such unlimited powers, given to whose interest forces them to abuse the trust.

A national bank, as proposed by President Jackson, would leave the profit in the hands of those who paid for it and produced it; that is, the public, and I have no doubt that this profit would equal the amount of the United States' and States' necessary expenditure. But how to ensure faithful and honest management of such a weighty and complicated concern is the vast difficulty. There is no national bank in any country, except the bank of St. Petersburgh, Vienna, Copenhagen, etc., which may be called national, as the governments have made them the medium of issuing their paper money. All the profits of the banks constituted like the banks of England and France, are for the benefit of the share-holders, the nation is only a customer like any individual who pays for his accommodation; the nation not being responsible for the paper, any more than the government of the United States is for that of the bank of the United States. A national bank of discount and deposit would be subject to the same abuse as a chartered bank. It might be possible to have an issue of paper, all the profits of which would belong to the nation, without distributing it by way of discounts to individuals. A bank of transfer and deposit, might be established by the federation in the capitol, under the control of the federal government; and the same kind of bank might be fixed in the capitol of each state, under the control of the respective states. The quantity of paper made *to order* might be limited to the sum supposed necessary to facilitate all transfers of property sold and delivered, which might be loaned on mortgages of real property, or on deposits of moveable or personal property, as is practised by the banks in Holland and Hamburgh. A scale for the valuation of such property might be published from time to time, and a list of the loans might be kept for public inspection; as there ought to be no secrets in a free country, where it is the interest of every individual to know the actual situation of every other person, all mystery is only encouraging fraud or deceit. For the facility of transporting money from one part of the Union to the other, they might have the power of issuing as many bank post bills as the public wanted, on being paid for the same; the duties on which, the loans on mortgage or deposits, might be made convenient to the finances of the bank, and a short process of bringing to sale in case of a want of punctuality, would furnish a circulating medium sufficient for all regular transfers of property, without being subject to any of the evils of a great surcharge of circulating paper, far exceeding the intrinsic value of the property to be transferred by it, which encourages hazardous speculations ending in bankruptcy. It would likewise secure the public against all losses by forgeries, and by torn and worn out paper, which cannot be less, in all the Union, than sixty millions of dollars annually. It would discourage all anticipation of riches, which tempts to extravagant expenditure at the expense of others, and would be a certain means of reducing luxuries within the limits that each individual could afford, bringing to a level that assumed superiority which false credit creates, and promoting equality, without which freedom is but a sound.

 Gold and silver, like all other property, is the representative of the quantity of labor necessary to procure it, and as such is used as a scale of value for other property. When the power or exclusive privilege is given to one or more individuals to stamp any value they please on a piece of paper intrinsically worth little or nothing, they become possessed of all the power and prerogative attached to the quantity of labor necessary to produce property to that amount.

For instance, a banker issuing paper for 10,000 dollars obtains the value of the labor necessary to produce, in the western country, 100,000 bushels of Indian corn. This, estimated at 500 bushels for each laborer on ordinary land, shows that the banker, by signing his name, in a few seconds would acquire the value of the labor of two hundred men for a year, and in proportion of every kind of work. This, though the most expeditious mode of creating a great inequality, is only one of the many hundreds restorted to by the few to rule the many. As a circulating paper is necessary to facilitate trade, and the profit arising from it is entirely owing to the public agreeing to take it at its nominal value, in common justice the public ought to reap all the benefit. The people's representatives will not do their duty if they do not endeavor to have the profits placed in the public treasury.

DIVISION OF PROPERTY FAVORABLE TO FREEDOM.—SOUTH AMERICAN GOVERNMENTS.

March 21, 1830.

Statistics is the only well-defined part of history; reduced to figures all understand it. France contains as follows:

32,000,000 inhabitants who possess an aggregate revenue of 6,396,000,000, which is divided as follows:

22,500,000,	of the poorest, at 7 sous per day, or 127 francs per annum, is	2,857,500,000
450,000	proprietors of 1000 francs per annum, is	550,000,000
300,000	of the richest class at 2,500 francs per annum, is	750,000,000
8,750,000	of the middling class at 267 francs each per annum, is	2,338,500,000
32,000,000		6,396,000,000

Such an equal division of property is scarcely to be found in any nation on earth. I wish our statistical gentlemen would attempt a statement of our relative population and revenue, if only to show the relative benefits of our revolution and that of the French. The present age divides knowledge in the same proportion. When all species of arbitary power, or hereditary monarchy, will rest on a foundation of sand that cannot possibly withstand the attacks of freedom and equality, the combination of foreign force may prolong the time of uncertain, troublesome and precarious rule, but the crisis must come. Seven hundred and fifty thousand moderately rich persons, possessing 1,200,000 francs a year, against thirty millions eight hundred thousand of working people producing all, possessed of a property of 5,196,000,000 per annum, is an equality that must control all power, but what they may please to delegate to their governors, and thus confirm the political axiom,—the division of property divides knowledge, and both divide power equally, which is freedom.

By the right of voting at elections being attached to property in France, the whole elective part is put into place by the votes of about thirty thousand; which, for the want of the prop of primogeniture and entails, most probably will diminish every year; while the great body of the working classes will increase both in number and riches, forming an immensely strong public opinion, without any legal mode of manifesting it. This must in the end break through the legitimate bounds by a physical revolution, produce war and blood-shed.

It exhibits in the strongest possible point of view the immense advantages of universal suffrage, where the moral revolution does not advance one atom before the knowledge of the day; and every class, by information, is prepared for the place he is required to fill by the majority of his fellow-citizens, without any pretensions to superior birth, privileges or power. He surrenders the trust as he found it, convinced that he had no better title to it than any other, and that the division of power is indispensable to freedom. It is the place that gives dignity to the man, and not the man who clothes the place with reverence and respect: and when he retires he leaves all the power and consequence to his successor, without pretending to any more influence than his real merit and knowledge entitle him to. In this, as well as in every thing else, an elective government differs from a hereditary one.

In a country just emerged from the mire of slavery and despotism to the theory of elective government of freedom and equality, the change is too sudden to secure the practice. And those who, from civil, military, or religious force, usurp the power of their former tyrants, create anarchy and confusion, attended by plunder, rapine, and cruelty, in opposition to the constituted elective authorities, are ambitious chiefs, who are permitted by the ignorance of the millions to wield the armed force of their recent tyrants; and though it is evidently the expiring struggle of despotism, yet the enemies of the liberties of mankind throw the blame on freedom and equality, though it is evidently the abuse of both, for a time replaced by the force of the bayonet. All such violent measures are carried by parties attached to the personal merits of the chief, in imitation of their late subjection to hereditary power. All men join the party they think the strongest; when they take the weakest party it is for want of foresight and is an error in judgment. All people who are under arbitrary power are accustomed to consider the military force the strongest, and are disposed to join any collection of armed men that may support a military chief.

This aggregation of force, rules despotically until another, more popular, can raise a greater force, and live and revel at the expense of the party subdued. This alternation of masters is always at the expense of the rich, and becomes a violent mode of equalizing property, which, though injurious and perhaps unjust to those who have accumulated property, is perhaps one of the most expeditious modes of creating that equality so necessary at the foundation of freedom. All the above theories will be elucidated by the future forms which the governments of the states of South America will take, after being instructed in their real interest, by the fortunate circumstances that are placed around them, by our vicinity, and by their intercourse with civilized Europe.

PRODUCERS AND CONSUMERS.

April 22, 1830.

The poverty and hard oppressive labor of the industrious producers, are in proportion to the number and riches of the consumers or non-producers, and every law, monopoly, fund, charter, etc., which enables a greater number of the society to live without labor, in the same proportion increases the toil, labor, and oppression of those who do labor. All laws of entail, right of primogeniture, monopolies of banks, charters, etc., priviledged orders, armies, navies, learned professions, merchants, etc., in any state of society, formed by, and for the benefit of such non-productive orders or establishments, must in the like proportion increase the toil and labor of those that feed them, and supply all their wants and luxuries. Of all the above enumerated modes of transferring the produce of the industrious laborer into the pockets of the idle consumer, a national debt is the most burdensome and perhaps the most unjust. It is an invention of the moderns, not to be found in ancient history, and it may be queried, whether the present generation has any right to burden posterity with the cost of their follies, luxuries, and extravagance, all of which falls on the industrious producers, who benefit little or nothing either by fees, perquisities, pensions, or salaries, in the division of the spoil at the time of expenditure.

Suppose a nation to have a population of eighteen millions, of which, by an accumulation of partial laws, a large national debt, privileges, monopolies, etc., as in Britain, six millions of the inhabitants are enabled to live without productive labor, supported by the industrious workmen; it is evident that every two laborers must furnish all the food, clothing, luxury, and expenditure of one of those idlers; the amount of labor necessary to produce which must depend on the amount of income they expend. For instance, as in Britain, for every two hunderd dollars per annum, each laborer must earn one hundred dollars, over and above his own expenditure for food, clothing, etc., for himself and family, which would require him to work at least double the time, and produce double the quantity that would be necessary for his own consumption. This sufficiently accounts for the poverty and misery of the operatives in Britain. Suppose a state of society, as in France, the consequence of the revolution. With a population of thirty-two millions, the division of property is so equal, that only 750,000 inhabitants are enabled to live without productive labor, which leaves the task to forty-one industrious producers to feed, clothe, and administer to all the wants, luxuries, and extravagances of only one idler or non-producer: and supposing the expenditure, the same as in Britain, two hundred dollars per annum, each productive laborer would only have to furnish less than five dollars per annum to the support and maintenance of the consumers or non-producers in France, where so much equality has been produced by the revolution, that the industrious producers, each on an average, possess property to the amount of thirty-six dollars, over and above the wages he earns, and there are about ten millions of land proprietors, nearly one-third of the population in France.

Let us examine the injustice of one class of citizens mortgaging the labor of posterity, by borrowing money for the public service of the present day. To bring it within the limits of every one's comprehension, suppose 100,000 acres of land cultivated by one thousand tenants or cultivators, and owned by ten proprietors; and suppose a conqueror or robber threatens to take possession of it. The ten proprietors seeing their all at risk, would endeavor to interest the one thousand cultivators in the defence of it, (who, not being so knowing as the ass in the fable with the two bundles of hay, when urged by his master to go faster and escape the robbers, inquired if the robbers would make him carry three bundles,) to which the cultivators agreed. "But you must give us arms, ammunition, clothing and provisions, whilst we are performing this extra service for you." "No!" answered the proprietors, "we will lend you money to buy those articles, on condition that you and your posterity pay us yearly interest, which will double the rent of your lands, and only oblige you and your posterity to labor double the time and produce double the property for us and our successors to spend." This is the real state of all national debt, borrowed from individuals of the nation. When borrowed from a foreign nation, in case of the total inability of the nation to support the expense, is a different affair, but the rich lending is a proof that they have wherewith to pay expenses, provided taxes were laid in proportion to property, as equal justice requires in all countries.

No exact statistics of our Union permit me to state, with any great degree of correctness, the relative situation of the industrious producers, and of the consumers or non-producers; but the following approximate statement of expenditure may be found to be sufficiently accurate for our purpose.

Religion, with expenses of churches, salaries of clergymen, etc.	$20,000,000
Lawyers, judges, and their attendants,	40,000,000
Physicians, etc., etc.	20,000,000
Legislators, officers, civil and military, of the federal Union,	20,000,000
Twenty-four states, county towns, with all their civil and executive officers,	48,000,000
Merchants, traders, their churches, servants, etc.,	40,000,000
Circulating paper of the Union, at least one hundred millions, at six per cent,	6,000,000
Loss on forged and defaced notes, five dollars each citizen,	60,000,000
Loss by failure of banks,	20,000,000
	$278,000,000

Suppose we take the population of the Union at 13,000,000, and that 500,000 of them are non-producers; there remains 12,500,000 to produce the 278,000,000 of dollars over and above their own food, clothing and other expenses, which amounts to more than twenty-two dollars for each man, woman and child in the Union. Suppose we deduct 78,000,000 for loss and destruction, that goes into no one's pocket, there will remain 200,000,000 of dollars, the produce of the workmen's labor, that fills the pockets of 500,000 non-producers, making 400 dollars for each of the consumers or non-producers; just double what was allowed to each of the consumers or non-producers of France or Britain. This in a great measure would account for the greater extension of luxury and extravagance over the Union; few being very rich, leaves a much greater number to make a show of riches, than could be expected in such a state of inequality as in Britain. By indirect taxation, the tax-gatherer being kept at a distance, few of our good, simple citizens will perhaps believe that they pay so much of the produce of their labor to those who expend and produce nothing; but let them only calculate the number of lawyers, parsons, officers of the United States, and of the state governments, etc., with the revenue they expend annually, and add the annual loss by forgeries, bad notes, etc., estimated by what they have lost themselves, and they will find the whole amount to a sum they could have had no conception of, in consequence of the different contrivances invented to disguise the truth, and make them believe that their affairs are managed with the strictest economy, far below the cost of any political association in Europe: which is not true if we compare them with the only government of Europe that has any pretension to being elective, that is Switzerland — we will find our expenses nearly ten times greater, even in proportion to our population. But our rulers are careful never to compare our financial, nor other situation, with that of any other country than Britain, the most extravagant, by many hundred per cent., of all the monarchies of the old world.

The consequence of a national debt to the interest, comfort, and happiness of the millions, has been disguised and kept out of view by most of the political economists since Smith, who treated the bipeds like their neighbors the quadrupeds, only investigating how their masters or rulers can make the most of them, without even considering the life, health, liberty, or comfort of man, so much as the interest of the farmer would force him to consult the well-being or prosperity of his cattle, perhaps because the assumed masters or rulers of freemen lose nothing by their disease or death, as the farmer would by the loss of his cattle.

It is high time, at least in elective governments of universal suffrage, that the great majority should occupy themselves with their own interest, and force the pride and presumption of the few to yield to the comfort and happiness of the many, that the hewers of wood and drawers of water should have consideration in proportion to their utility, by producing an equality that would make it necessary for the most of our species to hew their own wood and draw their own water. A state of society devoutly to be wished for; that can only be produced by the diffusion of useful knowledge amongst the industrious producers.

GREAT AND OBVIOUS ADVANTAGES OF SMALL CONFEDERATED GOVERNMENTS.

May 4*th*, 1830.

Simplification is perhaps the direct road towards perfection in morals and politics, as well as in science and mechanism. The simple machinery of the New-England townships, where every member takes an active part in producing the general good, is perhaps the greatest perfection in political associations that has been yet contrived; and in proportion as they recede from that simplicity of forms and number into vast kingdoms or empires, of great extent and corresponding complication, is the amount of injustice and abuse, producing in an equal degree the unhappiness and misery of the millions, whose comfort and well-being are in the inverse ratio of the extent and number of the association to which they belong.

Companies or associations for trade, manufactories, etc., when so extensive as to be out of the control of those immediately interested in the profit and loss, have generally failed. Such has been the fate of all the chartered companies for trading in Europe, except the British East India Company, whose territorial revenue supports them as yet, though all the profits of their trade would pay but a small part of their expenses. For some time, banks and insurance companies were supposed capable of being regulated under exclusive charters; but since the failure of all the chartered banks in Europe, except the British and French, it is doubted whether they are capable of being managed by directors not interested, nor responsible for the result of their management. This was the result of the experience of Europe, before our legislators granted exclusive charters to 500 banks without limitation of dividend, scattered all over the Union, 100 of which have already failed, and so confirmed the apparently well founded doubts,—their capability of being successfully carried on under the control of directors not interested, nor responsible for the result of their operations, and constantly tempted to lend the bank capital to their friends by way of discount, without sufficient security.

All the experience of the civilized world proves the vast superiority of small governments in extent and numbers, for the perfection of internal regulations, over the great extended kingdoms or empires, and a traveller can perceive the immense difference in passing from the frontiers of a widely extended empire into the territories of any small state, as from the Austrian or Russian into the small Saxon governments, or into the limited boundaries of Tuscany; the first house, hamlet or village, with their order, and comfort of their inhabitants, convinces the impartial observer that he has passed from an inferior to a superior state of civilization. The same conviction strikes the traveler on entering Switzerland from any of its neighboring countries. Thus we are forced to consider that all small states are ruled more agreeably to the interest of the millions than large ones, and the only objection to them is, the deficiency of protection against the injustice and oppression of their more powerful and ambitious neighbors. This serious objection can be obviated by a judicious and well arranged federation, where the protecting force of the whole can be collected, against every species of foreign invasion or interference, without the smallest meddling with the internal regulations of the individual states or members of the federal compact.

No one can possibly doubt, but that it flatters the ambition of all rulers to direct and manage large societies in preference to small ones. Of course, extensive associations with great power must be advocated, not only by those already in power, but by all those who in elective governments have the smallest hopes of ever being in power. This hope of office fortifies the ruling party with a hundred recruits for every one that will ever actually possess the place he aims at. In this, as in every thing else, the interest of the governed is in collision and direct contradiction with the interest of the governors, who think they gain by the accumulation of power inseparable from centralism, whilst the millions have an undoubted interest in the distribution of power over the whole body politic, so that every individual of every class should have justice and redress of grievances as near to his habitation as possible, and not be forced to go, at the expense of time and money, to seek a settlement of any difference he might have with his neighbor, to a great distance from the theatre of the transaction, all the truth and circumstances of which it is impossible to transport, or to find competent judges of all the minutiæ attending the transaction, remote from the place where it originated. This is one of the causes of so much injustice and litigation.

From the foregoing observations it may appear that the rich and influential, who may be called the aristocratic party in our country, in following their immediate interest, have thrown so much power into the federation as to become injurious to the rights of the individual states, and so much power into the state governments as to encroach on the rights of the subordinate authorities. This has occurred in all the states except those of New-England, where the rights and privileges of the townships protect them from the improper interference of the state's authority, in the prudent arrangement of their necessary and useful operations. If affairs have been hitherto so circumstanced as to produce much of the poverty and misery that pervades the Union, the line of conduct of the millions, when they acquire the majority in our legislatures, is marked by a broad separation of interest from the policy of the favorite few, who have as yet ruled our country.

Beginning at the greatest perfection to which political associations have yet arrived, as in the townships of New-England, the representatives of the millions would further the interest of their constituents by organizing similar ones all over the Union, adding to their power and privileges, the right of doing every thing for their own benefit, and laying taxes for defraying the expenses, enacting laws, rules and regulations for the government of their townships; which, being the will of the positive majority and subject to their amending or annulling, must be faithfully executed by the said majority. This would limit the state legislatures to a court of arbitration, to settle any dispute that might arise between the different townships. It may be objected by those who benefit by things as they are, that they would quarrel, and confusion and bloodshed would follow. Have any disputes arisen during the long existence of townships in New-England? On the contrary, are they not the best ordered, regulated, and managed societies in the Union? Have they not sent to all the states of the Union the most useful citizens, who have been enabled to fill the greatest part of the places of honor and profit? Is there not less vice and crime, in proportion to their population, than in the other states of the Union? Has not the long practice confirmed the great advantages of such institutions far beyond the reach of theoretical objections made by interested individuals?

In consequence of such arrangements, the federal power would be limited to their only useful authority, as in Switzerland, of arbitration in case of disputes between the states, and of keeping up all intercourse with foreign nations, collecting men and money from the different states, according to their population, in case of war.

Taxes would be levied for the expenditure of the states and United States by the townships, by the same direct contribution on property, by which they would supply their own expenditure, just as the New England townships have been long in the practice of paying for every improvement of schools, roads, bridges, etc., by a direct tax on property, the only just tax in any country, and above all, the only tax a free people ought to permit; as indirect taxation is the foundation of that inequality so dangerous to freedom. It ought to be avoided by all who value their liberty, which must depend on an equality, that is with difficulty maintained under indirect taxation. Many curious experiments are now making in the southern republics, that will throw much light on the dark subject of politics. Guatemala proposes a federation not unlike that of Switzerland. Columbia invests districts of 2,000 inhabitants with powers similar to our townships of New England, with a view to a federation.— Buenos Ayres is fighting for a federation. The army in Chili is fighting hard to convince all free states that it is not their interest to have any armed force but militia, and the influence of the town of Mexico is vibrating towards centralism.

NATIONAL EDUCATION.

May 6, 1830.

In imitation of hereditary Britain, the most of our gratis schools (excepting the township schools of New England) are for the poor, and are ranked under the invidious name of pauper schools. It would be necessary that the proper pride and independence of free citizens should be reduced by poverty and misery, before they could submit to the degradation of sending their children to them. The claim now making by the working classes, that a part of their property, yielded to the government in taxes, should be appropriated to a general and equal system of education, may be opposed by those who have as yet, enjoyed the monopoly of knowledge, property and power, under pretence that it will be disposing of their property, for purposes foreign to their interest. This assumption of the right of property, must be stopped on the threshold, by the inquiry how property, the produce of labor, comes into the possession of those who do not work? the answer may be, " by the laws, rules and regulations of society." " By whom made?" Answer. "By the rulers." "And who are the rulers?"— The non-producers and consumers, who granted charters, monopolies, corporations, privileges, themselves in the possession of that property, which originated out of the toil and labor of the great, industrious, producing and working classes. With these classes, the possessisn of the greatest part of that property would have remained, if the laborers, by the elective government of universal suffrage, had been rulers and legislators; and unless they succeed to put a great majority of votes into the ballot boxes, in favor of those who from a similarity of occupations, education and opinions, feel and advocate the same interest, they will not be able to carry any of their measures, but must continue to labor for the benefit of the non-producers, as they have done for the last fifty-three years, with the additional mortification, of having attempted to relieve themselves, and failed from ignorance and want of union. Let us hope for a better esult of the exertions now making, and that the equality of knowledge will be secured by a rational and equal education. Had all or any of the attempts, to make children feed, clothe and educate themselves with the produce of their own labor, succeeded to the expectation of those who tried the experiment, it would have been a further convincing proof how independent ought to be the condition of the laborer, when even children could free themselves from all dependence on parents or friends for support, during their weak and hitherto helpless state of minority. It would have been a strong accusation against all the regulations of both church and state for organizing society so unjustly, appropriating and misapplying the produce of their labor, as to leave the adult laborer deprived of the necessaries of life, in a state of wretchedness and misery, and to cause the suffering of the millions, to be commensurate with the extent of our boasted civilization. If the exertions of the children have not been so judiciously applied in this country as to produce all their necessaries, (as has been effected in others, and I have little doubt will, in time, be in this,) it is only common justice, that the labor of their parents should supply the deficiency, by the institution of free schools adapted to all classes of the society, at national expense, in place of endowing colleges, universities and seminaries, for the benefit of the rich and privileged, who are non-producers, are least of all the classes entitled to the benefit of public expenditure. Such schools, even if the salaries of the professors, and other expenses be drawn from the state or public treasury, should be under the complete control of the inhabitants of the vicinity, who are to benefit by them, who would then have the electing by universal suffrage, of the school-masters and other officers, the fixing of the locality and the directing of how and what should be taught.

But it will be time to dwell on the construction of the schools, when the working classes shall have the legislative power of creating them to suit their own interest: when they shall have persevered in close union at the ballot boxes, to elect into power the best informed of their own class, in spite of the high sounding words of sophistry and declamation, trumpeted forth by the mouth pieces of aristocracy, pretending that it requires vast learning and knowledge to legislate for the public good. There is not one line of either ancient or modern history that is applicable to the present state of the Union. All our knowledge must be drawn from the facts that exist, evident to the senses of all, on the surface and within the reach of the comprehension of every one the least practiced in observation. True logic is only the arrangement of facts, in a chain of reasoning, so that the last is supported by the preceding. All arrangement of words unsupported by facts is mere insignificant sound, sophistry and delusion, an insult to the common sense of the audience. The truths of the exact sciences of chemistry, natural philosophy, natural history, etc., are extensive, multifarious, and require much time to study; but the true interest of majority in legislation, is in a nut shell, and known to every individual, who has only to advocate his own interest, or the interest of his class, which, if the majority, must be just and right. To prove that the interest of the few is the interest of the many, the end and object of most legislators that have yet existed, requires a command of words, oratory and eloquence. To make an ounce of truth gild over a ton of falsehood, and to make it palatable to ignorant credulity, requires address and management, with all the force of sounds and legerdemain of public speaking. But the minority persevering in carrying every point dictated by their own interest, have not the smallest necessity for either oratory, rhetoric or eloquence. Attempting to convince the majority, who equally act on their ideas of their own interest, is in vain; the majority of the votes carries it in favor of the interest of the majority, in all bodies political or otherwise. The credulity of the millions in the cause of the day-and-night-long speeches in congress, not the hopes of changing the members. Ignorance values a speech as he does his land, by its length and breadth, and feels flattered that his representative makes a noise on the floor of congress so many hours or days; and the strength of the lungs is substituted for the strength of intellect.— While electors take sound for sense, they have no right to blame the elected for paying them in their favorite coin; in a word, under an elective government of universal suffrage, the people are unjust and unreasonable to blame any but themselves, for the faults, blunders, plundering or extortion of either church or state. All governments prove, that the interest of the consumers is opposed to the interest of the producers. If the people elect the consumers into power, and expect they will act for any other interest than their own, they show a most indign ignorance, both of themselves and others, and must submit to be wrought hard for the support of those who have cunning and combination to make dupes of them. If the millions do not acquire useful knowledge sufficient to manage their own affairs, they must pay doubly high for other classes, who substitute their own interest for the interest of the millions. Fortunately the abilities or ingenuity, requisite to discover their general interest in public affairs, is not equal to the talents and industry necessary to make a good house carpenter.

Not only the working classes of this side of the Atlantic, but the working classes of all the civilized world, are essentially interested in the success of this first experiment of practical equality. If it produce only one-half of what it promises, it will spread freedom and happiness over the millions in every region where the knowledge of it comes.— Our revolution was only the theory of self-government, this will complete the practice, against which all the sophistry of tyranny and despotism will strive in vain. All eyes are upon the effects of the experiment; the hopes and happiness of mankind are staked on the result.

KNOWLEDGE INDISPENSABLE TO FREEDOM. THE PRODUCERS OUGHT TO BE THE DISTRIBUTORS OF WEALTH. MISCHIEFS OF GREAT INEQUALITY.

May 8, 1830.

Freedom is a word that can only be understood by those who are well informed, and can only be enjoyed by those who learn thoroughly its rights, privileges, equality and toleration, both physical and moral. The millions are mostly subjected to the caprice of the hereditary one or few, transferred to their children or heirs like a herd of cattle, and it is a mockery of common sense, to pretend that they enjoy any of the attributes of freedom. Where the hereditary power is extended, by granting the right of suffrage to property, the idea of liberty is equally delusive; it only sweetens the pill of taxation, by making the people believe they empty their own pockets into the public treasury. Witness the enormous taxation of Britain, Holland and France, where nature has so far conquered artifice as to introduce the theory of equality. The practice as respects the millions is an illusion without knowledge; which is power and freedom.— Knowledge, power and freedom, and their inseparable consequences, must succeed one another, as certainly as the light follows the sun. If we abstract knowledge, then power and freedom are but sounds, bottomed on delusion. Equality begot universal suffrage, and put all mankind on a par as respects political rights; but it was a vain attempt to elevate our species to the dignity they ought to possess. The leaden weight of ignorance kept them groveling in the mire of misery; the knowing few, fell heirs to the hereditary power, with this difference; being tenants at will, they drained the public for the benefit of their children and heirs; the children and heirs of hereditary power, being provided for by the right of force, often called divine right, were not forced to accumulate for their progeny; which makes an elective government, when accompanied with the total ignorance of the millions, much more expensive than a hereditary one, as exemplified in most of the governments of the South American states, and even in our own during the last war. All of which extravagance, plunder and pillage will be saved, when those who produce all by their labor have the directing and distributing of all public expenses; an experiment only yet tried in the New England townships; but it has succeeded so completely in them, as to warrant the expectation that it will be equally advantageous to the millions, on a more extensive scale.

After fifty-three years of patient submission to the imitation and adoption of the laws and regulations of subjugated Europe; after fifty-three years impartial observation of the progress of artificial and self-created aristocracy, based on monopolies, exclusive charters, and unconstitutional privileges, producing great inequality of property, certainly succeeded by a similar inequality of knowledge, and followed by a monopoly of power. The assumed superiority of the few over the many, had completely pervaded all sects and classes of society: the separation of ranks was becoming marked with a broad line of distinction, and degraded equality durst not show herself any where or at any time but on the day of election. Our working classes fearing, that in time the last resource of freedom, the ballot boxes might be shut against them, agreed to make a trial whether one hundred votes of the hard hands of industrious labor would not control the one though ever so polished and refined, backed by all the pretensions to superiority.

Our industrious producers found legitimate equality and freedom in the ballot boxes, and by union and perseverance they will no doubt succeed in securing as complete a control over the distribution of wealth, as they have had at all times and in all countries over the production of property. This will introduce a practical freedom and equality, different from all other revolutions, which were limited to plausible theories, only masking the injustice of arbitrary power without protecting the millions from its apprehension. In the success of this first experiment of practical self-government, all the people on earth are interested; for the daring theory, of mankind being capable of taking care of their own interest, being first promulgated on this side of the Atlantic, and spreading rapidly in all directions, the practice that naturally follows the theory, may equally pervade the civilized world, and cause an immense change for the better, in the relative situation of our species, by fixing the scale of utility as the measure by which all things shall be valued; that the extension of private interest, constitutes public good; and that self-love and social are the same in practice, as has been so long asserted in the theory.

The very great inequality of property, knowledge and power, is the cause of a great part of the opposition, jarring and contradictory interests of mankind. In proportion to the equality between the governors and the governed, the producer and consumer, the master and servant, would be the assimilation of their interest, and the less the temptation either physically to oppose, or undo what others are doing. The more equality between the rich and poor, the less power have the rich to oppress the poor, and the smaller the inducement of the poor to retaliate on the rich; preventing vice and crime, by lessening the temptation, in place of the temporary cure of jails, penitentiaries and houses of refuge.— The greater the equality, the more justice and honesty; neither can be said to exist without it. The brutal ignorance of the laborers was formerly considered as an insurmountable bar to their improvement by self-government. But since the road to useful knowledge is only through the senses, and the senses of the many are equally accute, if not more so than the senses of the luxurious few, knowledge is spreading.— "The school-master is abroad," and the enemies of the improvement of their species, make no use of the cabalistical word, *passions*, to express the utter impossibility of any melioration in the lot of humanity. How to control, how to eradicate the baneful effects of men's passions? Passions are the expressions of sentiment or feeling, and whether instinctive, innate, or taught by experience, like all other sentient vibrations, they originate in self-interest and are less or more under the control of our ideas, of our interest, to court pleasure and avoid pain and must be regulated by our acquired knowledge of what promotes our real interest.— Passions figure both the good and bad sensations, and when we are taught that it is our interest to nourish and extend the benevolent passions, and to annihilate or depress the hateful and violent passions, it is only the application of our knowledge to the promotion of our own happiness; the neglecting of which would be ignorance of our essential interest. So that the mystical word "passions" is only ignorance, is a sound less comprehensible.

THE NAPOLEON CODE OF LAWS.—THE COMMON LAW.

May 10, 1830.

Lawyers may be expected to reform laws when bishops agree to abolish tithes; but unfortunately for mankind, few have attempted any change in them, excepting those who are interested in maintaining and increasing every abuse, because they gain by every addition they can make to the complication, difficulty, or litigation, either of the laws themselves or in the execution of them. Not the least of the many benefits which the French revolution bestowed on the millions, is the Code Napoleon; which has changed its name, and as much of its nature, as public opinion would permit, by being executed by judges appointed by those who wish to eradicate every amelioration in favor of the millions, introduced by a short period of elective government. Fortunately for mankind, the French code, as it is now called, was made under the direction of one who had an interest in saving his subjects from the extortion of the lawyers, as is manifested in the tariff of fees attached to it. All laws, however good, when executed by corrupt judges, must appear bad to the mass of superficial observers; and laws, however tyrannical and injurious, will appear comparatively good when executed by a jury who have no interest in litigation, as all delay costs them time and money, for which they have no adequate compensation. Since the restoration in France, the laws have been executed by judges appointed by the Bourbons, who would obliterate every remembrance of the revolution, and annihilate every advantage the people gained by the existence of a popular representative government. The code, made by a man whose memory they endeavor to vilify and by every means, direct and indirect, to calumniate, can have but a small chance of impartial execution under the creatures of such chiefs. Yet, under all these disadvantages, it is one of the principal causes of the present prosperity of France, by maintaining and propagating that equality so necessary to the comfort and happiness of every class in society; as is strongly evinced by the few crimes or breaches of the laws in France, when compared with their neighbors on either side.

When the code Napoleon was introduced into Holland, it was executed by judges, appointed by a king inimical to the improvements introduced by the French revolution; yet it has completely corrected the injustice and confusion of a complicated, multifarious, and litigious aggregation of laws, accumulated by the strife and contention of centuries, between an atom of civil and religious liberty, fighting against a strong hereditary and monied aristocracy; the first left by Spanish masters, the second introduced by successful commerce. The same code has wrought a moral revolution in the Prussian provinces on the Rhine, though subject to the same bad and defective administration, under judges named by the despotic government of Prussia. On a view of all the prominent facts which the cunning intrigues of the most expert lawyer cannot hide from the most common observer, what immense advantages would be derived from such a code executed by a jury friendly to freedom and the public good, elected and chosen by elective officers, independent of all power but that of the people who put them in place. How happy might the people be who could combine such reasonable, simple, and well-defined laws, with an impartial and fair execution by twelve men, influenced by no consideration to swerve from their joint understanding of justice, and from their mode of appointment removed from every attempt at bribery or corruption, there being few honest judges in any country, except those kept so by the presence of juries. What infatuated blindness must pervade the millions in an elective government of universal suffrage, who neglect to benefit by such favorable circumstances and adopt so rational a code, which experience, under all unfavorable circumstances, has proved so beneficial to other nations, and who are deterred by the impudent sophistry of those who live and thrive on the excess of every abuse that can possibly be introduced into the civil, political, religious or moral institutions of their fellow men.

Bentham, who was the first to expose the absurd injustice of the common law, though since followed by the first in the profession, is ridiculed by every pettyfogging attorney on both sides of the Atlantic, who preach by the year on the great and mysterious science of right and wrong, which they pretend cannot be understood, but by those who have studied the hundred thousand volumes of feudal precedents, recorded during the existence of barbarous, tyrannical despotism, and who have so much confidence in their law logic, as boldly to assert, that society would be unhinged by abolishing, even in associations of freemen, those chains and trammels, invented by a diminishing aristocracy to perpetuate their tyranny over the millions, beyond the time that their physical force permitted them to keep their fellow beings in bondage.

Some of the British lawyers, who have lately been endeavoring to defend their craft, have given credit to our lawyers for their liberality in not subdividing the profession into all the intricacies which the exorbitant number in Britain has forced them to split the trade into, that all might have a chance of living, and have adopted the term *flexibility* as a new property of the common law of England, a term which is supposed to have been made use of by our lawyers; and there is little doubt but the property of being easily twisted, to mean anything or nothing, originated the lawyers' toast, "The glorious uncertainty of the law." That "birds of a feather flock together," and that the British lawyers should cordially join with ours in opposing every infringement on that craft, is completely within the nature of men and things; but that the many, who feed and support them, who labor and toil to maintain them in luxury and extravagance; in return for which they only reap litigation and oppression, should continue any longer to tolerate such a swarm of non-productive consumers, who revel on their property, is as contrary to the nature of man in search of happiness, as it is to common sense and reason. In a free country, where universal suffrage gives the millions the legitimate right of regulating every thing to suit their own interest, and to support the freedom and equality left them as their birth-right, one of the greatest props to such advantages, is the adoption of a simple, well-defined code of laws; and the strongest argument in favor of it is, that the lawyers oppose it, as a certain proof that it is against their craft, and as certainly in favor of all the other trades and professions that compose society.

All temporizing or cobbling of old laws, many centuries behind the knowledge of the day, would be like the placing in a steam-boat one of the old steam-engines, with one of a late invention; an arrangement which would only retard and diminish the power, while it increased the expense. The steam-boat is under the direction of the proprietor, who furnished the expense; the law is under the management of those who not only do not pay the expense, but gain in exact proportion to the amount it costs the rest of society.

Why should a people, who never have made any change either in physics, politics, religion, or morals, without reaping benefit, by all the experiments which surrounding circumstances induced them to make, (as might be elucidated by all the changes, from the burning of witches and flogging and hanging of quakers; from the representation of property in the old states to the representation of persons, and the adoption of penitentiaries in place of the sanguinary laws of Britain) object to the enacting a simple code of laws, which every one could have in his pocket, and know when he transgressed any of them; particularly as said code has been translated into many languages, and successfully transported and made the rule of conduct of many different people, whose rulers had strong prejudices, both against the author and the times in which it originated, having, in all countries where it has been adopted, given general satisfaction, and advanced the civilization of all nations, where its wise precepts and just statutes prevail.

FREEDOM OF THE PRESS. — COMPLICATED LAWS.

May 15*th*, 1830.

The incorrect definition of words is the cause of many errors, and of almost all disputes. The words—*free press*, one would at first suppose meant a press open to the free discussion of all subjects on religion, morals, politics, and physics. But where is such a press to be found? Hardly in our country, the foundation of whose political institutions ought to be freedom and equality. All presses that have yet been called free are trammelled by two kinds of restrictions; laws, and the prejudices of public opinion in favor of certain religious dogmas, party politics, etc. In a country where the publishing of truth is considered a libel, and punished as such, the press cannot be called free; or when publishing any thing contrary to the dogmas of any species of religion is a crime, punishable by fine and imprisonment, the word *free* applied to the press is certainly a misnomer. In all nations, any one may publish in favor of the ruling politics or religion, but in few is any one tolerated to publish any thing against them; he is either physically punished by law, or morally injured by the persecution of those who, differing in opinion from him, assume the right of slandering and calumniating him for opinion's sake. Complete toleration, physical and moral, exists nowhere; and often where the physical restrictions are most rigorous, the moral are most tolerant. Almost all the presses in our mercantile towns are hired and paid by the advertisements to advocate the monied and mercantile aristocracy, free and open to every thing in favor of their supporters, and shut against every species of reasoning, be it ever so true, that can militate against them. All such presses cannot pretend to be called free. Great part of our country presses, supported by the subscriptions of the rich and influential, are forced to advocate the aristocratic party, and cease to be entitled to the appellation of free. All political party, or sectarian religious presses, are excluded from the title of free presses. All this is in the nature of men and things, and cannot be prevented in the present state of society; but why boast of the free press of the United States, when there is not one in a hundred that has the least pretensions to the honorable title.—Would it not be better, and save much error and deception, to call every thing by its proper name, that would designate its properties? For instance, this press is supported by the monied and mercantile aristocracies, to advocate their interest; that press is in favor of the government of the few over the many, one is in favor of the election of one president, and some of another; one is in favor of one religious sect, and some of another; let us not permit the shop that deals only in whiskey to pretend to sell bread.

All words that have no phenomena to represent them are insignificant, and words represented by phenomena vary agreeably to the immense diversity of said phenomena. For instance, the error in making the vast multiplicity of laws, in hopes of suiting the words to the immense variety of circumstances that surround every transaction or incident that complicates all the intercourse between one man and another, is in vain, as there are no two exactly alike; the discriminating power must be left somewhere, and whether it is safer with one judge, who expounds and explains the laws, or with thirteen of their peers, who judge by the common sense circumstances of the case, for the interests of the millions, may perhaps be decided by the corrupt state of the administration of justice in most countries where the judges are not under the control of a jury. A certain proof that no law can possibly suit the circumstances of every case is, the recourse that lawyers have to precedents, in adopting the common law, which is the decisions of many thousand judges, without any explanation, reasoning or motives, for an indefinite period, given under various controling circumstances of force or fraud, according to the dependence of the judiciary on superior and arbitary authority, exceedingly probable in all hereditary governments, and almost certain in hereditary aristocracies, such as most of the governments of Europe.

Even supposing that justice and reason presided in all the British decisions, unwarped by the feudal tyranny of the privileged orders, who is to judge of the analogy between a present case and one that happened 1500 years ago, when customs, habits, and opinions (that dictate all the received principles of right and wrong) were so contradictory to every thing that exists at present? Does not the great uncertainty of the similarity, leave the decision entirely to the judge, who might as well be left to his own opinion, under the control of a jury, and thus save the court, jury and audience, all the fatiguing litigation of time, of the lawyers quoting the various contradictory opinions of judges, appointed to suit the arbitrary purposes of kings and tyrants, who in no age or time have been scrupulous of the means they made use of to execute what their immediate interests dictated to them.

But granted that it was the interest of kings, privileged orders and lawyers, to keep those ancient checks to the freedom of the millions, and to counterbalance and retard the liberty which the knowledge of the day claims for all civilized nations, it certainly cannot induce a people, whose political institutions are founded on freedom and equality, under an elective government of universal suffrage, to tolerate such trammels on the course of justice, and to submit to be ruled by the arbitrary precedents of barbarous feudality, the complicacy of which is such, that not even those who have spent their lifetime in studying it can fathom it. It is a legal trap set in the public path of the whole society, to catch all who offend against laws which it is impossible for them to know. When a rich man is caught, he must pay well to the lawyers for extricating him, and is consoled with the gratifying consideration of the facility it affords him to oppress the industrious poor who pretend to independence. The benefit of the law is as far out of the reach of the poor as the exorbitant fees of the lawyers are beyond their means; so that such laws are an instrument in the hands of the rich to oppress the poor, with as much effect, and far more security, than the military force applied by despotism. For that reason, intricate and expensive laws are substituted in all countries, when the information and spirit of independence of the people will not submit to the tyranny of physical force. The intricacy of the laws has been in the ratio of the quantum of freedom; which has forced our millions, as yet, to pay dear for the small share of practical liberty their rulers have permitted them to enjoy, being frittered down and diminished by stock and land speculations, bank monopolies, by that practical and unfair indirect taxation on consumption which takes the greatest part of the public expenses from the pockets of the laborer; and the immense yearly addition to litigation and chicanery by the thousands of contradictory, verbose, and undefined laws passed by twenty-four legislatures, laboring in conjunction with the federal congress to complicate our jurisprudence, already far beyond the forbearance and patience of reasonable beings.

The immense impulse given to codification by the French revolution, and its succeeding consequences, will diffuse its beneficial effects over the civilized world; and though we, from our pride and presumption, may be one of the last who will adopt a simple code of well-defined laws, within the reach and open to the inspection and understanding of all classes, yet we must, amongst the other radical reforms, come to it, and the sooner, the greater will be the advantage we will derive from it.

GREAT TALENTS NOT NECESSARY TO OFFICE IN AN ELECTIVE GOVERNMENT.

June 3, 1830.

Every government, whether despotic or free, can have but two modes of ruling; that is, by the few or by the many. In arbitrary governments, the interest of the few is forced upon the many, by the physical force of coercion, with dexterous combination and close union, to prevent the many from acting in concert to assert their interest. Those governaments depending on the means of coercion will last as long as they can collect taxes to support armies; that is, to bribe one part of the millions to keep in subjection the rest. This requires force in the ratio of the diffusion of knowledge, and ingenuity, and talent in the rulers to muster that force and pay them, in proportion to the number necessary to subject the many to the will of the few, which must be in the exact ratio of the spread of knowledge. This fact is evinced at the present day by the large standing armies which the European powers maintain, requiring great taxation, and more troops to protect the collectors; so that the means of paying and maintaining requires the augmentation of the standing armies, which again demands an increase of taxation, and a consequent increase of force, ad infinitum. This contradictory and unnatural order of things, where the many are kept toiling to maintain the few, requires considerable abilities and knowledge, in those few, to keep up the delusion, and make it appear that their interest is the interest of the many; their good the public good. This has originated the idea, that none but men of great abilities and talents are fit to govern; and certainly, when it is necessary to persuade the producers that it is their interest to work hard from sunrise to sunset to maintain the non-producers, great oratory, rhetoric, and eloquence are necessary to make meum appear as tuum.

In governments where the many rule by universal suffrage, the case is entirely different. The only talents or eloquence that the great majority have any use for, is a knowledge of their own interest, so as to make laws for their own benefit; and when they are tired of the logic of the minority let them call for the question, and pass the law, as is done in the British house of commons, and in every other legislature where there is a decided majority. Freedom and equality, enforced by rulers elected by universal suffrage, have no need of eloquence in passing their laws, nor of standing armies to enforce the execution of laws made by themselves for the benefit of all. In popular governments, all must yield to the will of the majority, *vox populi vox dei*, the majority cannot be wrong, unless they injure themselves, which is impossible in the present state of the civilization of the country. All the faults laid to the charge of elective systems, are owing to the confidence of the electors in a class of men who have an interest different and opposite to the interest of the millions, and abuse their confidence. All the absurdities, and cruelties of the French, as well as of all other revolutions, have been perpetrated by the demagogues whom the people elected into power, by following the habits instilled into them by their former tyrannies; and it has required fifty-three years of freedom and independence, to relieve us from the routine of colonial subjection, in electing such representatives as from profession, opinions and education, were opposed to the interest of the great majority of the electors.

When one person assumes the right of governing five hundred or one thousand, it requires much greater talents, and management to convince the millions, that it is their interest to labor hard to maintain the men in power, than are necssary to direct the millions in the pursuit of their interest. A small degree of common sense to observe daily occurrences, teaches them their interest which their majority enforces, whithout the aid or artifice of eloquence, and renders the task easy for the great number of producers to rule and dictate to the few non-producers, by the ballot boxes. The working classes producing all, have the right to distribute all of which they have been deprived by hereditary power, and by its influence on the young converts to liberty and equality, not understanding the advantages universal suffrage gives them, but proceeding in their elections to trust their affairs under the management of the same classes, that would have fallen heirs to power under the hereditary system. This impolitic and irrational imitation of the aristocracies of the old world, has not only deprived us of nine-tenths of the advantages of freedom, but has thrown obloquy on liberty and equality, that has much retarded its progress, and may be injurious to the cause of the working classes, now that they begin to claim their long neglected rights, by the pretention of the rich and influential to a monopoly of that knowledge required in those who govern; which even admitting it to be necessary to keep in subjection the millions of European subjects, it is not either useful or necessary, to enable the millions to govern themselves agreeably to their own interest in our free country. With a majority in the ballot boxes they can do every thing, without it they can do nothing, but be laughed at by those who live on the fruit of their labor.— Union and perseverance are the qualities that can alone obtain their just rights. When they shall have obtained a majority in the council or legislature, they must sit together on one side of the house, consult and arrange their plans, and not permit any but the producing class to interfere. They must remain firm on the elevated ground that they produce all, and that they have a majority that are determined to distribute all, in accordance with their interest and the interest of their constituents; that all species of property was produced by them, which has been wrested from them by unjust laws, monopolies, and privileges, which they are in future determined to abolish, and to retain the produce of their labor in their own possession, for their own benefit, by putting all taxation on real property and income, not permitting any exclusive charters or privileges, or any thing that will in the smallest degree derange that equality, which is the only solid foundation of rational freedom.

It is not one of the least errors attending the imitation of European aristocracies, to suppose that equal abilities are necessary to govern in an elective government of universal suffrage, as would be required to keep the privileged few in power; or because that standing armies and forests of bayonets, are the only means of protecting arbitrary power, the same means are required to defend the millions in the exercise of their freedom and equality through universal suffrage, and still stronger combination of universal interest. Britain has a large fleet to protect her island against her powerful neighbors, (which has cost her the amount of her national debt, the cause of the misery and poverty of the working classes,) and likewise to maintain and increase the patronage of the privileged orders, therefore we must, forsooth, have a fleet, though the patronage infringes on our equality, and it is almost impossible to imagine any state of things, that would tempt any power on earth to attack us. Britain, hemmed in within the limits of an island, was forced to extend herself on the ocean, and become a trading nation, in which their small share of freedom, while all their neighbors were slaves, gave them industry and means of succeeding: therefore we, on a continent not one 200th part inhabited, with all latitudes, and every variety of production, must also be a commercial people to the neglect of our internal resources. Patronage, that enemy to honesty, economy, freedom and improvement, ought to be abolished in all free states, and every office of trust or profit, ought to be filled by the votes of the majority amongst whom its duties are executed. This would strengthen and perpetuate elective governments, as the right of appointing to offices of power and profit consolidates hereditary power. Friends and supporters of arbitrary rule, heap all power on the few; but friends and protectors of freedom and equality, ought to give the choice of all officers, holding places of profit, to the millions, as the only means of equalizing power.

Our government founded on liberty and equality, is new and unprecedented; nothing similar ever existed before, and it must be supported by laws, customs, regulations and practices, naturally flowing from the original source. All copies of laws, practices, etc., derived from systems different and opposite to ours, must create disputes, confusion and eternal warfare; such as aristocratic laws, habits and practices of the Romans, Britons, or any other nation ancient or modern, the foundation of whose civil, religious and political institutions, were based on principles, opposed to all the ground work on which our political institutions repose. All our political errors have arisen from fifty-three years accumulation of precedent and practice, copied from an order of things, at variance with the simplicity and justice of our declaration of independence; the only radical cure, is a return to first principles, and to reform all laws and customs, that operate against the great principle of all men being born free and equal and entitled to the same share of freedom and equality through life.

PROGRESS OF FREEDOM.

June 5, 1830.

Perhaps in no period, noticed in history, has there been so great a propensity to change, in the civil and religious principles of mankind; so great a movement towards reform; so much comparative ascendency of the moral over the physical as at present; and all founded on knowledge, introduced by the wide spread of instruction, and the facility of education to all classes. Without going farther back than the revolution which separated the British colonies from the mother country, we shall include an era pregnant with more events in favor of the civilization, freedom, and happiness of our species than a thousand previous years, where the millions of pages of history are stained with the bloody combats, and butcheries of the many for the pleasure and apparent advantage of the few. The emancipation of North America was an epoch; then, for the first time, the interest of the millions entered into and formed a part (though small) of the motives that urged on resistance to oppression, a resistance that savored of temerity and rashness, without estimating the protection afforded by the combatants, or the thinned population scattered over an immense wilderness, which at first was considered as a weakness, but was found by experience to be a tower of strength that no combination could subdue.

All the adherents and officers of royalty, joining the British, deserting freedom as the weakest side, thinned the aristocratic ranks. This, with the national bankruptcy of paper money, and other equalizers of property, diminished the wealth of the few, without much injuring the poverty of the many, produced an equality favorable to democracy, which all the schemes and intrigues of the favorite few have not been yet able to annihilate. From the force of long habit, the representation was founded, as in Britain, on property, (except in Pennsylvania, where the good sense of the Quakers prevailed,) yet the first new state that was created after the revolution (Vermont) gave hopes of reformation, by adopting universal suffrage, and only one legislature. During the struggle, the necessity of union produced the fortunate coincidence of a federation, which, though it completely succeeded in securing the independence of the country, was considered too slow and weak to repel an active invading foe in possession of part of the territory, and when peace was made lost its authority and retired. The individual states, freed from the colonial restrictions on commerce, and pushed on by the theories of freedom and equality announced in their declaration of independence, made astonishing progress in all the useful arts of civilization, and spread the fame of their prosperity over the Old World.

At this time, the chiefs of the revolution thought a strict union of the states' energies would be more powerful, assembled a convention of the wisdom of the nation, all of whom, born and educated under the colonial system, formed two parties; one disposed to imitate the British constitution, and the other in favor of something more congenial with their declaration of independence. After much debate they produced a compromise; a mongrel between a centralism and a federalism; an actual representation of numbers and metaphysical representation of states, which endangers agreement by the different proportions of power as two is to six.

The free and elastic movements of freedom and equality producing such unprecedented prosperity, wakened the sleeping apathy of the Old World, enchained as it was by the shackles of arbitrary monarchy; and, electrifying the French people, struck out the enthusiasm of the French revolution, gave so violent a shock to ancient prejudices, as to leave them yet quivering from north to south; alarmed the chiefs of arbitrary power, who combined to combat the principles of liberty by military force, and by repeated coalitions beat the French into a military nation, that could only be guided by a military chief, who, grasping the power, courage, and enthusiasm of the revolution reduced to a focus, enabled him to overrun Europe, and spread the contagion of liberty far and wide. Intoxicated with such singular success, and not content with ruling Spain peaceably by his ambassador, he attempted its conquest, and roused the sleeping pride and courage of the nation, who, in the absence of their kings, had recourse to the elective power of the Cortes, under the liberal constitution of the first French convention, collecting the energies of the people, fighting under the banners of a species of freedom, and paralized all his attempts at subduing them, and were the cause of the first reverses of the conqueror of Europe.

The spark that electrified the Spanish nation under the Cortes flew on the wings of the language across the Atlantic, and awakened the energies of the mixed race, so long oppressed by foreign rulers; produced a revolution similar to that of their northern neighbors, whom they seemed disposed to imitate. And as their civil, political, commercial and moral interest are the same, they ought to be united in the closest bonds of friendship and amity. The same ditch protects them from the encroachment of the tyranny of the Old World, as their freedom and equality, supported by an elective government of universal suffrage, guards them against all the evils that have as yet tormented mankind, under the usurped tyranny of despotism.

This hemisphere being separated from the rest of the world by immense oceans, and still further removed by the system of freedom and equality, existing nowhere else, is relieved from the burdens of hereditary kings or rulers, and from the toil and labor of supporting privileged orders, without apprehension of revolts, rebellions, or conspiracies of the citizens, because no change could possibly put them on a better or more elevated situation than an elective government of universal suffrage. It is free from all the fears of anxieties and cares of arbitrary, hereditary governors, and they may therefore dispense with a great many of the props necessary to maintain their precarious authority; such as armies, fleets, partial and unjust laws and customs, made and maintained to support their arbitrary authority, all of which is not only useless, but injurious to a system of universal suffrage, founded on universal interest and the general welfare of all. Such an order of things, founded on the convenience, interest, and happiness of the millions, is completely independent of all the expensive trappings both of church and state, the providing for which wastes so great a proportion of the labor of the working classes, and only adds to the tyranny of the few over the many.

A long struggle ended by the muscular strength of the continent, supported by the purse of Britain, in forcing the Bourbons on the French nation, and banishing Bonaparte to the island of Elba, whence he returned and took possession of France in a post-chaise, driving off the Bourbons, as a singular proof of their want of popularity. But force once more restored the Bourbons to a throne, on which they have been combating in vain to extirpate the scions planted by freedom. The seed sown by the revolution is flourishing, nourished and supported by a soil labored and manured by equality, are of the remaining fruits of the revolution which, being destructive of the rank weeds of despotism, may at last eradicate them, and cover the whole surface of equality with the wholesome grain of freedom, scattering part of this prolific seed among their neighbors.

Whilst the contrast existed between freedom and monarchy, the Spainards experienced both alternately. First the despotism of monarchy, then the freedom of the Cortes, to drive out Bonaparte; the second return of despotism under the reign of Ferdinand; then the second revolution of the freedom of the Cortes, which was changed by the money and bayonets of the Bourbons to a third despotism. By these means, the Spanish nation have five times made the practical comparison between freedom and despotism, during the short period of half an age; an advantage that has not been enjoyed by any modern nation. It must have produced a degree of civilization in Spain; a great contrast to what might have been expected on the old routine of calculation, though not to be observed by the common lookers on, yet it will most probably be found, that, under the despotism of Ferdinand, the millions in Spain are advancing farther towards civil liberty, than ever they did under the mild dominion of the Cortes, and that the tree of liberty, transplanted from the New to the Old World, has only been pruned of its useless suckers, by all the fierce sabres of monarchy, to make it more luxuriously productive of freedom and equality, for the benefit and advantage of future generations.

Freedom and equality have not existed long enough in any country for the millions to gain a sufficient knowledge of their power and rights, and to put in practice their interest through the ballot boxes of universal suffrage. All former revolutions have stopped at theories, leaving the practice, distribution, and purse, in possession of the same class of non-producers who had the control under the aristocracy before the revolution. Theories without practice are words devoid of sense; sounds that tickle the ear without satisfying any of the other senses, which the non-producers permit the hard laboring producers to make use of, and boast of their constitutions and laws: but none of them will willingly tolerate the practice of freedom and equality. All the rights of universal suffrage must be forced from them, by the constitutional privileges of the ballot boxes, which the millions have the complete control of, whenever they unite to reclaim the performance of their constitutional rights. If, from ignorance and want of union, they will suffer power to remain in the hands of those that have no common interest with them, they must expect to be harder ridden than if they had not made this stand for their rights.

CODE NAPOLEON.—ORIGIN OF THE WORKING MEN'S PARTY.

June 19, 1830.

Had the Code Napoleon been a British fabrick, or even manufactured where our language was spoken, it is more than probable we would have had, ere now, the advantage of its well-defined, plain, and simple regulations. But because it was promulgated in French, and by a man against whom the aristocracy of the civilized world had conspired, it may be ages before our millions will have the information or power to benefit by it, though it has already been adopted by both the Dutch and German nations, and serves as a rule of conduct to people who speak the Flemish, Dutch and German languages, accelerating the progress of civilization, and adding to the comfort and happiness of the millions, in every country that has had the good sense to copy it. On such slender threads hang the destinies of nations, and such silly prejudices obstruct the circulation of the most useful knowledge.

Adam Smith (on the wealth of nations) was one of the first who analyzed society into producers and non-producers; but his work was too voluminous and abstract to reach the comprehension of the millions, and was read and understood only by those of the consuming classes, who had no interest in applying the practice for the benefit of the millions. John Gray's first lecture on human happiness, first published in London, and afterwards in a cheap stereotype edition in Philadelphia, giving a general view of the British nation, as divided into producers and consumers, was the first practical knowledge of such a division of mankind that came within the reach of our working people, in the year 1825. This gradually produced, in 1829, the mode of reasoning of the mechanics and working classes in the different towns of the Union, and the practical application of such reasoning to the ballot boxes. And though John Gray did not find it his interest to offend the British aristocracy with a continuance of his lectures he has put the millions on the direct road to their interest, which fortunately on this side of the Atlantic is not barred or obstructed by any physical force, and has only to wrestle with moral prejudices, which vanish before reason and experience, easily put in execution by universal suffrage. This is the only system by which a peaceable or legal reform can correct all abuses, and enable us to practice the principles of freedom and equality, the theory of which we have so long had in our political institutions and constitutions, without ever attempting to bring into action the power vested in the millions by universal suffrage. Deluded by the sophistry of our upstart aristocracy, who compare our situation with the oppressed European, and take credit to themselves for allowing our working people so much independence, always reasoning as if the property produced by the laborers belongs by right to the consumers, on the principles of all the political systems of the Old World. These principles firmly attach all our assumed aristocracy to the imitation of the laws, customs, habits, and practices of subjected Europe.

CORRECTION OF POLITICAL ABUSES.—SWISS FEDERATION.—THE ABUSE OF BANKING.—THE ABUSE OF TAXATION.

June 20, 1830.

Whether the claims made by the working people, of their rights in having their due proportion of legislation and distribution, or whether a synchronous propensity of thought, has produced the investigation of so many very interesting topics, there has certainly been lately, both on the floor of Congress and of the state legistatures, discussions most interesting to the productive laborer; and as such they ought to have been agitated long since. They are crowded into the present time; an era big with ominous changes on both sides of the Atlantic. The people begin to enquire into the collision between the interest of the United States and the states' sovereignty; the use and abuse of banks; the injustice and partiality of indirect taxation on consumption; the tariff; free trade, etc. Though all these subject have been treated by our different representatives in the European fashion, favoring the nonproductive and consuming classes, yet the door is open to discussion, and I have no doubt our industrious producers will be able to take their own part in the dispute. Many two and three days' speeches have been made, on the various meanings that can be put on the federal constitution, like all other speeches, made up of words, one-half of which are undefined and undefinable, the dispute about which might last for ages, without coming nearer to a settlement. Had they put to one side the passive, wordy, and undefined document called the constitution, and examined the active causes of dispute, they would have found the judiciary and laws of the United States, their mode of taxation, recruiting and disciplining the army, interferes with the interest and internal regulations of the states, and are the causes of collision, which cannot possibly be removed by any number of long speeches, on the variety of metaphysical, legal, or grammatical explanations of that instrument; which was originally intended to favor the construction of the contending parties who made it. Having impartially ascertained the real cause of dispute, and that the theory of the constitution, as promulgated in the written document, would not work well in practice, common sense would recommend to search for some other instrument that was more perfect, and which time and experience had proved to be fit for the intended purposes. Such an organization they will find in the mountains of Switzerland, where liberty first broke through the crust of despotism in the old world, and where there is still the only unmixed power of representation in Europe. There they will find a federation that has peaceably united in the bonds of amity and friendship, pure democracies and hereditary aristocracies, without a symptom of collision or dispute, for upwards of 500 years. All which peaceable union and perfect agreement, is owing to the powers of the federation being limited to foreign intercourse, entirely separate and distinct from all interference with any internal regulations of any of the federate cantons; the federation having no right to recruit a man, or raise a cent, or hold courts of justice in any of the cantons. All causes of collision between the federation and the federate members, were thus annihilated. If 500 years successful practice does not prove that the political association is as perfect as our nature will permit, it would be difficult to find a better test, and civilization is too far advanced for the sophistry of either church or state, to argue that the difference in the locality, makes any great difference in the nature of man.

Banks, like every thing else, may be generally useful to the whole population, or useful to an exclusive class, at the expense of the great majority—like the chartered banks without a limitation of dividend, for discounting mercantile paper to furnish artificial or fictitious capitals to tradesmen. The universal utility of banks is to afford a means of transferring and removing of property, easier, safer, and at less expense than with specie.

The deposit banks of Amsterdam, Hamburgh, and Bremen, effect this object in a safe and convenient manner for the public interest, by advancing on actual deposites, without raising speculative, fictitious capitals, by the discount of paper for traders or merchants. Giving the power to directors, no wise responsible for their conduct, to issue as many notes, and discount as much paper, as their friendly disposition for their intimates will force them to do, must be abused either by a national bank or by a joint stock company; the premium for betraying their trust in both, being the same, must have similar effects. All the discount, chartered banks in Europe, except the British and French, have failed, and it is doubtful whether they could withstand any political revolution as the banks of Amsterdam, Hamburgh, etc., have done. All the reasoning of the advocates for the rechartering of the bank of the United States, and against national banks, was founded on the false supposition, that there was no other useful bank but the discount bank, for the benefit of merchants and traders. Whereas the experience of Europe has proved them to be the most liable to abuse, and therefore the most dangerous even to monarchies and aristocracies, and much more opposed to the equality on which freedom is founded on this side of the Atlantic. These gentlemen pleaded for the present stockholders, and the mercantile interest, like lawyers who had a retaining fee; not like impartial and well-informed legislators, for the general welfare, which can only exist in the interest of the millions.

Countervailing duties for the encouragement of one production in reference to, and at the expense of the other products, has even in monarchies been lately considered as unfair; though from the nature of their arbitrary powers, supported by indirect taxation on consumption, it was their interest to adopt tariffs, as the best excuse for their favorite indirect taxation. How much more dangerous to the union and peace of federate sovereign states, is the pitching the interest of one-half against the interest of the other. The least foresight of the consequences, ought to have crushed the project when it was first proposed in congress by the advocates of the interest of the comparatively few manufacturers; but once passed into a law, self-love, pride, and want of candor to confess being in the wrong, will probably prevent its being changed by the present members of congress. All the industrious producers concerned in manufactories, are interested in the abolition of the tariff, as well as all other indirect taxes on consumption, which put the greatest part of the burden of public expenses on them; and all those not concerned in manufactories, are doubly interested in its abolition; first, because it raises the price of the articles they consume; and secondly, as an indirect tax, it burdens them with much more than their just proportion of the public expenses. So that all the producers have a double interest in direct taxation, as it reduces their proportion to a small per centage on the visible property, not one-tenth of what they pay by indirect taxation on what they consume, and in free ports and free trade, supplying them with all foreign articles, at one-half what they pay through the medium of custom-houses, diminishing patronage, and in the same proportion, public expenses. It is certainly the interest of all merchants and traders to have free ports, and to be relieved from the expending of time and money, required by the routine, and often arbitrary inspection of custom-house officers, restricted to certain days and hours; which retards the operations of every species of trade. All these facilities would increase much the quantum of trade, and quick returns, as ships need not lay in the ports as many days as they are detained weeks by the ceremonies of the custom house. The people would likewise benefit by their share of the economy of public expenses. Farmers would have all their supplies much cheaper, and a quicker and easier circulation of their produce, which would not cost so much freight by the despatch given to every vessel in a free port. On an impartial examination of all circumstances, and weighing accurately the interest of all classes, it will certainly appear that free ports, free trade, and direct taxation, advance much the interest of every class of the governed; and it is only the actual governors, and those who expect to be in power, who can have an opposite interest, as their authority over the governed is in proportion to the difficulties they can oppose to the free circulation of property and knowledge; the patronage of places in their gift, constituting their profits, power, and means of perpetuating them in the place, must attach the rulers of all countries (where public opinion can be manifested) to the species of taxation, fleets, armies, etc., that give them the nominating of the greatest number of officers, enjoying good salaries.— Under the popular ignorance that tolerates despotism, the same patronage is not necessary to the power of those who govern, and we find the expense of their government is less. The waste and pillage of public property in Europe, bears some proportion to the share of freedom allowed to the millions; for they must not only pay the expenses of those in power, but must pay the necessary bribery to induce a part to subjugate the whole. Not far removed from this state of parties will be the elective government where the few rule the many, by monopolizing property, knowledge and power. The effects are the same whether it arises from hereditary power, founded on the physical force and conquest of their ancestors, or on the combination of deception, sophistry and intrigue, practiced by a class to monopolize power; which latter is the most dishonorable and worthless of the two. Once in possession of the power, they use it for their own purposes, contrary to the interest of the millions; and the only effective remedy, is for the millions never to elect a man twice into any place of profit or trust, so that he shall be perfectly convinced, that all the laws he makes and taxes he lays, while a ruler, he will have to obey and pay, the rest of his life as one of the ruled.

APATHY OF THE PRODUCERS. NEGLECT OF THE COMFORT OF THE PRODUCERS. IMPORTANCE OF OUR EXPERIMENT OF SELF-GOVERNING. TRICKS AND SOPHISTRY TO DECEIVE THE PRODUCERS.

June 21, 1830.

It is sufficient to convince an infidel of the existence of original sin, and that the sins of the fathers, are visited upon the children to the third and fourth generation, to see that many of the political abuses, and all the legal corruption that torments old mother Britain, have been entailed on her progeny, on this side of the Atlantic, aggravated immensely by the consideration that the millions have the power to reform every abuse, and to legislate agreeably to the dictates of their own interest. Whilst their forefathers in Britain are chained down to hereditary power, from which they cannot be released, without a union of force and violence, which their subjugated state will not permit, their offspring on this side of the Atlantic, have only to will it, by universal suffrage and it must be done. But hugging their chains, and submitting to the arbitrary laws, customs and habits of Britain, argues an apathy more morbid than can be found in the quiescent Chinese; in whose country a similarity of climate, may predispose towards a similarity of moral affections and physical propensities which the stimulus of freedom and equality may tend to correct. The influence of climate on both the moral faculties and physical properties, has not yet been sufficiently attended to.

Long before John Gray had dissected society, and shown its real elements, by analysis of the British nation, little short of chemical accuracy, Latrobe was arranging the scheme of furnishing the city of Philadelphia with wholesome water, in the manner of the new river company of London, by making the millions, first pay by the produce of their labor, for the erection of the works, and afterwards pay an exorbitant revenue to the capitalists, for the use of the water.—On explaining the utility of the building in the centre square for the steam engine, Latrobe suggested that public baths could be added for the accommodation of the working people, at little or no additional expense, as the water could be heated by the same fuel that raised the steam for the engine, hinting that all nations, both ancient and modern, had public baths and other accommodations for the use of the great mass of laborers, who could not conveniently purchase those necessary means of healthful cleanliness themselves. The town council got much offended at Latrobe for hinting at such an improper mode of spending their money, and forced him to erase every word concerning the baths, before they would receive his estimate. Would any town council, put in power by the votes of the millions, venture to act so aristocratically at present? So far we are changing in favor of freedom and equality.

In all political associations that have preceded us, whether free, mixed or despotic, the governors have had some consideration for the convenience and pleasure of the laboring producers, and public fountains, public walks, public gardens, public exhibitions of the fine arts, etc., etc., are all open gratis to the whole population; there a perfect equality prevailed, and he that had not a cent in his pocket was on a par of gratification with him who wallowed in wealth. But money is the god of our country, he who has none in his pocket, is shut out from all walks, exhibitions, gardens, pictures, music, etc., etc. Even water must be purchased in our large towns. Every species of amusement is monopolized for the individual benefit of some one or other of the aristocratic class, or one that is forced by the combination of their influence to join them and promote their interest.

In a government founded on freedom and equality, there must be some radical defect in the nature of its materials, to produce so great a contrast in the practices of the social order, and must be either in the qualities of the governors or of the governed, and most probably in both, depending on surrounding circumstances. The governors are all elective, holding the places of honor and profit, on a precarious and uncertain footing, and therefore forced to make the most of their time to accumulate property, of the chance of which they may soon be deprived. The number of expectants, being perhaps some hundreds for every place worth the possession, increase in the same proportion the advocates for power and perquisite, under no responsibility but from laws, made and executed by themselves, and public opinion, from the ignorance of the millions, being completely under their own control, they, like the tenants at will, drain the soil of all its substance, regardless of the interest of those who come after them. The governed by universal suffrage, having all the power, are dupes of a more intricate, active and deep laid intrigue, imposing on their ignorance and want of union. Both church and state hunt in packs, and run down their prey singly, when the ignorance of the millions neglects to protect their class. It was both prudent and polite in the millions to begin the moral revolution, through their hall of science to equalize the knowledge of the present generation, and to secure a still greater equality of property, knowledge and power, which contains all the ingredients of freedom and equality.

On the success of the working classes' experiment, is staked the happiness of the civilized world. The theory of a people governing themselves, first promulgated by our revolution, spread afar, and was supported by the prosperous results. The present claims to practical equality will be diffused through all nations, and will awaken the oppressed producers to a sense of their utility, rights, and power. The facility of communication to every part of the globe, transports every ray of useful knowledge to the smallest ramification of society, and benefits the mass of mankind, by the experimental knowledge of every individual state. Thus the ages of the world are watching the improvements in each nation to benefit by it, and the interest of mankind become a unit, by the judicious adoption of federalism, where the interest of the few is forced to yield to the interest of the many, and the interest of one modifies by his happiness the interests of all.

Where the millions rule, the interest of the millions must at last prevail. Nothing is more easy than to govern people according to their interest; nothing more difficult than to rule men contrary to their interests. Men having been always governed contrary to their interest, originated the idea of the great difficulty, intricacy, and mystery, in the act of governing. What address, finesse, and intrigue is necessary to make the interests of the few appear the interests of the many: to make the interest of the laboring producers appear the same as the interests of the idle consumers; what hocus pocus, legerdemain, to magnify the hundreds into the size and consequence of the millions. In London, when the war was declared against the French revolution, what farcical tricks and ingenious contrivances were played off, to make the will of the privileged orders pass for the will of the millions. A meeting was called in the excise office, and all the clerks had a holiday, to fill the hall, which was completely occupied by the friends of war, so that no others could gain admittance; petititions to the king were to be signed, and the emissaries of government dragged the John Bulls to sign them. Amongst the rest, they attempted to force a hatter to sign for a French war; but he asked, if these Frenchmen, they were going to fight with, had heads? On being answered in the affirmative, "Don't think," said he, "I am such a fool as to help to kill my customers."

INTERESTED OPPOSITION TO IMPROVEMENT. — THE INTEREST OF THE PRODUCERS OPPOSED TO THAT OF THE NON-PRODUCERS.

July 21, 1830.

Against the very few civil, political, or religious changes that have yet been made in any country, in favor of the industrious producers, the non-productive consumers, who, from force, cunning, or accident, have got possession of power, make a number of objections, which they pretend arise out of the passions, prejudices, or ignorance of man, laying all the blame on human nature, forgetting that they themselves are part, and perhaps the most corrupt part of mankind. During, and for long after our revolution, they asserted the impossibility of any society being capable of self-government: when experience proved them in error, they were forced to acknowledge that it might do for our half-peopled desert, but could not regulate any civilized society. Freedom was transferred to France, and the same objection, enforced by the bayonets of the civilized part of Europe, gave them a momentary triumph, only to prove in time (the adage, "A man convinced against his will, is of the same opinion still," the folly of attempting to change opinions by physical force. The moral experiment of the penitentiary at Philadelphia was opposed by the same class, and on the same grounds of the great defect of our species, perhaps taken from the religious dogma of original sin; but the perseverance of the Quakers succeeded in spite of all civil, political, and religious oppositions; and though it has effectually improved the state of society in all countries where it has been introduced, such as all the states of our Union, Britain, France, Holland, and Switzerland, yet there are beings who ought to be rational, who pretend that it would not work well in some countries, because the people do not speak the same language, have a different mode of acting in church, or are of a different color; though all possess the same senses, physical appetites, and much the same moral capacities. Among the number of beneficial changes made during the French revolution, the code Napoleon, was one of the most useful, and has benefited all countries that had the good sense to adopt it, such as France, Flanders, Holland, and part of Germany. Its original language was French, which has been translated into Flemish, Dutch, and German; and because it has not found its way into any country that speaks our language, neither Britain nor our Union are likely to benefit by it for ages. The young converts to freedom in South America are now making the code Napoleon speak Spanish, and will most probably reform their antiquated feudal laws, forced upon them by their foreign masters, some ages before our Union: will release themselves from the oppression of complicated, undefined, and litigious laws, nearly a thousand years behind the knowledge of the day, and in contradiction to the theory of all our simple political institutions.

Is it the interest and egotism of the rulers which prevents reformation, or the prejudices and ignorance of the ruled? In all governments that have yet existed, men in power find it easy to direct public affairs according to their own interest, and have found precedents in every page of history, to sanction their usurpation and sophistical reasoning in abundance, to prove that their interest is the public good. The world having been ruled by arbitrary and despotic power, there are a thousand examples to refer to as precedents for one that is to be found where any species of freedom was permitted to prevail. Had it been the interest of the privileged few who rule our Union, that all the western associations should be begun on a footing of equality, they would have adopted the British mode of settling uncultivated lands, and would have defended the imitation by a far superior reasoning than they can produce for the civil, political and religious copy they have taken from old mother Britain. If it had been the interest of the non-productive consumers to instruct the industrious producers, our continent would have been as amply furnished with free schools for the children of the millions, as it is now with universities and colleges richly endowed for the education of the children of the ruling rich. If it had been the interest of our assumed aristocracy, who have as yet governed us, to simplify and define our laws, by a plain and easily understood code, our working people would not be tyrannized over by a mysterious, incomprehensible crowd of crude precedents, invented in the barbarous ages of feudality to subjugate the feudal serfs.

Where hereditary power transfers the glebe with the men and oxen that feed upon it to a weak successor, the millions have no resource but passive obedience to the will and caprice of their governors, by divine and hereditary right. But in an an elective government of universal suffrage, the interest of the few, must yield to the interest of the many; the source of power being completely changed, all rules and regulations which flow from it must be equally changed, and often reversed: for the interest of the few non-productive consumers is evidently opposed to the interest of the producers, as is every act, principle or product, which emanates from the two irreconcilible systems; and nothing but the cunning of the few, and the ignorance of the many, could have left so self-evident a problem so long unsolved.

Every page of history attests that the interest of the great mass of industrious producers is opposed to the interest of the few non-productive consumers, and that national wealth, power, and dominion, have only been an accumulation of riches, influence, and artificial superiority of the non-productive few, over the producing many, whose poverty and misery, in all countries, are in proportion to the extravagance, luxury, and grandeur with which they are forced to maintain the consuming classes; that all wars, victories, and conquests add to the glory and renown of the rulers, at the expense of the peace, freedom, and happiness of the ruled, as is sufficiently proven by the results of the Roman conquests down to the effects of the extensive empire of commercial Britain. What has been the advantage to the millions of the high sounding names of freedom and equality, introduced by our revolution, and that of the French and Spanish? Has it not been limited merely to the change of mode by election, not the change of men? Has not the same class of society governed by universal suffrage, who used to govern by divine and hereditary right? What have the industrious producers gained? The boasted faculty of having the power to release themselves, by self-governments, from all injustice, tyranny, and oppression, without having the knowledge, judgment, or courage to practice it. Will it not rather lower than advance our species on the scale of intellect?

Let us hope that a new era approaches; that the diffusion of knowledge amongst the industrious producers will enable them to take care of themselves, and to entrust their civil and political affairs with such as have the same interest, and a fellow-feeling with them, and change them as soon as the intoxication of power forces them to swerve from the duty they owe their constituents: that the practice of freedom and equality will originate amongst the same people, where the theory began half a century ago; that our operatives will have the merit of giving an example, that most probably will be followed by all the working classes in every country. The stake is immense which depends on their success. Not only their own and their posterity's happiness, but the comfort and happiness of hundreds of millions yet unborn hang on the union and perseverance of our industrious producers, who first have the good sense and courage to claim their rights, and show the inappreciable advantages of universal suffrage, when practiced with judgment, firmness, and moderation, at **the** ballot boxes.

NECESSITY THE MOTHER OF INVENTION. — DISTRIBUTION OF THE PUBLIC LANDS. — LEGISLATORS MAKE LAWS IN THEIR OWN FAVOR.

July 14, 1830.

It is a deception in the property of riches, that has been propagated and maintained by those who possess them, that money can command all things. In no country is wealth so much the *summum bonum* of life as in ours. And although it can purchase many things, it is the paralizer of all talent and genius. Hereditary wealth presses on the extinguisher of merit in proportion to its weight; and both hereditary wealth and hereditary power incapacitate the possessor for all mental or corporeal exertion, useful to himself or others. It has been remarked, that there never was a lawyer who inherited £500 or more a-year who ever made any figure at the English bar, and the same observation will no doubt hold good in every other trade or profession. The spur of necessity produced a Franklin, a Watt, an Arckwright, etc., etc., and all those who have benefitted mankind by their ingenious inventions. It is the nature of repletion to produce indolence and the excess of physical indulgence, which riches facilitate, to debilitate both body and mind, which descends to their offspring, and shows the injury done to society by permitting any thing liable to abuse to descend to the weak and imbecile progeny of luxurious parents. Fortunately, nature, when left to herself, tends to equality, when not counteracted by the unjust laws of primogeniture and entails; for there have been scarcely any family riches, consequence, or consideration which last two generations, since our revolution, and much the same may be said of France, since the equalization of the French revolution.

Is there the smallest reason to prevent our farmers, mechanics, and working people from trusting the management of their political affairs in the hands of the best informed of their own class, who have their interest, and have a fellow-feeling in promoting it? What interest has a lawyer — a dealer in words—to forward the interest of a dealer in things, the real value and utility of which being understood, must lower the value of his stock in trade? During the two or three days' speeches in Congress, on the right to the management of the uncultivated lands, it was never mentioned how it was the interest of the millions to have them divided, though that was all the millions were interested in. Once fix how the interest of the immense majority could be served by the distribution of them, and it is not so material what artificial body of the states, or of the United States, have the execution of it, provided the mode of distribution was so well defined that the interest of the many could not be injured. All of this would be well taken care of, if they were properly represented by their own class. The mode of treating that question, like every other, depends on whose interest is to be preferred: If the interest of the few non-producers and consumers, they must advocate the sale to the highest bidder; as capitalists, they have the advantage in speculation, the money going into the treasury, they as rulers have the benefit of distributing it. The interest of the laborers or producers is, certainly, that the lands may be equally divided amongst all who can cultivate them, and that the beginning of society in the West should be an equal division of property, by giving to each settler 200 acres, at a small consideration to pay for surveying them, on condition, that if they be not improved by a certain time to revert to the state; which would prevent all speculative monopoly. But the few favorites of fortune may say, it will be a defalcation of the revenue. Let the revenue be collected from those who own property, not from the poor, whose circumstances force them to cut down the forests, and to suffer all the privations incident to a new settlement. Such a mode of distribution would be a perpetual resource against poverty and misery, and would not force our industry to seek refuge in Upper Canada, where this mode of granting lands, in spite of the bad climate, has peopled that country with our citizens. In all affairs that come before our legislatures or congress, there is the same opposition of interest. It is no doubt the interest of every man, who has the smallest expectation of being president or member of congress, to heap power and patronage on the federation, no matter at whose expense: but it is the interest of the industrious producers that all should go on peaceably and smoothly, without friction, well knowing that they must pay dear for the oil necessary to lubricate the political machine; they are therefore interested in preventing the interference of the federation with any of the internal regulations of the states.

Examine every law, or legislative act, bank, or monopolizing charter: all are for the interest of the few, and against the interest of the many. Nor have the many any right to complain, after electing such representatives as had interest opposed to them; one might as well blame another for eating and drinking as blame him for following his own interest, when left to his free choice, as is the case with all elective officers. The vague word *duty*, means anything or nothing, according to the interest of the party, and is never construed to mean anything disagreeable or offensive to the interest of the acting party in practice, whatever may be the fine spun theory of moralists, who judge of man according to their imagination of what he ought to be.

Sweden is the only country where half the elective power is kept in possession of the industrious producers. There are four houses, each having one vote: the peasants, in which none is allowed to represent a peasant, but a peasant; burgers, in which none is allowed to represent a burger but a burger; the clergy, and the nobles. These last are in constant dispute with the king; the two efficient causes of tyranny, by their opposition, form an arch under which the people circulate more freely than in any other country in Europe. Where universal suffrage gives the right to the millions, to be governed according to the dictates of their own interest, and they by giving their votes to a monied aristocracy form an artificial privileged order, all impartial observers, foreigners as well as others, have a right to say, such people conscious of their inability to govern themselves, are forced to surrender their birthright, to a class instituted to rule over them, which class, if it were hereditary, would save much time, money, and trouble. It is thus that the practice hitherto of the United States has thrown much obloquy, scandal, and distrust on freedom and equality; and sanctions the enemies of human happiness, in asserting that man is incapable of liberty and self-government; they instance the result of the only fair experiment that has been allowed to be made, and that this disgraceful and unaccountable order of things has been allowed to exist for fifty-three years, confirming the disrepute in which all such experiments have been yet held.

GREAT EXPENSE OF INDIRECT TAXATION. BRITAIN COMPELLED TO MODIFY IT.

July 30, 1830.

Necessity is the mother of invention; it is likewise the corrector of errors; it elucidates truth, curtails corruption, promotes investigation into political and other public abuse and misrule. Since the great distress of the millions in Britain has become so obvious, the parliament has been occupied with partial and temporary reforms. They have abolished the indirect tax on beer, leather, and cider, to the amount of £3,400,000, for which the minister takes the credit of relieving the public burthens to the amount of £5,000,000; which is a frank confession, that the expense, trouble, tyranny, oppression, and loss of time in collecting £3,400,000, by indirect taxation amounts to £1,600,000, or nearly fifty per cent. on the sum collected. By a similar calculation, if the accumulating strength of public opinion should force the British government to change the forty millions of indirect taxation (now paid principally by the working classes) into a direct tax on all kinds of property, (which would be paid principally by the rich non-producers) the government might take credit for relieving the millions of 60,000,000 of expense or burdens. This is a truth which nothing but dire necessity could force an aristocracy to acknowledge; and the only reason why it has not been put in practice is, that the rich non-producers, possessing all power in the governments that have yet existed, do not choose to tax themselves, but lay all burdens on those they think it their interest to keep poor and ignorant. Political economists make their books in favor of the rich, who are alone able to buy them. Turgos' Political Economy endeavors to prove, that the land pays all taxes at last (which the present situation of Britain seems to verify), and that therefore it saves much trouble and expense to lay the taxes direct on the land; hence this work exhibits the only system of political economy and taxation in favor of the millions. During the enthusiasm of the French revolution, they began by adopting Turgos' system; but it was abolished when their representatives felt might, and forgot right. Nor has the influence of the millions been sufficient in any political association, either before or since, (except the New England townships) to give a fair trial of Turgos' system: though there can be no doubt, that its tendency to the equalization of property would constitute it the best possible security and protection of freedom and equality; and as such it ought to be adopted by all free nations who value the advantages of their rights and prerogatives as an independent and free people.

When the British aristocracy take off part of the indirect taxation as the only mode of relieving the distresses of the working people, and propose further to commute a certain part of the indirect taxes into a direct tax on income, to alleviate the burdens that oppress the industrious producers, now in a state of starvation from the enormity of indirect taxes, which load them with the greatest part of the public expenses: this must be taken as an irrefragable proof of the unfairness of indirect taxation, as being extorted from those who can least afford it, and who by their industry produce every species of property, and at the same time it must be taken as an equally undisputed acknowledgment that, direct taxation is the only just and equitable mode of raising the the public revenue. When these great truths have flashed conviction into the minds of the most aristocratic society in Europe, how much more interest have our electors by universal suffrage in the total abolition of every species of indirect taxes, and the substitution of direct taxes on every species of property in their place. Ignorance of the common rules of arithmetic, cannot be the reason why our industrious producers have suffered the federal expenditure to have been so long collected by indirect taxes; it must rather be the total absence of the stimulus of necessity, which has paralized all the mental faculties, and left our industrious producers in a state of indolent apathy as respects their pecuniary and political interests.

CANALS AND RAIL ROADS. THE VETO.

August 18, 1830.

How long will both individuals and nations be in acquiring knowledge in the cheapest, most certain, and most useful manner, by the experience of others. No country was ever in a situation to benefit more by what has been done before them, than ours, removed as it is so far from the contagion of local circumstances, free to choose the best, and most appropriate arts, inventions and practices, moral and physical, which the civilized world has proved (in some instances by their dear bought experience) to be the fittest, and best suited to produce the benefit required, in a comparatively new state of society, where the prejudices and blunders of antiquity have not had time to take root.

What is the reason that scarcely a turnpike road in the Union pays an interest on the money it cost, and that many of them do not even pay for the necessary repairs? It is, evidently, because the thin population of the country does not afford a sufficient circulation of either people or property, to pay the expense of making roads paved with stanes. If so, prudence, economy, and good policy would council to bestow the labor on something more productive. Will the multiplicity of roads, canals, or rail-roads, increase the surplus produce to be transported on them, or provide sufficient markets for it when so carried? The answer must be in the negative. For the labor put on the means of conveying is taken from the means of producing, and therefore retards it, and there is no necessary relation between the mode of transporting and the market which consumes it. When we began to speculate on the utility of canals and rail-ways, it was natural, and rational, to inquire what the few roads we had made, produced, towards paying for the expense of constructing. This producing no great encouragement at home, perhaps a few sanguine speculators might imagine to find it abroad.

The two nations in Europe, nearest to our own in their thin population in proportion to their extent of territory, are Russia and Spain. Russia has one canal of about a mile between the Wolga and the Neva, to join the Caspian sea with the Baltic, facilitating a navigation of nearly 2,000 miles. Spain has no canals, and scarcely any navigation on the rivers, equal to what the population had in the time of the Romans. Our speculators might imagine that the vast extent of our continent would make up for the want of population; and that we might expect to reap the benefit that Britain and perhaps France have obtained from canals; and some hundred years hence they might perhaps be right in their conjectures. But even then they must follow exactly the British mode of making canals, by allowing individual enterprise and industry to make them, when the quantity of produce which shall be ready to be transported on them, will pay all the expense and a reasonable profit for the outlay of money. That is, first to ascertain the existence of the materials, the carriage of which shall pay the interest of money laid on and the repairs of the canals, and likewise the certainty or great probability of a market. These are the requisites to render either roads or canals profitable to the undertakers, without which they cannot extend far or be a public good. In a country where there is so much uncultivated land, and labor scarce, to employ it on any unprofitable works must be considered as a public loss.

"Internal improvement" is a popular phrase, which seems to mean exclusively the making of rail-roads and digging canals. It may be doubted, whether the expending of ten or twelve millions of dollars in digging a canal, where the nature, value, or quantity of produce to be transported on it, will not pay for the necessary repairs and for the interest of the money it cost, may be considered an internal improvement or the contrary, even if the money was in the peoples' treasury. But where the poverty of public funds forces us to have recourse to a loan, to mortgage posterity for an expenditure not immediately required by the situation and circumstances of the present population, nor even by their successors perhaps for ages, it would appear to be premature. Had the Erie canal, coasting along the shores of lake Ontario, been allowed by the New York legislators to be made by the abundance of capital and enterprise of individuals, it is more than probable it would have been deferred for ages, before it would have been considered the most necessary amongst the great number of improvements wanted. The same remark may apply to Pennsylvania, and to all the other states who have mortgaged posterity to dig canals or make railways, before the population of the country was sufficient to pay for them. In every situation where coal or any other bulky material, gave a probability of paying for the expense of a canal, it has been made by individual industry and enterprise, as at Richmond, the Schuylkill, Lehigh, &c., &c. and would have been made under like circumstances every where, at the proper time, without the interference of government. As the French merchant said to Colbert, when asked what he could do for them, answered, "let us alone."

Account of the tolls and expenses of the Erie canal, taken from the Banner of the Constitution, Washington.

Expense in 1826,	- - -	$1,121,286 96
Tolls, do.	- - -	715,245 80
	Loss,	106,143 86
Expense in 1827,	- - -	993,436 50
Tolls, do.	- - -	846,651 73
	Loss;	146,711 81
In 1828 balance against the canals,	-	92,269 81
1829, do. do.	- -	110,632 51

Debts contracted for making canals in the state of New York, $10,272,316 76.

Adding the four years deficit canal debts, &c., in 1830, was $12,237,399 70; showing a cost of canals over the produce, of nearly two millions.

The interest on the debt contracted for digging the canals will always be the same, but the expense of keeping them in repair will increase, as in the fourth, fifth, and sixth years all the wooden portion will decay, of which part of the embankments, bridges, aqueducts, &c., are made. This canal has likewise a rival in the St. Lawrence, the natural outlet of the lakes, which may force them to lower their tolls. Lakes Michigan, Huron, and lake Superior, will find a more convenient and economical outlet by the river Illinois, and lake Erie by the Ohio canal, or by the one proposed by the river Wabash. Those short canals which unite extensive navigation, ought to be first constructed by a scattered population, enjoying the benefit of such immense navigable rivers, the beds and channels of which, ought to be cleared of all bars and obstructions, as the most natural, and cheapest mode of communication, in a country situated, and peopled as ours is, who ought to make the most of their natural advantages before they think of imitating Britain or any other country, that, forced by circumstances, depends on artificial resources.

It is more than probable that the productions, all over our continent, will supply the consumption in every district, when property and knowledge are allowed to find their level; that is, when our rulers cease to bribe, by premiums, planters to grow sugar, or the manufacturers to make what can be bought cheaper elsewhere. It must then be the foreign market on which we must depend for the consumption of our surplus produce. Already the diffusion of knowledge has deprived us of Spain and Portugal as customers for our bread stuffs, and a little extension of the same useful information to South America will annihilate civil war and bloodshed, and will equally deprive us of that market for our flour. It is probable that the increase and diffusion of useful knowledge through nations, will decrease the necessity of foreign trade, and the equalization of knowledge through the same nations, will equally diminish the necessity for home trade, by teaching every nation and every district to supply its own wants in a greater degree. So that even if our canals and railways would pay now, in consequence of the great inequality of the means of production, they may cease to pay, when both property and knowledge are nearer a par with both individuals and nations.

We have had an instance of the effects of the diffusion of knowledge, in our supplying ourselves with cotton manufactories, and will very soon have a further elucidation, by having woolen and iron fabricks erased from the list of our imports. And it is even probable that before long we shall be independent of all countries for our consumption of wine, oil, dried fruits, and silk. As from our extended latitude we can have the products of all climates, it only depends on our own knowledge and industry to supply ourselves with every species of natural production to be found in any parts of the earth. Then our foreign trade will be small, and there will be but little necessity for fleets to protect it; materially diminishing the cares and expenses of government.

President Jackson, by rejecting the act authorizing the subscription to the Maysville road, gave a very fortunate check to legislative extravagance in voting away the people's money for what has been called internal improvements; begun by sanguine speculators, in hopes that government would put the burden on the peoples' shoulders by furnishing the money to complete the work, many years before the population of the country could support it, and giving to the state of Kentucky an advantage, which could not with justice be refused to all the others: thus opening a door to a vast expenditure out of the federal treasury, at the option of each individual state who might find it their interest to make internal improvements at the expense of the Union. By the judicious exercise of his negative, the president has benefitted his country, and will deserve the thanks of the present as well as of future generations.

CORRECTION OF OLD ERRORS. IMPROVEMENTS FOR THE SUCCEEDING GENERATIONS.

August 29, 1829.

In the present rapid progression of useful knowledge, satire loses its sting, by the correction of old vices, follies, errors and opinions, and the adoption of new, to which the old satire will not apply. Can there be any thing more foolishly ridiculous than Don Quixotte in the present day? even the satires of Voltaire on the catholic christianity are lost on a great majority, as well as the ridicule cast on our forefathers, by the Spectator, Tatler, and other similar publications called classical, from the supposed purity of their style. The music of words and literature, changes with the knowledge of the day, and fiction, in order to amuse, must now take the form of reality; as the success of Scott's novels has proven: and many of the errors of the present day, which our ignorance prevents us from correcting, will, in the next age, be considered as a shame and disgrace to this. Amongst the most injurious and absurd of our present system, may perhaps be considered the multiplicity, intricacy and complication of our laws, filling many thousand volumes, and feeding myriads of lawyers, rendering the possession of life, liberty, and property, dependent on a quibble, and searching into the registers of dark and barbarous ages, to obtain a rule of conduct for this; thus losing every advantage gained by civilization; whilst many of the old nations, whose political and religious prejudices, place them centuries behind us, have had the good sense to adopt a simple, well defined code of laws, contained in a pocket volume, which every one can read and consult, so as to know what he has a right to do, and when he transgresses the laws of the country, without consulting those, who, from their education, profession, and habits, have an interest in deceiving them. Our successors may consider, the expenses of two legislatures unnecessary, when one might do the business with less risk of collision; to employ two men to cut down a tree, one holding the handle of the ax, and the other the head, is labor and time lost. Our indirect tax on consumption may be thought, by our descendants to be unfair and unequal, as there is no proportion between a man's property and what he consumes: very often, those who have the least, spend the most. A laboring man, with a wife and ten or twelve children, consumes more than a bachelor with 100,000 dollars a year, whose property is protected by the government, without his paying any thing to support it. In justice, taxation ought to be in proportion to protection. Our children may object to the double, triple, and often quadruple expense of having collectors for the United States tax, for the state tax, county tax, township and town tax; and may have the ingenuity to contrive a method of having all the public revenue collected by one set of officers; thus reducing both the expense and the patronage, so injurious to that equality on which real freedom can alone be founded. The next age, convinced of the benefit they will have derived from the small number of free schools, may insist on more of ther money being appropriated to maintain free schools for the education of the millions, and less expended on colleges and universities for the instruction of the rich.

Coining money by bank monopolies, may be considered throwing property into the hands of the few, without paying for it by labor, deranging the natural equality, and tending to create a monied aristocracy; to prevent which our successors may divest their legislators of the rights of granting monopolies, privileges, or charters, if not altogether, at least, limiting them to the time they are elected into power, and prohibiting any act of one legislature from binding the next, being a royal prerogative they have assumed, which if extended, would leave nothing for their successors to do, but to look at the execution of the acts passed by their predecessors. Generations to come, with the experience of this, may decide that a standing army is unnecessary for the protection of freedom, which is safer, and more surely maintained and defended by a militia, who enjoy all the benefits of its equality, comforts and happiness. By the future publicity of all public acts, and national transactions, ambassadors may be useless, as the intrigues of one nation against another, cease to be profitable to either. Political labor may, in time, be reduced to a par with other labor, and be paid in a medium less subject to vary in value than money. This will diminish the intrigue and violent scramble for place, by making the salary a less object of contention. To effect this desirable object, the best and perhaps only way would be to put no one into office for a longer term than a year, without a legibility to be re-elected. As fleets are more for aggression than for defence, and as no people can possibly benefit by conquest, considerate descendants may dispense with that expensive and troublesome appendix to freedom, and also avoid the expense of fortifications; as the best defence of freedom are the arms of the free.

The probable consequence of adopting all or any of the foregoing improvements or changes, will be, the luxury and vices of the rich and influential will be diminished, and in the same proportion an addition will be made to the comforts, and independence of the millions. It is gradually taking from the one the superfluities that injure him, and giving to the other the necessaries of life, that would do them much good. But it is a desideratum to be wished for, more than to be soon expected with us, in consequence of the strong phalanx of organized opposition of the few, against the apathy and slowness of intellect of the thoughtless many. Mexico, in its political infancy, is perhaps nearer to a beneficial change of the speculative system of politics and religion, than those nations, who from long continued habits and practice, have so intervowen their errors with their existence as to make them second nature, not to be eradicated but by a strong physical shock, or by a long moral experience. The old aristocratic faction in Mexico was broken up by the expulsion of the Spaniards, and there has not been time, industry, or talent, to form a new party, strong enough to compete with the numbers and natural advantages of the democracy. There exists in the nation an equality of knowledge and power, rarely to be found in old societies, which will in time most probably produce a greater equality in property. This new order of things, will be much accelerated by the great proportion of property belonging to the church, which in the other States of South America, has been considered as public property, and employed as such. Great advantages to future generations may be expected from the population that will most probably settle their lands, not one two-hundredth part of which is yet cultivated. Induced by their fine climate, and other natural advantages, the cream of the civilized world may be expected to immigrate.

On this side of the Atlantic, our system is founded on equality of rights, and on the other side, on the inequality of hereditary power. Our operations, both political and religious, are carried on by the mutual interest of the many; in the old world by the combined force of the few, coercing the divided strength and exertions of the many. In the one all is free will and a community of interest, on the other all is force and a contradiction of opinions, habits and interest. It appears natural for our descendants, removed one age further from the customs of their forefathers, to reflect seriously, whether the laws, armies, fleets, policy, political and religious institutions, &c., necessary to support and protect the system of violence and coercion, practised for many centuries in the old world, are either useful or necessary to the existence of our free institutions and constitutions, and if no ways useful, they might be injurious, tending more or less to the establishing an order of things similar to the systems they were contrived to support. Convinced by experience of the truth of such conclusions, it would not be astonishing if our successors, in the next age, should endeavor to release themselves from the moral trammels and fetters of antiquity, and invent laws, rules, regulations, habits and customs, more congenial to their freedom, and erect a system on the broad basis of universal suffrage, that would consolidate and perpetuate our free institutions, and augment the comfort and happiness of the millions.

POLITICAL SELF-INTEREST. OFFICE HUNTING.

August 7, 1829.

All men are actuated by their interest, as far as they understand it. Hence it follows as a certain consequence, that he who possesses the most knowledge, and the greatest and most accurate foresight into the consequences of his actions, will pursue most accurately his own real interest, and that all deviations from it must be in proportion to the quantum of ignorance, or want of thought, reflection, or foresight of the individual. Men are checked in following their interest at the expense of others, in exact proportion to the state of equality of the society, and are licensed to injure one another in the ratio of the great inequality that force, fraud, or superior powers, have established amongst them. In many countries, the millions seem disposed, to make an exception to the general rule of selfishness, in favor of their rulers; the class of men, who, from their situation, power, and physical force are out of the reach of retaliation, and by their superior privileges are exempt from the check of equality, which controls others that are forced to obey.

One of the last lessons that experience teaches us, is that men are all the same, when under the control of similar circumstances; and that liberality, generosity, patriotism, philanthropy, &c., are words that only mean different modifications of self-interest, according to the kinds of pleasures, gratifications, or habits, which we may have contracted in pursuit of our own happiness. If mankind had coolness, patience, and impartiality enough, to examine and analyze, the various ramifications of self that actuate them as motives, they would have no difficulty in substituting, *my* for *public*, in all the speeches of politicians, from the grave senator, through all the grades of office, down to the stump orator of a back woods election. Our self-conceit and self-love deceive us relative to the disinterestedness of our own actions, and justice and impartiality, induce us to attribute the same superior motives to our friends, however ready we may be to condemn the selfish motives of those we think our enemies. On this pivot of ideal benevolence and generosity, whirls all the delusive sophistry of both church and state.

Fix the movements of society on truth and reality, and the whole scaffolding of deception falls to the ground, and would save the millions the trouble of investigating the intricate question of public good, limiting their inquiries to finding out whether, from the habits, opinions, or profession of the candidate for office, he is likely to further their interest, or whether acting on a motive founded on his own interest, he may be disposed to oppose the interest of the electors. With such forethought, it is more than probable, that neither a farmer nor a tradesman would give his vote to a lawyer or a divine, to represent them and make their laws.

In our country the scurrility of some of the newspapers, in abusing the candidates for power, the eagerness of place hunters, in endeavoring to live on the labor of others, is carried on with a violence and want of decorum, hardly to have been expected in a free country, (where common sense and common decency ought to rule,) until the successful candidate is ascertained, when the dispute ceases in a great degree, until the next approaching election, and the fortunate majority scramble for the partition of the loaves and fishes, whilst the minority calculate how they can become the strongest party at the ensuing struggle. Not the smallest hint is given of a change of government or measures, but a change of those who live on salaries out of the people's purse is the whole, bone of contention.

SELF-INTEREST THE REGULATOR OF OUR ACTIONS.
August 8, 1829.

We have in abundance, for all useful purposes, chemical, physical, and other instruments, tests and reactives, invented by our men of science to facilitate the judging of the qualities, properties, and component parts of matter with expedition and certainty, without requiring the speculative theories of either church or state, to interfere in the common sense results of these positive experiments. But our moral rules and guides are more or less founded on a mistake in the conception of our nature. They are rather applicable to beings independent of wants, and are designated under the doubtful and ever varying denominations of "duty and love we owe to God," and "duties to our fellow men," without permitting self-interest to be considered as a motive of action; thereby sanctioning the most immoral and detestable crimes, under the pretence of public good and the salvation of souls; whilst the real motive, the self-interest of the perpetrators, being known, would unmask the deception, and prevent any individual being ignorant or depraved enough to execute the malice and criminal propensities of others. Under the mask of this duty and love, have all the horrors, massacres, butcheries of both church and state, been perpetrated. Under the pretence of the good of this, or of their other world, have all the slaughters, burnings and persecutions been committed.

Most of which disgraceful and barbarous acts, would have been saved to humanity, had the real selfish motives been known and avowed. Military chiefs, exciting to carnage for the good, and glory of their followers, or religious bigots preaching extirpation for the love of God, and saving the souls of the sufferers, could not have found men ignorant or wicked enough to have executed their tyrannical cruelties, had their true motives been known, and the whole mask of religion and the mysterious veil of national policy, been torn from the hypocrite.

By founding the motives of man's actions on the true basis of self-interest, every one would have credit for the effects that were evident and well understood by every observer, in place of taking merit for mysterious motives, seldom understood by themselves and certainly hidden from all others. It would destroy the deceptions too often practised, to make dupes of the ignorant, contained in the words patriotism, philanthrophy, benevolence, disinterestedness, charity, &c. We would have as good a right to claim merit for eating, drinking, or sleeping, as for doing any other action that pleases ourselves; for if it were not to obtain pleasure, we certainly would not act to procure pain; and a perfect neutrality is inconsistent with our nature. Few are capable of impartially investigating their own motives. Self-conceit offers a ready decision. Once persuaded of their own disinterestedness, they easily admit their friends to a participation in the merit, however sparingly they attribute such praiseworthy motives to their enemies, or indifferent acquaintances. We generally deceive ourselves, before we allow others to deceive us. It is so pleasant to glide into opinions that flatter our self-love, that we readily believe ourselves actuated by motives which long habit has induced us to think of a more refined and superior order. Influential men, and those in power, who amuse themselves in granting favors to their dependants, are shocked at the idea of any thing selfish, existing as a motive of their actions, as it partly conceals the claim to remuneration or gratitude. These are powerful supports to the principle of disinterested motives and have deterred many from avowing the result of an impartial analysis. Rochefoucault and some others have ventured to hint at the influence of self-interest on the conduct of men; but they were cried down and reprobated by the governors of both Church and State.

 The principle of disinterested motives, which favors the interest of certain classes, gives the utmost latitude to that species of deception which tends to lead astray public opinion, by giving a sanction and plausibility to the sophistry of every religious and political quack, to advocate his own selfish interest under the disguise of philanthropy, patriotism, &c., keeping out of view the true reason of private benefit, and inducing the nation and the public to believe, that the public good is their only object, leading astray the attention from the effects easily judged of, to the motives that are difficult to find out, concerning which the only safe way to act, is on the conviction that every individual is for himself, and prosecutes his own interest as far as he knows how. By fixing the foundation stone of men's motives, in the centre of self-interest all the radii that emanate from it the circumference of all the various incidents in the social order, will repose on a solid base, and confine the investigation of the plans, moral or physical, of all speculators to their general utility, without any confidence in the motives or abilities of the projector, taking it for granted that both will conduce to his own advantage, so far as his foresight would permit him to perceive. This would narrow the field of examination, and exclude the judgment of all those who base their opinion on their faith in merits of others, and would confine the decision to those particularly informed of the true state of the question, and payers, not receivers, could have no interest in exaggerating the expense.

 It would make men cautious how they embarked in any thing they did not understand, and they would look still more to the situation, education, probable interest, and opinions of those they consulted. If they should get into dispute, the lawyer is the one of all others that would benefit most by an expensive process: if sick, the physician would be one of the greatest gainers by prolonging the disorder: if some wood work were required, the carpenter is more interested in the profits of the job than in the filling of your purse; and so on; through all arts and professions, the man we employ has a retaining fee from self-interest, against the economical success of our cause. It may in many cases be modified by respect for reputation and character, previous habits of honor and honesty, &c., but still the bias gravitates towards self, and can be only radically rectified by every one being taught the elements, principles, and practice of every art or profession, which his situation in life may force him to resort to. This will lead to the great advantages of a practical, general instruction. It will occupy the time of youth in acquiring knowledge in proportion to its utility, associating pleasurable sensations with every necessary or useful operation, and rendering their plays and pastime subservient to gaining information, so that a moment of their most precious time may not be lost, in advancing their future happiness and prosperity. A careful attention to the healthful practice of Hygæa, a frugal table, will keep them out of all dependence on the physician. As we are cursed with a labyrinth of intricate and complicated laws, the only safety is avoiding all contact with them. Let no temptation induce you to have any transactions with a dishonest chicaner. Be particular in having all your bargains well defined on paper; always take receipts and keep short accounts: when a man refuses to settle, he is an unsafe one to deal with. Make yourself master of every thing connected with your object before you undertake it, and do not neglect the obtaining of every kind of information, it will most probably be of use sometimes. All truth, health, wealth, prosperity, and happiness, are concentrated in knowledge, and all falsehoods, abuses, errors, evils, misery and crime, are the legitimate children of ignorance. Inequality of knowledge, by lavishing a sufficiency on the few to follow their self-interest at the expense of the ignorance of the many, gives birth to most of the evils and misfortunes that torment mankind. Divide knowledge by giving every member of society enough to take care of himself and protect his own interest, and the natural level of equity would be undisturbed; but the smallest usurpation of the rights or interest of one, would be immediately checked by its obvious infringement on the rights of the whole, and society would be kept in a just equilibrium, consonant to the amount of comfort and happiness, which they are capable of enjoying.

FEAR, A CONCOMITANT OF SLAVERY; DESTRUCTIVE OF FREEDOM. FLEETS AND ARMIES. PREJUDICIAL REVERENCE OF ANTIQUITY. UNTIL THE MANY SHALL BE EDUCATED, THEY MUST CONTINUE TO LABOR FOR THE FEW.

September 5, 1829.

Ignorance is too often the parent of fear, and fear is the motive of most of our cruel, shameful, and thoughtless actions. It is the lever, by which we have been taught to move all our four-footed neighbors to our purposes, as well as to drive the weak of our own species into the nets and trammels which our ambition, avarice, and tyranny, have laid for them. Possess an animal with fear, and you can mould him into any form you please. Make a nation afraid, and the rulers can have full use of the persons and property of the people. This is an act of taming the fiercest, and sometimes inducing the most indolent to be active. But knowledge of the reality dissipates the fear, and converts this craven passion into moral courage. Both church and state have acted on this principle, by their rooted aversion to the diffusion of useful information to those they wish to govern.*

---

*A scientific man gave a memoir to Villelle, minister of the Bourbons, on some useful discovery in mathematics and mechanics, and observed, that he did not expect his excellency to examine it himself, but that one of the chiefs of his office might give a report on it. The minister said, if he knew any one of his clerks to be capable of making such a report he would discharge him immediately.

On the extended shore of the young political society of Mexico, landed three or four thousand of their former tyrants, with the avowed intention of reducing them to their former slavery. Eight millions of freemen are panic struck, dissolve their legislature, invest a dictator with absolute power, in imitation of their former despotism, recur to the violence of forced loans, raise as many soldiers in the federation and in each state, as would be sufficient to annihilate the enemy, were they five times the number, even of men fighting for their freedom, in place of for their tyrants; a distinction we have not learned fully to appreciate. At Madrid, in the late Spanish revolution, four thousand of the guards, the best troops in Spain, had been kept by the king's party at a small distance from the city, on purpose to surprise it; they were introduced at midnight, by the guards at the gates, and entered the great square in the centre of the city, before they were discovered by the militia who were on guard, who first fired on them, and afterwards charged them with the bayonet, drove them through the streets, and forced them to take refuge in the king's palace. Thus five hundred defenders of freedom, who had never been in action, beat and dispersed four thousand of the slaves of despotism, though old troops inured to warfare, and strict discipline. Although in every page of history, from that of the Greeks to the French revolution inclusive, freedom has always been attended with heroism, as slavery has been characterized by baseness and cowardice, yet the moderns, who have wrested their freedom from their former tyrants, have not enjoyed it long enough to value its advantages, or to get acquainted with its inestimable properties, but on all occasions, with the pusilanimity of their former infancy, wait for new experience to support that confidence, which ought to be founded on the experience of all former ages. It is this ignorance of their own force, that induces freemen to permit their rulers to fortify their frontiers, and establish fleets, at the great waste of labor and money, only to follow the example of despotism, whose subjects or slaves, having nothing valuable to fight for, are conquered as soon as an enemy can enter the country. Fortifications are more for the support of tyranny and oppression, than for the defence of any thing valuable that the millions possess, and on this side of the Atlantic may be safely dispensed with, and will, no doubt, be abolished as soon as the free nations of the present day have the confidence in their strength and courage, that the small state of Sparta had, who not only proclaimed the theory, but supported it, with successful practice.

The inhabitants of this extensive hemisphere, possessing some hundreds of times more land than they can cultivate, can have no object in increasing their territory. Rather losing than gaining by adding power to their rulers, they are removed from every possible temptation to make conquest. The only rational excuse for supporting either fleets or armies must be defence against the unprovoked attack of some nation, who are so ignorant, or misinformed, as to invade so powerful a Union, at so great a distance, with the intention of subjugating upwards of thirty millions of freemen, who, when less than one fourth of their present population, were strong enough to break their chains, and release themselves from the dominion of some of the most powerful nations of the Old World. It is high time that the "glory" of subjugating their fellow-men, was expunged from the dictionary of freemen, and in its place, something permanently useful, both to themselves and others, substituted.

Mankind are twice children; returning in their dotage to the follies and fictions of their nurse, unfortunately for their descendants, at the very time when the reverence for age, gives them most weight and consideration in society.— Whilst we had rulers who had been educated under the prejudices of colonial aristocracy, nothing better could be expected, than a slavish imitation of the laws, customs, and follies of our grandfathers; but now that the revolution of time has placed all those ancients under ground, and both church and state are under the management of the eleves of our revolution, something original, and on a par with the knowledge of the day may be expected. The present generation may begin to think, that a law does not suit the economy either of church or state, merely because it was made by the Romans, and adopted by the British: that family dignity or respect does not descend to a profligate son, because the father professed some occupation of law or gospel in the non-productive classes, though sanctioned by the hereditary rights of the privileged orders, riveting the honor and profit of the father on the sons, to the third and fourth generation. They may perhaps examine what the millions have gained, by an elective government of universal suffrage. Are they not ruled by the non-productive classes of lawyers, and others who do not work? and who are much like the privileged orders of the Old World. Can the interest of the laborer or mechanic, be represented by one who has an opposite interest? Is not respect, profit and consideration bestowed in exact propotion to the uselessness of the class? What use has the word freedom been to the millions, but to allow them to change one master for another, whose education and habits, equally remove him from any participation in the interest, comfort, and happiness, of the great majority; and though the many have all the power, they are still governed by the interest of the influential few.

Whence comes all those contradictions, all those causes of mischief and misery? From the ignorance of the producers, who permit their representatives to expend the money of their constituents, in colleges and universities, for the instruction of their own children, and little or none for free schools for the education of the children of the laborer, who produces all. This is the true original sin, which descends from father to son and pollutes generations yet unborn.

EVILS OF OVER POPULATION. GREAT EXTENT OF TERRITORY OR OF POPULATION, FAVORABLE TO TYRANNY.

February 6, 1830.

By every imitation, or slavish copy we take of the laws, customs and habits of the old world, we sacrifice part of the comforts and happiness we derive from our natural and artificial advantages, of soil, climate, freedom and independence. None is attended, perhaps, with more trouble and inconvenience now, or more serious consequences in future, than attaching merit to the raising of children: giving an artificial premium to a strong natural appetite, in the indulgence of which, all animals are disposed to commit excess. When Madame De Stael asked Bonaparte who he thought was the most meritorious woman, she received for answer "the one that has raised the greatest number of children." This sentiment was in perfect concordance with his interest, as well as with that of all other conquerors, to esteem merit in proportion to the supply it afforded of articles they most want, and of which, in their wars, they consume the most. Fortunately for humanity, very few have so direct an interest in the multiplication of our species. There are two nations in Europe, where the moral check (according to Malthus) of population, has existed from time immemorial, and though hardly dealt with by nature, inhabiting an indifferent soil, and climate, yet the millions enjoy a greater sum of positive happiness, than falls to the share of any other European nations. How much of that comfort and enjoyment arises from the moral check to population, and the habits and practices following from it, I shall not venture to say. But if you enquire of a laborer in Sweden or Switzerland, why he is not married, he will answer, "it is because I cannot afford to maintain a wife and children." Yet their great class of industrious producers, are better fed, clothed and lodged, and better instructed in those two nations, than in any other in Europe.

Church and state, in all countries, have framed laws, and established customs, in favor of the abundance of population;

but no nation has so rigorously enforced such laws, with punishment for defalcation, as the Chinese: which forces them to permit the mother to destroy as many of her progeny as she thinks proper, to prevent the dreadful consequences of an over-stocked population. And even with that privilege, starvation and famine frequently occur, and at no time is the whole population fed.

An extensive empire or kingdom, flatters the self-love and vanity of the political or military chief who rules uncontrolled the subjugated millions; but always at the expense of the comfort and happiness of the ruled. Misrule, corruption and tyranny are nearly in proportion to the extent of surface of the empire, and of the number of subjects, over whom their arbitray power domineers. The chain of power falls heavier, and is more oppressive in the ratio of the distance from the seat of authority; and is lighter and more tolerant, when the authority is circumscribed to narrow limits of surface or population. It is only necessary to compare the moral and physical condition of the subjects or slaves of the Russian and German empires, with that of the small governments of Saxe Weimar, Saxgota, Denmark, etc., to be convinced that tyranny and misery are co-existing in the ratio of surface and population, though the political chiefs of all the above mentioned countries, are equally arbitrary and uncontrolled in their authority over their subjects.

EXPENSIVE POMP AND PARADE OF PUBLIC OFFICERS, OBJECTIONABLE. BANKS AND BANK NOTES. COLLISION OF THE STATES AND UNITED STATES.

June 26, 1830.

When the great numerical majority shall rule, considerable changes in the customs, habits, and practices of society will take place, in favor of candor and frankness. Much of that verbal politeness, bordering on hypocrisy, will be dispensed with, tending to economise time, money, and sincerity in the intercourse between classes, as well as between individuals. Men in public offices will not obtain much respect, or consideration, for the luxury, pomp, and show they make at the expense of the people's money. Each laborer will be able to distinguish, how much of the produce of his labor is wasted in the external ornaments of his public agent, who can only have a momentary enjoyment of such gaudy trappings, to add to his disappointment and mortification, when the necessary rotation in office deprives him of them. All superfluous expenditure in objects of luxury and parade, will cease to bestow honor or consideration on the possessor, when the source whence they flow, shall be perfectly known by the millions of shrewd observers, capable of correct analysis, much of the showy and splendid materials of dress, furniture and equipages necessary to support the artificial aristocratic superiority of the consuming few, may not be either useful or necessary to maintain the authority of the millions, founded on universal suffrage and universal interest, having the good of the immense majority for its object.

In the late discussions of the utility of banks in our congress and state legislatures, the bias in favor of old mother Britain is conspicuous. They seem to consider banks only as the means of furnishing artificial capitals to a few speculative merchants by discounts of paper specialties, though the British mercantile spirit was the first that substituted paper for property by bank notes, national loans, etc., (for which they are now paying dearly) the greatest part of the chartered banks in Europe, facilitate the circulation of property by advances on deposites, neither circulating notes nor discounting mercantile paper, considering these as a risk that bankers' profits do not pay for. This is proved by the great number of discounting banks that have failed.

On the collision between the States and United States, they seem vainly to endeavor to conciliate the opposing interests without removing the cause, which is the interference of the United States in the judiciary, taxation, and military, of the individual states, which must eternally create collision, until, after the example of the oldest federation (Switzerland, that has existed five hundred years without any dispute) they form a federation, that shall have no power to raise a man, or a cent, or hold courts of justice in any of the states. To attempt to remedy the evil and yet to have the cause in full force, would appear to be too far behind the knowledge of the day.

DIVISION OF PROPERTY. THE MILLIONS WITHOUT SUFFICIENT KNOWLEDGE TO GOVERN THEMSELVES AGREEABLY TO THEIR INTEREST.

June 26, 1830.

All property is produced by labor. Even the wild fruits and animals would not belong to any person, unless labor was bestowed to gather and hunt them. Those who labor produce all, and those who do not labor produce nothing; but live on, and consume the produce of other's labor, and are therefore dependent on the producers for the means of existance. Suppose the consumers of any country to expend forty, the producers must toil and labor ten times more to support them, than in another country where the consumers only expend four. This is exemplified at present, in the two great rival nations, Britain and France. In Britain the great inequality of property, caused by an enormous national debt, indirect taxation, monopolies, exclusive privileges etc., has pushed the whole population into the two extremes of poverty and riches, so that the laborer cannot support the weight of idle consumers thrown on his shoulders, and at the same time feed and clothe himself and family. But the consumers, having the command of the bayonets, must be supplied in all their extravagance, while the producers must starve. In France, in consequence of the division of property, produced by the revolution, with the consequent equality of the just laws, abolition of tithes, of feudal rights, etc., property is so equally divided, that the number of positive consumers is small in proportion to the number of producers; the great bulk of the population, producing nearly what they consume, have the toil and labor of the producers in France equal to four, on a comparison with that in Britain where it may be equal to forty: though the millions of both countries labor under the same disadvantage of being governed by the consumers, who have the distribution of the whole wealth created by the producers.

In all countries, climates and situations, it must be the interest of the consumers, to appropriate as much of the labor of the producers for their own use, as they possibly, by fair or foul means, can effect. It must be equally the interest of the producers, to diminish that quantity, as it diminishes their quantum of toil and labor, and at the same time retains for their own use, more of the produce of their labor. This is a natural opposition of interest, which sophistry, rhetoric and eloquence cannot reconcile. It must follow as a consequence, that all people governed by the consuming few, must be ruled by an interest opposed to the producing many; necessitating a great superiority in the abilities, cunning, dress, and address, of the governors; with all that great exterior pomp, show, and grandeur, to dazzle and deceive the millions; keeping up that artificial superiority on which much of their authority depends, and making the force of armies, navies, forts, and citadels, the *sine qua non* of the few ruling the many. Has there existed, in what has been called the civilized world, any political association where the few have not ruled the many? can the many, legally govern under any form, except that of elective government of universal suffrage? has any such existed before the United States of North America? have the millions governed themselves by the rights and power given them by universal suffrage, for the last fifty-three years in our Union? Truth forces us to a negative on all the foregoing questions. It must therefore be considered as an indisputable fact, that in any grade of civilization, the millions or the immense majority, have not yet possessed sufficient knowledge or union, to exercise the right of governing themselves according to their own interest; but have foolishly suffered themselves to be ruled by the will and agreeably to the interest of the consuming few.

How the millions will conduct themselves in their self-government, which is a novelty in the annals of mankind, there may be much said, and speculated upon on both sides, but the result of the experiment can only decide. When travelling in Switzerland, with a Genevan, who, like all his townsmen, was hostile to Bonaparte, insisting that he had ruined the country, arriving at Zurich after the table d'hote, we dined in our room at double price; when the landlord, as is customary in England, came in with the first dish, and waited to give us all the information concerning the country we might require, I asked him how went trade, etc. etc., he answered, that fellow Bonaparte has ruined us all. I said, I had been over the canton, on the borders of the lake, etc., and found the people all contented and happy. So they may be, said he, "those clod hoppers who are only fit to raise potatoes and cabbages, pretend to govern themselves, legislate, make speeches and laws, etc., whilst we towns people, who are educated to govern them, have lost our places and are ruined." So may the nonproductive classes, that have arrogated the privileges of ruling, complain, as the royalists, who hold their places under the hereditary king of Britain did at the commencement of our revolution, and as the priests with the privileged orders lamented the French revolution, and all who lose by any change must be allowed to complain, and make a great noise in proportion to their deficiency of right or reason; all of which is re-echoed as sound logic, by the fellow feeling of all the same classes in all countries, who having the control of the press, inundate the civilized world with their bitter recriminations. The same game will be played by the monopolizers of property, knowledge, and power, against our working classes, for attempting to assert their rights, and with as little success, as the enmity of our royalists, or the fury of the privileged orders, against the French revolution, had they not been assisted by the combined bayonets of Europe.

The millions in all countries, have toiled and labored long enough for the benefit of their masters: it is high time they should begin to do something for themselves, before they may be deprived of the means, the universal suffrage, when a physical and violent revolution would be necessary, in place of a mild, legal and moral revolution through the medium of the ballot boxes. Without equality there can be neither equity, justice nor virtue. The equality of power is completely within the control of the ballot boxes, and the future equality of knowledge, must follow the power given to the millions of establishing free, equal, and rational schools, where all the children of the nation are to be fed, clothed, and instructed at the expense of the people's treasury, or what has been denominated the public, and in some countries the government treasury. When the bars and obstructions to the free circulation of property shall be taken away, by the abolition of monopolies, exclusive privileges, unjust mode of raising revenue by indirect taxation on consumption, and the reduction of the wages of political labor to a par with other labor, the equality of property must be insured as far as is necessary to equalize happiness; for perfect equality of any thing is impossible as long as there is such a variety in our physical and moral organization, and only to be found in the exaggerated sophistry of those enemies to all improvement, who pretend to argue, that because men cannot be perfect, they ought to make no exertion to relieve themselves from the vices, corruption and miseries entailed upon them by the tyranny of church and state.

WAR OPPRESSIVE TO THE PRODUCERS. TAXATION OF POSTERITY. INDIRECT TAXATION. IMPROVEMENTS ARE EFFECTED BY THE PRODUCERS.

July 15, 1830.

Most wars are made for property: either to defend it against enemies disposed to plunder it, or to plunder and pillage the property of others, who appear weak, and unable to defend it. Common justice therefore requires, that the expenses incurred by all wars, should be paid, either by those who have property worthy of defence, or by those who benfit by the pillage or plunder gained by conquest. What class of society possesses property to be defended, or divides the spoil wrested from the conquered? Through all the pages of history of the Medes, Persians, Romans, feudal Barons, down to the chiefs and rulers of the present day, it has been the non-productive consumers who have property requiring defence, or who benefit by the plunder and pillage taken from the conquered. The millions of the industrious producers have all the toil, labor, and risk, of fighting as soldiers, without having any property necessary to protect, or participating in any part of the spoil; so that in war as in peace, they labor and produce every thing, for others to consume and enjoy the fruits of their toil. In peace the producers only maintain, feed, and support the consuming classes by their own labor, but in war, by the artful invention of a national debt, contrived by the moderns and unknown to the ancients, the non-producers, mortgage the toil and labor of the descendants of the industrious producers, for the payment of principal and interest of that debt contracted to protect their own property, or to add to it by the spoils of warfare. By this unjust political trick, not only the sins of the fathers are visited on the third and fourth generation, but the folly and extravagance of the non-producer, is visited on the children to the thirtieth or fortieth generation of the industrious producers, until the accumulation of wretchedness and misery can be borne no longer, and the spring of revolution restores the natural equality of our species.

Hereditary power and wealth, may have some resemblance to an excise for loading their posterity with their debt in return for the inheritance of the toil and labor of their subjects, which they have left to their heirs; but an elective government, where the rulers are in power only for one or two years, to assume the right of binding their successors by any law or act of theirs, either as a loan which their descendants must pay, or as monopoly, which their descendants must uphold, sacrificing interest to the maintainance of its exclusive prerogatives, nothing but a slavish copy, taken from nations originating in the physical force of conquest, could possibly have introduced such unjust and irrational usurpation on the rights of others.

British subjects oppressed by the weight of an immense national debt, (principally contracted to deprive other nations of the blessing of freedom,) and aggravated by the mode of raising the interest by indirect taxation on consumption, are reduced to a state of wretchedness and poverty, which contrasted with the non-productive consumers, wallowing in wealth, and gorged with every luxury, is starving in the midst of superfluous abundance, and is a state of temptation that must have an end. Even they are goaded on by the misery resulting from such an unnatural and unjust order of things, in spite of the bayonets which coerce them, to query the right, justice, or policy of submitting to be loaded with the debts of their ancestors. Such subjects are freely discussed in their public prints, the medium through which public opinion is first promulgated, before it ripens into action. They begin likewise to perceive the injustice of indirect taxation, and had they the advantage of universal suffrage, such an enormous oppression on the millions, would disappear immediately after the first election.

How long will the interest of the few prevail over the interest of the many? How long will the inappreciable advantage of universal suffrage be lost to the millions, by intrigues at the ballot boxes? How long will the millions be oppressed with that unjust and partial mode of collecting the revenue, by indirect taxation on consumption? How long shall the millions be deprived of the benefit of free ports, and a free circulation of knowledge and property? How long shall the millions be under the tyranny of complicated undefined and litigious laws, which they cannot understand, or afford to pay those who pretend to explain them? Just as long as the ignorance and apathy of the millions of producers suffer themselves to be the dupes of the cunning artifices of the few, the non-productive and consuming classes—a period devoutly to be wished terminated; and though society, particularly on this side of the Atlantic are making rapid strides towards it; yet the patience and forbearance of mankind are so inexhaustible as to make it difficult to foresee the time, when such a moral revolution will be accomplished.

Our working people, from their share of liberty and equality, their education, situation, and information, are much better fitted to govern themselves, than any state of society that has yet existed. They ought therefore to build their success on their own merits, without reference to the precedents taken from any former civil, political, or religious association; which being congregated by chance, and organized under the influence of ancient prejudices, are composed of materials quite different and opposite to our institutions, that are improved and framed on the highest state of civilization that then existed; which ought to deter all classes of our citizens from taking any example from their laws, habits, or customs, originating in the darkness of barbarous ages.

On examining to whom mankind are indebted, for the civil, political, and religious labor, which has advanced the civilization of our species, it will be found to be the work of the lower and middling ranks, in all countries. The promoters, supporters, and actors, in our revolution, both civil, military, and religious, were all from the lower and middling ranks of life. When the spark of freedom crossed the Atlantic, and exploded in the French revolution, blowing into atoms the crust of ancient prejudices both of church and state, all the civil and military officers, who conducted this violent change, were sprung from the lower and middling classes. Many of them from what was then called the very lowest, such as stable boys, grooms and waiters. Even the great chief who grasped the energies of the revolution, and drawing them to a focus, scorched the ancient aristocracy to the utmost bounds of civilization, was, as well as all his officers, from what was then called the lower orders of society. Britain, that hot bed of aristocracy, owes the greatest part of her pre-eminence and national superiority, to the facility afforded to the lower orders, of advancing by their merit to the first places both in church and state. If their nobility had not been constantly recruited from the lower orders, they would have been, ere this, as insignificant as the grandees of Spain.— For instance, the great Bacon was a Franciscan friar; Newton a farmer's son; Shakspeare a link boy; Brindley a wheelright's apprentice; Arkright a barber; Pope a linen draper's son; S. Johnson a bookseller's son; Cardinal Woolsey son of a butcher; Burk son of an attorney; Curran son of a low man at Newmarket; Peel son of a calico printer; Lord Nelson son of a clergyman; Lord Eldon son of a coal fitter; Lord Stowel son of a coal fitter; Lord Chief Justice Abbot son of a barber; Lord Lindhurst son of an artist; Lord Thurlow son of a butcher; Lord Ashburton son of an attorney; Tillotson son of a clothier; Arch-Bishop of York of obscure birth; and many thousand others. All of which proves that without the work of the industrious producers, neither civil, political, religious nor moral labor, would have produced the comforts, convenience, or happiness of their species.

Ridicule is often used in the absence of reason; and the silly vanity of ignorance allows it to pass current, and to have some effect. It will most probably be lavished on the working people by their opponents, with all the wit and satire they are masters of. The best way to treat it, is by silent contempt; answering otherwise only keeps it alive, and gratifies the jester by showing it has some effect. The millions of industrious producers ought to go straight forward to their interest, and bear down all opposition by the weight of their numbers.

THE ART OF TEACHING. OPINION. PERSECUTING FOR OPINION'S SAKE.

July 29, 1830.

All teachers of men, as well as instructors of children, tell their pupils what to think, but none tell them how to think.—Without reasoning, or permitting others to reason, they give their opinions as a rule of conduct for all; most probably because they were taught so, and there is not one in a thousand, but is convinced that the mode or system of his own education, was the best possible; for it requires great impartiality, and mental exertion, to think otherwise. Church and State, in all countries, climes, and latitudes, have monopolized the instruction of young and old, that their opinions founded on their interest, might descend unimpaired to posterity. The *ipse dixit* of the nurse, parent, schoolmaster, priest, and governor, regulates the conduct of beings, who possess five senses, but are allowed only the exercise of their ears. A boy in Philadelphia, who had been taught after the Pestalozzian system, was put to a master of the old school, to learn some more mathematics. He got his lessons better than the others by the rules, but was always asking the master the reason for the rules; which his master, not having learned himself, could not give him, and told his father that he was a good scholar, but one of the most troublesome, he ever attempted to teach. Rules are reasoned on by the judgement of those who made them, but are only attached to those who learn them, by rote, by the memory, and are forgotten as soon as learned. The self conceit of having learned them, is all that remains, only to prevent acquisition of any further knowledge. Mystery and fable may amuse as far as they have some resemblance to truth, but when they are contradicted by the evidence of our senses they cease to convey information, and become delusions of the imagination. Adopting the opinions of others, without knowing the why or wherefore, is like a shopkeeper with his shelves full of merchandize, who, when a customer demands the price of any of them, is forced to answer he does not know.

Positive knowledge of matter, motion, and mankind, is truth. The correctness of opinions depends on the accuracy of the observation, judgement, and experience of those who form them, and may lead to utility, or augment the mass of prejudice, according to the surrounding circumstances of those who opine. *It is therefore probable, that positively useful knowledge, conveyed through the medium of our senses, ought to be the chief object of all systems of education.* And there are many strong and convincing reasons why natural history is the most solid foundation on which all subsequent knowledge ought to be built. 1st, because the study of it consists of simple ideas, arising from the direct use of our senses; 2dly, it pleases and amuses the pupils, and can be taught without the force of punishment or coercion; 3dly, it gives them the habit of diligently observing, and accurately examining, on all sides, every thing they wish to be acquainted with, and teaches them not to suppose that they know any thing, until they have thoroughly investigated all its properties; thus saving them, in the future occurrences of life, much trouble and loss, and restraining them from acting on a careless smattering of the qualities of both men and things; 4thly, it makes them familiar with the useful properties of surrounding objects; 5thly, the endless variety of nature, furnishes complete, innocent, and useful recreation and amusement, which banishes all that irksome *tedium* and *ennui*, the inclined plane that glides into vice and debauchery. A naturalist is never without healthful, and respectable, as well as useful occupation, which strews the paths of life with flowers.—When visiting Dr. Priestley at his residence in Northumberland, in company with Dr. B. S. Barton, and T. Smith—Dr. P. went with us on all our botanical and geological excursions, and said he found an amusement in natural history that he wanted, "and if you will remain with me a few weeks, I will begin to learn it; for books, and even chemistry, cease to have that novelty to me, which I perceive I could find in the study of nature." But no professor will condescend to teach it, unless he has received pleasure and gratification in the practice of it; for most of the literati think it below their notice. As one of our ministers to the French court, said of one who found an amusement in natural history, "what can you think of a character who amuses himself in gathering pebble stones." Arithmetic by head or memory, excludes the dreams of the imagination, and may be taught along with natural history. The first, disciplines all the faculties of the mind, while the last teaches accurate observation, and gives the habits of examining on every side, and ascertaining the properties before concluding that you understand the object or subject; an exceedingly useful habit, the want of which is the cause of many of our errors and misconceptions. The elements of writing, and designing may be best learned, by making all kinds of figures on a slate; as straight lines, dividing them into equal parts; squares, parallelograms, triangles, etc.; turning the superficial contents of any square or parallelogram into a triangle, etc., by the accuracy of sight, without the aid of calculation or instrument. This practice gives an ease and facility to the acquiring of writing, and likewise to that only defined language, drawing, so useful in all trades and professions. Accurate mensuration of space and distance by the eye, is easily acquired when young, but very difficult afterwards. All the above are simple ideas, acquired by the use of the senses, completely within the reach of all children whose senses are unimpaired by any physical defect, and perhaps ought to be the first things taught them, as a solid foundation for more complicated ideas. The beginning with reading and languages, before the child can have any distinct comprehension of the complex meaning of words, is laying the foundation of future acquirements on a quick sand, that endangers the stability of all future acquisitions, and fills the mind with hypothetical opinions, and vague descriptions, in place of the fixed and sensible properties of things, so easily understood by the examination of the substance or its representation.

Nothing but positive knowledge ought to be taught in schools. The inculcating of opinions, is burdening the next age with the errors, superstition, and delusions of the present, and impedes much the progress of intellect. Teach the youth every kind of useful knowledge, and leave the application, until future circumstances dictate the conveniency or necessity of acting, or forming opinions. Advising any one how to act in such or such circumstances, is only declaring what you think you would do in a like situation, and is therefore liable to mislead; as the previous habits, temper, disposition and opinions, not being the same, the council most probably will not suit. The safest way, on being asked for advice, is to give all the knowledge you possess on the subject, when the individual is the best judge how to act. Opinions are so various, contradictory and changeable, depending on incidents, temper, constitution and situation, many of them beyond our control, that they ought not to be the subject of a dispute, much less impressed on the plastic minds of children during their education. Change of opinion ought to be a proof of more accurate information; but as it is a confession of being formerly in the wrong, our self-conceit is opposed to the avowing of it, and ignorant people attach some weakness and disgrace to those who change their mode of thinking. Suppose a preacher or schoolmaster, or any other teacher of men or children, had for ten years taught certain doctrines and opinions, which on obtaining a better information he found to be wrong; have not his hearers, and pupils the right to blame him for leading them astray, and teaching erroneous doctrines? how much better would it have been for both teacher and pupils, had they confined their lessons to unchangeable truths.

Nothing is more changeable or precarious than opinions. One who obtains possession of power, has not the same opinions, as when he was subjected to obey power. One who obtains riches, does not hold the same opinions, as when he was poor. When a man is sick, he thinks differently from what he did when in good health. A weak man thinks differently from a strong man; a young man from an old man; a wise man from a fool, and any and every man who acquires more correct information, must change his opinions.

Change circumstances and you change interest, and as certainly change opinions. One may as reasonably quarrel with another for having a nose longer or shorter, as for having an opinion different from his own. Yet the arbitrary assumption, that all ought to think with the strongest party, (for the weakest party never think of persecuting for opinion's sake) is the origin of all intolerance, and persecution. From what propensity arises this rage for conversion, which has seized on all sects of Christians? must we suppose it is for the purpose of recruiting and strengthening their party? like a general whose success depends on the number of his soldiers; or must we make it an exception to the general rule of self interest? Taking it on the disinterested motives of doing good to others, would be to place it in opposition to all the ascertained motives of human actions.

OBSTACLES TO THE INTRODUCTION OF A SIMPLE CODE OF LAWS. IMPRISONMENT FOR DEBT.

July 30, 1830.

That inexplicable common law, perhaps the most uncommon of all the anomalies of the British empire, is now undergoing revision and a kind of reform, as far as the attachment of the lawyers, to their fees will permit. Many thousand acts of parliament have either been abolished or consolidated into a space at least within the reach of the gentlemen of the law. But the adoption of a well defined, simple code, within the comprehension of all as a rule of conduct, will most probably not take place until the pride of the nation has forgotten that their rivals on the other side of the channel, were the first to make use of such a code. We, on this side of the Atlantic, have no dread of the principles of the French revolution, nor any envy or jealousy of the French nation, to prevent our copying or adopting any of their laws, arts, sciences, or practices, that may suit us. The strong attachment of lawyers (who as yet have been our rulers) for large fees, and the monied aristocracy to their superiority over the working classes, prevent the introduction of a simple code of laws, which would place society nearer to a level of equality. It can scarcely be from the ignorance of our industrious producers that they have not long ago relieved themselves from such an accumulation of oppression; but rather from the total absence of the spur of necessity; for what physical want or necessity can possibly exist in any country, where the value of an acre of land, is little more than a dollar. All moral incitements to action are slow and weak, paralyzed by the sophistry of both church and state, whose moral influence with us, is strong in the ratio of their physical weakness, in the humble imitation of feudal tyranny as respects laws, where a citizen can be incarcerated for life for a debt of a few dollars. The cruel and tyrannical Roman laws, which gave the right to a creditor to sell his debtor; were more in favor of the industrious poor, by placing them in a situation to pay their debts by their labor.

Why did the feudal barons of Europe adopt the Roman laws, where property was every thing and personal freedom nothing, as the foundation of their code? (for the same reason that a system of liberty and equality ought to consider property as nothing, when put in the balance against freedom,) because the despotic Roman laws, best suited their system of keeping in bondage all the industrious producers, who as serfs and slaves, were at the command of their feudal chiefs in peace or war. Like the rich, luxurious patrician in Rome, with thousands of debtors at his heels (all of whom he had a right to sell as slaves) ready to execute any arbitrary act at the nod of their patron. If the penury of intellect will force the republics of the present day to recur to barbarous antiquity for a precedent, let them imitate the Athenians. There the first orators of the republic were appointed to plead the cause of the poor against the rich gratis, as the only means of preserving any kind of equality, where law was to be obtained through the medium of lawyers. But the superior knowledge and civilization of the day, is not reduced to the humiliating situation of imitating the barbarous practices of the dark ages of antiquity. Freedom and equality, only brought into precarious existence by our elective government of universal suffrage, ought to have a corresponding system of laws, rules, and regulations. The comfort, happiness and liberty of the many debtors, have been, by aristocratic laws, sacrificed to the luxury, extravagance and dominion of the few creditors. Where the many rule by universal suffrage, the principle ought to be reversed, and the interest of the few ought to yield to the interest of the many. Perhaps the shortest remedy, would be to exclude all coercion for the collection of debts, without a corresponding deposite, and an expeditious mode of selling the deposite, for the payment of the debt for which it was guaranteed. "This would put an end to all credit, and commerce that depends on it," cries the merchant who trades on others' capital. It would certainly curtail the credit of the rogue, who wishes to live on the produce of others' labor, but the honest punctual debtor, would lose none of the confidence his conduct merits.— "There are two bad pay-masters, he who pays before hand, and he who never pays." Giving credit is paying before hand, and the profits must be equal to the risk of loss by dishonesty, carelessness, imprudence or extravagance. That is, the honest, punctual man who pays, must make good the deficiency of the rogue who never pays. The law coercing the payment of debts, tempts creditors to trust characters who would have no credit on their honor or honesty, and burdens the honest punctual debtor, to make good the defalcation of the unpunctual rogue. It would abolish that system of enticing a workman to run in debt and making him a slave to his master; a practice common in most countries.

OPPRESSION PRODUCTIVE OF FREEDOM. STANDING ARMIES. ARISTOCRATIC EMULATION AND IMITATIONS.

July, 31, 1830.

In the present state of civilization, on both sides of the Atlantic, the government of the few consumers, over the many producers, is like the two ends of a ballance; when the folly of the rulers lowers their end, that of the people rises in the same proportion. This is proved by all modern history. The ancients were under a barbarous system of masters and slaves, which excludes them from being precedents to the present state of society. Without going farther back into the dark ages of ignorance, we may begin with Switzerland, whose freedom arose from the tyranny and oppression of their masters, protected by their mountains, the cradle of liberty in all climates. What has been called the revolution in England, commenced by the feudal tyranny of the barons, and weakness of the king. The little liberty the Dutch conquered, was wrested from the religious bigotry, superstition and tyranny of their Spanish masters. Our revolution might have been retarded for ages, had not the British government insisted on taxing America, without the consent of representation, thereby going contrary to one of [the pretended principles of their constitution, that taxation ought to be commensurate with representation. The premature breaking out of the French revolution, was prompted by the pride, folly, and obstinacy of the clergy and privileged orders; a small relaxation of their unjust pretensions at first, would have contented the millions, who were totally ignorant of their power, until forced to make use of it. Have the severe lessons, given lately to the nonproductive classes, made them more prudent or cautious? or have they "learned nothing and forgot nothing," as Talleyrand said of the French emigrants, on their return at the restoration. The Bourbons, both in France and Spain, by attempting to govern in opposition to the knowledge of the day, are giving their people more effectual lessons of their own interest, than ever the revolution in either country could effect. Since the return of the government of the few, the civilization and information of the many have made more rapid progress, than ever they were allowed to make under the government of the represented millions; for they are emancipated in proportion as their knowledge enables them to retain what they get, and make a proper use of liberty without abusing it—which is often the consequence of too rapid a change from despotism to liberty; and the moral revolution in both countries will keep on a par and be graduated by the knowledge of the day. In Britain, public opinion and the mode of manifesting it, through the long toleration of the press, are a kind of safety valve, that has as yet prevented explosion; but they may temporize one day too long, and the military ceasing to act as mercenaries, becoming imbued with a fellow feeling, may refuse to fire on the citizens; when both church and state will be in great danger.

Even in our comparatively free country, the power of the artificial and monied aristocracy, might have been tolerated much longer, by the ignorant apathy of the millions, had they had any moderation in the exercise of their usurped prerogatives; but the exorbitant avarice of making money, and the power attached to it, forced them so far beyond the limits prescribed to their class in Britain, as to make five hundredtimes more chartered exclusive banks to coin paper, and give them the monopoly of the circulating medium; all this joined to indirect taxation and other exaggerated copies of European abuses, alarmed and aroused the working classes to claim their rights of universal suffrage at the ballot boxes. Their union and perseverance will exclude the non-productive monied aristocracy, from all places of power and profit, and make all laws, rules and regulations in favor of the immense majority of producers.

—

In the late emancipated free states of South America, where the military still retain the preponderance, which the contest for their liberties gave them, the despotic conduct of the standing army, constantly fighting against the constituted authorities, to elevate into power some one of their chiefs, will at last arouse and awaken the sleepy objects of three hundred years oppression to a sense of their own interest, which they will find they can claim by universal suffrage through the ballot boxes, and reduce the soldier to a par with the citizen, and raise each citizen, by the use of arms to a level with the soldier, constituting the militia the only military force, under which freedom can be secured.

In Europe, where the large standing armies must be increased in proportion to the increased dissemination of useful knowledge, they act first in making the governments unpopular by the exorbitant taxes necessary to their maintenance, and are afterwards (if raised by conscription) but an unsafe protection to the rulers, against the overt acts of the ruled, who, taken from every family, with whom they still keep up a constant intercourse, naturally partake of the popular opinions, and have a fellow feeling, that may induce an unwillingness to act against them in case of disputes. This has already happened in Bavaria, where the king, refusing to sign a popular law, the people assembled round the palace; the troops were ordered to fire and disperse them, but they refused; the king signed the law, and was more popular than ever; losing no part of the esteem and affection of his subjects by that act of condescension. If this has taken place in Bavaria, where the king is constantly occupied in doing good to his subjects, has no guards, but mixes with the peasantry in the market place, and inquires into the wants and opinions, what may be expected of conscript armies in despotisms, where the subjects are treated as slaves. The spread of useful knowledge is so wide, that the old maxim of soldiers having no right to think, is obsolete and out of fashion since the French revolution; so that the contrivance intended to facilitate the raising of armies, may render them unnecessary for keeping society in subjection. It is only copying hereditary aristocracies, for governments founded on universal suffrage, to keep standing armies in pay and in unproductive idleness.

The many cannot possibly wish for any change; having the whole power, any change must be to curtail their power: but the aspiring few are interested in having a force at command, to coerce and make slaves of the many. It is therefore the interest of the many not to keep in pay any such force; but to have an equal division of armed force, on purpose to secure an equal division of property, knowledge, and power, without which there can be no real freedom.— The most economical, simplest and best protector of liberty, is a militia, where every soldier is a citizen, and every citizen a soldier, and taught the use of arms.

How fortunately situated are the inhabitants of this side Atlantic. They are out of reach of the corruption and tyranny of the old world, and free to pick and choose of their laws, habits, customs, arts and science such as suit their interest. How have all the settlers on this side of the Atlantic benefited by this inappreciable privilege which nature has bestowed on them? Have they imitated any thing in favor of the great industrious producing classes?— Have they taken the advantage of the only elective government that approaches their own (Switzerland,) in collecting their expenses by direct taxation, and defending themselves by a militia? Or by simplifying the forms and economising the produce of the workman's labor? Truth forces us to put a negative on all such questions. They have copied the hereditary aristocracy of Europe, in their indirect taxarion, their complicated and incomprehensible laws in in their standing armies and military schools, in the organization of their legislature's power, and perquisites given to their rulers, in the forms of public offices divided into departments, in their luxurious and extravagant expenditure, in their fashions, customs and manners, in their monopolies and exclusive privileges, in their commercial avarice, in their food, lodging and raiment; scarcely an original habit has sprung from the great source of human happiness, freedom and equality. The reason must be cogent why art differs so far from nature; why practice contradicts theory on this side of the Atlantic. Yet nothing is plainer or more easily understood. The interest of the non-productive consuming classes, rules both sides of the Atlantic; the one by hereditary power, the other by elective; although the sources from which they obtain their power are different, they are forced, by their interest, to take much the same means of reaping all the benefits.

THE WORKING PEOPLE GRADUALLY OBTAINING THIER RIGHTS. GREAT ABUSES YET REMAIN TO BE CORRECTED.

August 4, 1830.

There are strong symptoms lately, of the increasing influnce of the industrious producers, on the operations of both church and state, on both sides of the Atlantic. Austrian edicts ordering the establishment of free district schools to teach all children to read and write; without which accomplishments no couples were to be married, or servants hired. In Prussia the king has granted to the large towns, municipal representations to regulate their affairs, and has tolerated the Napoleon code in the Prussian provinces south of the Rhine. The King of Holland established free schools in every village, both in Holland and Flanders, and adopted the Napoleon code of laws, with many other changes in favor of the millions. In France, though nominally under the dominion of a power disposed to be arbitrary, yet virtually, from the equality of property and knowledge, they enjoy the freedom of the press, and a representation opposed to every encroachment on liberty, though elected by about 50,000 voters out of a population of 32,000,000. Schools and public instruction flourish in spite of the violent opposition of both church and state. All their exertions to stop the revolutionary ball, only accelerate its motion. The king of Denmark proposes to give his subjects a constitution; and the pacha of Egypt has given his subjects a representation. Even under the dark curtain of despotism, in both Spain and Italy, some sparks show that the revolutionary fire is not extinguished. And when the children, born and taught in revolutionary times, arrive at the top of society, by the decease of the old school, changes in favor of the millions may be expected. The British parliament taking off some of the indirect taxes, and contemplating the converting more of them into direct taxes on income, to alleviate the distresses of the working people, with the reform of their expensive, complicated laws, all prove that the diffusion of useful knowledge amongst the laboring classes, begins to force their rulers to attend to their interest, in their laws, rules and regulations.

On our side of the Atlantic, the changes are considerable in favor of the producers or democracy, which are synonymous. The state of New York adopting universal suffrage, passing a lien law, and acts in favor of instruction to all classes; the state of Connecticut adopting universal suffrage; the legislators of Pennsylvania are rather inclined to change their pauper school for something less aristocratic, and have made resolutions to revise their complicated laws by a commission, mostly of lawyers, which will make it only a partial improvement; but any thing that will make a breach in the iron bound towers, of tautology, mystery and litigation will finally facilitate their destruction. Virginia has made a new constitution, which, though not what it ought to be, is yet more liberal than the old one, granted them when a British colony. In Louisiana they have made a criminal code, and propose adopting a civil code, which, though not free from the intricacy of ancient law, is yet much better than the confused mixture of French, Spanish and British precedents. A little improvement exists in the mode of enacting laws in some of the western states, by annulling all the previous acts, on the same subject, and including all the necessary rules and regulations of the latest law.

Our congress, after a tedious debate on uncultivated lands, decided to sell them to actual settlers at seventy-five cents per acre, (these most probably will be working people,) and to speculators a dollar per acre. (These most probably will be consumers.) It would perhaps be better to annihilate speculation in uncultivated lands, and to grant them in small portions to actual settlers. But the decision is something in favor of the millions, that shows their increasing influence. The congress voted by a majority, to lay on the table a resolution declaring the bank system prejudicial to the working classes and dangerous to freedom, and that the charter of the Bank of the United States ought not be renewed. Some debates on the tariff seem to hint that the power granted the federation to interfere with the interest of the states, approaches it to centralism: which most probably was not the intention of the original framers of the constitution, nor of the states that agreed to it: a hesitation that may ripen into a reform. All those partial and gradual changes in favor of the industrious producers (so contrary to the former course of political events,) clearly demonstrate a propensity in the civilized world towards a moral revolution, to relieve the oppressed millions, from a weight of burdens forced on them by a domineering aristocracy, either hereditary or elective. Whether the attempt of the working people to claim their rights and privileges at the ballot boxes, has or has not accelerated many of these changes with us, does not belong to the present inquiry. Effects only interest, as the best understood and easiest perceived; motives are always hidden and mysterious, and even if it were possible to ascertain them, it would not in the smallest degree change the good or bad consequences of the effects. Mankind seem to be fond of mysteries beyond their comprehension. The dogmas of all religions are contradicted by all the laws of nature that have come to our knowledge. State policy and intrigues are often as unnatural and unreasonable, and even when we attempt to dive into causes, the most mysterious and least understood, are often preferred. Had the industrious exertions of intellect, been limited to the knowledge of things within out reach, useful knowledge and the civilization depending on it, would have made much greater progress, and the situation of our species for comfort, convenience and happiness, would have been much farther advance.

It is encouraging to our people, that public opinion generally in the civilized part of the old world, is aiming at the same end, though with far inferior means, and that they by the help of universal suffrage, will have the advantage of taking the head of all nations, in the practice of freedom, equality, and true independence, as they were half a century ago, the first to promulgate the theory of liberty and equality. Their companions in art, trades and affliction on the other side of the Atlantic, must contend with the unequal struggle of unjust and partial laws, supported by a well combined military force, while the millions on this side, are maintained in their equal and legal rights and privileges, by all our political institutions, laws, customs and habits. Legitimacy, which is against the natural rights of their class in Europe, authorizes the assumption of every privilege that can add to the comfort, convenience or happiness of our working people; such a manifest situation ought to confirm them in the determination of persevering in a well combined union at the ballot boxes, to obtain a participation in the distribution of their wealth, commensurate with the share they take by their labor, in the production of it.

All the intrigues, deceptions and electioneering tricks are known to the most unskilful, having been practiced so long through the whole Union; the sophistry of words, endeavoring to prove that *meum* is *tuum*, that the interest of the few is the interest of the many, and constitutes public good; assuming the truth of the thing disputed, and reasoning accordingly; all of which are easily counteracted, by leaving the words and examining the nature and properties of the things. How are the working people benefitted by the exclusive privilege granted the banks of issuing paper money? do they obtain the use of paper currency by discounts? or all the advantage thrown into the pockets of their masters, to increase the weight of their oppression? How are the working people benefited by the patronage made necessary by the collection of the revenue by indirect taxes on consumption? does it not load them with the greatest part of the public expenses? while it furnishes their rulers with the corrupt means of bribing at elections and constituting the place an object of violent strife, contention and fighting. What do the people gain by the luxury and opulence of commerce, or by all that speculation which enhances the value of the article they buy? what did they gain by the funding system, but being compelled to pay principal and interest of the debt out of their hard earned wages of labor? what do they gain by all wars, but the risk and toil of fighting? how are they benefited by complicated mysterious and litigating laws, which their means cannot purchase the use of, but the mockery of being told all are equal in the eye of the law; like a tavern keeper proclaiming the equality of his guests, provided they have dollars in their pockets to pay him his perhaps exorbitant charges. It is an insult to common sense and justice, to pretend to equality where the laws are so undefined, confused and multiplied, that ninety-nine in a hundred cannot afford to pay the fees of a first hearing; and those who can pay the fees, may litigate for ages.

ACCUMULATION OF PROPERTY ON CREDIT. LABOR THE ONLY TRUE BASIS OF WEALTH.

August 7, 1830.

All property is produced by labor: even the wild fruits and animals, are gathered and caught by the labor and industry of some part of the society, before they can be a property useful to man. Those who labor produce all, and those who do not labor produce nothing, but live on the produce of others' labor. All the ingenuity of the well born artificial aristocracy have not been able to find any other source of wealth than labor. The monopoly of land by force or fraud, before the contrivance of either money or its multifarious representative paper, was the first store-room that hoarded up the accumulating produce of the labor of one age, to be expended by the next: since which, the number of idlers to be fed, clothed and lodged by the industry of the producers, became so great by the progress of civilization, that the landed property, though seized upon by the few, was not sufficient for their maintenance. It was then that the precious metals, and other rare productions of nature were resorted to, to increase the stock of wealth in store for the use of the non-producing consuming classes. At last in our time, the number of idlers created by the luxury and extravagance of church and state are so great, that the monopoly of the land, the precious metals, with the rare productions of nature (all of which have their limits, beyond which they cannot be produced,) were not sufficient to satisfy the artificial wants, avarice and cupidity of those who were entirely occupied in finding out modes of consuming what was brought forth by the soil and labor of others. Borrowing on the mortgage of land, and deposites of moveable property, originated rents and the interest for the use of money, which extended the means of administering to the extravagance of the consuming classes; all being short of the property those in power wished to expend, the representation by mercantile paper and latterly by the circulation of bank notes, they have continued to anticipate the produce of labor for ages, and waste all, on the fancies, whims and superfluities of the day (for this paper representative is so easily made as to be without limits,) depending on the confidence of those who never expected to labor for the payment of it.

Governments, seeing how easy it is to live by anticipation, and mortgage posterity for the expenses, by far too great to be borne by the present generation, borrowed on public securities, and formed a funded stock of national debt far exceeding all the produce of land, paper or bank notes, filling all the reservoirs of anticipated necessary wars, luxury and extravagance, in hopes that the future generations would pay for all; in which however the European creditors are disappointed. Not one of the nations has paid one cent of debt but by a bankruptcy, and perhaps their successors may query the right they had to burden others with the expenses of their follies. This vast addition of a national debt to the store room of forestalled labor, supports an immense number of unproductive members of society under the garb of lawyers, officers of the army, navy and customs, preachers and pretended pilots in the best road to the other world; all of whom to have some pretensions to giving something for what they receive, make a complicated mystery of their trade, and do more harm to society by their deceptions and delusions, than even by expending the people's money. One of their favorite deceptions is to pretend that they feed and clothe the working people; and they ask, how would the laborers live did we not spend our money in consuming the produce of their labor? In this false reasoning, they are supported by a certain class of political economists, who to get the favor of the rich, have invented the figure of the feet depending on the stomach; assuming that those who live on the labor of others, are represented by the stomach; forgetting that the feet, head, stomach, and every other part of the body, are fed and provided with every thing by labor. The monarchs of the old world, pretending to rule their subjects by divine right, are not more absurd than the rich in pretending their property came to them or their ancestors, by any other means than labor, in the shape of force or industry.— Trace the origin of any of the few rich that are to be bound in our Union, and mostly it will be found in their own earnings. Since the abolition of the laws of primogeniture, and entails, property scarcely ever descends to the third generation. Examine into the origin of the riches in civilized Europe, it is all founded on the force of conquest, and confiscation by the strongest from the weakest, accumulated on their descendents by entails; otherwise nature would have long ago, made a more equal division of it.

CAUSE OF THE INCREASE OF CRIME. REMEDY.

August 10th, 1830.

Very few in our country have a right to live without labor of some kind; which makes the struggle for property violent and uncivil, there being twenty brought up to nonproductive professions, where one would suffice in a rational, and economical state of society. This accounts for the misery and crime of our large mercantile towns, there being more robbing, theiving, swindling, and forging in New York at present, than was on our whole continent before the invention of stock, land and bank speculations. There are many towns in Europe, in which there is more misery and wretchedness, but perhaps not one of the same population where there is more crime, in spite of the various remedies applied, of penitentiaries, houses of refuge, and asylums. These are like drugs, given to cure diseases, that are not considered worth our moral prevention, which is a conviction of the necessity of great moderation in the indulgence of the physical appetites. One of the great causes of multiplicity of crime, is the false pride of parents, who are ashamed of giving their children a useful trade, that they may live honestly by their labor. As far as my observations have yet gone, nine-tenths of the criminals are men, brought up without any productive trade, being reduced to poverty, must steal or rob to live. If a register was kept of the trades and professions of all criminals, it is probable that a great proportion would be gentlemen, who had no honest means of living. This would point to the cause and elucidate the case. The theory of equality which for reasons too long to mention here, has never been supported by practice, has created such an erroneous stock of false pride without practical equality to maintain it, that all would be on a par without the means of paying for it; and failing in their attempt, are reduced to all lawful and unlawful means of gaining their end. Had the state of society, and the slavish copy we have taken of corrupt Europe, permitted our primitive simplicity (on the broad basis of which our revolution begun) to have continued, the natural equality would not have been deranged by the stock, land and bank speculations, aggravated by indirect taxes on consumption, and exclusive privileges granted by our legislators to their friends and companions. Every citizen would have had a little property, and none would have had too much, to dash and squander under the eyes of his less fortunate fellow-citizens; taking airs of superiority because he could live without being useful and endeavoring to depreciate every useful occupation, and bring them into disgrace: in which they were assisted by the foolish conduct of some of the working people, who, ignorant of their interest, force or utility, submitted to the dupes of the few idlers.

I think I hear the class who have so long monopolized power say, "a fool may find fault, but it requires a wiser man than the writer to find a remedy." This may be true; for fault finding is treated as Utopian and is tolerated, while remedies to abuse, touch those who live by them to the quick, and must be strangled in the birth. Yet it would appear in a government of universal suffrage, that nothing more is wanted to correct all injustice or abuse, than every citizen to follow the course pointed out by his own interest. Then the majority of interest would carry all, which is the only rational intention of universal suffrage. "But," say the monopolizers of wisdom as well as power, "the working people do not know their interest;" an unqualified assertion that might pass, where the whole population, above sixteen years of age, make the laws, as in the small democratic cantons of Switzerland: but to assert that in the many millions of working people in this enlightened age, there are not a few well informed men to legislate for the interest of their class, is too much deception even for spoiled children to attempt.

DEMORALIZING INFLUENCE OF POWER.

Power is a poison which intoxicates all men, and it is doing them great wrong and injustice, in an elective government, to give an elective officer more power than his head can carry with propriety and steadiness. As it is difficult to find out how much power any man can make a good use of, and almost impossible for every elector to choose amongst the exagerations of pros and cons during an election, the best rule would perhaps be, never to put a man in power twice; but to choose a new representative every election. This would diffuse the practice of governing, and keep all right by having some dozens of old members at home on their farms, to watch over the conduct of those in place. It would prevent the possibility of an executive, forcing the majority by patronage to act as his interest might direct; for the patronage necessary to satisfy a new legislature or congress, every election, would be beyond the bounds even of the British patronage. This calls to my recollection an anecdote.— When travelling west, we came to the foot of the blue ridge in a light waggon, and enquiring at a log house if we could pass the ridge before dark, the answer in the negative forced us to put up for the night. An old man on the *stoop* smoking and drinking his pint of cider, presumed by our carriage that we were from Philadelphia, and enquired how John Adams was going on; we answered very well for himself perhaps, but bad for us; it is your fault for putting in such a congress; the president does nothing but by the authority of congress. "That is true," said he, "when this federation began, my district in New Jersey, that had a right to send a member to congress, consulted, and we sent one of the best, and as we thought an honest man. During the first session he changed all his opinions, and voted contrary to our interest. We then kept him at home, and chose the next best man, who was spoiled in half a session. Considering well the evil of corrupting all our good men, we sent the one back that had been already spoiled." At present the poverty of intellect is not so great as it was forty years ago, when the electors of New Jersey were forced to return the member that had previously felt might, and forgot right. The working people have now an abundance of common sense, individuals who know perfectly the interest of their class, and will steadily follow it during an election. Never trust any one without a necessity, is a good rule in life, and never more necessary than in politics.

ORIGIN AND PROGRESS OF FREEDOM.
August 21st, 1830.

Politics and religion are the two great speculative objects of men's researches, and it would appear, from the immense variety of opinions, no two nations or scarcely two individuals thinking alike, that there is no fixed principle, no well ascertained series of truths, as a foundation of those opinions on either of those topics. Religion, consisting of an assemblage of dogmas, out of the sphere of the laws of nature, and as various as the imaginations of those who live by them, cannot be reached by any of our five senses, and perhaps must remain without elucidation or explanation until we can acquire other means of perception. Politics professing to be the means of securing our peace, comfort and hapiness on earth, its laws, rules and regulations, ought to be founded on the nature of man, and to conform to the interest of the majority. That it has been the reverse in all countries, is perhaps the only truth to be learned by the innumerable pages of history, and almost every contrivance, and artificial arrangement, seem to be as opposite to the nature of our species, as to their peace, comfort and happiness. The origin of all the nations, from the Medes, Persians, Greeks and Romans, down to the Russians, etc., has been by the union of physical force, under the title of conquest, which, stript of its heroics and delusions, is the strong taking possession of the property, and making slaves of the persons of the weak. The power thus usurped, has been perpetuated, under the various relations of tyrants, and subjects, masters and slaves, by the consummate policy of the cunning combination of the few to force the many to work for them, which has hitherto kept the producer both poor and ignorant.

It is worthy of remark, that the first attempt at any kind of rational freedom amongst the moderns, was made by the energies of a people, relieving themselves from the despotism of a foreign yoke. As in Switzerland, where the purity of the mountain air, joined to the sterility of the soil and climate, have assisted their spirit of independence, whilst they lessened the temptation of their neighbors to conquer them: and in the emancipation of Holland, where an equal spirit of resistance was manifested, inspired by religious enthusiasm, but could not stand mercantile riches and corruption. In our struggle for independence, far removed, by geographical position, from the arbitrary interference of the old world, commenced a new era in the destinies of mankind. Our declaration of independence, was the first public promulgation of independence, liberty and equality, and our constitution emanating from it, the first attempt at fixing the limits of power, within the security of person and property, corresponding to the universal interest and freedom of all classes of society. The theory established by these documents might have served as a solid foundation, on which to build the practice of freedom and equality, had not the laws and habits of the mother country contrived for the support of a hereditary aristocracy, opposed, and in some measure counteracted the adoption of a practice conformable to that equality, on which alone, the independence of the great mass of producers, can have any permanent existence. As colonies of Britain we were divided into provinces, under the system of a trinity of powers (it is perhaps as difficult to form a unit in politics as in religion) two of which in imitation of the mother country, were hereditary, or deriving their power from the British king, and one elective under the denomination of governor, council, and assembly, subject to all the laws, rules and regulations, that had been accumulating for upwards of 1000 years, for the protection of the British monarchy, and feudal aristocracy. At our revolution these provinces, with the same boundaries, and distinguishing names, were changed into States, and the trinity of political powers were made all elective, and called governors, senate, and assembly, or legislatures, with all the complicated, litigious laws, retained as the basis of jurisprudence, on which each State has been building every session two or three hundred acts, on the same tautological system as practiced in Britain, until the labyrinth of legislation is so intricate, that few of our lawyers can extricate them from the mazes of contradictory precedents, much less can their clients.

After the States had remained four or five years recovering from their losses and expenditures of the revolutionary war, under their former economical governments, it was thought expedient to form a Union, by something that has been called *federalism*, but which, by the powers granted to it by a compromise of parties, is nearer to centralism; having the right of interfering with the internal governments of the States, in their judiciary, military, and fiscal departments, which has been the cause of collisions and disputes. This Union kept up the trinity of powers, and took the form of the British executive in its different departments and many of their parliamentary rules and regulations, not specified or perhaps not authorized by the constitution, unless by constructive explanations, assisted by precedents taken from the British common law, which has been declared in the House of Commons, to be so confused, and mysterious, as to be understood by no one. This imitation of monarchical principles, has existed for half a century, in spite of universal suffrage, owing to the electors giving their votes to the same classes of society who govern in aristocratic Europe, that is, the non-productive consumers; who having the same interest with their European compeers, adopt the same measures for accomplishing their ends. By a greater diffusion of knowledge amongst the great class of producers, they have got a more correct view of their real interest, and of the legal power by the ballot-boxes, of putting in execution whatever may conduce to their peace, comfort or happiness, which will induce them to unite their suffrages, to elect such representatives, as from similar professions, trades, or education, have similar interest and fellow feeling for the working people, who are the producers of all wealth, and ought to have a corresponding influence or control in the distribution of it.

A new field of experiment has been thrown open to the trial of political improvements, in the emancipation of South America, with a population of nearly twenty millions added to the weight of liberty and equality in the scale of nations.— These new converts to freedom having been rescued from a foreign despotism, can have little or no attachment to the laws, contrived by their foreign tyrants, to subject them to their usurped right of conquest, and of course will be easier induced to adopt all practices, moral and physical, that are on a par with the knowledge of the day, which will much conduce to their rapid progress in civilization, as there can be no good reason why the framing of governments should not be perfected by practice, as well as the cobbling of shoes, or any other art which improves by experience. The southern half of this hemisphere, is now trying all forms of political systems, and will no doubt finish by holding to what best suits the great majority. "Fools and children ought not to see half done work," is an old adage, which never was more completely applicable than in what has been said, written, and predicted, concerning the revolution of the South American States, and the probable consequences. Few are competent judges of the result of a fermentation of heterogeneous materials, consisting of the remains of despotism, dregs of slavery, mixed up with a confused idea of liberty and equality, under the control of the military who invest with power, those they believe most in their favor for the moment. To judge by the temporary success of any of the parties would be a deception leading to error. Chili began with centralism, and after being peaceable for some time, was thrown into confusion and civil war, by the ambition of the military chiefs. Peru has a central government, which has been revolutionized several times by the military. Buenos Ayres has been vacilating between federalism and centralism. Columbia has been tolerably governed under the dominion of Bolivar, but is now separated into States, and seems to wish for a federation. Guatimala has had a federation too expensive for the poverty of the States, which has forced them to seize on the property of the church, and think of a more economical federation. Mexico adopted our federal constitution, which interfering with the States, and being too expensive, they have ceased to support it, and permitted the military chiefs to take possession of power, contrary to the articles of the federal constitution; but the disorder has been limited to Mexico the capitol of the federation; each state continuing to govern itself according to its constitution, which proves one of the advantages of every species of federation, and teaches the whole states, the incompatability of a standing army with freedom.

KNOWLEDGE HOSTILE TO THE GOVERNMENT OF THE FEW.
August 25th, 1830.

Of all the States of the Union, it was in New York where Church and State ruled with the most arbitrary sway. There the hierarchy was organized nearer the principles of the Old World. There the number of churches, the influence and wealth of religious establishments, were nearly on a par with the junction of Church and State in Europe. There the hereditary aristocracy of families prevailed; even political parties took the name of their chief, such as Livingstonians, Clintonians, etc. There the habits, customs, opinions and fashions of Europe predominated, and coerced public opinion. To that mercantile emporium was attracted many Europeans who found there a state of society nearly similar to what they had left at home. In every town of the Union, speculation is carried on beyond all profitable or prudential bounds, but in New York it is pushed to the utmost pitch of extravagance. There a man's feet cannot keep pace with commercial changes, but a vast number of hacks are constantly driving from street to street in search of the object of speculation. There the quantity of paper securities is multiplied *ad infinitum*, and a whole street to the very garrets is peopled with money brokers. It is irrelevant to the present purpose to enquire, whether the fact of its being the quarters of the British army during the revolution, may be the ultimate, or its local situation the proximate cause of this turmoil and bustle, so exceeding the operations either of church or state in their neighbors. It is sufficient to ascertain, that the political, religious, and mercantile influence, and dominion, was better combined, and more artificially united, to put into successful operation, all or any of their aristocratic plans, than in any other part of the Union; and notwithstanding this powerful combination against freedom and equality, New York is the first place where the working people have had any success in asserting their claims to rights and privileges, given them by all their political institutions; but which have lain so long dormant, as to have become obsolete.

In our southern states, slavery has annihilated equality and monopolized all freedom to the master, who is of the nonproductive and consuming class. The life, persons, and property of the producers, are possessed as a lawful inheritance by their owners, and the broad line of distinction of color, seems to place an insurmountable bar to general emancipation. The aristocratic monopoly of political rights, wealth and power in the hands of the white descendants of Europeans, destroys all means of a gradual and peaceable improvement in the state of society, removing this unnatural and unjust state of the population, out of the reach of all moderate or temperate means of a change, towards the equalization of property, knowledge and power, the *sine qua non* of rational freedom. This great difference of the rights and immunities of the population, widely separating their relative interest, may perhaps be the cause of a reform in our federation. By removing the cause of collision and dispute through the right of interference in the affairs of the individual state governments given by our present federal constitution, which might be done without weakening the federal tie, as the great interest which the states have in union would be augmented by the great saving and economy of a federation similar to Switzerland.

Our northern states, the nursery of population, long habituated to the equalization of knowledge, through the means of their township schools, which has produced a corresponding equality of property and power, and given them great influence over the other states to which they emigrate, have been gradually ameliorating their political institutions, so as to acquire the denomination of the country of steady habits; thinking themselves further advanced in civilization than their neighbors, they may be longer in making any great change, though the working people begin to claim the remainder of their rights even in New England, and must make every thing bend to their interest, by their numbers in the ballot boxes.

While the federation was ruled by the interest of the same class of society from both the north and south, the acts of congress were considered partial and unjust towards the ministry by the mode of taxation. How much more reason will the southern minority have to complain, when the congress are controled by the interest of the great class of producers, who will most probably charge the rich consuming classes with their full share of public burdens by direct taxation. The producers in the southern states, being slaves without any political rights, property, knowledge, or power, must be governed by the interest of the consuming class, whilst the north, will most probably be ruled by the interest of the great class of producers. These two interests being in all countries opposite, and irreconcilable, will be the cause of a constantly augmenting collision between the interest of the north and of the south, which can only be remedied, by preventing all interference of the general government either in the judiciary, military or fiscal departments, of the individual states, leaving each state to be regulated by its own laws, defending its own militia, and to lay its own taxes, according to the will and interest of the majority, as in Switzerland.

It must certainly be false logic, to reason that the Union will be weakened by making the compact more agreeable to the interest of the contractors, by giving them a constitution, that leaves them more independent at far less expense, and with equal protection, as has been fully proven by the five hundred years experience in the federal constitution in Switzerland. To assert that making the federation more conformable to the interests of the individual states, is a dissolution of the Union, would be equally absurd as to insist that all the reforms made in the state governments are their annihilation. The framers of the constitution aware] that it would require reforms to fit it to the knowledge of the day, only stipulated that it should have an undisturbed trial for ten years, before any change. That all those who now benefit or expect to reap any advantage by the patronage and expenditure of the federal government should advocate its extension of power and privileges, is perfectly agreeable to the nature of our species; but that the millions who pay and obey, who must work harder and live more sparingly in consequence of the extra expense of the federation, should be in its favor, requires more apathy and ignorance, than one would expect to find in a country where there are so many facilities of instruction.

Formerly it was thought that a political association, so cunningly organized in favor of the consumers as was New York, was much more secure and lasting, than one in which the influence of democracy was greater, and the interest of the producers more respected. But with the diffusion of knowledge, most things must change; the greater the power of the few, the greater the abuse, the sooner it will exhaust the patience and forbearance of the millions; who in governments of universal suffrage, have only to will it and it must be done. Even in despotic tyrannies, when the forbearance of the people is exhausted, a revolution must succeed; from which it would appear that in the present state of civilization, the propensity to the equalization of property, knowledge, and power, is in exact proportion to the spread of useful information, and as that is extending wider every day, so will the improvement and amelioration of mankind. It was the privileged orders of church and state, having the power and abusing it, that was the cause of the French, and all other revolutions. The more information and useful knowledge is diffused amongst the people, the less injustice and oppression they will tolerate. As the influence of the moral increases the power of mere physical force must diminish; and the moral revolution must be substituted for the physical, which has too often forced an equalization of power, before the equalization of property and knowledge was fit to support it.

The increasing power and influence of the millions, even in Europe, is evinced every day by the stand the people, through their representatives, make in France against the hereditary power, though sometimes by a charter, at first acknowledged under the military coercion of the combined aristocracy of Europe. The late triumph of representation over the divine right of kings in Holland, and the symptoms that even the tyrant of Spain cannot govern his kingdom without the aid of representation, from the reports of his calling together the Cortes to settle and adjust the affairs of the country, that are in complete anarchy and confusion at present: all these circumstances evidently prove, that any nation that has been once ruled by any kind of equal representation, never can submit peaceably to divine right or hereditary power.

DIVISION OF PROPERTY. UNSETTLED LANDS. JEWISH GOVERNMENT.

August 15, 1830.

Equality of property begets equality of knowledge, and both establish equality of power, which is freedom. Nature, when left to herself is the equalizer of property; and consequently a state of freedom and equality is the natural condition of man, if freed from the oppression of force, maintained by unjust, partial and unequal laws to favor the few at the expense of the many. Our experience since our revolution, proves the truth of these natural consequences, as nearly as the prejudices of the people, and their attachment to ancient laws, habits and customs would permit. For though immense exertions have been made by the influential rich, by obtaining power, and through the means of stock, land, bank and other monopolizing speculations to create a monied aristocracy, yet property remains nearly as equally divided as formerly; that is to say, there are few very rich, and as few miserably poor, keeping out of the calculation the overflowing of European wretchedness, the consequence of arbitrary power and its injustice, which in every thing is opposed to the results of our system of liberty and equality. This brings to my recollection what happened in the penitentiary prison of Philadelphia; before the neutral trade had inundated the county with speculations and paper, there were only 123 convicts for the whole state. One of the directors who was solicited by the convicts to be "allowed to keep St. Patrick's day," answered, "what have you to do with St. Patrick's day, there would have been some rationality had you wished to keep St. Tammany's day;" when the solicitors replied, "you know very well the greatest part of us are from the dear island." The present state of France is another proof of the equalizing propensity of nature.—Property since the revolution is more equally divided than in any other civilized country; knowledge is now dividing; and when both are equalized, power must be in the same proportion. So that it is more than probable, the French nation cannot be governed peaceably by any other than an elective system, and at present all civilized Europe seems inclined towards representation, which must be the consequence of the diffusion of knowledge; for it must be evident, that if the many who produce all property, had as much common sense, ingenuity and contrivance to retain it, as the few consumers have used to deprive them of it, equality could only be deranged, by the superior industry of the few individuals during the age they lived in, to be reduced to a level by the extravagant expenditure of their children in the next age. Since the working people have attempted to claim their legal rights, which their number and utility entitle them to in all countries, the cry of the monopolizers of property and power has been, "agrarian laws;" that the poor were going to pass laws to rob the rich, judging by themselves, how they would act if in the situation of the poor, with their legal power, by universal suffrage of doing what they please.

Though the poor have been, in all countries, some thousands in numbers and physical force, more powerful than the rich, yet history only records two nations that founded their political institutions on agrarian laws; these were the Jews and Spartans. The Jews divided equally the land they conquered, and to perpetuate that equality, they passed a law that no man could sell his land for longer than the jubilee year, which was every fifty years; at that period all land sold during the term, was returned to the original proprietor. So that every fifty years they all started on a principle of equality of landed property. On the adoption of the laws of Lycurgus, the Spartans divided all the lands of the republic, by an agrarian law; and the nature of their money, the equality and community of their clothing and feeding took away all temptation, or ambition for the monopolizing of property, which gave Sparta the superiority over Greece for nearly five hundred years, without any great change in the form of government. The children of Israel retained their equal and pure democracy for about four hundred years.—The Roman people often claimed their share of the lands conquered by their bravery and exertions, but the aristocracy of Rome was sufficiently powerful, to deny them all participation and to sacrifice their leaders: which has been more or less the fate of all people who have claimed their rights ever since.

On the settling of our uncultivated lands, there is the fairest, easiest and most equitable opportunity, of establishing society on the broad basis of equality, without interfering, in the smallest degree, with the rights, property or privileges, of any sect, class or description of citizens. The soil being purchased from the Indians, the original proprietors, with the people's money, cannot possibly be better disposed of, than by an equal division, that will assist in perpetuating freedom and equality. This might be accomplished by a simple law of congress for any territory, that no individual shall be permitted to own or possess by purchase or otherwise, more than two hundred acres of land, or the quantity that may be judged most appropriate for the equal division. There is nothing new in this principle. It is as old as the settlement of the Jews on the conquered lands of Canaan, and the laws of Lycurgus, which in both instances established freedom and equality, without any change for upwards of five hundred years. Yet as some may be afraid of so great a deviation from former modes of legislation, a trial may be made in only one territory, for the purpose of showing how God's chosen people were first governed by judges; to which no good Christian who believes in the bible can object. For the political system of the Jews by the advice and council of the God of the Christians, was the most practical demonstration of freedom and equality, that has ever existed, either before or since. They began by the agrarian law, which was renewed every jubilee or fifty years, by annulling all sales of land, made during that time, and returning the land to the original proprietors. They were ruled by elective judges; no mention is made of pay, perquisites or privileges. They had no nobility, nor any who possessed hereditary power or dominion, no army, but every Jew was a soldier when occasion required; no lawyers, the judges arbitrated all disputes without fee or reward. Perfect equality reigned through the whole Jewish territory. No mention is made of taxes, except in favor of the Levites; who in consequence of their having no share in the division of lands, had a tenth part of the produce, as a religious contribution, which was separate and distinct from their political institutions. The Jews waxed vain, capricious and dissatisfied, and called out for a king, that they might be like other nations; and the Lord gave them a king to punish them, and by the mouth of Samuel told them how that king would oppress them; that he would take their young men and their young women (as David did Beersheba,) their men servants, and their maid servants, to be his servants, their oxen and asses; that he would lay taxes of a tenth, and seize on every thing of the best for his own use; that he would make commands of fifty and one thousand to fight his battles. And Samuel gave the children of Israel an exact description of what every king has done since. The greatest proof of the poverty of the human intellect, and the depreciation of our species, is the submitting to be ruled by hereditary power, under the denomination of emperors, kings, nobles and patricians; for in exact proportion to the unlimited power they usurp, is the misery and wretchedness of the people they govern. That the peace, comfort and happiness of the many, should be sacrificed, without adding to the happiness of the few rulers, is evidently in contradiction to common sense and reason.

One of the most singular anomalies in the history of mankind, is the immense number of different sects of Christians, who all implicitly believe in the prophecies and dogmas of the Jewish bible, and whose faith stretches to all the mysteries and miracles of their religious worship, yet none of them have imitated the perfection of their simple and economical political institutions, nor taken example from their pure democracy based on perfect freedom and equality so conducive to the peace, comfort and happiness of the whole human family. The great respect and reverence to the forms and ceremonies of their religious worship, which though it might be useful to them, cannot benefit the present state of society, contrasted with the total neglect of their perfect civil institutions, argues a disposition for man to do wrong, yea as the sparks fly upwards. That the Jewish bible is a revelation from the divinity, and that he gave the first form of the government of the judges, to his chosen people as the most perfect, is generally believed by all sects of Christians, yet that none of them have attempted to imitate the civil institutions, established by divine authority, cannot be accounted for on any reasonable or consistent principle. Our mode of settling our territories, resembles more the manner in which the Jews took possession of the land of Canaan, than any thing that has happened since. Nearly the same driving out of the original inhabitants, taking full possession without any mixture of the native race, etc., would seem to render the adoption of their civil institutions, more easy and appropriate.

SUGGESTIONS RELATIVE TO SCHOOLS FOR THE CHILDREN OF THE MILLIONS.

Sept. 1*st.* 1830.

Supposing that the working people of the Union, should continue to gain in strength at the ballot-boxes, in the same proportion that they have, from the time of the New York election in November, where they carried only two of their tickets, to the Albany election in April, where they succeeded with five out of six, it is more than probable, that in a very short time, a great majority of both the general congress and state legislators, will be put in place by them, and disposed to act according to their interest. In that case their plan of universal education, on an equal, free and most liberal principle, will be carried into effect—when all the children shall be fed, clothed and instructed at the expense of the people's purse, formerly called the public treasury. As this will be the most active reformation, where a new system is to be introduced, the abolition of monopolies, exclusive privileges, etc., constituting improvements, it is perhaps the duty of every citizen to contribute his mite, by making public the result of his experience on this most important subject, essential to the comfort and happiness of all. It is perfectly new in the annals of modern civilization, though practiced in Greece, as at Sparta, etc., but totally neglected in the copy the moderns have taken of the ancients; like many other of their good practices favoring equality, not suiting any political system, founded like most of the European governments on the feudal system. It is probable the Lancaster or monitorial system will be preferred for its cheapness, on which may be grafted, gradually, the Pestalozzian method, as has been practiced with great advantage in the Kildair street schools, Dublin, from which they sent sixty school-masters every month, to teach in the different parishes and district schools in Ireland. Country localities will be preferred most probably to towns for this description of schools, as much on account of the health of the children, as being removed from the vicious practices, so common in our large towns, which the apish propensity of children are disposed to imitate, and being less exposed to be led astray, from their more useful studies, by the constant abstraction from the idle amusements of large and luxurious societies. All being fed and clothed by the establishment, the vicinity of parents is not necessary, and the schools may collect the children of a large district to the number of some hundreds, and each would serve in place of twenty or thirty small district schools, when the children eat and sleep at home. An immense saving of time and improvement in the amount, quality, and economy of instruction peculiarly suited to a country so thinly peopled, where the greatest part of the children's time is wasted in going and coming at least once a day to a school necessarily at a considerable distance. The locality might be chosen in a healthy situation, removed from swamps or stagnant water, on or near canals, great roads, or navigable rivers, surrounded at least by two acres of land for every child, as a productive farm, from which they might obtain wherewith to feed them. Joining muscular to mental exercise, by the alternation of moral and physical labor, the activity, strength, and dexterity of both, are kept in a constant state of healthy vigor, much more conducive to the comfort and happiness of the individual, than the perpetual separate occupation of either our mental faculties or our corporeal energies. By this useful and agreeable change, every moment of the time of the pupils may be advantageously employed, and no place left for the introduction of idleness, the mother of mischief, and contriver of vice and crime. For the purpose of varying the corporeal occupation, and giving the pupils a choice of the useful art they prefer, teachers of all the useful arts and professions might be attached to the school. As it is not probable that suitable buildings could be found on the seats that combined all the requisites, they must be built expressly for the purpose, and the arrangement and commodious position of the work-shops, houses, court-yards, gardens, etc., are by no means indifferent to the successful execution of the plan.— The materials ought to be solid and durable, as little wood employed in the construction as possible, both on account of its perishable quality and its being a harbor for all kinds of noxious insects. A parallelogram or square may be thought the best form for centralising all the inhabitants, that the least time might be lost in changing place. A court-yard would occupy the centre and all around the buildings would be the gardens, both for the convenience of culture and collecting the fruits. However the systems of instruction may change to keep on a par with the knowledge of the day, the buildings and other conveniences will be permanent, and ought to be constructed with the most durable materials, the area and buildings so placed as to be easily enlarged to suit the growing population of the district. Pisa, a mixture of gravel, sand and clay, rammed solidly between a shifting frame, might perhaps fulfil all the requisites of durability, health and economy for buildings. The materials are to be found every where in nature, without any preparation, and in such abundance, that a wall four or five feet thick could be made with much the same labor, as a wall of one and a half feet thick, the common thickness of our brick walls, which does not protect the inhabitants from the intense cold of our winters, nor from the extreme heat of our summers. The pisa wall being a non-conductor of heat, and made at small expense to any thickness, would guarantee the inhabitants from the unhealthy effects of the rigorous extremes of both our winters and summers. The longer it stands, the harder and more compact it becomes, resisting all absorption of moisture, and retaining its equal temperature. With a coat of white-wash, it has the solid and handsome appearance of a stone building, and might be roofed with tiles or slates that would make it fire proof. It might be heated by hot air or steam by the latest improvements in the construction of the kitchens.

Such buildings would be a useful example and pattern of the best and most economical mode of arranging dwellings, the knowledge of which would add much to the useful instruction of the pupils.

It is well ascertained that immense advantages are gained by all kinds of manual labor and manufactories being on an extensive scale. This is still more evident in schools, where the saving of labor, fuel, etc., in cooking, washing, making clothes, furniture, etc., in wholesale, is comparatively with small establishments, greater than in any species of art or trade. One master by the monitorial system can teach five hundred children as easy as five, with the same expense of apparatus, only the locality must be larger. One professor can lecture to five hundred on chemistry, mathematics, mechanics, natural philosophy, etc., as easily as to five. Now that so much of the teaching of children is by substances and their representations of models and prints, the quantity, quality, and perfection that can be put to the making of every species of instruments for the elucidation of those departments of learning, must be incalculably superior to any thing that the small parish schools can possibly afford to buy. By assembling the children into a numerous, and what may be called a scientific aggregation, the improvement in their health and physical constitutions, would keep pace with the rectitude of their moral conduct. An experienced physician with a fixed salary, would be enabled to practice the hygean or prevention of diseases—which would be assisted by the regularity of their meals and healthfulness of their food. Removed from the constant temptation to excess given to children in the kitchens of their parents, by the foolish fondness of their mothers, while the absence of all vicious and depraved examples, so common in the admixture of children and adults, which are imitated with avidity by the young, their morals would be secure from that contamination unavoidable in mixed societies, where the vices of the old are perpetuated to the young; and all the advantages of the infant's school would be extended to an age when reason takes the rule.— There is nothing that has yet existed so sublime and beautiful as such establishments in theory, and let us hope that now the practice of real equality is begun to be advocated by the great producing class, they may carry it through all the ramifications of society, and imprint it on the plastic minds of their children.

Who shall be trusted with the execution of so noble, useful and permanently advantageous a system, to the present and future generations? those that are immediately and ultimately to reap the benefits of it, the parents of the children that are to be instructed by it. Are there any political associations, that for their limited extent, habits, customs, practices and opinions have been familiar with the management of such an establishment? or must new districts or divisions be created? The new England townships are the nearest to such political divisions, and with the extension of their powers, and a small alteration in the organization, might suit. In extent, allowing two hundred acres to each family, they may support one hundred families, at five children each would be five hundred children, who would be instructed in one school in the centre of the township, that would not be more than three miles from the furthest habitation. The possibility of making the labor of the children feed and clothe them, and the rational improvement that might be made in the forms of clothing, feeding and amusements may be noticed hereafter.

THE CAUSE OF THE MILLIONS WILL BE MARRED BY TRAITORS.

Sept. 10*th*, 1830.

Equality has been considered, as the best and most sure prop to freedom, and as such has been ridiculed by the enemies of mankind, who have always represented any approach to equality, as producing anarchy, confusion and crime, as being contrary to the nature of man, and incompatible with any regular order of society. It was to throw it into a ridiculous point of view, and at the same time to create enemies to freedom, that the royalists, at the height of the French revolution, exaggerated all the vulgar symptoms of equality — Geoffroy and others paraded the streets of Paris with red caps, and coarse clothing, spread their tables before their doors, and invited all the passing crowd to dine with them. Some such tricks as that may be attempted by the aristocracy to bring the working people's claim to equality of rights into contempt, as a thing unprecedented and impossible: forgetting that universal suffrage, when the Quakers adopted it in Pennsylvania, was unprecedented and considered impossible without confusion, riot and bloodshed. They will most probably hire one of the democratic editors and authors to exaggerate all kinds of plans to establish perfect equality, and, under pretence of giving advice, endeavor to take the lead in the working people's councils, criticising and underrating all true friends of moderation, as enemies to freedom and equality, and thereby endeavoring to split them into two or more parties, who will waste their strength against one another, in place of uniting for the general good. These secret enemies of the working people will endeavor to exaggerate the necessity of reducing to equality the rich and those who have until now enjoyed all the power, by insinuating the necessity of having all their children fed, clothed, and educated, the same as the poorest. They will dwell on every circumstance in the contemplated change, that can humiliate and irritate those, who, acting from an opposite interest, are disposed to counteract the will of the majority.

They will bring forward consequences that may perhaps occur in the progress of events, as projects that are immediately to take place. They will interfere, and nominate candidates whom they know will refuse on purpose to make it appear that the working people are at a loss to find any one to represent them. They will talk loud and bluster, whilst their paper will be open to all the crafty insinuations of the people's enemies. All such over officious and busy bodies, ought to be suspected, and all their proposals well weighed and examined, before they shall be adopted; for if they tend to forward the people's cause, it must be by chance, and contrary to the aim of their employers.

As the working people, who produce all, are the great majority in every country, their interest ought to be represented by an equal majority in the councils of all nations.—Fortunately universal suffrage gives them the means of being so represented in our country. To effect and secure that power must be the first object, and all schemes or plans that may increase the opposition or render the obtaining of such an influence in the legislation more difficult, ought to be postponed for the present, and the whole force applied to the ballot-boxes, to obtain the power to regulate public affairs, agreeably to the interest of the great majority.

PUBLIC SCHOOLS. PROBABLE EFFECTS OF THE PRESENT ADVANCING MORAL REVOLUTION.

It is presenting the butt end of the wedge against the old prejudices of society, in place of the small end, in attempting to remove moral as well as physical obstructions, to advocate a Spartan education, that would not suit the present state of civilization, any more than their iron money, but might tend to increase opposition, by striking against the prejudices of a greater number. The equality necessary to freedom, may be obtained by elevating the producers, without depressing the present consumers. Schools on the most improved plans may be formed with the people's money, to feed, clothe and educate all the children in the country, and the rich may be left in full possession of their old monkish colleges, hundreds of years behind the knowledge of the day, as one of the most effectual means of producing the equality of knowledge, which must be followed by equality of property and power. This moral revolution differs from the physical one which preceded it, in as much as, having no physical force to oppose it, deliberation is permitted, gradually to follow the improvements of the age, without violence, or depriving any one of his rights or property: on the contrary every one will be enabled to enjoy the fruits of his labor, by the abolition of all artificial monopolies and exclusive privileges, and it may end by the removal of all restrictions to free trade, free ports, and a free circulation of knowledge and property barred at present by indirect taxation on consumption. All interference of physical force is out of the question; the working people are legally and constitutionally authorized, and forced by a due regard to their own interest, to give their votes only to those, whom they consider to have a corresponding interest with themselves, and therefore disposed to legislate for their benefit and advantage.— The monopolizers of wealth and wisdom, may declaim that the ignorance of the working people is such as to incapacitate them from acting agreeably to their own interest, etc., but the diffusion of knowledge and the progress of civilization, is too far advanced for such sophistry to have any effect.

Once possessed of the majority in the legislatures, and seeing that expensive, complicated and litigious laws deny justice to all who cannot pay the extravagant fees, whilst it completely prevents their knowing or understanding what is law or not law, thereby giving a vast advantage to the rich consumer, they will have the right, and their duty to their constituents will force them to reform those intricate and mysterious laws, and to substitute any simple and plain code that may have been practiced by any modern nation long enough to prove its advantage. If they shall find that the influence of the non-productive consumers, has hitherto thrown the greatest part of the public burdens on the industrious producers by indirect taxation on consumption, their duty to their constituents will oblige them to change that indirect taxation for direct taxes on all species of property. So that each individual should pay towards the expenses of government, in exact proportion to the amount of his property, protected by the powers, vested for that purpose in the rulers, the exercise of which powers caused the greatest part of the public expenses. If, on examining how the State of Vermont is governed by one legislature, they should think the division into two, with distinct powers to the Senate and Assembly, only caused a loss of time and money, in the legislative operations, they must, for the interest of their constituents, simplify the machine, by reducing the legislature to a unit, and save expenses by annulling the possibility of collision. If, on reviewing the history of our federation, they should be of opinion that the cause of all the collisions and disputes between it and the individual States is from the powers given to the federal constitution, to interfere in the judiciary, fiscal and military establishment of the States, they ought so to reform that constitution, as to prevent, in future, all interference of the federation with the governments of the individual States.

Hitherto all the operations of the State legislatures, as well as the federal congress, have been conducted by the non-productive and consuming classes, agreeably to their views of their own interest, and too often in direct opposition to the interests of the great producing classes. All the pages of history attest, that all advocate what they conceive to be their own interest, as the interest of the classes they belong to, and our consuming classes, in their legislative proceedings, do not contradict that historical truth. As the few have hitherto ruled the many, according to the interest of the few, so the many have a right to rule the few as their own interest dictates, when by their immense majority at the ballot boxes, they get possession of all the legislative and executive power. All governments are professedly made for the benefit of the majority, which is the origin of universal suffrage to ascertain that their interest shall prevail; therefore whatever conduces to the interest of the majority must be right, and the only thing to ascertain is, what is for the interest of the majority. Of this the majority in elective governments must be the sole judges. It could only be for that purpose that elective governments were formed; particularly those founded on universal suffrage; any yielding to the will or interest of the minority, is a dereliction from all the principles of representation, and an abandonment of the immense superiority it has over the hereditary system, where the interest of the many is constantly sacrificed to the interest of the few, because the very small minority rule.

SALUTARY REFORM WILL STRENGTHEN THE CAUSE OF THE MANY.

Sept. 15th, 1830.

Our working people will most probably be supported in this moral revolution, by the necessary reforms they will be enabled to make in the various contrivances of the ruling consumers, to deprive the industrious producers of the fruits of their labor. The two great engines which engross the fruits of the producer's labor, are, the monopoly of property, knowledge and power, and taxation. The first consisting of legal monopoly by the charters and exclusive privileges, granted by the legislatures to certain individuals or companies to do what others are prohibited from doing; with the favorable conditions of being free from responsibility beyond a limited term; whilst the public are liable to lose without limits. This kind of monopoly granted by the people's representatives, may be annulled by the same. The other monopoly, founded on the combination of superior wealth, wisdom and management, can only be reformed by equalizing knowledge; which may be affected next age, by the free, equal and universal education of all the children in every class.— Taxation can only be lessened by a reduction of the expenses; though a change in the mode of collection from indirect to direct taxes, would relieve the producers from nine tenths of what they pay at present, and is completely in the power of the majority to do; as well as reducing the public expenses, which might easily be accomplished, by curtailing the agency of the federal government; limiting them to intercourse with foreign nations, and to settling any disputes that might arise between the individual states, like the federation of Switzerland, that has existed without any dispute or change for five hundred years. This would prevent, the federal interference in the judiciary, fiscal or military establishments of the states, the cause of constant disputes and encroachments on their independence, besides saving the double expenditures of States and U. States' judges, lawyers, collectors of revenue, and military establishments, which would be a saving to the people of nearly the whole of the present federal expenses, without adding any thing to the expenses of the States, as they are now under the necessity of keeping up all the above mentioned establishments. This would produce another beneficial change to the working people, by forcing the States to raise all their revenue by direct taxation, on every kind of property; by which they would not pay above one third of what is exacted from them by indirect taxation, and would save nine tenths of the expenses of collecting; thus reducing the patronage of their executive in the same proportion. They would establish free ports, free trade and free circulation of property and knowledge from one end of the Union to the other, leaving every one to enjoy the fruits of his labor, and to transport them how and where he pleased, without being subject to the search and suspicions of custom-house or any other officers in power, which cannot effectually be put in execution, without clothing some of the citizens with the arbitrary power of favoring their friends and punishing their enemies.

INJURIOUS EFFECTS OF HIGH SALARIES TO PUBLIC SERVANTS.

A people whose dignity, character and independence, rests on the broad basis of liberty and equality, can reap no advantage, nor add to their consideration either at home or abroad by the luxurious splendor, show or pomp of the servants they choose to manage their affairs, for the limited time of one or two years. On the contrary, by adding the authority of wealth to the authority of office, gives a double temptation to the abuse of power, and the time spent in expensive amusements, is so much deducted from the public duties.—Therefore, reducing the wages of political labor on a par with other useful occupations, would guarantee the faithful execution of the public trust, and would not remove the public servants so far above the level of their fellow citizens, as to make them regret the loss of their places, or incapacitate them from following productive trades or professions in an elective system where the legal and peaceable change, of rulers, tends to that division of power, property, and knowledge, so essentially necessary to the comfort and happiness of the industrious producers. That constant succession to office and authority, on which alone the vast superiority of an elective government depends, must create violent competitions, intrigues, and corruptions at elections, in proportion to the emoluments obtained by the place. This is strongly exemplified, by the experience of all the States of the Union. The governors of Connecticut, Virginia, and some others with small salaries and little or no patronage, are canvassed by few, and no undue influence is used to obtain them; whilst for the governors of Pennsylvania, New York, etc., etc., their elections are like an arena of gladiators; violent strife, ill will and hatred, encouraged by the newspapers which for months before are filled with all the lies, scandal and calumny which the ingenuity of the different rivals and their friends can invent, disparaging the characters of all the candidates in the most opprobrious terms, taxing them with every vice and crime, bringing an elective system into disrepute both at home and abroad, by inducing the candidates to corrupt and demoralize the electors by grog shops, bribes, and promises of places, which afterwards forces them to put into authority, men who have no other merit than being dexterous at the shameful, deceitful and injurious trade, of an expert canvasser for public trust.

RESPECT IS DUE TO THE OFFICE RATHER THAN THE OFFICER.

The dignity, honor or consideration of an elective officer, is not attached to the person of the magistrate, as it is in all hereditary systems, but to the authority vested in him by the confidence of his fellow citizens; which cannot be increased or diminished by his mode of eating, drinking, clothing, lodging or traveling. Whether he be clothed in home-spun or foreign lace and embroidery; whether he sits down to a table with a simple joint, or to two courses and a dessert; whether he drink small beer or foreign wines; whether he lodges in a log house or a palace, travels on foot or in a coach and six horses, the independent free citizen ought to have the same respect for the man of his choice. This deference and respect ought to be much greater for those who waste little, either of time or money in luxurious living, being well convinced that the more time they spend in parade, ceremony or attending levees, routes or dinners, the less they will have to attend to their public duties; which is what interests most the industrious producer, who does not participate in those fashionable amusements.

REPUBLICAN SYSTEM OF EDUCATION.

Sept. 7th, 1830.

All animals whilst awake are constantly occupied, morally or physically; and even when asleep, their mental faculties are agitated in dreams, volition being the only faculty that is suspended. Perfect neutrality is perhaps not in our nature. Actions therefore must either be useful to ourselves or others or useless, beneficial or hurtful. It follows, that the restless activity of children, when not occupied with something useful, will most probably be employed in something injurious, mischievous, or at least useless. Habits acquire unconquerable obstinacy and strength by time. Good habits cannot be too early acquired, and the habit of useful industry cannot be too soon instilled into children; as the future basis of prosperity, comfort and happiness, constant useful occupation is the most certain, and prevents them from injuring themselves or others.

Children lose patience, their attention is fatigued, and their good will exhausted, by being kept too long at mental exercises, and their instinct suggests the necessity of keeping up the equilibrium between the vital power or force expended by muscular action, and the intellectual exertions: out of which, necessity originated their love of play and amusement, though requiring harder labor than their scholastic studies, such as crooked stick, hand and foot ball, cricket, etc., all creating violent competition, and the useless ambition of being pre-eminent in a struggle which tends to no utility, but serves to strengthen and excite the malevolent passions of ill will, envy and hatred, habituating them to the unsociable eeling of gaining pleasure by others' loss, which is the immoral feature of all amusing contention and gambling. When a little older they follow the sports of men, fishing, shooting, horse-racing, cock-fighting, bull-baiting, etc., all tormenting cruelties, finishing by blood and slaughter, strengthening and augmenting the brutal propensities, which seem peculiarly adapted to our species, from the Roman gladiators, down to the British boxers. It would be more rational to amuse themselves with the trade of a butcher, because the plea of necessity might excuse that cruelty, which cannot be advanced for such amusements. It is more than probable that all such pleasures and pastimes, are the remains of savage barbarity, kept up by the idle and tyrannical consumers, imitated by the ignorant and foolish producers, and perpetuated and enforced by long habit; for it is a query, whether any one at first, reaped either satisfaction or gratification in being spectators or actors in such wanton exhibitions of force against weakness. Probably training and discipline, by perverting habits, were necessary to associate pleasurable ideas to such revolting sights of barbarity.

If pleasurable ideas can by habit and practice be united with such mortifying exhibitions of human depravity, where every result is annihilated the moment the action is finished, how much more easy would it be for teachers, to imprint on the tender minds of children, the union of pleasurable ideas with the useful occupation of some mechanical art. This would furnish the necessary muscular exercises, so conducive to health, while, at the same time, the gratification would be prolonged by the permanent benefit obtained by the utility of what is produced, and securing pecuniary independence in being capable of practicing a productive trade in case of necessity. The being taught to make shoes or coats, does not force the possessor of such knowledge to be a shoemaker or tailor, any more than learning mensuration or navigation obliges him to become a surveyor or sailor. They are all acquirements good to have in case of necessity, and in no state of society, is that necessity more likely to occur, than in our system founded on liberty and equality, where the only bar to the most complete equalization of the whole population, is the ignorance of the great producing classes, which however is vanishing rapidly before the increasing means of obtaining useful knowledge; an d children ought to be trained, and educated to suit the probable situation, which the circumstances of the next age may place them in. Even at present, all our farmers and manufacturers, ninetenths of our population, would be very much benefitted by possessing one or two of the mechanic arts, suitable to their occupations.

Besides all the foregoing reasons for the introduction of the useful arts into the schools, there remains the great economy of enabling children to feed, clothe, and educate themselves by their own exertions; thus rendering them independent of the labor of others, and establishing an equality founded on each administering to his own wants from the most early age, which would continue through all the wants of life, and would effectually prevent one class of society from tyranizing over another.

All those who think their present riches will keep their descendants above the necessity of manual labor, may object to making the useful trades a part of the instruction of the children; but they are a very small minority, and as long as they retain the aristocratic ideas of their great superiority, they will not, most probably, put their children to such equalizing systems. If the children can nearly produce their expenses, which there can be little doubt, with judicious management they can, under the control and parental inspection of those who benefit by the school, those children whose parents will not permit them to work, will have no right to be at the school, and the proper management of such establishments will free all the working people from their dependence on those who have already accumulated wealth; and will dry up the source of inequality of property in future.

In all free countries, every citizen ought to be trained so as to be a soldier when required, as the only means of protecting their freedom. In those schools the pupils should be taught the manual exercise, marching, and countermarching, forming squares, parallelograms, triangles, and all the geometrical figures with exactitude and rapidity. They ought all to learn to swim, and ride on horse-back, by wooden horses so poised as to require equal address to balance on them, as on the living horse. They ought to acquire an accurate idea of heights and distances at the first sight, by carrying a measure in their walks, each guessing at the height or distance of any object, and measuring to find who is the nearest. By this practice they will acquire an accuracy of sight, so as to determine within a few feet the distance or height of any object. These exercises in the useful trades, will make a habit of muscular motion, that will aid insecuring health, wealth, comfort and happiness during their progress through life.

In such schools the scale of utility, may with more ease and probability of successs, be used, by which to measure the value of things, than in the contending interests of common society. The absurd, extravagant, and worse than useless whims of fashion, in eating, drinking, clothing, recreations, pastimes, etc., may be corrected without interfering with the prejudices of the present age. The food might be the most conducive to health and vigor, cooked in the most simple manner, abstracted from all that complicated mixture and variety of stimulants contrived to provoke excesses of all kinds. Drink might be the only two fluids furnished by nature, water and milk, which are the most healthy. All the artificial liquors, such as beer, cider, wine, and spirits, are taken for their stimulant qualities, which are very bad for adults, but poison for children. Clothing, in place of the long tight coat with a high collar, and sharp pointed shoes, that cramp and paralyze all muscular motion, might be made to sit easy to the natural shapes by plaits and folds, giving an elasticity that would yield to the natural change of forms by muscular motion. The shoes, like the feet, might be made broadest at the toes, and shaped diagonally from the great toe to the little one, so as to allow the toes to spread at every step, which would facilitate the elastic spring of exertion, by affording a broader and more solid base, and would conduce much to health, by permitting the fluids of the extremities a freer circulation. The shoes would last double the time; for when the toes are confined, nature insisting on freedom, bursts the shoes before they are half worn. The same argument applies to every part of dress that confines or constrains the natural movements of the body. The Turks, though half barbarians, have a more rational dress than any of the boasted civilized nations.

Schools on the above general principles, might easily be so organized, by the judicious variety of instruction, avoiding to fatigue the attention by more than one hour's application to any one study, so that the children might be induced with pleasure and the utmost good will, to be occupied in acquiring useful knowledge from five in the morning until eight o'clock at night, with the exception of three hours to meals. This is no speculation of mine, it was in full practice by Pestalozzi at Yverdun, before his system was adulterated by the folly of parents, and old schoolmasters, that he was induced by the public to employ.

IGNORANCE OF THE ARTS AND SCIENCES, AT THE CLOSE OF OUR REVOLUTION. UNPRECEDENTED IMPROVEMENT SINCE.

Sept. 10*th*, 1830.

For the instruction of those who were too young to observe, and of those whose recollection is obliterated by the glare of an immense progress in all the arts, sciences, agriculture, navigation, commerce, etc., since our revolution, as well as to encourage other states just emancipated from foreign bondage, and who are experimenting on the effects of freedom and equality, it may be necessary to give a short sketch of our situation as regards the arts, sciences, etc., etc., immediately, and for some considerable time after our revolution. Every instrument of iron for use, within or without the house, from a hob nail to an anchor, was imported from Britain.— All species of clothing, from head to foot, bed furniture, pewter, glass, earthen-ware, carriages, saddles, harness, etc., etc., were all from Britain, and we used to import into Virginia hundreds of bundles of brush handles and mop sticks made in London, from Norway pine, every year.— Most articles of German and other continental manufactories, came to us through Britain, not having the correspondence or credit to import them direct from the place where they were made. Our agriculture consisted of cutting down the trees, impoverishing the land with four or five crops, and leaving it as an old field, to enclose more of the forest.— Even our garden vegetables were exceedingly scarce, particularly in the slave states. Our navigation consisted of a few sloops and schooners. On the first anniversary of our independence at Philadelphia, the largest vessel they could find to hoist a flag upon, was a top sail yard arm schooner; and the first vessel we sent to China was a sloop of about 100 tuns burden. Most of the trade of the southern States was carried on by foreign bottoms, mostly British, and our merchants consisted of those who sold goods by the piece, and those who sold by the yard. Few ran sea risks, but those who carried on the trade of the southern states. Our carpenters to the eastward were without work, and a subscription was raised to build ships to employ them. No periodical works, either on literature or science, were published; our books were mostly imported from Britain, and newspapers were almost the only publications that issued from our presses. There was not a paved road or canal, from one end of the continent to the other for long after our revolution. The Richmond canal, and Lancaster turnpike, were amongst the first, neither of which paid any dividend for a great many years; so little was the trade that passed through them.

When I was a merchant, having business that forced me to visit Virginia twice a year, I visited Richmod in company with Dr. Scandala, an Italian gentleman; seeing Mr. Latrobe at the hotel, I enquired who he was, but was warned by my friends not to make acquaintance with him, as he was a crazy man who gathered weeds and stones in the woods. On making his acquaintance, I found him a man of merit, who did more in less time, than I had known done by any one before; but his talents at that time, were lost at Richmond. He next year visted Philadelphia, and I requested him to draw a handsome edifice and put it in perspective. He put on paper what was afterwards the marble edifice of the bank of Pennsylvania: after it had remained some time over my chimney piece, I sent it to their discount room, where it remained for two or three years, until they thought of erecting such a building. The directors then requested me to send for Latrobe. He came and gave the dimensions of every marble slab that was to be put into the building, to the marble cutters, which was new to the stone masons and against which they complained much, and also said the lime was rotten, and would not hold. There was no wood or any thing combustible in the building; all was arched. To groin the arches, the bricks were to be cut; the brick-layers stopped work declaring it was impossible. Latrobe took a trowel, cut the bricks and laid them. Had he not been a practical, as well as theoretical architect, the building would have stopped from the ignorance of the workmen. At this time he gave three different plans for bringing the water from the Schuylkill into Philadelphia: the town council chose the worst of these because it was the cheapest; which has been since changed. When making my geological map, as I was breaking a rock on the road side in Virginia, a traveller who observed me, stopped at a respectable distance, and went out of his road to a tavern, to tell them there was a madman on the road, breaking the rocks with a large sledge hammer.— When I got to the tavern, no one would take care of my horses, and made their escape when I went into the house: nor was I able to explain my object in breaking the rocks to their comprehension, so that I left them under the idea that I was mad, but not violently so, excepting when I met with rocks. The only cabinet of mineralogy in Philadelphia, at that time was a very small one, which Dr. Seybert brought from Gottingen, with specimens about the size of a thumb. In 1805 I enabled a young Frenchman, (Mr. Godon) to go from Paris to the United States. He delivered in Boston and Philadelphia, the first lectures that were given on mineralogy in any part of the Union. Excepting a little botany and zoology, understood by a very few, all the other branches of the Natural Sciences were almost as well understood by our Indians, as by the civilized inhabitants of our states. The charters of all our colleges being copies of Oxford, had no chair for the exact sciences of chemistry, natural history, etc. The first coal pits that were wrought, were above Richmond in Virginia; and about thirty years ago a collier from New Castle in England, taught them how to clear the mine of foul air, by a fire at the mouth of the shaft.

For the few first years after the revolution, before the people were burdened with federal expenses, the States under their economical governments and free trade, recovered the losses and destruction of the revolutionary war, so as to lay a foundation for an unprecedented prosperity in the annals of mankind. The fruits of freedom, augmented the resources of the country, far beyond any thing before. The rapid and surprising increase of the population, the equally great augmentation of their agricultural, manufacturing, and every other species of production, with the increase of their navigation and commerce, astonished the old world. The gigantic strides made in the useful arts and sciences—the immense extension of their roads and canals, with their great improvements in river navigation by steam boats, far exceeds what the most fertile imagination could have foreseen. The last forty years experience of the United States, places freedom in a superior point of view to any thing that could be imagined, and the rapidity of their progress compared with any thing that preceded it staggers belief.

Even these wonderful effects are the consequence of freedom, although deprived of the aid and assistance of her handmaid equality, crippled by the prejudices, fashions and frippery of arbitrary systems, where the few rule and consume the production of the many, where long habit and custom have subjected them to the laws, opinions, manners and practices of the aristocracy of the country whence their forefathers came, continuing the inequality of property and knowledge, by submitting the industrious producers to the rule and control of the idle consumers, wresting from the industrious many, the fruits of their labor; thereby causing poverty, disease and misery, without adding to the comfort or happiness of the ambitious few; only enabling them to commit all kinds of excesses in the physical appetites, finishing a life of care and anxiety by disease and regret, despising and branding all the productive occupations necessary to the existence of mankind, as disgraceful and scornful in proportion to their utility, whilst the luxurious waste and extravagance of dissipation, vice and crime, are bedecked with the consideration, respect and approbation of society.

If freedom alone, separated from equality by so many artificial and cunning contrivances, has been able to effect such astonishing improvements in the condition of our species, what may not be expected, when the diffusion of knowledge and civilization shall have made a more equal division of property, knowledge, and power; when the two extremes of society, poverty and luxury, whence issue all mischief, vice and crime, shall be compressed into the honest and respectable middle ranks, above poverty and below luxury; when equality (without which there can be no justice) has made it the interest of all to be honest and upright in all their transactions, as the only mode of acquiring the respect and esteem of their fellow-citizens, so essentially necessary to the comfort and happiness of all social beings. Let those who sneer and deride at such predictions as Utopian dreams, look at the progress of humanity for the last fifty years, and tax their ingenuity for some sophistry to prove that it cannot continue in an accelerated motion; let those who by artifice and combination have usurped a temporary superiority over their fellow-citizens, consider that their power is founded on the ignorance of those they control, which is every day dissipating by the various means and facilities of acquiring useful knowledge.

155

CHOICE OF PARTY.

Sept. 15*th*, 1830.

All men of independent minds, who have the moral courage to think for themselves, make choice of their political party by their opinion of its strength and power, either of numbers, reason, justice or some superiority which they conceive they have over their opponents. The timid mass of mankind follow and augment the current, which the designing and cunning few, have had the address and power to direct into the channel of their own interest. This iniquitous stream wears down its bed deep in the substance, prosperity, peace and happiness of the industrious producers; overflows and deluges all opposition, until the mass of the population, over whom it has swept with the broom of destruction, and has worn out all their patience and forebearance, rises up and throws it out of its usurped bed, changing the direction of all political events. Surrounding circumstances influence and form all our opinions. I began to think, during our revolution, seeing justice, reason and numbers on the side of the people, and tyranny and oppression enforced by the bayonets of their former rulers, that there was neither merit nor demerit in becoming a democrat, which the success of the revolution tended to strengthen; and a residence in the different European nations, where less or more despotism prevailed, confirmed and consolidated all by democratic principles, and united them to that powerful stimulant self-love; considering myself interested in all that concerned my party, which the European revolutions (most of which I was an eye witness of, from pure curiosity) though not so successful as the friends of humanity could have wished, yet tended to fix and rivet my democratic opinions; which, the little time I have, most probably, to remain above ground, cannot materially change.

POLITICAL COWARDICE OF THE MANY, FAVORABLE TO THE FEW.

The first struggle against vulgar errors, which the influence of the few has impressed on the ignorance of the many, is the most difficult. When once our working people shall have obtained a majority in any of the states, the tide of popularity will be augmented in their favor, by the accession of that great mass of apathetic population, who follow suit; and so strong is their fear and ignorance of consequences, that they are never satisfied of being safe but in the midst of multitudes. This artificial aggregation of numbers kept together by the fear and ignorance of consequences, has been the chief support of both Church and State: the first subjecting the moral pusillanimity, the last overawing the physical cowardice so as to overwhelm justice, reason and utility; stopping the diffusion of useful knowledge, by reducing the intellect to feed on the poison of their imaginary chimeras, hunting down any isolated individual who may oppose their political or religious creeds.

ARISTOCRATICAL LAWS NOT SUITABLE IN AN ELECTIVE GOVERNMENT.

Sept. 18*th*, 1830.

Are there any of the laws, rules or regulations, made for the support and perpetuity of arbitrary power in the privileged orders of hereditary monarchy or aristocracy, that can suit, or be with safety adopted by a free people, under an elective government of universal suffrage, where political institutions are bottomed on freedom and equality? It is probable that that question must be answered in the negative by all the friends of freedom. In hereditary power, abuse accumulates from father to son, through ages without any change. The very name of change strikes with horror all the privileged orders. They can see nothing but destruction to their exclusive prerogatives, in every melioration to the lot of humanity. Their subjects have not the right to dispose of their persons; their sovereign claims them as his property wherever he can find them: all is chained down, and permanently fixed as a perpetual inheritance of the hereditary chiefs. All this is reversed in elective governments of universal suffrage. Constant changes of men and measures at the will of the majority, constitute its essence, life and pre-eminence over all others. The power and prerogative being equally divided amongst the whole population, no one has a right to encroach on another's share, by perpetuating his authority beyond the time he is elected. Hereditary kings and legislators possessing all the power, and most of the property during their lives, may with some appearance of justice, leave it with certain restrictions, to their heirs agreeably to the rights claimed by parents in most countries; but elective legislators placed in power for one or two years, are tenants at will, having no property in the power they exercise for that limited time, nor can they leave any of it to their heirs, any laws they make to bind their successors, encroach on the rights and prerogatives of those who take their places, and assume both a power and a property which do not belong to them, being wrested from the share of their successors, leaving them *minus* of all the power and prerogative their predecessors had usurped.

Owing to the checks and balances in the British government, the friction is great, and the oil necessary to lubricate expensive, and from a variety of concurring circumstances, during a long period of mercantile prosperity, the wages of political labor increased with the wealth, real or artificial of the inhabitants, so as to be perhaps four times more than in any other country. Our leading men, particularly the gentlemen of the law, during, and for some considerable time after our revolution, were educated with a great reverence for British institutions.

It is therefore not to be wondered at, that our elective system is grafted on many of the abuses of hereditary aristocracy, and that our declaration of independence, promulgated during the first burst of popular enthusiasm, should be almost the only public document, where inequality is acknowledged as one of the props of our political system. From the beginning of both our State and United States' legislation they assumed the rights and prerogatives of the British Parliament, and copied many of their forms and usages, borrowed money and mortgaged property without consent, for purposes, from many of which their successors could reap no benefit; granted exclusive privileges, and charters for long periods, so as to monopolize the prerogatives of their successors; thus acting in many cases, as if the temporary power delegated to them, was an inheritance fixed and permanent, in them and their heirs.

As long as the States participated in this sweeping authority, all went on pretty smoothly; but as soon as the federation assumed the place of a hereditary sovereign, and placed the States as subjects that were bound by the act of their predecessors half a century ago, then some of the faults and inconveniences, foreseen and predicted by Patrick Henry and his party on forming the federation, began to appear.— Though previous collisions had occurred between the federation and State courts of justice, yet the dispute was settled by compromise; but the federal exercise of taxation, touching the interest and independence of the States in the most tender and sensible parts, has placed the interest of the south in opposition to the interest of the north, the interest of the manufacturers against the interest of the agriculturists, etc., which perhaps, will not be so easily settled by compromise. while the federal government had the right to interfere with the judiciary, fiscal, and military, of so many independent states, whose habits, customs, climates, productions and of course interest were so different and various, a union of opinions could not be expected to exist long: nor can the same species of taxation be equally just and impartial in every part of an extensive territory. For instance, the paying one dollar in the western country, where wheat is at half a dollar per bushel, and corn at less than a quarter, requires more labor than the paying two dollars in the Atlantic States where wheat is at one dollar and a quarter, and corn at seventy-five cents per bushel; nor could any thing short of the tyranny of force collect such a tax in the extensive bounds of the Russian or Austrian empires. But that bayonet executive is out of the question, in elective systems of universal suffrage, and therefore all our institutions ought to be so organized as to work freely, agreeably to the interest of all, without the application of a force which freedom and equality cannot tolerate. This is only the commencement of the many inconveniences arising from the adoption of the policy or laws of arbitrary aristocracies, which must increase with the extension of our population. The patronage of the federal executive before we reach the Pacific, will be too exorbitant to be wielded by an elective officer.

Fortunately all the useful purposes of a federation can be accomplished, without permitting them to interfere with the judiciary, fiscal or military establishments of the independent States, by assimilating our federal government to that which has regulated, without a dispute, the affairs of Switzerland for nearly five hundred years, by which we could save almost the whole expenses of the federation; most of which is a double expenditure, for judges, lawyers, collectors, and military; each State keeping up an establishment of the same kind for their judiciary, fiscal and militia, which would require little or no additional expense to extend it as far as would be necessary for the maintenance of all. The reason given for fixing a federal judiciary in every State is, that strangers and foreigners may obtain more impartial justice from a federal judge than from a State's judge; as the jury who decide every thing, must be a State jury, it seems to throw obloquy on the judges of the States, without benefiting the foreigners; the late extension of their powers to settling any disputes between the States and the United States, has not been sanctioned by the States. All direct taxes were at the option of the States to collect, by the constitution; only indirect taxes were to be collected by the United States' officers, to prevent the States from the collisions of taxing one another. But by adopting direct taxation as in Switzerland, immense benefit would accrue to the Union, by free ports, and the free circuation of property and knowledge, without the inquisitorial search of revenue officers, which too often does injury to the articles, and is always attended with the loss of time, temper, and money.

The federation, except in time of war, would have no occasion for troops, having no duties to execute which could require the application of force: and in case of hostilities with any foreign power, they would have the same means of forcing the States to furnish their quota of men and money as they have now: that is, by the force of the majority of the States, without which no kind of federation can compel compliance with the conditions of their Union. Nations are feared and respected in proportion to their moral and physical force, exhibited by their quantity of productions, not by the show, pomp or extravagance of their rulers, which diminishes their power of defence, as well as of aggression. Freedom does not require the support of privilege, patronage, or monopoly; all officers ought to be elected by the votes of the majority, under whose eyes they serve and do their duty, being the best judges of their merit, gaining by the faithful discharge of their duties, and suffering by their negligence or incapacity.

THE FEW EXCHANGE THEIR OPINIONS AND DOGMAS FOR THE HARD LABOR OF THE MILLIONS.

Sept. 20th, 1830.

On looking coolly, in the sense of the interest of the millions, one can see nothing in the operation of both church and state, modern or ancient, but ingenious contrivances to rob the millions of what would add to their comfort and happiness, and which added to the ruling influential few, diminishes their happiness, increases their care, anxiety, and trouble, by placing them in an unnatural and uneasy posture, with respect to the multitude who surround them, on whom they are dependent, not only for their artificial wants and luxuries, but even for their necessaries, without which they could not exist. Their dangerous dependence has been for a long time concealed, under the thick veil of their own ignorance and that of the millions; but now that the facility of acquiring useful knowledge, has disseminated information among the millions of their rights, privileges and utility, and at the same time opened the eyes of those who formerly ruled, without reflecting why or wherefore, their situation becomes doubly painful and precarious, by attempting to remain at the tottering height where the presumption of their present race of ancestors placed them. If we examine and analyze all the dogmas, principles or pretensions of the church, we shall find them to be resolvable into a quantity of air, modulated into sounds, which when tested by the evidence of the senses, evaporate into invisible, incomprehensible, metaphysical, immaterialism, for the pretence of solving which, and piloting t to paradise, the priests exact, in many countries, nearly one-third of the solid production of the toil and labor of the industrious producers, on which they revel in luxury and idleness, tyrannizing, domineering, and insulting those who feed and support their extravagant affluence. Each sect, of which there are so many thousands, monopolizing the gifts, and what they called the blessings of paradise, which they exchange for the real and solid food, raiment, lodging, luxuries and other commodities of this world, being without bounds or limits as inexhaustible as the currency they pay with.

Search into the arcanum of state policy; there you find a corporation, in most countries, distinct and even contrary to the interests of those who support them, dividing the property of the people with the church, and affording each other mutual protection. The greatest part of the law is made in favor of the rich, and of the few that might benefit the millions, so enhanced by the exorbitant fees of lawyers, as to be out of the reach of the working people. You will find that life and liberty are sacrificed to property, because the rulers have an interest in preserving their property, but none in protecting the lives and liberties of the people; instead of property being responsible for property, and life for life.—

An honest debtor is incarcerated for life for debt, and the miserable, half-starved thief is hanged for taking a few dollars perhaps to buy bread for himself and family. The equitable punishment, and the best to deter others, would be to make him pay, by his work, the damage he has done. His death benefits no one, and is not even an example to deter others, being forgotten the next day. This monopoly of wealth and wisdom, leaving no other birth right to the millions, but poverty and ignorance, is an artificial creation of the rulers, supported and maintained by unjust laws against all the propensities and exertions of nature to continue the original equality of our species. It would be foolish in any people to expect their rulers to do any good, but to themselves; doing good to others is not their province, though under that specious pretence, they often prevent the people from doing good to themselves. All their useful duties ought to consist in maintaining the natural equality, and checking evil, leaving the millions free to do good to themselves; as they never interfere under pretence of doing good, without doing harm. Civilization has only yet contrived artifices to push society into the two extremes of poverty and riches, depriving the one of necessaries, to heap on the other superfluities, removing both from equality, from justice and happiness.

Our revolution was the first successful attempt to restore the natural equality; but the opposition was not sufficiently strong to scatter and divide property; only political equality was accomplished. Whilst the consequences of retaining most of our habits of inequality, joined to the monopoly of the national debt, state lands, and circulating paper, created an inequality which the exertions of nature have not been able to equalize.

The French revolution was the next violent push at the monopolies of church and state, and the reaction against the force and violence of aristocratic opposition, such as to scatter both property, and proprietors, and establish a degree of equality unknown before under any state of civilization.

It has produced a corresponding equality of knowledge, and forced a proportioned equalization of power, the end and aim of the present revolution, which most probably will finish by an elective system of universal suffrage, as the only kind of government that can suit the equality so completely pervading the French nation.

EDUCATION OF THE PEOPLE.

In physics, when the pendulum is forced far on one side, it re-acts nearly as far back on the other, passing the bounds of moderation in the middle. The same may be remarked in the moral movements of mankind, vacillating at first between two extremes, they often pass the centre of reason, before experience teaches them the advantage of moderation. This is evinced by the contrast between the present and former opinions on the education of the working people. Formerly little or nothing was done, either by themselves, or others, to procure a rational education for their children. But during the late few months, education has become a rage which absorbs all the energies of society, and the continent is to be covered with boarding schools for the whole race, at the expense of the whole population; certainly an event devoutly to be wished for, and when put into judicious practice, it will be one of the greatest and most beneficial revolutions that ever improved the destinies of mankind. To all novelties, however, there is opposition nearly in proportion to the extent of the change from the old to the new, and the difficulties of execution are nearly in the same ratio. No one can doubt of the vast superiority of having children lodged and boarded in the school; of the advantages much greater than the difference between twenty-four hours and the four hours occupied by the old confinement on a stool without movement, which cramps both the moral and physical powers; from which prison they are released only to retaliate on their jailors, by every act of destructive mischief their fertile activity can invent. But it may be well to consider that this old fashioned folly has existed for centuries, and most of our ideas of right and wrong have been beat into us by that clumsy machinery; that at present there are houses built both in the towns and country, sufficiently capacious to lodge father, mother, children, servants and attendants; that by transporting all the children with their necessary nurses, and menials to those new gymnasiums, you must leave four-fifths of the old buildings empty and in some measure useless. All this would only injure the owner of the houses in those unnatural aggregations of mankind, large towns, and prevent them from enjoying the benefit of the monopolies, which power and numbers have enabled them to usurp. This may perhaps do little harm to the whole population, but the expense of erecting new buildings, calculated to suit this new mode of education, is rather a serious consideration, which would require a skillful converter, to make as much as possible of the old in changing them to suit the convenience and necessities of the new order of things. All this is only the opposition of inert, dead matter and its proprietors; but there is another set of opponents, in the active intrigues of the old schoolmasters, a combination of obstinate and persevering individuals, having an interest opposed to giving knowledge cheap, and more strongly riveted to their ancient power, dominion, arbitrary laws, customs and happiness, than any other class of the community. Long accustomed to reign by the dread of punishment over their innocent pupils, out of the reach of a superior or even an equal, it will be difficult to find many of them, willing to submit to reason in an establishment organized on rational principles, guaranteed from fear or abject submission; which if permitted to be introduced into these extensive seminaries, will be an evil increased in the ratio of the extent.

165

THE AMOUNT OF DIRECT TAX ON EACH INDIVIDUAL WOULD BE ABOUT ONE FIFTH THE AMOUNT OF THE PRESENT INDIRECT TAX.

October 8th, 1830.

When traveling in the different countries of Europe, I used to think they had formed erroneous opinions of the state of society and civilization of the United States, from the merchants and supercargoes, who were the principal travelers at that time, whom they judged by their proficiency in positive knowledge of natural history and the exact sciences; studies very little attended to at that time in our Union. On a fair comparison of our learned professors and others, who could live without manual labor, I found there was little to boast of; but our mechanics and working people, I insisted, were far superior to any of the same class they had in Europe: at which they shook their heads, and inquired if we were not governed by an elective system of universal suffrage, and if the principal parts of our revenue were not raised by indirect taxes on consumption, which they considered as a proof of the ignorance, rather than the superior knowledge of the working people; "for," said they, "give our laborers the advantage of election by universal suffrage, and all our indirect taxes would be changed into direct taxes on property the first month, as it was at the commencement of the French revolution, which would have continued in France, but for the perpetual wars waged by the combined powers against French liberty:" they then repeated an anecdote of a foreign traveler, conversing with one of our mechanics, who in boasting of the superiority of our country, exultingly said, "we pay no taxes." The foreigner asked him, how much he paid for his coat; he answered, "twenty-five dollars," "mine is as good for fifteen dollars in my country, where coats do not pay taxes, and you pay ten dollars tax on your coat." "But," says the mechanic, "I do not see the tax gatherer." "You may not choose to see through the cunning of your rulers, who employ the wholesale and retail shop-keepers to collect the taxes. The latter not only make you pay the tax, but their profit on it also, which augments it nearly fifty per cent."—The great aversion to direct taxation has been remarked as an anomaly in the character of the North Americans. This brings to my recollection a caricature I had planned at the close of the last century; which in consequence of having been educated in an old school, that is, having learnt little or nothing that I could make use of when I left it, such as Latin and Greek, but not the best defined and universal language of drawing, I could not execute my caricature. Though our working people have learnt much since, they are still deficient in the true result of taxation, and as a description may induce some draftsman to delineate it, it may be some utility to give it here.

I represented a mechanic sitting at his work-bench crying out, "I pay no taxes," blindfolded by a bandage, with this label, "state intrigue," with a label on his coat, 40 *per ct. tax*, on his cotton pantaloons 50 *per ct. tax*, on a bar of iron 50 *per ct. tax*, on a box of tea 40 *per ct. tax*, on a barrel of sugar 100 *per ct. tax*, on a bag of coffee 90 *per ct. tax*, on a bushel of salt 100 *per ct. tax*, on a bottle of brandy 60 *per ct. tax*, on a bottle of wine 50 *per ct. tax*, on a case of salad oil 30 *per ct. tax*, a bale of hemp 25 *per ct. tax*, on a pack of wool 25 *per ct. tax*, etc., etc.; a wholesale shop-keeper on the right side of the mechanic, slyly picking his purse out of his pocket, and counting the money, giving half to the treasury, and putting the other half into his own pocket, saying, "what a profitable thing, to be in the service of the public;" a retail shop-keeper on the left side, with his hand in the mechanic's pocket, saying, "how easy it is to make money in partnership with the treasury."

With the tariff before us, let us try to make out a mechanic's account of taxes, for one year for himself, a wife and three children; but in all things of this kind, it is better to be under than over the mark, viz.

Two suits of clothes, coat, waistcoat, pantaloons, shirt and hose, cost $15, each at 33⅓ per ct. the average tax, with shop-keepers' profit, etc., etc. $30 at 33⅓ is 10
Two suits for his wife at the same value, 30 do. is 10
Three children at $15; $5 each, 15 do. is 5
One hundred lbs. of sugar pays $3 tax, 3
Eight lbs. of tea pays 100 per ct. or half a dollar per lb., 4
Twenty lbs. of coffee at 5 cts. per lb.,' 1
Fourteen gallons of brandy, at 53 cts. per gal. is 7½
Five bushels of salt, at 20 cts. the bushel, is 1

Paid by the consumer, by indirect taxation for one year, $41,40
Deduct for smuggling on our extensive frontier and for the profits of all the shop-keepers, through whose hands it passes, 21,50

$20,00

Twenty dollars to five persons, five dollar per head on all the individuals of the Union, which goes through the treasury, and nearly ten dollars per head which they pay by indirect taxation for mere political labor, that vanishes the moment every one has got his salary; exclusive of the cost of roads, bridges, canals, paving of towns, public buildings, etc., for which some improvement useful to the people remains for the money expended.

If the accuracy of our statistics would admit of our making a general bill of the union, such as is made out by the states of Virginia and Vermont, for the collection of their direct tax, for the state expenses, then every individual in the Union, when the amount of the yearly expenses was declared, would know what proportion of it he had to pay, by the per centage on the value of his real property. But as that under present circumstances, cannot be done, we must be contented with making out a sketch, as near as our present information will admit, in hopes that it may serve as a proforma for some of those acute politicians, who intrusted in the present state of things, may choose to counteract all those who incline to what they think a useful change, by showing the errors in their calculations.

The general bill of the property of the Union, on the east side of the river Mississippi; allowing all property on the west side to make up the deficiency, may be stated thus, viz:

About 800,000,0000 of acres of land valued one with another, at $3,	$2,400,000,000
All houses in town or country, with the stock and implements on the land,	2,600,000,000
Five hundred chartered banks, having on an average half a million of capital,	250,000,000
All other companies, such as insurance, roads, canals, mercantile, manufacturing; mortgages, all that recording is necessary to legalize,	150,000,000
Mercantile capital, value of shipping, etc.,	600,000,000
The general property of the Union for taxation as a foundation for a direct tax, may be supposed at least to amount to,	6,000,000,000

Though there may be great errors in these different items, which may furnish cause of contradiction and dispute for those of different opinion, whose interest binds them to the indirect taxation, yet the whole property of the Union cannot be supposed less, as the value put on property in Britain has been 20,000,000,000 of dollars. Considering our quality of land, great division of property, which prevents it from making so great an appearance, yet increases the whole amount, it cannot be less than two-thirds of the property in Britain, where there is not more than about 50 per cent. more population, nine-tenths of whom possess no property.

Considering the reduction in the expense of collecting, by the adoption of direct taxation, and the saving of almost the whole expenses of the federal government, by abolishing the double expenditure for judicial, fiscal and military, 30,000,000 of dollars would be a large allowance for the expenses of political labor, to include all the cost of governing, naval and military fortifications, etc., exclusive of the useful improvements of roads, canals, bridges, paving of towns, public buildings, etc.; which $30,000,000 would amount to one-half per cent. on the 6,000,000,000, the general bill of property requiring each citizen to pay one-half per cent. on the property in his possession. Perhaps five hundred dollars, averageing one with another, might be a sufficient sum to allow for the property of each working man of the Union; but as we have a large margin we shall suppose one thousand dollars, which at one-half per cent. is five dollars, that each laborer would have to pay by direct taxation, in place of forty-one dollars and fifty cents, which he pays at present by the indirect taxation on consumption ; and all the injury to his pride prejudice or self-love, would be that the tax-gatherer, who might be the sheriff, as in Virginia and Vermont, would call once a year for payment, in place of the different species of shopkeepers surreptitiously emptying his pocket, which his careless apathy prevents him from seeing. The two principal causes of the poverty and misery of the working people in Britain, are the immense national debt, the dividends on which at least double the number of consumers to be maintained by the producers, and the raising the revenue to pay the interest on said debt by indirect taxation; both of which great evils the working people of the Union can prevent by universal suffrage at the ballot-boxes.

ON THE ABUSE OF POWER. IT IS THE FAULT OF THE PEOPLE.

Oct. 10*th*, 1830.

"Self-love and social are the same." It would have been more consistent with the present state of society, or any that has yet existed, to have said, *ought to be the same.*— What has prevented the utility of all to be useful to every one? Is it the artificial inequality, and unjust division of property, knowledge and power? Or has nature decreed servitude and slavery as the lot of the many, and dominion and power as the privilege of the few? Nature has ordained that all our species shall come into the world weak and helpless; and that the capabilities of the industrious many shall be more perfect and less adulterated, than the physical force and moral faculties of the luxurious few, who being enabled to indulge in all the physical excesses, are depreciated, body and mind; as is fully evinced by the state of the nobility in all civilized countries. It is a true observation, that all perfection is in the middle ranks. The two extremes of luxury and poverty, meet in vice, depravation and crime. Any state of society that will compress the two ends towards the middle, must effectually tend to reconcile the interest of the whole with the interest of every one. These two extremes can only be approximated by the equality of property, knowledge and power, which has been prevented by the two great regulators of human actions, church and state. The one placing the fulcrum of its lever in the next world, the other in this, push society into the two extremes of sin and crime, as sinners and criminals are less independent and easier tyrannized over than honor and honesty. To perpetuate such a state of things, hereditary power was invented, as the most complete bar to the strong propensity of nature to the equalization of property, knowledge and power.— Whatever may be the reason why hereditary power pushes society into the two extremes of poverty and luxury, there can be no doubt, that in all hereditary governments there are only to be found, masters and slaves, monarchs and subjects; and that the elective system is the only one where freedom can be permanent.

An elective government by universal suffrage, brings the whole population as near equality as the nature of men, or their laws, rules, regulations or constitutions, will permit. If the majority allow any artificial superiority, by the monopoly of wealth, wisdom or power, it must be their own fault, and they have no right to blame the few, who take advantage of their physical or moral qualities of superiority, to induce the industrious producers to labor hard to feed, 'clothe and lodge the consumers. These latter can remain in idleness with more justice than the privileged orders of hereditary power, who use force to compel the laborer to give up the greatest part of the fruits of his industry; whereas universal suffrage makes it a free-will gift, a *quid pro quo*, which entitles the non-productive consumer to assert, "if you could live without us, you would not pay us; but your ignorance is such that you cannot manage your own affairs, and are necessitated to educate us to rule over you."

When you complain of high fees, and expensive litigation to the lawyer, he has a right to say, "Is it your pleasure to have mysterious, complicated and intricate laws, which require the reading and studying of a great many thousand volumes to understand, when you might have a simple, well-defined code, which each individual might have in his breeches pocket, and perfectly understand, like the French people have at present as one of the fruits of their revolution. I am educated to decypher those mysterious hieroglyphics for you, that you may have justice; it is by that I live, and it is your agents or representatives who multiply the laws every year, and increase the expense."

Your rulers who shift the public burdens from their own shoulders to yours, by indirect taxation, may say, "It is your will and pleasure, rather to pay four dollars by indirect taxation than one dollar by a direct tax on property, and as we possess the greatest part of the real property, it is our interest to comply with your wishes."

Bank share-holders, directors and merchants, who have the monopoly of six per cent. on the circulating medium, besides the profits and power which the use of it gives them, may say, "It is a privilege given us by your agents or representatives, and you cannot blame us for accepting so great a boon."

Political labor is so much higher than other useful and necessary labor, because you, the working people by universal suffrage, being the hirers of the political laborers, allow them to fix their own wages as well as the amount of the patronage of those they choose to appoint to do the work;

which expense augments with every complication or difficulty they can throw in the way of public business: it would be a great ignorance both of yourselves and others to expect otherwise. Who, of all your tradesmen, if left to fix their own prices, without any competition, would not exact as much as their customers would bear? Your rulers also have the temptation of following the example of the hereditary aristocracy of Europe; where there is in fact only one that has any pretensions to the elective system, which is Switzerland, whose expenses are too economical to be copied by the rulers of any people who have the fixing of their own salaries.

The comfort and happiness of mankind, depend much more on the equal division of property, knowledge and power, than on the quantity. A small amount of property and knowledge equally divided amongst the population, produces infinitely more happiness, than ever so much, unequally divided. For the greater the amount of property and knowledge when unequally divided, the greater the quantum of poverty and misery; as is proved by the history of all nations and strongly exemplified by the present state of Britain.—Now property and knowledge have been much more unequally divided since, than during or immediately after our revolution, in spite of that freedom and equality, proclaimed by the declaration of rights, as the basis of all our political institutions. This interests much the industrions producers to enquire into.

The funding speculation was the foundation of a monied aristocracy in the United States, augmented by the land and much increased by the greater number of bank speculations; all of which originated in, and were authorized by, the representatives of the people, favored by the various individual neutral trade speculations, which created an inequality of property, unknown before on our continent. The great inequality of knowledge originated equally in the representatives of the people, who richly endowed universities and colleges, with the people's money, for the education of their own children, and neglected to establish free schools for the instruction of the children of the working people. From this it would appear, that the servants or agents of the people were the principal cause of the accumulating inequality of property and knowledge, and that the exercise of a small quantity of common sense and self-preservation on the part of the producers, would have prevented most of the consequences of such an inequality.

At last the great majority are worn out, and they seem determined to try the force of universal suffrage in the ballot-boxes. If they fail in carrying every thing according to their interest, after seeing that the French people have returned a great majority against hereditary power, though not one in six hundred had any right to vote (of course the control of the elections was in the hands of the richest) it will evince an ignorance, in the great mass of our population, that half a century of freedom and equality have not been able to correct, and at the same time give currency to the aristocratic scandal so often published and repeated in the old world, that freedom is a state incompatible with the nature of our species, who must be ruled by fear and force. An opinion which the supineness of our industrious producers, has contributed to spread over our Union.

As it only requires a union, which their interest imperiously demands, and the advantage of which seems well understood by all the gregarious animals, let us hope that our industrious producers will not be so low in the scale of intellect, as to allow their opponents to split them into parties, and waste their force and energy in disputes with one another, about principles and projects that at best are premature, until they acquire a majority in the legislatures to execute what may then appear to be their interest. In all matters of warfare and contention, it is injurious to discuss what may be done, previously to being in possession of the power of acting: as the old proverb says, "to show your teeth before you are ready to bite." All men who do not by the labor of their hands, augment the utility or value of the materials they work upon, cannot be denominated productive; agreeably to the signification put on the word by Smith, operatives are not always producers; a man may operate as diligently in destruction as in production.

PRESIDENTIAL ELECTION. INFLUENCE, CORRUPTION AND BRIBERY AT ELECTIONS; HOW REMEDIABLE.

October 16*th*, 1830.

In all elective governments of universal suffrage, bottomed on freedom and equality, every citizen has the same right to be chosen into power, as the only means of perpetuating the equality essentially necessary to freedom. All assumption of superiority by one class over the political rights of another, all pretensions to monopolize power by intrigue, deception, falsehood or corruption, is derogatory to the essential principles of liberty and equality, and destructive of the comfort and happiness of a free people. When we conlemplate the rapid increase of intrigue (softened down by the denomination of canvassing) for office, violent in proportion to the power and patronage attached to it, which has taken place since the formation of our federal government, and look forward to the accumulation of influence and patronage that must accrue to the federal executive, by the immense population that must fill the void between the present settlements and the Pacific, something ought to be done to lessen the wages of party, and of course their violence and immorality, before it exceeds the bounds of peaceable reform. Washington's popularity made him President without any opposition; the Vice-President succeeded with very little; the popularity of Jefferson raised a successful contention a little before the election, and his two friends Madison and Monroe into the Presidential chair with little opposition. Four candidates so divided the people's votes at the next hard-contested election, that no one had the majority of the whole, and the choice of one fell to congress, where it is said intrigue gave the place to the one who would not have had the majority of the people's votes.

The last election was between two competitors, and the contest began nearly four years before the time of election, creating a violent agitation over the whole Union. Tavern orators declaimed in every grog-shop in favor of their party, and vociferous scurrility, mixed with the fumes of whiskey, produced much ill-will, hatred, spite and malice, the shameful effects of the violence of the supporters of both sides. The intrigues for the next presidential chair have begun long ago, and extended further than ever. The power, patronage, and profit of the federal chief, seem the ruling motives which actuate all the state elections, and split each state legislature into two parties. From the superiority of either party in the State legislatures, is calculated the party that will prevail in the next general election for President, as if the election of President, was by the states, or that some unchangeable hereditary authority prevented the voters from altering their minds. This overwhelming federal influence, involving all the state authorities, leans much towards centralism, and verifies many of Patrick Henry's predictions.

The editors, and of course readers, of our party newspapers, act a disgraceful part in these scandalous intrigues and disputes for power. They blow the flame of discord and disunion, by asserting scandalous and malicious calumnies and falsehoods against their opponents, whilst plastering with fulsome flattery and adulation their patrons or employers, all under the mask of public good, which they surreptitiously use to cover their cupidity. Britain, from whom we copy our political faults, has two parties; the powerful and those who wish for power, the outs and ins, etc.; but no periodical publication descends to propagating the individual scandal of an electioneering falsehood; those scurrilous productions are left to the unblushing handbills of the day, distributed about the hustings, by those individuals, professed canvassers for the polls. Our editors of newspapers, become the prize-fighters and champions of these patrons, sacrificing truth, honor and honesty, to the success of their patrons, on which depends their reward, in some place or appointment, the power of granting which is gained by the election. Were the spurious sheets only emitted on the day, and scattered over the locality of the election, and afterwards sent to the grocers, their scurrility would be buried in oblivion, but it is accompanied by the history, records and statistics of our country for many years, and is scattered over the globe, to many people who know nothing more of us than what they learn from these prints, which authorize them to believe that our rulers are immoral, vicious and profligate; bringing elective governments into disrepute where their practical utility is not known, and giving currency to the exaggerated falsehoods propagated by aristocracy against them.

Immediately after our revolution I was at Norfolk in Virginia, and had a store at the great bridge, for the collection of timber, (at that time one of the principal articles of export,) under the management of a clerk of the place. The inhabitants of the district solicited me to permit my clerk to represent them in the legislature of the state. At that time most citizens accepted if elected, but no one solicited votes. Political labor was low in profits or patronage, and not even high in consideration or respect. The complicated machinery of federalism, approaching to centralism, had not been thought of. Great as had been the increase of our agricultural, manufacturing and mercantile productions, it is probable that the increased value of political labor has been still greater; which ought to be paid in something of a more fixed and permanent value than money, for one dollar now when flour is at three dollars, is equal to four when flour was at fifteen dollars.— Perhaps the most equitable and impartial mode of raising revenue on so extensive a continent, as well as paying political labor where there can be no competition in price, would be by bushels of wheat, that would always require nearly the same quantity of labor to produce them.

The application of money or any other inducement, (after the example of Britain or any of the other aristocracies of Europe,) to prefer one candidate to another in the elections of a free people, may be considered equally disgraceful and dishonorable to the party who gives and he who receives the bribe. It is traficking their part of freedom and equality, which belongs conjointly to the whole nation, for a base coin which does not return any thing to the joint stock, equal to the risk the whole runs by the bad conduct of an immoral or incapable ruler. Bringing barrels of whisky to the poles, or feeding the voters by open taverns, is so groveling and swinish an imitation of the poor deluded subjects of hereditary aristocracies, as to require no other refutation of the shameful practice than the mere mentioning of it. When Esau sold his birth-right for a mess of pottage, he got something which nourished him; but he who sells his birth-right for a glass of whisky, gives it for what injures both the moral and the physical man. Those who are influenced by the flattery, promises or predictions of the candidates, or their agents, the editors of newspapers, sell their birth-right for words that never were intended to be realized to them; though the editors of newspapers, if they have preached their patrons into place expect their reward, and often change sides if they do not receive it. It would be foolish to find faults with men for following their nature, by living at the expense of those who require least labor from them, and pay them best; but it is those who pay them much for doing little that are to blame. For the governors of Virginia and Connecticut there are seldom two candidates, because their pay, perquisites or patronage is scarcely worth the soliciting. Reduce all the political labor of the Union, as near a par with other labor, and you annihilate intrigue or bribery either to the moral or physical appetites. Election for every office of trust or profit, is the only way of reducing patronage and securing the faithful discharge of the public trust. It is not the governor who is injured by the defalcation of the officer he appoints, but the people amongst whom he does his duty, who are the best judges of his merit, and consequently the fittest either to place or displace him, according to the advantage they receive from the faithful performance of his duties, or the damage they sustain from his neglect or incapacity. No objection can possibly be made to this, but an objection that will be stronger against the election of all the great officers; which is, that the ignorance of the voters incapacitates them from being judges; but certainly, if they are allowed to be judges of a president or a governor, they must be still better judges of a post-master or a collector, who does all his work under their immediate observation, and the nature of which is such that the most of them are judges of the good or evil that must be the consequence. It would simplify the political machine, and put it under the management of those who, providing all, are alone interested in its working well.

CONJECTURES ON THE CONSEQUENCES OF CONSCRIPTION.

October 26*th*, 1830.

Amongst the many equitable and fair distributions of the public burdens, introduced by the French revolution, the conscription for recruiting the army, was perhaps the most just, and in its ultimate consequences perhaps the most beneficial and favorable to every species of popular reform. It has been adopted by most of the civilized nations, Britain and the United States being the only governments that have retained the ancient mode of mercenary troops, bought with money, and bribed by their pay to serve those who employ them. As the pay of soldiers in all countries, is much beneath the wages of other labor, and at the same time, their rigorous discipline, and strict obedience, too often to arbitrary commands, make their situation irksome and unpleasant, being subject to the caprices of their officers. Consequently none voluntarily enter the army who can do any thing else, and it becomes the refuge of all, who from drunkenness, loss of reputation, deviation from morality, or any other bad conduct, are forced to take a trade, where character has been considered of little consequence, and thereby depreciating the general reputation of the troops below the par of any other trade or profession, inducing them to act like mere machines, agreeable to the impulse given them by their leaders, making them the willing instruments of despotism and oppression.

An army of conscripts, consisting of an individual from almost every family of the nation, with which they keep up intercourse and exchange of opinions by correspondence; who serve their country for the fixed term of years, because it is a duty imposed on all, is a good average sample of the morality and information of the nation, and is most probably in unison with the popular opinions of their fathers, mothers, brothers, sisters, and relations they left at home, and to whom they expect to return when their time of service is finished. A corps of troops so formed under any species of government, is not likely to become the instrument of passive obedience, to enforce tyranny or oppression with their bayonets, against the will of their fellow subjects or citizens, but is imbued with the general principles and opinions of the nation to whom they belong, more than to their rulers or officers.

Recent events have sufficiently characterized the difference between mercenary and conscript soldiers. In the British dominions, where the troops are all mercenary, bought by a premium, and fight for their pay, at the will of those who pay and support them, they have in every instance fired on the people at the command of their officers. But in Bavaria, where the troops are all conscripts, when first ordered to disperse the people by firing on them, they positively refused; and the king was obliged to sign a popular act, though he had refused to confirm it when passed by the representatives of the nation. Lately in France, all the troops of the line, who were conscripts, not only refused to fire on the people, but joined them in opposing the king's foreign guards and others, not raised by conscription, who obeyed their officers, and fired, killing a great many men, women and children in the streets of Paris.

Arming the conscripts as soldiers, is confiding in, and trusting the safety and protection of the nation, to those who have both character and property at stake in the public prosperity; but mercenary soldiers have only their pay to induce their exertions, which are exercised for the benefit of those who command and pay them. In conscription there is an equality, which raises men to the dignity of freedom, but in the purchase of mercenaries, men are degraded to a state of slavery, which influences all their actions, propensities and passions. When peace comes, and there is no more necessity for maintaining armies, disbanding mercenary troops, is filling the highway with robbers, because they have neither house nor home to go to; but disbanding conscripts, is diffusing the knowledge and experience they have acquired in the service, throughout the smallest ramifications in society. When traveling in France, I knew whether a particular laborer or mechanic had served in the army, by his dexterity and expertness in his trade. So that for cheapness, safety, utility, respectability, morality and security, an army of conscripts is vastly superior either in peace or war to an army of mercenaries.

Most of the monarchies at present in Europe are maintained and kept steady in their ancient routine, by a much greater proportion of soldiers than they used to have before the French revolution, the greatest part of which is raised and recruited by conscription. On this side of the Atlantic, where universal suffrage has given the millions as great a share of liberty as they can possibly possess, free from all apprehensions of revolutionary changes, because the majority at the ballot boxes, can make any change their interest dictates, without recurring to force or violence, in this inestimable state, we can coolly speculate on the present crisis of civilized Europe, and foresee some of the consequences of the discontent of the people, when the arbitrary power has nothing to protect it but an armed force, raised and recruited by conscription.

Beginning with the south, where indolence and superstition have long made the seat of despotism of both church and state. The French revolution will most probably penetrate into Spain, Portugal and Italy, and break down all the implements of tyranny; these have been accumulated for centuries by the ingenuity of civil and religious chiefs. The new order of government they may probably adopt, will be nearly a copy of what the knowledge and experience of the French people enables them to contrive for their own happiness and security.

When the rulers have had the wisdom to place themselves nearer on a par with the knowledge of the day, in a prudent and peaceable reform, by opposing a check to the arbitrary hereditary power, and giving a share to the people by election, as in Bavaria, Wirtemberg, Baden and Holland, called limited monarchies, it is probable that the elective power will increase with the diffusion of knowledge amongst the electors, and so restrict the hereditary authority within the comfort, convenience and happiness of the millions, by following the knowledge of the day, in a gradual, slow and imperceptible reform, suited to the times, and in unison with the various degrees of general information, and thus avoid any sudden or violent revolution, in which the people in a few days, demolish the accumulating tyranny of centuries. Sweden, by its poor soil and indifferent climate, joined to its representation, is guaranteed from all violent convulsions or revolutions, and the parental prudence and economy of Denmark, will most probably imitate the limited monarchies of their neighbors.

Prussia has become one of the largest kingdoms of Europe, by the aggregation, by conquest, of a great many small principalities, under different laws, customs and regulations, and can only be consolidated into a permanent union by federation, to which the Saxon and Westphalian states might be joined. But as it is too soon to expect such perfection in the rulers that be, the probability is that the provinces south of the Rhine, which remained for some time under the dominion of France, will participate in the opinions and movements of the great nation, and may serve as a bridge or inclined plane to introduce a revolutionary spirit into the rest of the Prussian dominions, which nothing can stop but reasonable concessions on the part of the rulers, to the demands of a population, too far advanced in civilization and a knowledge of their real interest to submit to the control of hereditary power in possession of an individual; and it is probable that a much smaller concession on the part of the king, on the suppression of the freedom of France by the allied powers, would have satisfied the people of Prussia, than will now, after the French people have reconquered their liberties.

Austria, like Prussia, is an aggregation of small states, bound together by the galling tie of force and conquest, and can only be permanently and solidly united in the sense of their interest by a federation; but from which their state of civilization removes them farther than in the case of Prussia. Though the diffusion of knowledge would require some change in the arbitrary power which rules them, yet their distance from the center of civilization, and proximity to Russia retard their improvement much longer than the other civilized nations of Europe. Poland perhaps approaches nearer to a division of power by something approaching to a popular government, than any of the Austrian provinces, owing to the small atom of representation, given by Bonaparte to the Duchy of Warsaw.

Britain and Russia, the one at the head, the other at the foot of European civilization, by the artificial elasticity of the first, and the stiff, inflexible, barbarous rudeness of the last, may keep them longer from any change, and make it difficult to conjecture how and when it may be effected; but as every thing is progressing, improvement may reach the extremes in time, and bring all mankind nearer a par of equality in the arts, sciences and civilization.

THOUGHTS ON THE PROGRESS OF REVOLUTIONS.

October 30th, 1830.

When giving an analysis, in a former paper, of the great and equal division of property amongst the population in

France, for the purpose of showing that such an equality of property, and consequently knowledge, did not afford a solid footing for the peaceable existence of any species of hereditary power, I found by statistics, there were ten and a half millions of land proprietors in France, eight millions of whom paid a land tax of twenty one francs, and under forty thousand paid from five hundred to one thousand francs, and the highest seventeen thousand, paid from one thousand francs and upwards in 1815, when the land tax was nearly one-third of the rent. The whole population of twenty-two millions, possessing less property than the land owners, were averaged to be worth from one hundred and fifty to one hundred and eighty francs each, over and above their wages. So equal a division of property, never existed before in any civilized country; it was entirely owing to the French revolution, removing all obstructions to the free circulation of property, by destroying all monopolies and exclusive privileges, leaving nature to act by the uninterrupted accumulation of labor and industry, the only producers of wealth.

Since which the two powers, elective and hereditary, united by the cannon law, and bayonet logic, of the holy allies, have quarreled, and the people, taking the part of their representatives, as they must always do, drove off the king; who, deprived of the support of a rich hereditary house of peers as in Britain, was foolish enough to attempt to build up a similar constitution without any material. It is said that the chamber of deputies, elected under the ancient royal charter, by the choice of about one to every five hundred citizens, and forced on the people by foreign bayonets joined to the house of peers, appointed by the former hereditary power, have made one of the Bourbons king of the French; binding the people by a new charter without their consent. That is what Napoleon in all his glory and victorious course, did not dare to do, but consulted the public opinion as consul for life, and emperor.— When we consider the three or four hundred thousand foreign bayonets, which enforced the charter of Louis XVIII, over a people whom revolutionary spirit had cooled down by so active a drill sergeant as Napoleon, and compare it with the surrounding circumstances of the present charter, we can scarcely argue it a different fate. Had not the spirit of liberty been broken down to subjection by such a dextrous rough rider as Bonaparte, who bound down the French nation by every hair in their heads, surrounding them with a quintuple net of legion of honor, gendarmerie, commissaries of police, prefects and mayors, the cords from all which, came direct to him by different channels, without interfering with each other; he could tighten or restrain them singly or the whole, as he found opinions to agree with or to be contrary to his interest. These various modes of knowing the opinions of all classes, were a substitute for a free press. It is probable if the Bourbons had not laid hold of this well contrived machinery, in place of reigning fifteen years they would not have been able to resist the impulse of freedom three.

On considering the progress that the division of property and knowledge have since made, not only in France but on the continent of civilized Europe, the numerous practical political lessons, which the French people have had, both by their own experience, and that of their neighbors, the great change in the leaders of society, from the old who were educated under the influence of the ancient despotism, (now mostly dead,) to the young *eleves* of the revolution, who sucked in freedom with their mother's milk; when one reflects on all these circumstances, tending to strengthen and fortify the propensity to liberty and equality, one would be disposed to conjecture, that the French people will not be satisfied with any thing less than the first constitution given them by the national assembly. Even if they are disposed to tolerate hereditary power for the sake of peace with their neighbors, against the adoption of it, besides their own dear bought experience, they have the direful effects before them which it has produced in Spain and Portugal, the many collisions and disputes that have arisen between the elective and hereditary power in all unlimited monarchies of Europe, which has passed the Atlantic, and occasioned the quarrels between the legislators and governors of Nova Scotia and the Canadas: the military tyranny that has embroiled South America in civil war, is only the spawn of hereditary despotism of their former masters the Spaniards: after so many proofs of the incompatibility of the two great sources of power, elective and hereditary, remaining peaceably in the same body politic, one would be cautious in believing that the experience and knowledge of the French people, would risk it under the present circumstances.

Nature has ordained that the whole human race should come into the world equally weak and helpless, and that the same equality, when not controled by artificial bars and impediments, should merely continue from generation to generation through life; that is, the small superiority of talent and industry, which raised the father a little above the common level, should be dissipated by the folly and extravagance of the children.— Nature is therefore an equalizer of property, which equalizes knowledge, and divides power in the same proportion, which is freedom. Mankind have only to acquire sufficient knowledge of their real interest and remove those tyrannical and unjust obstructions to the free circulation of property, in order to lay the road open to rational freedom, without any let or hindrance from barriers, custom-houses or toll-bars.

Universal suffrage is the key stone of freedom, the permanent, solid and broad foundation of the liberties, rights, and prerogatives of our species. It was adopted by our revolution, transplanted into Europe by the French and Spanish revolutions and diffused over South America, so as to pervade at present nearly one half the globe. The fortunate results in the unprecedented prosperity of our country, although the theory has only yet been known, has given it a hold on the opinions of mankind, that all the sophistry of hereditary tyranny and despotism will not be able, in any civilized country, to eradicate. Now when the practice of freedom and equality, so long deferred by the indolence and ignorance of our people, is put in force at the ballot boxes, by the great mass of industrious producers, and all laws, rules and regulations, as well as all naval, military and judiciary operations are made and ordained for the benefit and interest of the great majority, the immense reform in the condition of mankind that will radiate from our country and diffuse its benign light and influence over the whole earth, will be incalculable from any data we can obtain in either ancient or modern history, even the wildest conjectures of the most enthusiastic imaginations, may fall far short of the effects that may be produced on the convenience, comforts and happiness of mankind.

Fortunately the spirit of freedom, following the diffusion of knowledge into the smallest ramifications of society, does not now permit the experience of our country to be lost to the inhabitants of any other, and may induce the people of different nations to combine for their mutual interest, in imitation of the despotic rulers, who under the mask of the holy alliance, united to protect their usurped power. The immense improvement of rail roads and canals on land navigation and steamboats on sea, so shortens distance, saving the expense of both money and time, as to bring the means of traveling within the reach of all classes, which could only be afforded by the richest. Thus all events, both physical and moral, conspire to raise mankind into a more rational, comfortable and happy state, than ever they were before, and to elevate all ranks to that degree of dignity and respectability, as to be above falsehood, vice and crime.

RAPID ADVANCE TOWARDS IMPROVING BOTH CHURCH AND STATE.

November 3d, 1830.

Considering the equality with which all men come into the world, we are astonished at the great inequality with which they go out of it. Some are thrown into a ditch like a dog, whilst others are embalmed, enclosed in metalic, incorruptible coffins, conveyed to the place of sepulchre by great processions of both horse and foot, attended by crowds of priests, preaching, praying and singing. These are the same priests who profess to be servants of a religion of equality, by which the poor and helpless are proclaimed to be the favorites of heaven, and whose laws and authorities on which they claim an existence, declare, that "it is as easy for a camel to pass through the eye of a needle, as for a rich man to enter the kingdom of heaven," yet these priests intercede daily for ages for the salvation of these rich men's souls; that is, as long as they are paid. That the physically weak, and not even morally strong few, should cozen and rule the many, must astonish all who trust to the evidence of their senses. No less surprising is it that the heterogeneous union of the Christian church and state, should usurp despotic rule over the millions; the first possessing all humility, meekness and forgiveness, pretending to obey commandments strictly prohibiting, under the pain of external punishment, every kind of murder, pillage, plunder, robbery and all violence; the last founded and supported by violence, transforming (by the few cabalistic words, *a declaration of war*) slaughter, rapine, pillage, plunder and robbery, into the heroic virtues of patriotism, for which they are entitled to honor, fame and renown. The same meek priests will sing *te deum*, and return thanks to the Author of nature, for the massacre of millions, the plunder of their property, and in many countries even yet, (not long ago in all,) the enslaving of the persons of those whose lives were spared.

With the aristocracy of the Mexican union, and perhaps with the same class in all South America, it is a favorite phrase, "that the government ought to be surrounded with *Prestiges*." By the dictionary I find that *prestiges*, means jugglers' tricks, hocus pocus, legerdemain, deception, delusion, etc. Though all churches and states that have yet played their part on the theatre of the world, have surrounded themselves with every description of slight of hand, it is only in primitive states of society; such as in South America, where they would have the candor to confess it. This jugglery is cunning, complicated and refined, in exact proportion to the common sense possessed by those they mean to deceive. The clumsy jugglers of the Russian empire would not succeed in Britain, France or Holland: nor would the physical quackery of the ornamental saints and virgins of the Roman Catholic religion, cheat the superior understanding of a protestant population. But by the moral jugglery of sounds without sense, words without meaning, they effect their purpose of deceiving the senses by drawing off their attention from them, like the mountebanks among their audience, with fictions and fables, whilst they pick their pockets; the one acting in the small scale of individual speculation is disgraced and destroyed; while the other, exercising the same tricks on a great national scale, is honored, reverenced and applauded. The poor half starved robber is condemned to death, whilst the conqueror, who plunders and murders by wholesale, is loaded with fame and honors, through all the pages of flattering and falsifying history. All this originates in taking words for things, fictions for facts, phantoms of the imagination for realities of the judgment. The shortest and easiest remedy for all these delusions of fancy, would be to teach children, the most acute use and exercise of their senses, and how to improve the application of them to the acquiring of as perfect a knowledge of animate and inanimate nature, as their capabilities will permit, and to consider all that is directly or indirectly out of the reach of their senses, as immaterial and useless to their well being.

Those who doubt of the rapid approach of mankind nearer to perfection, have only to examine our state of utility to ourselves and others, at present, and before our revolution; the situation of France now, and before their revolution; the civilization of Flanders and Germany during the same epoch; all within the short period of half a century, to be completely convinced of the vast progress, moral and physical, that our species have made, and must continue to make; for who that has attentively observed the immense improvement in every art and science, can easily set bounds to their progress.

The two greatest obstructions to useful improvements have been church and state, religion and politics. The great ruling members of both, having more than their share of good things by the present distribution, fear a smaller share by the least approach to equality, and oppose every change; and it is but lately that men began to test their pretensions by the scale of general utility. In all those countries where justice and impartiality, free from brutal force were permitted, all those have been condemned who assume power without the consent of the industrious producers, as usurping the rights and prerogatives of their fellow men; which in fact is in part confessed by the subterfuge of hereditary power asserting their divine right; an acknowledgment, that if they cannot make good that pretension they have no other.

A great many experiments are on trial at present to improve both church and state on both sides of the Atlantic, from which it is probable that oppressed human nature may be benefited. As the interest of the millions speaks too loud to be longer neglected, the first topic in consequence and importance to us, is the working people claiming their rights to a share of the distribution of wealth, equal to what they have always had in the production of it. The capitol of the Mexican Union has been deranged by military tyranny, but the ravages have been confined to federation as the most imperfect of all their constitutions: which, bad as it is, has protected all the states from participating in the disorders that, under a centralism, would have pervaded the whole.—Guatamala has made the property of the church useful, stimulated its members to produce part of what they consume, and aim at a more rational and cheap federalism, suited to the poverty and circumstances of the people. Colombia, in spite of Bolivar, seems disposed to avoid federation. Buenos Ayres is verging towards a compromise of their differences in a federal union. Chili and Peru are smarting under military discipline, which will probably prove the incompatibility of freedom with a standing army. In Europe revolution has awakened after refreshing slumbers, and the French people have reconquered part of their liberty without political equality; but the complete equality of property and the great equalization of knowledge, will guarantee them against the monopoly of power. The amenity, moderation and unanimity of this second revolution, will recommend it to their neighbors, and both principles and practice may spread to the south, east and north, as the surrounding population, by the general diffusion of knowledge, are much better prepared for the reception of freedom and a popular government, than they were forty years ago. Even the unchangeable laws, habits and customs of Britain begin to yield before the knowledge of the day; and although their great inequality of property, with their corresponding inequality of knowledge and power, have been a bar to improvement, yet the vast weight of poverty will press on the rich, and the necessity of relief will curtail the exorbitant revenues derived from the national debt.

OBJECTS OF REFORM FOR THE WORKING MEN WHEN THEY SHALL HAVE OBTAINED A MAJORITY IN THE LEGISLATURE. OBSTACLES TO THE INTRODUCTION OF A GENERAL AND USEFUL SYSTEM OF EDUCATION, WHICH, HOWEVER, MUST ULTIMATELY PREVAIL.

November 17*th*, 1830.

It may be, perhaps, considered as certain that the industrious producers will at last succeed in obtaining a large majority in the Legislatures of all the free states of the Union. In the slave states, where most of the producers being slaves, deprived of all political and other rights, the consumers, or non-producers may retain the majority;

which will widen the breach already begun, between the northern and southern interest, and shows more clearly, the inconvenience and impolicy of giving the federal congress power to interfere with the fiscal, military or judiciary, of the individual, independent states. The federal congress being a representation of numbers, the superior population of the northern free states, will give them the majority, and enable them to pass regulations and laws agreeably to their views of their interest. But in that metaphysical representation of states in the senate, the slave states may have a majority, and the collision will demonstrate the inconvenience and the unnecessary impolicy of dividing the legislation, only to create the trouble and difficulty of uniting them; for until they are united they cannot act; as Franklin predicted, "two horses before the cart, and two behind, and if they both draw, the cart must stand still." It is therefore probable that this contradiction of interest between the north and the south, may make some change in the federal constitution necessary, to prevent all interference in the affairs of the states, and at the same time show some of the evils attending the division of all the legislatures of the states (except that of Vermont) into two distinct powers, which have only been induced to act as a unit by compromise, which cannot be expected to be easily effected in any great question of national importance.

When the working people, in all the free states, shall have obtained a majority in all the legislatures, as they have an undoubted right to legislate according to their views of their own interest, they may abolish imprisonment for debt; they may form a simple, well defined code of laws, suited to the equality of persons and things, agreeable to their political institutions, and annul all those old laws, founded on the privileged aristocracies of Europe, and some of them may even prevent the interference of the force of law in the collection of debts, and adopt the rational and peaceable method of the Quakers. After which, should the federal judiciary continue to judge in every state by different laws, enacted by the federal congress, agreeably to the interest of the southern slave states who may have the majority, there must be a constant contradiction and dispute, an *imperium in imperio;* two sovereigns in the same body politic, neither of whom being willing to cede, must endanger a violent dissolution of the union; a catastrophe easily avoided, by adopting a federal constitution, resembling the simplicity and economy of the federation of Switzerland, as explained fully in some of my former essays.

In effecting the great object which the working people have in view, an universal, free and equal education, where all the children of the state shall be fed, clothed and educated at the expense of the people's treasury, there are some difficulties which may as well be foreseen and endeavored to be remedied in time. I do not apprehend any hindrance from the want of money; if the working people legislate agreeable to their evident interest, in reducing the price of political labor on a par with all other labor, and substituting direct taxes in place of indirect, there will be a sufficient saving of expenditure to establish schools on the most extended system of utility. But the teachers necessary to the well conducting of such establishments, men whose information and liberality are on a par with the knowledge of the day, free from the old monkish routine of our colleges, and not imbued with the prejudices and reverence for useless antiquity, those necessary materials for the well being and general utility of such schools, will I fear, be difficult to be obtained in the present state of scholastic institutions.

Most men are thoroughly convinced, by the prevailing ascendency of self-love, and self-approbation, that the method by which their own education was conducted is the best possible; and that all deviations from it must be wrong and injurious to youth. With those fixed principles, they will persevere in following as near those, by which they themselves were taught, as possible; and, mixing the old course of instruction, by the coercive discipline with the late improvements, they will depreciate both, and create confusion and anarchy, which has been sufficiently proven in all countries, where the late meliorations of instruction have been left under the direction of school-masters, reared and taught by the barbarous superstitions, and unnatural methods, handed down to us by our tyrannic and ignorant forefathers. Having no moral schools for the instruction of school-masters, that might have been kept near a par with the knowledge of the day, we are forced to take teachers trained in our colleges, whose characters are copied from the English Universities at Oxford and Cambridge, originating in the civilization of the fifteenth century, where little or nothing is taught that can be practically useful to the present generation, however necessary *then* for the privileged to plead their clergy, by being able to read Greek and Latin, the languages through which the little useful knowledge, then existing, circulated. It is to be presumed, that the dead languages as well as all imitation of barbarous antiquity, will not form part of this general, equal and rational instruction, which the working people intend should be the solid and permanent foundation, of that equality, so essential to the existence of freedom. To induce such teachers with good will, and without it nothing can be well done, to forego the supposed advantages gained by seven or eight years study at college, and to substitute useful instruction, little or none of which the most part of our colleges afford, will be one of the impediments and difficulties opposed in the organization of the schools. Our sectarian clergymen, in such numbers and variety, who all teach different routes to heaven, each pretending that his own is the only true path, having hitherto had much control and direction of the education of both young and old, will most probably oppose all innovation, in the teaching of their religious creeds, which are so varied and contradictory, as to create in any one locality the confusion said to have happened at the building of the tower of Babel. All those varied and different principles of preaching, which will most probably be supported by the superstition and bigotry of their hearers, will with difficulty be reconciled to that union of action, so essential to the success of so great and beneficial an establishment, particularly as many of their dogmas hold the wisdom of this world, (which without doubt will be taught in these schools,) as foolishness.

By endeavoring to teach the useful arts and sciences, the acute and accurate use of the senses, with a rigorous discipline of all the mental faculties, more as a foundation, on which to build that knowledge which their future experience might make necessary to their comfort and happiness, than as dictating the application to any specific employment, they would dispense with the interference of most of the learned professions, which could be best acquired by the youth after they left school. By strictly limiting instruction to utility, nine-tenths of the learning of the old school is thrown to one side, and a common sense farmer or mechanic would be the best and most useful teacher. The teaching children what they never are to practise as men, is filling their intellectual store rooms, with what pays no rent, and which they get rid of as soon as possible by forgetting it, leaving only the delusion behind that they know it because they once learnt it; which only prevents all attempts of acquiring a knowledge of it.

MONOPOLY IS CONTRARY TO THE PRINCIPLES OF OUR GOVERNMENT AND PROHIBITED BY THE CONSTITUTION OF SIX STATES.

November 24th, 1830.

Monopoly is an exclusive privilege, of doing, transacting, or professing some art, trade, or occupation, the right or liberty of carrying on which, is denied under penalties to all others. The word monopoly is an invidious term, including something unjustly partial, and has been disguised under various denominations. Hereditary power is a political monopoly. A state religion is a religious monoply. An exclusive privilege of trading is a mercantile monopoly. A bank charter is a banking monopoly. Corporations, insurance and manufacturing companies by charter, though not exclusive, are privileges having a prerogative over common companies without a charter. Even patents are a monopoly for the time they last, perhaps more prejudicial to the community than is generally supposed, which is proven by the few civilized nations that have adopted it, having no superiority of inventions over the Germans and others who have given no such encouragement. The effect of all monopolies is to create a much greater artificial inequality of knowledge, property and power, than could possibly arise out of the natural advantages of industry, talent or merit, and as such ought to be cautiously avoided, and even detested, by all people, who have the smallest knowledge of the advantages of freedom and equality. In the United States the political usurpation of power is by combination, cunning and intrigue, which though equally injurious to the millions, as if possessed by a hereditary monopoly, yet being by the consent of universal suffrage, cannot be called a monopoly. Of the numberless religious sects, though all are striving at monopoly, none has yet obtained it. In trade all are endeavoring to annul competition, by seizing on all the articles in which they deal, at market, thereby to enjoy a partial monopoly, but being without authority or privilege, cannot be called such.

It would appear that in the United States there is no positive monopoly, but those given by charters to the banks, insurance and manufacturing companies and corporations.— The first is the only kind which has an exclusive privilege, the rest have the advantage that none of the interested are liable for the debts of the company beyond the sum they put in the stock, though they may contract debts to the public for ten times the amount, for which the public have no security, the charter absolving all concerned from any responsibility. The inhabitants of no country can be called free and equal, when such charters are granted to the favorite few, who can contract debts to an amount, for the purpose of dividing, under pretence of profits, amongst their shareholders, and afterwards close their office, with a declaration, that there is no more money remaining in the vault; though the directors, and other share-holders, may have drawn, by way of dividends, a great deal more money than would have paid all their debts; as was practised in the south sea bubble in England, which was the only charter that was ever granted without a limitation of dividend in Europe; yet all our bank and other charters, permit the stockholders, through the directors, to divide what they please, by way of profits.

Besides the constructive evidence, that the principle of all the elective governments of liberty and equality in the Union, militates against, and is opposed to, every description of monopoly, there are certain prohibitions in the constitutions of the following states, viz:

Massachusetts—part 1, article 5. No man or corporation, or association of men, shall have any other right or title to obtain advantages, particular or exclusive, distinct from those of the community, than what arises from the consideration of services rendered to the public, etc.

Connecticut—declaration of rights, article 1. That all men, when they form a social compact, are equal in rights; and that no man, or set of men, are entitled to exclusive public emoluments or privileges from the community, etc.

Maryland—declaration of rights, article 39. That monopolies are odious and contrary to the spirit of a free government, and the principles of commerce, and ought not to be suffered.

North Carolina—declaration of rights, article 3. That no man, or set of men, are entitled to exclusive or separate emoluments or privileges from the community, but in consideration of public services. Article 23. That perpetuities, and monopolies are contrary to the genius of a free state, and ought not to be allowed, etc.

Kentucky—article 10. That all free men, when they form a social compact, are equal: that no man, or set of men, are entitled to exclusive, separate, public emoluments or privileges, from the community, but in consideration of public services.

Tennessee—declaration of rights, article 23. That all perpetuities and monopolies are contrary to the genius of a free state, and shall not be allowed, etc.

In elective governments by universal suffrage, founded on liberty and equality, that one in many thousands, clothed with a little temporary authority, by the suffrages of their equals and fellow-citizens, should assume the right of making laws, granting exclusive privileges to the few, which are denied to the many, thereby counteracting and destroying that equality on the authority of which alone, they have a right to legislate, is an astonishing anomaly in legislation and the history of nations. It may cause posterity equally to wonder at the usurpation of the few, and the subjection of the many, who have tolerated for half a century such encroachments on equality, without which freedom is but a sound, and that the many should tolerate so long, such gross abuse in their servants, whom they only clothed with a little brief authority, to legislate for their benefit and according to their interest, but who extend their usurped authority to twenty times the period they were elected to rule, by granting charters of exclusive privileges for twenty or thirty years, thus attempting to bind their successors to legalize their usurpations. All this deviation from justice, and the acknowledged principles of elective power, can only be attributed to the slavish imitation, by both electors and elected, of the laws, habits and customs of the old world, subjected to the arbitrary will of the hereditary power, all men though elected only for a year, must wish to participate. The only remedy for that natural propensity, is for the electors to fix it is an unalterable rule, that no man shall be twice elected, but must retire to an equality with his fellow-citizens, to hear the criticisms and remarks on his conduct as a ruler, to pay the taxes he may have helped to lay, and to obey all the laws he may have assisted to make, during the rest of his life. There is no other possible mode of reconciling the interest of payer and receiver, the obeyer and the maker of laws.

It would appear by the essential principies of all the constitutions, and the express prohibition in six of them, that none of the legislatures are authorized to grant exclusive privileges; nor can they claim the power from the orders or permission they may pretend to have had from their constituents. They are even deprived of the excuse of acting thus for the benefit of the great majority, as I have endeavored to show, in some of my former papers, that they have sacrificed the interest of the many industrious producers, to the few consumers and nonproducers, in every instance where they have given any species of exclusive privilege. In consequence, all said exclusive privileges must be unconstitutional and illegal, and subject to be annulled and abrogated by any subsequent legislature, who may think them injurious to the interest of the great majority of their constituents or derogatory to the public good. All the rules of hereditary despotism, concerning the sacred, unchangeable nature of their laws, are, like any other principle of arbitrary power, reversed in elective governments of universal suffrage, when every thing must give way to the interest of the positive majority. Change is the essence and chief attribute of the system, and no law, rule or regulation, can exist for a day, if contrary to the interest of the great majority, of which they are the only judges, deciding at the ballot-boxes;—all other interference is an usurpation of the people's rights and prerogatives.

UNIVERSAL AND PRACTICAL EDUCATION NECESSARY TO MAINTAIN EQUALITY.

December 1st, 1830.

Education is a word, by long habit, applied to the knowledge acquired within the walls of a school-house, too often as circumscribed as the locality which coercion has made a prison, evinced by the slow sorrowful pace in which the children go to it, and the hilarity they exhibit in escaping from it. Now, since more freedom is permitted to both men and children, the word that expresses the acquiring of knowledge, might, perhaps, be *instruction.* Certainly the physical energies and healthy movements are paralyzed by confinement, and the moral faculties not less injured, by irksome constraint, generating discontent, and all the attendant petulant vices, and they rush out of school seemingly determined to take their revenge on all they meet, for the many privations they have suffered during their confinement. As the equal expenditure of vital force between the sensorium and the muscular movements, is positively necessary to the enjoyment of health, the gymnastic or physical exercises ought to proceed on a par with the moral instruction of all ages, and rather precede the moral during the early period of childhood. For this purpose they ought to spend much of their time out of the house, in the open air, occupied with a variety of bodily exercises to which might be joined, the disciplining of the moral faculties, by giving a rapid, and correct use of all the senses, in applying them to an accurate definition of all the properties of surrounding objects. In their walks, one day they might practice the acuteness of vision, in deciding on the distance or height of objects; by each guessing, and afterwards measuring, they would become so exact as to determine the distance or height of any object within the fraction of a foot. Another day they might take exercise with a pair of scales, guessing at the weight of a stone, by poising it in their hands and afterwards weighing it; they would thus become so expert, as to know the weight to the fraction of an ounce, by handling, of any object they could lift. Another day they might walk out with a theodolite or compass, and guess at the angle of the corner of a field, etc., then ascertain who was nearest: by which practices they would become good judges of space and dimensions, without the trouble of surveying. At another time they might collect specimens of rocks and ascertain their vulgar and mineralogical names, plants, insects, reptiles and objects, in all the branches of natural history in the same manner; for all the useful part of natural history, is to recollect the name, and some of the useful qualities of the thing when presented to their observation. Extending the knowledge to a thousand objects which you will never come in contact with, nor have occasion to use, is more for amusement than utility, for recreation rather than profit. All the above practical knowledge can be acquired without the aid of any learned professor, merely by a vigorous use of the senses, and the habits of close and attentive examination, the medium through which all useful knowledge comes, and the only kind of instruction children can be induced to study with pleasure and without compulsion.

Description requires much exercise, and the habit of speaking, and even with all the literature that can be acquired; language is so vague and imperfect, that the nature, form, figure or properties, of any natural or artificial body, cannot be described accurately, to the right understanding of adults, and much less can description, bring the knowledge of any thing the least complicated, within the comprehension of children. I recollect, that when young, I never got a correct idea of any thing by description, and that the few distinct ideas I obtained of objects, were from an examination of themselves, or accurate representations of them. With this conviction, I no sooner began to amuse myself with endeavoring to reform schools, than I tried every mode of introducing representations in place of descriptions, to give accurate ideas to children, and for the facilitating of which in the United States, while traveling in Europe, I collected many thousand prints, and about 1,500 copper plates, capable of drawing off about one million and a half of prints on all subjects. Many of these I gave to schools, but without being able to convince any one school-master of the advantages their scholars must derive by transferring the image from the print, directly to the mind, without the laborious task of delineation from imperfect description, conveyed in still more imperfect language. The very superior advantage of giving correct ideas of things without the *ipse dixit* of the master, may perhaps be the reason why all school masters objected to make use of it, and pretended to depise it, some of them giving as a reason that it gave ideas too cheap; for not only is it the most correct mode of imprinting ideas on the mind, but also the most durable, the image long remaining after the words or sounds of the description, have escaped all possibility of recollection. All children are fond of examining representations, and are never tired of inspecting them, never fatiguing their attention, which is very soon exhausted with dry description; the labor of reducing sounds to an image or figure in the mind, very soon disgusts them. Most men, when they open a book, the prints are the first things they look at, as the shortest and easiest way of getting an idea of its contents. As improvements advance the number of prints put into books increase rapidly.

Scholastic education, in most christian countries, has been in the hands of priests, who have warped it, towards the object of their profession, theology, metaphysics, the dead languages, etc., etc., and for a long time the clergy was the only class, who had any education. Their 'knowledge constituted their power, which has made them oppose the diffusion of knowledge, and consequently the civilization of their species. The time is come when the interest of the few must yield to the interest of the many; when children of all classes must be practically taught, what will be necessary for their existence as men, which will most probably be some productive trade; for we find the freest nations of antiquity enjoyed the greatest equality, and practiced the greatest economy. In Athens the rich man could not be distinguished from the slave by his dress, and the most wealthy citizens and greatest generals went to market. As society returns to the natural equality, by the abolition of all unjust, partial and monopolizing laws, property, knowledge and power, will be so divided as to render it necessary for every individual to produce something for a living. Indolence, luxury and extravagance are the fruits of riches, and the certain result to the next generation is poverty, when not prevented by tyrannical monopolizing laws. All the props which sustain the monopoly of wealth and wisdom, will be abolished by this moral revolution in the United States, and consequently unprecedented equality must follow; when all the establishments of schools, at the expense of the people's money, ought to be so organized, as to suit and maintain that equality, so essential to freedom. If the schools are made for the benefit and advantage of the industrious producers, production will be one of the principal objects to be obtained, and useful and profitable labor the only means; which, under judicious and economical management will support and maintain all the expenses of the establishments. The first expenditure for arranging the locality, and some outfits at the commencement, would be the only expenses out of the people's purse. The children would be beholden alone to their own exertions for their maintenance, which would lay the foundation of a highly useful equality and independence; and would continue and strengthen through life, so as to raise them far above all vice and crime; for the great and unnatural inequality of property, knowledge and power is perhaps the cause and origin of all force, violence and crime, where civilization has made any progress.— Sin and crime have ever been the chief support of both church and state, as far as civilization has yet advanced.— We may perhaps be allowed to hope that the great radical, moral reform now begun, will secure the greatest happiness to the greatest number, as the most important result for abused humanity.

LEGISLATORS LIMIT THE FREEDOM OF THE PEOPLE UNDER PRETENCE OF BENEFITTING THEM.

December 9th, 1830.

All governments are in theory, made for the use and benefit of the governed, but in practice, most of them appear to be contrived for the use and advantage of those who made them, and who are always the governors. These have so cajoled the many producers, that the real use of governments, has been masked and obliterated by the innumerable abuses, introduced by the rulers at the expense of the governed. Man with all his wants, appetites, passions and desires, both real and imaginary, to satisfy, must be so essentially selfish, as to leave no place for a disinterested motive for any of his actions. It would therefore be folly to expect any species of rulers to do good to the people they govern, merely for the sake of benefitting them, without being actuated by some one of the numerous interested motives which regulate the conduct of mankind. On an impartial analysis of our nature, which pervades governors perhaps more than governed, being less exposed to the check of equality, it must result, that it is not the province of those in power to do good to those they govern. The only benefit that can be reasonably expected from any kind of rulers, is to remove all natural or artificial obstructions, that can, in any way prevent the governed from doing good to themselves.— There are two different sources of those artificial obstructions placed in the way of people doing good to themselves;— one is individual violence against person or property, by robbing, thieving, and other vices and crimes; the other, which is by far the most injurious, arises from the abuse of power, by the governors feeling might and forgetting right; complicating and extending their influence, under pretence of teaching the governed how to follow their own interest. This restrictive system of tutorage is exactly in the ratio of despotism.— As freedom consists in the right each individual has of following his interest in his own way, provided he does not injure others, it is therefore injured and diminished by any law or authority dictating to him how he must follow his interest.— Most of these restrictive regulations are applied, through the military, fiscal, religious or legal divisions of arbitrary power, which naturally interferes with the individual concerns of the governed, forcing them to substitute the interest of the rulers for their own.

Under the head of military, are all wars, which the governors wage against one another, to gratify their ambition and love of power, at the expense of the governed, who are armed and disciplined to cut one another's throats, with a certainty of increasing their subjection and burdens, by the additional force of large armies at the command of their governors, to enforce their despotic measures. The millions in no country, ever have or can gain by a war, be it ever so successful, but must lose all the value of their blood and treasure, wasted in carrying it on, besides the injustice, plunder, cruelty and rapine it creates, brutifying and demoralizing human nature below the level of our four footed neighbors, who never fight but for the purpose of satisfying some natural appetite, except when man trains them to gratify his own wicked propensities. The hatred, enmity, and all the angry and violent passions of our nature roused against another, whose interest it is to be on friendly terms, is the remnant of our barbarous habits, which the depraved amusements of our governors retain, like the pleasure the Romans had in the fighting of the gladiators, or the savage amusement of some of our fashionables, in cock fighting, horse racing, etc. If those who make war were obliged to fight in it;—or those who laid taxes were obliged to pay them, the one would be much less frequent, and the other much more moderate, which will be the result of a judicious exercise of the right of universal suffrage, in dividing property, knowledge and power, more equally.

Fiscal, or unjust and arbitrary modes of collecting the revenue by indirect taxation, paralyzes industry, and interferes more with individual interest, than perhaps any other operation of government. It authorizes a crowd of revenue officers to search and impede the transportation of all articles, from the place of growth to the place of consumption, under pretence of preventing smuggling; offers a temptation to fraud, which leads to demoralize, both the officer who ought to secure the revenue, and the citizen who ought to pay it; is a loss of time, temper and money, to all parties; damages the property by the mode of inspection; favors the fraudulent who evade the payment; costs a great expense, only to add to the patronage of the executive, who fees his friends to support him, right or wrong; falls heavily on the laborer, who consumes nearly as much as the rich, and helps to reduce him to poverty and wretchedness, while it favors the accumulation of wealth in the hands of the few; obstructs the free circulation of property, knowledge and power, and deranges the natural equality so essential to freedom.

Religion, by its arbitrary laws and regulations, prevents men from following their interest by depriving them in all christian countries, of one seventh part of their time, and in some, nearly one half; infringing on the interest of the great mass of freeholders, much more than on the habits of the cnosumers, the exercise of whose professions being in the house, making no noise, and the division of their time, allowing of many holy days or idle days. From the variety and uncertainty of every thing beyond our comprehension, it is the cause of eternal disputes, ending in war or bloodshed. It interferes with that friendly and social intercourse, so essential to the well-being of society. It creates a consuming corporation, who, living on the produce of others' labor, have an interest opposed to the general welfare, and use perpetual intrigue to seize on as much of the fruits of the producer's labor, as their cunning combination can effect. Their interest being in contradiction with that of the community, obstructs the progress of civilization and diffusion of knowledge.

Legal obstructions to the peace, comfort and happiness of the whole human family, have accumulated immensely in the progress of civilization, more particularly in such political systems, as permit a small quantity of theoretical freedom.— By the mysterious complication and intricate litigation of the laws, the expense is out of the reach of the pockets of the industrious producers, and enables the rich to tyrannize over the poor, more safely and securely than under any despot acting by the force of hereditary power. The tyranny of the laws is substituted for the tyranny of despotic power, in all countries where the people have obtained some freedom; and in spite of universal suffrage it has been pushed as despotically with us as any where else. Where lawyers alone, know any thing about laws, they have as complete a monopoly of justice as the emperor of Morocco or any of the judges of a despot; no one can have justice without paying the extravagant fee of the lawyer, or the equally extorting bribe of the judge, and as to those who have not wherewithal to pay either, justice is equally out of their reach.

All these and many others, are the artificial contrivances of governors to circumscribe the freedom of the governed, under pretence of doing them good. All these complicated inventions of the non productive consumers, are practiced on purpose to monopolize as much of the fruits of the labor of the industrious producers as will maintain their luxury and extravagance. Limit the business of governors, to their positive utility, in removing all natural and artificial impediments to the individual happiness and prosperity of the governed, and you would remove all those lets and hindrances which prevent the governed from doing good to themselves, and which originate in the acts and regulations of the governors. You would thus simplify the political machine, so that any man of common sense could regulate it, and if the electors would establish a fixed and unalterable rule, never to put the same man twice into power, they would completely take away every temptation to complicate or render difficult, the administration of public affairs: as no one would take the invidious trouble of enhancing the value of the place to his successor, when positively certain of never enjoying it himself.

WHAT IS NOT UNDERSTOOD, IS IMPROPER FOR PUPILS. PROPER OBJECTS OF TUITION. EQUALITY INDISPENSABLE IN SCHOOLS. EXPERIMENTS NECESSARY ON THE BEST MODE OF TEACHING.

December 14, 1830.

Let any one impartially reflect, how much of his scholastic education he ever made use of during his occupations as a man. He will most probably find it limited to reading, writing, and the four rules of arithmetic, all of which may be learnt in six months; and even the two last have been but imperfectly taught, for he must learn a current hand writing, and a more practical and shorter mode of calculating after he leaves school. This is all that ninety-nine in 100, perhaps 999 in 1000, gain by being imprisoned within the walls of a school house five or six hours every day for four or five years. The instruction children obtain themselves on the out side of the school house, though perhaps the most useful, not being obtained under the ferula of the master, is not considered as education. All the words or sounds that are nailed to their memories by the hammer of authority, attempting to designate imaginary opinions or fanciful ideas, as far beyond comprehension as they are out of the reach of their senses, can be of no use to them either as children or men, however necessary they may be to the continuance of the authority of the master. Teaching must include some kind of knowledge, but what we do not understand, is no species of knowledge to us, their forced attempts to communicate cannot be called teaching or instruction, though it may have long passed for education.

Happiness is the end and object of all rational beings, who cannot begin too soon to accumulate the materials necessary to the enjoyment of it, nor to avoid, too early in life, all that would tend to diminish or interfere with our happiness. All our comfort, peace and happiness which depend on others, are precarious and uncertain, and it would be wise to limit the sphere of our gratifications, as much within our own circle as possible. There can be no happiness without wherewith to satisfy the physical appetites. The means of production ought therefore to be the first to be attended to, by learning some useful and productive trade that might be recurred to in case of necessity. Under the wise regulations of moderation and economy, the quantity of sustenance strictly necessary for health, strength, and real enjoyment, is but little, not perhaps one fourth of what is usually wasted; the surplus creates disease and misery; to avoid which children cannot be too early taught the great advantage of moderation in eating and drinking, first by having nothing but plain, simple food on the table, with milk or water, and carefully avoiding all artificial stimulants. This wholesome regimen should be prescribed rather by example and the moral constraint, than by physical privation, which only strengthens and excites the physical appetites. When any of them by indulgence to excess, bring on an indigestion, sick stomach, head ache, etc.; a lecture should be given, showing the pain and misery that result from gormandizing. All physical restriction, either in quantity or quality, creates imaginary desires far exceeding the real ones; to prevent which, of the simple food set before them they ought to have as much as they desire of all or any of the dishes, so as to leave no void for the imagination to work upon. Preventive is better than cure; much of the future happiness depends on a healthful and well regulated diet, which cannot be learned too soon. Physical exercise conducive to health may be taken by acquiring dexterity in all the occupations they may have occasion to practice during life, never for a moment losing sight of the useful.— Their questions ought to receive satisfactory answers at all times.

I believe all that we know of morals is the fruit of education, or appetites: all realities are bounded by utility and necessity; but imagination has no limits, nor the labor of satisfying it any end. Morality by being yoked to religious dogmas, has been driven from its original and natural foundation, which is the interest of mankind, and placed on the artificial base of duty, benevolence, doing good to others, etc making all moral obligations disinterested, and placing them in opposition to the selfish principle, which rules and governs our species. All great inequality of property, knowledge or power, encourages immorality, by placing certain individuals above retaliation, correction or punishment. Equality is the true source of morality, which perhaps cannot exist without it and in the same ratio. In a state of equality, it is easier to convince a people of the necessity of honesty, and that it is their interest to have as many friends and as few enemies as possible, to obtain which, they must do as much good and as little harm as possible. The violence against person and property is less in France for its population, than any where else in Europe: because there is more equality. There is more crime in Britain than in any place of its size, because of a greater inequality. The quantity of crime in our mercantile towns, is a proof how far the artificial inequality of our moneyed aristocracy has been carried.

Morality is easier taught in schools where nearly a perfect equality exists, than in schools where the distinction of rank, creates jealousy and envy on the part of the inferiors, and assumed superiority, bordering on contempt, without being supported by merit, from the usurpations of the others. This tends to sour the temper of both, and alienate them from that social intercourse, so necessary for the acquiring those friendly and amiable habits, which strew the rugged path of life with flowers. Equality in schools is as much more necessary and useful, than in adult societies, as the impressions are stronger and more lasting; and to remove any temptation to partiality, it might perhaps be well to exclude the children of masters or professors from their own school, as much for their own good as for the benefit of the school. Equality leaves fair scope for competition; just and impartial decisions give a useful stimulus to exertion.

When general and equal free schools shall be established gratis for the benefit and advantage of all the children of the state, there will be a fair opportunity of experimenting on the most useful system of instruction for the children of a free people, whose government is founded on liberty and equality, provided the management and selection, be left to the townships inhabited by those who are to reap the benefit if good, or suffer the loss if bad, and of course are interested in improving and changing to suit the knowledge of the day. But if it be left to the state legislature to form a system which is to regulate the whole, it will become a job in which the priests and old professors, will have their interest more attended to than the people or their children; and when once established by law, no change, however necessary, can be made but by law, and the difficulty of obtaining that unanimity necessary to change the law, would allow a bad system to go on long after it was proven to be insufficient, besides restricting the experiment to one system. Whereas, if left to the townships there would be many hundreds to choose amongst, each township trying who could give the best and most useful system of instruction to their offspring. Legislators, lawyers and the learned professions may be allowed to be the best judges of the education they wish given to their own children, but farmers, mechanics and working people, are the best informed of the kind of instruction that would suit their children to fit them for the situation they are to fill as men. Unless they verify the toast formed by the aristocracy when they thought their party the strongest, "the people, their own worst enemies," to remove all obstructions from the people following their own interest, is all that can be expected from rulers.— Unfortunately most of these inpediments are put by the rulers, which make them so unwilling to remove them.

DIFFERENT MEANINGS OF THE WORDS ORDER, REGULARITY, ETC. NECESSITY OF CHANGE IN EDUCATION AS WELL AS IN POLITICS AND RELIGION.

December 18, 1830.

The words, regularity, order and uniformity, seem to imply a perfection not yet *to* be found in human institutions. To that order and uniformity are too often sacrificed both common sense and utility. Regular government has been understood to mean the arbitrary power of military force, to quash all changes or political movements, though as necessary to the healthful state of the body politic, as fermentation is to liquors. The holy alliance was contrived to keep up the unanimity of despotism in Europe. The coalition of the allied powers against the French revolution, was to restore order and uniformity in despotism, which freedom has disturbed. The interference of the Bourbons with the liberties of Spain, was to restore the regularity of despotism. All the combinations of sovereigns have been to maintain the uniformity of oppression and prevent the practice of freedom from contrasting with their arbitrary power. The order and regularity of bad laws, bad habits and customs, only fortify and strengthen their mischievous effects, lengthen their duration, by preventing any trial or comparison with any better, and it may be questioned whether any of our religious, political or civil practices, are even on a par with the knowledge of the day, much less do they follow the rapid progress of civilization. So that every combination, under pretence of regularity, order and unanimity, to keep society in its present state, is an injurious bar to that comfort and happiness which men are capable of enjoying.

It is not perhaps so useful in morals as in physics, for men to march to the same step or tune, and pull all the same way. Morals are so far behind physics, that a little variety and opposition, like the percussion of the flint and steel, produce light. Make the application to the instruction of children, who are full of vivacity, activity and curiosity, all of which are paralyzed and compressed into the stillness of death, and the silence of the grave, by the order, discipline and despotism of the old school. All aggregations of men or children, in nations or schools, are only kept still and quiet by the force of tyranny; which perhaps is equally unnecessary in both, when governed by the dictates of their real interest. The result of instruction is not known in much less than an age. Before I adopted the Pestalozzian system, as the best I had found, I examined the conduct, talents and capabilities of at least fifty youths taught by that method, and ventured to attempt to propagate the system, only when convinced of its superiority over all others I had seen. If the legislatures of the states, even by the advice of the professions, are to fix an uniform system of instruction for the whole, and bind down the school-masters in trammels to follow the same routine that may be thought the best in theory for certain states of society very different from what we are fast approaching to, as it would require an age to find out the advantages or disadvantages of the system, much time might be lost.

Suppose a legislator was to dictate by a law, that all chemists should be compelled to follow the same methods of analysis and other operations in their laboratories, there would certainly be conformity; but as certainly there would be no improvement. The order and uniformity of the grammar schools of Eton and Westminster, where every one is flogged for the least mistake in a Latin or Greek lesson, cannot be denied, but it may be questioned whether all the desire of knowledge or study is not flogged out of them. The same observation may be applied to the rules and regulations of Cambridge and Oxford, of which most of our colleges are servile copies. Experiments ought to be made on a small scale, and the greater the variety, the sooner the best will be found out. All laws, habits, customs, practices or systems, contrived or invented for the support of the monarchies or aristocracies of the old world, are destructive of the system of freedom and equality executed by universal suffrage in the United States, and must counteract every principle on which the happiness of a free people is founded; and in nothing is that contradiction stronger, or more contrary to the public weal, than in the education of children, the base and foundation of the whole superstructure of society. As yet our systems of education, being exact copies of those of Europe, all changes we make to suit the simplicity of our political, civil and religious institutions, must be considered as experiments, inasmuch as no political association ever existed before, on the basis of liberty and equality.

I think I hear those whose lot has been fortunately cast in things as they are, exclaim, " changes are dangerous," etc.— Like the little French Abbe with a hundred thousand francs of revenue, at the commencement of the French revolution, when the people were crowding and grumbling in the streets, exclaimed, "what would the people be at, are we not all very well." Changes are only dangerous to those who, by hook or by crook, have seized upon more than their share.

I believe history will prove that there has been no change in the civil, political or religious state of society (always excepting what has been produced by the force and violence of conquest, which must participate of its savage and barbarous nature) for the last hundred years, which has not been for the advantage of our species. Our revolution was the first great change from hereditary to elective power, and no one can now dispute its being eminently advantageous to the whole population. The French revolution succeeded, equally advantageous to the millions, but was suspended for a time, by the bayonets of the allied powers, to re-establish the tyranny of the Bourbons, now resuscitated for the benefit of all, by the joint confessions of all Europe. The Spanish revolution was vastly advantageous to the people, but has been three times suspended by the tyranny of their neighbors. The Italian revolution was greatly in favor of civilization and the millions, but rendered for a time abortive by the bayonets of the combined allies, who introduced Austrian despotism. The changes in Bavaria, Wirtemberg, Baden and Holland, were much in favor of the millions, and because partly hereditary, were tolerated by the despotic allies. The freedom of the elective states of South America, for its extensive and beneficial consequences, is perhaps equal to any change that has as yet taken place on the globe. Civilization, knowledge and information, are now too widely diffused, to tolerate any change, but such as is for the benefit of the great majority, and such as will advance the interests of the millions, who by a knowledge of their great utility, and of the dependence of all other classes of society on the produce of their labor, are raising themselves to that station of respectability, which their productive usefulness has always merited, but of which they have been, as yet, deprived by their own ignorance, and the artifices of those who have usurped the power of ruling over them.

ORIGIN AND TARDY PROGRESS OF REFORM.

December 22, 1830.

History has been made for, and only gives an account of the governors and their interest; the mass of the governed are only mentioned as soldiers, to enregister the number that were killed, fighting for their master. Before the invention of printing, the rulers of the people were the only persons who could afford to read history; of course, like all other merchandize, it was made to please the customers, and has ever since been the favorite study of aristocratical power and prejudice, finding therein examples and every kind of encouragement and support of their arbitrary rule. The page of history teaches the consumers the various modes of filching from the producers the fruits of their labor, while it tends by comparison of greater injustice, to make the working people contented with their situation. In all reforms of abuses, it is the interest of those who lose by the change, to look back on their ancestors, while those who are benefited, are inclined to look forward to a still more favorable change; so that in every instance, the interest of the consumers and producers, the interest of the governors and the governed, must be opposite and contradictory. The governed have gained by the weakness and folly of the governors. The cause of the protestant reform, was the weakness and wickedness of the catholic priesthood. The liberty of Switzerland originated in the folly and injustice of the Austrian government. The *magna charta* of Britain was wrested from the weakness of king John. The emancipation of Holland sprung from the folly and superstition of the king of Spain. The freedom of our country might have been much longer postponed but for the weakness and obstinacy of the king of Britain. The ignorance and folly of the Bourbons, have been the cause of the two revolutions both in France and Spain, and all their consequences. Mankind have perhaps been more benefited by the weakness and folly of their rulers, and more injured by the brilliant abilities of the Cæsars and Alexanders of all countries, than our self conceit will admit.

The selfish principle, founded on our desires, wants and necessities, real or imaginary, forces all to follow their own interest; and the more knowledge and useful information we have, the more closely and directly we will follow our real interest. But the interest of the consumers, is opposed to the interest of the producers, and the interest of the governors, is equally in opposition to the interest of the governed, it must follow of course, that in all governments, whether elective or hereditary, all the information, talents or abilities, of the governors, will be exercised to forward their own interest, and more dexterously increase their privileges, at the expense of the governed, who have to contend with power aided by abilities. It would therefore appear, not to be the interest of electors to choose for their representative, a man of brilliant talents, nor an eloquent declaimer, who can make the worse appear the better cause, but a practical, common sense man of their own trade or profession, who would go straight forward towards their interest, in following what his previous habits and occupations, have made his own. This would appear to be the only possible mode of having the interest of the great majority to rule, which must certainly be the only aim and object of all governments of universal suffrage. For the right of voting would be a mere mockery, if not exercised for the good of the majority; and would only prove that the people are too ignorant to enjoy the benefit of so free a government.

If the people dare not trust themselves with power, but must have lawyers and other learned and rich men taught, at their expense, to rule over them, the hereditary power might be better, on the principle of the man who was attacked by musquitoes, who said to his friend who wished to clear them away, "Let them that are full of my blood remain, for if a hungry set come, they will be more voracious;" so are a new set of placemen, who are trained to live on the people's purse, the oftener you change, the more idle mouths you have to satisfy.

The claims which the working people are now making for their rights and prerogatives, a knowledge of, and a due regard for their own interest, would have forced them to insist upon forty-five years ago, before bank and other monopolies had created so much inequality of property; before the profits, patronage and salaries, attached to places, were thought worth intriguing for; when the people at the great bridge in Virginia solicited me to allow my clerk to represent them in the Virginia legislature. The equality of property, knowledge and power was such, immediately after our revolution, that the working people would have had their share of influence and consideration at the ballot-boxes, without a murmur; for all were necessitated to work more or less for a living; the classification of ranks or existence of office hunters was not then known, political labor not being so much more profitable than other useful labor, as to induce parties to scramble so violently for the possession of public offices. Fortunately it is for the producers, that they have at last made use of their senses, if they should remain hoodwinked forty-five years longer, it would be forty-five times more difficult to obtain their rights, for by the aid of the complicated, intricate, litigious, British common law, raising the revenue by indirect taxation, favoring commerce at the expense of agriculture, etc., etc., the working people of the United States, would be reduced to the same poverty and misery as the laborers in old mother Britain. To this end all the ingredients of luxurious riches, and their constant attendants misery and poverty, were fast accumulating, aided and abetted by the fortuitous neutral trade, which went hand in hand with the enormous circulation of bank and other paper, to derange that equality so essential to rational freedom.

It would appear that the late revolutions at Paris and Brussels were entirely owing to the exertions of the industrious producers. The rich and learned professions kept aloof until the day was won, and it is more than probable, that if it goes farther into Germany, Spain and Italy, it will be by the exertions of the working people. During the heat and enthusiasm of revolutionary movements, changes and improvements may be made beyond the knowledge and understanding of the producers; but the intrigues and combinations of the consumers, will soon abolish any thing useful to any class but their own, and nothing will be fixed or permanent until supported by the knowledge and conviction of the producers, that it is their interest to maintain it. If after the brilliant examples of their fellow laborers in Europe, conquering their freedom against the combined military force, disciplined and organized to keep them in subjection, our working people should fail in their attempts to regain their natural, constitutional and legal rights, requiring only a peaceable, moral exertion of their mental faculties, it must be owing to some defalcation of our soil and climate, that has depreciated the human energies, and left them a prey to indolence, pride and presumption. Let them not be satisfied with being the first who dared to walk alone and establish the theory of self-government; let them not sleep on their former laurels, forgetting that all things are comparative, and that in 1776, when they astonished the old world with their declaration of independence, freedom and equality, all civilized nations were immensely behind what they are at present. As it is only reducing the theory they have had for more than half a century, to the practice of that equality, without which freedom cannot long exist, we may entertain the well grounded hopes that a failure can hardly take place, after experience has taught them to distinguish friends from foes, and not to depend on persons, but adhere strictly to principles. The *ignis fatus* of agrarianism invented by the aristocracy, and advocated by one of their creatures, which rendered abortive nearly one-third of the votes, was a trick that can only succeed once; but they may expect deeper laid schemes to conquer their unanimity and perseverance. So long as the bank monopoly of coining paper money has the command of the circulating medium by the exclusive privilege of making a small piece of paper, not intrinsically worth one quarter of a cent, worth some thousands of dollars, they will have money in abundance in their hands, to practice every kind of bribery; against which the supposed patriotism of the editors of newspapers, is but a weak defence, when urged by the necessity of a scanty subscription, still more poorly and scantly paid: particularly too as all former advocates of the producers have lost both their money and advice, owing to the ignorance of those whom they wish to serve.

HABITUAL SUBMISSION OF THE PEOPLE TO THE TYRANNY OF CHURCH AND STATE. THE PEOPLE THEIR OWN POLICE. INEQUALITY PRODUCTIVE OF CRIME.

December 25th, 1830.

Our country being the only one perhaps on earth, that has been entirely free from all kinds of rebellion, conspiracies, mobs, anarchy or tumults for the last half century, and at the same time the freest, it has sometimes puzzled me to find where could arise the general opinion, that freedom descends to anarchy and is succeeded by despotism; a circle of vicious actions, contradicted by modern history, where despotisms are the seats of conspiracies, revolts, assassinations, etc., etc., where the slaves retaliate the cruelty and oppression of their master, when relieved for ever so short a time, from physical restraint. The remnant of my Latin and Greek education, is a recollection of the furious manner in which a reverence and respect for every thing ancient was flogged into me; how we read with reverential awe the poetry of Virgil, Horace,

Homer, etc., and almost defied the ancient ballad singers, placing them among their numberless gods and goddesses, the imitation of whose verses was thought the *ne plus ultra* of human wisdom. I remember the praises lavished on the perfection of Greek democracies, Roman republics, etc., etc., who without the pendulum of representation to regulate and equalize their movements, were mostly in extremes, sometimes wandering in licentious anarchy, but oftener oppressed by petty tyrants, though all dignified as the result and consequence of freedom; and all transferred with the name, and applied to the political, moral or religious circumstances of the present day. We might as reasonably propel ships by oars, and steer them by the stars, in place of steam ships with sextants and chronometers, as copy the opinions, laws, habits or customs of those barbarous ages, in the present advanced state of civilization. Yet so durable are first impressions, that we continue to act and think agreeably to our early lessons, long after maturer reason has soared above them. And those dogmas and creeds, both religious and political, based on no solid foundation, retain the control and direction of the human mind, and occasion that alternating mixture of absurdity and reason, folly and rationality, just as the memory of the past, or judgment of the present, prevails.

When men shall substitute the evidence of their senses, to the wild fancies of the imagination; the realities that exist, for the nonentities beyond our comprehension; when we shall judge from what we see, in place of by what we hear, trusting more to the other senses, than to the ears, we shall be astonished at the long continuance of the delusion that has led the human intellect astray, through the mysterious wilderness of deception, by the cunning intrigues of church and state. Strange that sounds presuming to teach incomprehensibilities, out of the mouth of a priest, should have so long induced men to feed, clothe, lodge and administer to the luxurious desires and appetites of this dealer in miracles, out of the fruits of their hard earned industry, or to furnish the implements of oppression to their governors, and bow the head or bend the knee to idols of their own making. When the diffusion of useful knowledge shall have reduced society nearer the par of equality and utility, and have taught them how much of this mystery, pomp, parade and ceremony, is for the advantage of their heavenly and earthly rulers, to mask and disguise their selfish plans, and how much labor it costs them to maintain in luxury and extravagance, such a number of nonproductive consumers, they will be more amazed at their former ignorance than the Christian of the present day is at the folly and ignorance of the Mahometan, in believing the fabulous doctrines of Mahomet, though there are more human beings who believe and regulate their conduct by Mahometanism than by the Christian dogmas; and the Mahometans are more constant, having only split yet into two sects, whereas the Christians are divided into nearly 100, most of whom hate, despise and persecute one another with more violence than they do the Jews and Pagans.

Every superstition and delusion that can be invented by the ingenuity of the church, is necessary to the support and protection of hereditary governments, who rule their subjects with despotic power. This makes the union of church and state a necessary compact for the maintenance of both, who mutually aid each other in the exercise of their usurped authority. The physical force of the state upholds and coerces obedience to the religious dogmas, laws and regulations of the dominant church, and in some countries prohibits under severe pains and penalties the exercise of any other. This intolerance is principally confined to Christian countries, whose zeal for converting all to the same worship has been conspicuous in all the great variety of Christian sects. In all elective governments of universal suffrage, founded on the interest of the positive majority, no combination, either religious, civil or military, is in the smallest degree necessary to sustain it in its pristine vigor and energy, the people having all the power must lose by any change, and have a decided interest to crush all attempts at usurpation the moment they perceive it.—During the sessions of the federal senate at Philadelphia, there was a senator who was suspected of some intrigue with the British ministers; on which he left town to go home; at Staunton the citizens stopped him, and we found him at the tavern under a guard, on the suspicion that he was making his escape, we advised the people to liberate him, as they had no authority for detaining him. The same thing happened frequently to Col. Burr, during his preparation, as it was said, for revolutionizing Mexico; which shows that free people, where equality prevails, have no use of a police to keep the peace; each citizen is an officer of police, to quash all symptoms of rebellion or conspiracy against the rights and liberties of the people.

As we have imitated the great inequality, luxury, extravagance and corruption of the European aristocracies in our large mercantile towns, such as New York, we are forced to follow them in our officers of police, jailors, etc., to regulate our well filled prisons, penitentiaries and houses of refuge.— Little or none of all this detection and punishment of crimes would have been necessary, had the equality of property, knowledge and power, remained the same as it was at the end of our revolution. For though the army was then all disbanded, and a number of men accustomed to the idleness and indolence of a military life, were thrown on the public, yet there were no robberies or crimes of magnitude in any part of the Union. When I left Philadelphia to go to Europe in 1799, there were only 123 convicts in the new jail, for the whole state of Pennsylvania, fifteen years afterwards there were 700, and 123 for forgery alone; so much had the inequality, created by bank and other paper, joined to the neutral trade, deranged the morality of the inhabitauts. This has been rather increasing than diminishing ever since, owing to the great number of young men brought up to the nonproductive professions, tempted by the profits of the neutral trade, which left them without the means of existence, having learnt no productive trade.

The temptation to crime is nearly in the proportion of the inequality of property, knowledge and power, which is great in the city of Mexico; where thieving, robbing and murdering are committed daily, both in the town and its environs. But in the Indian villages, where equality exists nearly in its natural state, there are no locks or bars, and scarcely any doors or windows to their houses, yet there is no thieving or robbing. And perhaps there are as many crimes committed in the town of Mexico in one day, as are perpetrated in all the Indian villages of the union in one year. Men have paid dear for civilization as far as it has yet gone, by the multiplication of artificial wants and the temptation to crime, injustice and oppression. The further progress of civilization may perhaps tend to the simplification and equalization of society, and in that case those now in the savage state, may perhaps be nearer perfection than those who pride themselves on a complication of wants and passions, the satisfying of which creates much labor, trouble and anxiety; and the excess and indulgence brings disease and misery.

CAUSES OF INEQUALITY. PROGRESS OF THE WORKING MEN IN THE ACQUISITION OF THEIR RIGHTS.

January 1*st*, 1831.

In my last, and some of my former essays, I noticed the connection between corruption, vice and crime, and the inequality of property, knowledge and power, and remarked that the degree of all kinds of immorality, is in proportion to the inequality of those three essentials to rational freedom, and of course, that their equality is the broad and solid foundation, on which the peace, comfort and happiness of mankind is founded. Beginning with the master and slave, and reviewing all the gradations of artificial inequality, we find immorality and vice, by the nature of surrounding circumstances, are pushed into the extremes of slavery and tyranny; and morality, peace and happiness must be looked for *equi-distant* from both. It would therefore be in vain to expect peace or rational freedom, from the heterogeneous mixture of tyranny and slavery, where the multitude are deprived by force of what would increase their happiness, and which adds to the care, luxury and extravagance of their masters, placing them as far beyond the medium point of happiness, as their slaves are short of it; an order of things that may agree with subjection under church and state, but which is at variance with every principle of freedom and equality.

As equality is perhaps the most solid and permanent foundation of human happiness, which is favored and befriended by nature, it follows that the origin and cause of inequality; must arise partly from the artificial laws and regulations introduced by civilization, and partly by violence. This last the savage state is liable to as well as the civilized, but does not produce so great an inequality, there being fewer objects for plunder. The three principal sources of inequality, are conquests, monopoly and wages of civil and religious labor. The first is a barbarous stain both on savage and civilized life; the two last belong exclusively to civilization, and seem to have swallowed up the greatest part of the fruits of industry, as far as civilization has yet gone, being mostly in favor of the few and against the many. Modern wars have been less sanguinary and destructive, since religion ceased to be one of the objects, and will be still more rare and less desolating, when the great utility of freedom shall be understood, and may cease entirely when the great majority have knowledge enough to regulate their affairs according to their own interest. Wars are waged to indulge the pride, ambition and passions of the few, at the expense of the many. No majority of a nation ever gained by the most successful war; hence, as soon as the producers have good sense enough to avoid playing a losing game, wars must cease. It only requires a small share of useful knowledge in the great mass of producers, to be convinced that all complicated and monopolizing laws, must be contrary to their interest;—and a still smaller share of wisdom to find out, that the more the consuming class of political and religious laborers are paid, the harder they must work to maintain them; and the higher and more luxurious they are kept, the more careless they will be in their duties, and in their civilities to those who feed and clothe them. So that every kind of equality and economy is in favor of the producers, who beget all kinds of property; but a knowledge of their power, a knowledge of their utility, a conviction of the dependence that all other classes of society must have on them for every thing they eat, drink or wear, must be forced into them before they can be brought to that elevated state of independence and superiority which their great utility and merit entitle them to. But the difficulty is how to engraft on the minds of the working people, whose vital or sensorial power is exhausted in muscular exertions for existence; how to induce them to be occupied with the saving knowledge of taking care of themselves; and how to counteract that unjust gravitation of the civilized and social order, that have loaded them with oppression, in proportion to the weight of their own production.

Divide and conquer, is the maxim of all who are ambitious to rule. If those who live by the labor of the industrious, had not the address to enlist as soldiers, etc., a part of the working classes to aid them in subjecting the rest to their views and interest, their power and importance would soon finish, or rather it would never have commenced. So that the union of purpose ought to follow the union of interest. Before this necessary union can be effected, so as to act efficaciously, there must be some degree of individual independence and competence to resist the various temptations which the present inequality of property holds out to them, until their knowledge of the advantages of union, will enable the producers, to throw off the great burden which the artifice of civilization has imposed on them. There are two roads to competency, one is by ingenuity, hard labor, out-working their competitors; the other is the most simple, healthy, moral and agreeable, without any competition, struggle or exertion, by moderation in the indulgence of the physical wants and appetites, reducing them as near the essential as circumstances will admit, as their experience, if attended to, must have convinced them, that all beyond necessity runs to physical disease and moral inconvenience. By utilizing all their time, physically to augment their prosperity, and morally to increase their knowledge they will avoid excess, vice and immorality. Being the great independent majority of the society, they might regulate their own dress and fashions to suit their occupations, and cease to ape the whims and extravagance of the idle consumers, which in all states that civilization has yet reached, is the principal cause of the poverty and misery of the industrious producers. Some such prudence and economy are necessary to emancipate the present race of laborers; to draw them out of the mire of misery into which the contrivance and intrigues of church and state have plunged them. Without some pecuniary independence, they must find it difficult so to unite, as to benefit by the advantages which universal suffrage gives them without as strict and well organized a union, as the talents and abilities of their adversaries opposes to them, they can scarcely expect to carry a majority at the ballot boxes, on which depends the execution of their theories of education and every other reform they propose.

It is rather to be feared, that the working men and their friends have not sufficiently appreciated the advantages of possession; which is proverbially called *nine points of the law*. The nonproductive consumers have long had the control of both church and state, which has given them the bank and other monopolies, with the disposal of the whole circulation passing for money, as well as a great proportion of the fixed and mercantile property; all of which will be used to keep the majority at the ballot boxes, and even after they are in the minority they will try hard, as they have often done, to procure a majority in the legislature. It is in the nature of men and may be expected, that as soon as any fortuitous circumstances add to the property of the working man, his interest changes with his riches, and he is admitted into the ranks of the consumers, and participates in all their artificial privileges. So that the working people will not only be forced by union and perseverance to obtain a majority at the ballot boxes, but a proper selection and a constant change of their representatives, to retain that majority in the legislatures, making it a fixed rule not to expose the same man two sessions to temptation, by re-electing him, let his talents and abilities be ever so prominent. The certainty of being in power only once, will lessen the value of the place, and diminish in the same proportion, the intrigue and influence to get it; whilst the having new men to influence every session, will make it more difficult for the parties to carry their measures.

Had all the people who enjoy the advantages of electing their governors, sense enough to perceive the great advantage that would accrue to them, by never re-electing any one, and to oblige him to pay the taxes he laid, and obey the laws he made as a simple citizen all the rest of his life time, it would be one of the principal articles in all free constitutions, besides the advantage of a more equal division of power, and the having in addition to their party at home, a great many old governors to watch the conduct of the new. This was an article in the first French constitution, the most favorable to the governed that has since been made, and the legislature that made it, was of the most liberal and enlightened that has ever been put into power either before or since. Though it was the first time that the French people exercised their right of universal suffrage, it tends to prove that people if left to their own good sense, without being warped by intrigue, as all the subsequent elections in France were, will always go straight forward to their own interest; and being the great majority, for whose benefit all political associations are formed, they must be right. All the succeeding legislatures, after the places were known to be valuable and to be worth canvassing and intriguing for, made constitutions every one more and more against the people, who finally lost the interest they at first had in freedom, and left it first to their own military and afterwards to the allies. The Spanish constitution copied the first of the French, in that article, and I believe carried it further, so as to prevent militia officers from being re-elected, until they had served one year in the ranks. It is partly adopted by all the free states in South America, and has prevented many cabals and much military tyranny at elections, by the exclusion of the rulers that have the power, preventing them from using the influence of their office to secure their re-election.

ELECTORS DO NOT OBTAIN LAWS FAVORABLE TO THEIR OWN LIBERTY. PERVERSION OF LANGUAGE. OPPOSITE INTEREST OF THE ARISTOCRACY AND WORKING MEN. THE LITERARY FLATTERY OF THE ARISTOCRACY MUST CEASE.

January 5th, 1831.

The few elective governments that have yet existed, have followed the forms and practices of the hereditary monarchies and aristocracies, as nearly as the ignorance of their constituents would permit them. Power intoxicates all mankind, and like all intoxicating stimulants, requires the dose to be increased to produce the satisfactory effects. It is therefore as natural for a man once in power, to wish for more as for a drunkard to increase his dose of ardent spirits. It is not the fault of those whom the people choose for their rulers, to follow their nature in stretching the power of doing good to themselves or friends, as far as their constituents will permit, but it is the fault of the electors; who having the right of measuring out the dose of power, and the time it shall be allowed to act, are to blame if they make it too strong, or suffer it to act too long, for the feeble resistance men are capable to oppose, to what appears to them their interest. Power and patronage cannot be too much divided. Prevention is easier and better than cure, was one of the sayings of those who thought our federation was clothed with too much power of inteference with the independence of the states, as it was easy to increase that power if found too little; but difficult to curtail it if found too much, which future events may prove.

No electors who have yet enjoyed the great advantage of universal suffrage, have had the wisdom to make laws, rules or regulations, calculated to support and protect their political liberty and equality, on which their free system is founded, but have been carelessly contented, to allow these rulers to adopt the laws, rules and regulations, contrived and invented for the purpose of perpetuating the arbitrary, hereditary power for which alone they were made; of course in favor of the rich and those of hereditary privileges, by whom and for whom they were enacted; the millions of industrious producers having to do with them, only to pay the taxes and obey the laws, the greatest part of which only serves to keep them in a state of poverty and ignorance, as hewers of wood and drawers of water, administering by their labor to the luxury and extravagance of those who assume the power, either by force or intrigue, of governing them. Changing the words and leaving the things; proclaiming freedom, and surrounding it with arbitrary, complicated, intricate and litigious laws, which none but lawyers understand, whose fees are so exorbitant, that not one in a hundred can purchase any kind of justice; boasting of equality, and laying all the public burdens on the industrious producers by indirect taxation; granting exclusive bank monopolies to the favorite few, authorizing them to stamp in a few seconds, on a piece of paper not intrinsically worth one cent, as much value as many thousand laborers could produce in a year; these are the solid privileges of the domineering few, with which they keep the deluded many in subjection. These are the perpetual sources of inequality which open the flood-gates of immorality, vice and crime; adding to the misery of poverty, the great contrast of opulence and luxurious extravagance, pushing all into two extremes, the one above, and the other below character, equally injurious to the comfort and happiness of both.

Besides the evils which depreciate and demoralize the present generation, the constant grinding of real practice against imaginary theories, may in future change the original meaning of words, and turn "freedom" into *the interest of the aristocracy,* "equality" into *the superiority of the privileged orders,* etc., etc. Books like all other merchandize are made to please the customers, who have as yet chiefly belonged to the aristocracies in all countries. Laws are enacted for the benefit of the class of those who make them, who have been the still higher class of aristocracy in all nations. Speeches and orations are delivered for the benefit of those who make them; education has been confined to those who can pay for it, more for ornament than utility, more for pleasure than profit. It would be foolish in the millions of industrious producers to expect any other class of society to sacrifice their own immediate or apparent interest for their advantage; and unless they have spirit and knowledge enough to take the management of their own affairs, universal suffrage is a mere mockery, adding disgrace and insult to oppression, and nothing short of universal suffrage can secure the rights and interest of the millions. Heretofore both church and state have been devoted to the interest of the aristocracy, and as their interest is in direct opposition to the interest of the millions of industrious producers, all the principles, policy and arrangements of former governments, must be reserved, to suit the interest of the millions. It is the interest of the aristocracy to expend more than they are willing to pay, for which they mortgage the labor of the working people to raise a loan, which pays them a revenue besides saving them the advance of money; but it is the evident interest of the millions of producers, that the money expended by the rulers, should be raised within the year. It is the interest of the aristocracy to collect all the public revenue by indirect taxation on consumption, by which they put the greatest part of the public burdens upon the millions of producers, which keeps them poor and ignorant, fitter for the subjection they are kept in; but it is the evident interest of the millions of industrious producers, that all the public revenue should be raised by direct taxes on all property, each individual paying in proportion to the amount secured to him by the protection of government. It is the interest of the aristocracy to have the monopoly of law and justice, by a complicacy and intricacy beyond the reach of the knowledge or pockets of the millions; but it is the evident interest of the millions, to have their laws so simple and well defined, as to be perfectly well understood, as their rule of conduct. It is the interest of the aristocracy to have a monopoly of knowledge, by endowing universities and colleges, with the people's money, for the education of their own children; but it is the evident interest of the millions of producers, to have all their money expended on free and equal schools for the support and instruction of all children, gratis. It is the interest of the aristocracy to have a mercenary army to enforce their commands; but it is the evident interest of the millions of producers, for every citizen to be a soldier, when necessity requires them to defend their liberties and property, which cannot be well protected but by a well organized militia. The aristocracy gain honor and profit by war; but the millions only expend their blood and treasure, without the smallest hopes of any advantage. All the popular themes of history, poetry, romance, and most other literary productions, so much in praise of aristocracy, and so strongly advocating their interest, are so completely silent and neglectful of the interest, comfort and happiness of the millions of industrious producers, that the mere reasoning on their utility or claims on society, risks being condemned as heterodoxy, and not long since was scouted as an unattainable paradox.

Our revolution awakened the first claims the millions made of their rights. The French revolution reiterated with a voice of thunder; and now returns to the charge with the aid of a more perfect equality than has existed since the commencement of civilization, which bids fair to extend over civilized Europe, and in time may embrace, in its happy consequences, the habitable world. When equality shall have brought the two vicious extremities of society towards the centre of utility more by the elevation of the industrious producers, to that rank and respectability their usefulness merits, than by depressing or deteriorating the non-productive, consuming classes, opinions, principles and practices of society must change.— That literary flattering of the foibles, whims and caprices of aristocratic superiority, will scarcely be tolerated, but must be replaced by something more useful to the majority, whose interest will then prevail. The millions of literary productions, to amuse and kill the time of those classes, whose opulence has left them little other occupation, will then cease to be in demand, and the whole trade of book making will change, approaching nearer the useful, as the scale of utility becomes the measure of value; so that a revolution amongst men, makes a change necessary in the physical and moral situation of all animate and inanimate things.

ON PAPER MONEY AND BANKS.

March, 1834.

Bank notes and other representations of property, are ingenious contrivances for peaceably transferring property from those who circulate and take them at their nominal value into the pockets of those who make them, and have the use of them, whilst they have credit to pass for their supposed value. All kinds of national debts, bank and mercantile notes, and all the paper representations of property, are of modern invention; a substitute for the physical force of the ancients, to purloin the produce of the industrious many, for the use and benefit of the consuming, nonproductive few. Most ancient nations consisted of slaves and their masters; the first produced what the last wasted, destroyed or consumed; it was an order of society so long and completely under the control of the sword and the scourge, that both slaves and masters supposed it to be as natural as the rising and setting of the sun; and no other moral or physical machinery was requisite to transfer the comforts and happiness of the many into the luxury, extravagance and dissipation of the few, but the sword and the whip. No charter of exclusive privileges of banks, commerce, manufactories or corporation was necessary to secure to the hereditary Roman patricians the fruits of the soldier or husbandman: no financial schemes of national debts to accumulate the war expenses on the millions to the ninth and tenth generations; no paper representations of property to augment the great and destructive inequality, of property, knowledge and power, limited only by the number and extent of the paper mills. The influence of the ruling few are bounded within the extent of real property, the produce of labor. Whilst the state of civilization enable the combination of brute physical force to enslave the millions, there was no necessity to resort to diplomatic legerdemain, incomprehensible dogmas of future punishments—complicated, intricate and expensive laws—indirect taxation on consumption, etc., to keep mankind in a state of poverty and ignorance, and render them the more obedient slaves.

In modern times, since the invention of the compass, gun powder, printing, and the various applications of the power of steam, which tend to break down the monopoly of knowledge, and place men on a par, the great unequal division of the then existing natural property being insufficient to support the monopoly of knowledge and power in the hands of the few, recourse was had to artificial property, in paper representations, to counterbalance, if possible, the paper difference of knowledge through the printing press. The first was assignable specialities such as bonds, mortgages, etc. followed by such as could be rapidly transferred through an extensive circulation over the world as mercantile bills or notes, national debts, etc. and though last, not least, bank notes payable to bearer, which circulated extensively, with the swiftness of confidence, without responsibility or the smallest obstruction. These artificial paper representations of property, had a vast advantage over real natural property, in facilitating the accumulation of it in the hands of the few monopolizers. 1st. It was possessed by the few who had power or credit to circulate it, who reaped the benefit and profit as long as it passed for its nominal value. 2d. It was produced with little or no expense of labor or material. 3d. Its limits were only the number and extent of the paper mills. 4th. It was easily concealed or kept out of the risk of accidents. 5th. It gave the issuers and possessors the full command of the circulating medium to bring it to bear, on the smallest obstruction, the diffusion of useful knowledge might oppose to their oppressive monopolies. 6th. It increased without limits the too great inequality of property, knowledge and power, originating in plunder, rapine and conquest, and perpetuated by cunning and intrigue of rulers of people who have some pretensions to freedom.

In despotisms, when the extortions and regulations of priestcraft do not counteract the industry of the millions, the legalized hereditary masters seem contented with the portion that military plunder and conquest has given them, and make little or no exertions to increase their property at the expense of the millions. But in countries where the more general diffusion of useful knowledge, has awakened the millions to claim some of their unalienable rights, both the hereditary and monied aristocracy cordially join their utmost exertions to keep the millions poor and ignorant, and make up for the great loss of physical arbitrary power, paralized by that increase of knowledge.

Britain was the first nation partially emancipated from the physical force of feudal slavery, and has the most dexterously organized moral substitute for the loss of that coercive power. It consists of laws accumulated to such an incomprehensible state of complication, intricacy and expense, that the millions cannot obtain justice; that the exorbitant feeing of the lawyers is as oppressive as the bribing of the judges in despotisms, with this addition, that they are tantalized with the phantom of equality in the eye of the law, though as completely under the feet of hereditary and monied aristocracy, as the utmost despotism can place them. Nine tenths of the exorbitant indirect taxes are extorted from the millions, and grinds them to the dust. The privileged orders of church and state, revel on the fruits of the industry, talent and enterprize, that the small atom of freedom confers on the millions.

Holland, snatched from the sea, and depending on it, enjoyed some mercantile independence, burdened by excessive taxation, complicated laws and oppressive customs, which bore hard on the millions, arrived at the *ne plus ultra* of a moneyed aristocracy. Now impoverished by the weight of their taxes and loss of trade, they are dwindling down to the insignificance of their territory. France obtained a more perfect equality of property by their first revolution, than ever before existed in any civilized country, and the wreck of their assignates frightened them for a time from adopting proper representations of property. But the Bourbons, in their endeavor to re-establish the abuses of church and state, called in the help of the monied aristocracy, who are now beginning to fetter the nation with paper representations of property, in imitation of their neighbors across the channel. Time must decide if the division of property and knowledge will not prevent a moneyed aristocracy, founded on monopoly, etc., against which the national character of France, economy is powerfully opposed.

In the United States of America, the hard struggle for their independence and total bankruptcy of paper money, left society in greater equality of property than existed at the time in any other civilized nation. But retaining the intricate and expensive system of laws of the mother country, adopting their political forms, indirect taxation, with their strong propensity to mercantile ambition, avarice and money making, through the medium of banks and other monopolies, very soon laid the foundation of a great inequality of property and knowledge. This was augmented by the long enjoyment of a profitable neutral trade, inundating the Union with a flood of paper representations of property, unprecedented in any other country. Seven hundred and five chartered banks without limitation of dividend, issuing as much paper and paying as much dividend as their short sighted interest tempted them, was the cause of the failure of 160 of them and thirteen fraudulent bankruptcies. Land, the foundation of property and knowledge in the old world, the object of the ambition, avarice and exertion of all thickly inhabited countries, is so abundant and produces so little over the expense of cultivation

isher of all physical enjoyments; should make gold their god on this side of the Atlantic, as to baffle speculators in their attempts to monopolize it, may be one reason for the exaggerated quantity and quality of the paper representations of property. Being of easy fabrication and accumulation in the hands of the few monopolizers, little labor being required in its production, it circulates with its full force and influence to every quarter, for the purpose of bribery, buying every kind of living or dead matter, without the appearance of any thing but confidence, it augments immensely the great inequality of property, knowledge and power, and weighs heavily on the industrious producers, who are now beginning to see and feel the burden. The union, after having witnessed the making of 705 banks, has experienced the winding up of but one, from any other cause than that of bankruptcy, and the president of the United States deserves well of this country, for adding to that useful lesson, by teaching the people what it is to wind up another bank, which will be the cause of the closing of many more, for the lack of confidence to keep their paper kites afloat.

BANKS AND PAPER MONEY.

April 1, 1834.

"You cannot eat your cake and have it," is an old proverb and like all old maxims, the condensed wisdom of ages. In no part of the world have the inhabitants anticipated on the cake to be produced by the labor of the industrious millions, so much as in the United States of America, by paper representation of property not yet in existence, and perhaps never will be forthcoming to relieve one-half of the paper engagements. The data on which to ground the estimate of the paper finances of the Union are very sparingly given, because those in the secret are interested to keep back the truth from the public. We must therefore draw conclusions from the few facts which have been stated at different times, to come as near the probable state of paper money as possible, in hopes that some one possessed of more information, may state facts either in contradiction or corroboration of a statement so essential to the peace, comfort and happiness of society. It appears that the bank of the United States and the numberless branches, had issued notes, before the veto, to the amount of forty-two millions, and augmented that issue since twenty-eight millions, making in all, seventy millions in circulation. Supposing that each one of the 705 banks on an average had issued half a million, it would amount to 352 millions, the promissary notes, bonds, mortgages, and other paper representations of property at the same, 352 millions, and cannot be reckoned at much less, would make the sum of floating paper amount to 704 millions, waiting to be realized by the labor and industry of about twelve millions of people making about fifty-eight dollars for each man, woman and child in the Union.

After deducting their expenditure (which is much greater here than in enslaved countries,) seventy millions of surplus produce yearly is as much as can be produced by the labor of twelve millions of people, so that the whole labor and industry of the Union will require ten years to realize the anticipated paper representation of property, which has accumulated for half a century, augmented by the luxury, extravagance, and dissipation, introduced by the neutral trade. In countries where there is no hereditary monopoly or exclusive privileges, there are only two scales on which to measure man's station in society, wealth and merit. The first is external, evident to the senses; he that runs may read it; the second is a moral, modest quality, requiring research to find, and judgment to appreciate, and is opposed by the envy, self love and conceit of those around them. It is therefore in the order of things, that a nation, founding their social system on the hitherto unknown base of liberty and equality, should look up to the scale they best understood for the discrimination and value of men and things; should make riches the summun bonum of life, as the purveyor and furn- and multiply the representatives of him, like all idolaters, to

lish an office with pens, papers, etc. Their shares are much as great an extent as the ignorance of the industrious millions, who pay for it at last, will permit. To labor on either land or mechanism to produce only 100 millions of the 704 millions, would require 950,000 men, at a dollar per bushel of corn, and at ten cents, the price in the western country, would require 2,500,000 men. He must be ignorant of his own nature or that of his species, who expects that the influential few, the merchants and other nonproducers, can continue to enjoy the produce of the millions of laborers, by signing, in a few minutes, pieces of paper. Can it possibly surprise, any rational being, that this class of consumers should augment, as much as possible, their means of indulging in luxurious extravagance, by so simple and easy an operation as signing their names to slips of paper? To expect that the rulers of church and state, the bankers, merchants, lawyers, etc., will cease making this admirable machine of paper money for transferring, peaceably and quietly, the produce of the industrious millions into their own pockets, would be to expect an effect without a cause. Even the partial, unfair page of history, with all its sophistry cannot disguise the fact that the millions owe all the little they have got to their own exertions. That they must work out their own salvation, and that none but the millions can benefit the millions. So long as the many work for the maintenance of the few; so long as one class labor and produce all, and another dissipates and consumes, so long must poverty and misery be in exact proportion to luxury and extravagance, to the diminution of the peace comfort and happiness of the two extremes.

What has become of all the riches that has been so lavishly anticipated by the paper representations in our Union? may be a rational question for all those who have not observed the progress of luxury in our great mercantile cities, or who may be too young to compare the simplicity and economy during, and at the end of our revolution, to the present unprecedented expensiveness in every (species of luxury, extravagance and dissipation. Deduct what has been expended in canals, roads and other public works, (which perhaps would not have been prematurely made but with the aid of paper money) all the rest is put into the stomachs or squandered on the backs of the few, who rise early enough to put themselves at the head of church and state, to the great increase of all the diseases produced by physical excesses. Compare the situation of a shop-keeper in Philadelphia, (for there were few or no merchants,) at the time there was only a topsail yard arm schooner to hoist the flag on, at the first commencement of independence, and the bankrupts Rob. Morris and Blair Maclenahan, were the richest men in the Union. Compare those honest times (when there was not as much crime in the whole Union as there is now in a single town,) with the present luxury, extravagance and dissipation of our merchants and consuming classes, in all the great overgrown towns of our Union.— This will account for the expenditure of the immense anticipation of property by paper representations, and prove that the production has not kept up with the consumption.

Now that one of the 705 banks is threatened to be forced to wind up its affairs, by a refusal to renew its charter of irresponsibility, the whole mass of the consuming classes, who are to benefit by the discounts, is in a ferment; and one bank curtailing their discounts, has caused the failure of a great many of the principal houses in all our commercial towns. A president and twelve directors of one of these money coining machines, to be revenged on the president of the Union, by rapidly curtailing their discounts, have bankrupted their customers and endangered perhaps half the capital of their stockholders. This rapid withdrawing of the aid which commerce depended on, has swept confidence from under paper representations, and has reduced the prices of property that had augmented on its faith nearly 50 per cent.: a proof that the fictitious value of it, depended on the food of artificial paper, with which the country was inundated, by 705 coining establishments without limits or responsibility.

It only requires the analysis of the origin of most of the banks, to explain the above, beginning in iniquity. A few speculators, in any of our cities or towns perceiving the profit of an exclusive privilege of coining, club together, and estab-

below par for each share would be liable for all the debts; and the most knowing, is sent to the legislature to solicit a charter; it is brought before the legislature and perhaps thrown out by a majority of fifteen or twenty, to whom this cunning agent applies by giving them shares at par or under, assuring them, if they grant the charter, the shares forty or fifty per cent., when they may sell out and pocket the profit: the charter is granted, directors appointed, who are principal owners of the shares; declare a dividend of ten to twenty per cent., raise the shares to forty or fifty per cent. above par, when the knowing ones sell out to as many dupes as they can make, like the South Sea bubble in England.

The general mode of forming mercantile firms, accounts for the great number of bankruptcies. Three or four clerks leap over the counter, form a copartnership, obtain discounts at six or eight banks of the town to the amount perhaps of $100,000, on which they trade. Having obtained a capital without working for it, or having any experience of its value, they dash into the market, twenty of them where there is only business for one, raise the article fifteen or twenty per cent., above what it will sell for at the place of consumption, lose the greatest part of their bank capital in three or four years, which, the bank finding out, insists on further security at every renewal, gets mortgages on any real property they may have speculated on, assignments on ships and cargoes they may have at sea, and then lets them fail by refusing to renew their notes. The banks get all, and the other creditors, whom the bank credit enabled them to borrow from, do not get a cent in the dollar. Neither the bank speculators, nor the merchants' clerks are to blame, for following their legal interests in endeavoring to better their condition. The legislators, for betraying their confidence their constituent placed in them, by sacrificing the public interest to individual cupidity, they and they only are guilty of a breach of trust, honor and honesty, which cannot be radically reformed until those who produce, have the distribution of the wealth and power they have brought into existence. This is one of the most melancholy effects of the want of responsibility in an aggregation of power. The lawyers are the only persons who benefit by these misfortunes, which may perhaps induce the people to abolish all suits for debt and lessen their profits on the losses of others.

BANKS AND PAPER MONEY ARE SUBSTITUTES FOR DESPOTISMS IN A FREE GOVERNMENT.

April 9, 1834.

Confidence in all species of paper representations of property, is the attendant of all kinds of liberty, and the drag which hinders the progress of freedom from benefiting the millions as much as it ought. It is the principal machine which enables the knowing few to enslave the ignorant many. The slight of hand which changes *meum* into *tuum*, and the art which realizes the deceptions and quackery of church and state. Despotisms, like Russia and Austria, force the circulation of paper money; but deprived of confidence, its depreciation is so rapid as to become a curse to the issuers, by lessening their revenue in the ratio of its depreciation, and requiring constant and accumulating issues, ending in bankruptcy, which equalizes property tending to the equalization of knowledge and power; a consequence as injurious to their interest, as it is unforeseen by the contrivers. But the paper representations of property, founded on the confidence attached to any kind of liberty, is supported, 1st, by the knowing ones who make it, circulate it, and get the use of it; 2ndly, by all the rulers of church and state, who find it a convenient machine for increasing their ration at the expense of others; 3dly, all merchants, traders and chapmen who acquire a capital without working for it; 4thly, the whole unproductive consumers, who live more easily and luxuriously, on the produce of others' labor, by the facility of transferring such anticipations of wealth. From which it would appear that as soon as any people have been so fortunate, by any concurrent circumstances, as to emancipate themselves from the despotism of physical military force, the paper mills and coining pressses of paper representations of property, are set to work, as a substitute for the loss of physical force, which could no longer tyranize over the portion of useful knowledge diffused amongst the millions.

Holland, with a dense population restricted within narrow limits, found the necessity of extending her trade far beyond her own boundaries; benefited by the portion of liberty necessary to commercial speculations, she extended paper representations of property in proportion as her little liberty afforded confidence to support it, and was the first after the independent republics of Genoa, Venice and Florence, to fund a national debt, and mortgage the produce of the industry of future generations for the premature expenses she had incurred, and by the exorbitant taxes to pay the yearly interest to the nonproductive consumers, oppressed the industrious producers, and originated much poverty and misery. King William took with him the funding system, with other paper representations of property from Holland to England, where it was sown in a fertile soil producing millions fold, increasing with the false confidence the people had in their House of Commons, inundated the country with poverty, until the pauperism of Britain was nearly equal to that of all Europe, and their poor rates nearly double the amount of their whole revenue before the adoption of the funding system. It has now become too heavy for all the industry, energy and enterprise of the millions to support and must tumble into the exhausted vacuum it has made under itself. Great will be the fall thereof; and the crash will frighten confidence from under the paper representations of all nations, who viewing the national debt as the cause of their activity, energy and industry, as the scourge applied to their backs, forcing them to that quantity of extra labor. They are blind to the real cause, the atom of personal freedom the British enjoyed for 150 years, whilst their surrounding neighbors were slaves. All are attempting to follow their example, an *ignus fatuus*, which will lead them astray from the direct road.

When the colonists crossed the Atlantic, free from the trammels of the hereditary aristocracy, and privileged orders of church and state, it was natural for them to adhere to their strong propensity for the creation of a monied aristocracy, the only substitute their influential rulers could get for the hereditary power of the mother country.— And though their distance from the corruption of the old world, and the broad basis of their representation, checked their propensity to wars and consequent accumulation of a national debt, yet the strength and superiority of their mutual confidence, arising from the unprecedented superiority of their freedom, laid the foundation of an immense superstructure of artificial paper representations of property through the medium of chartered banks, monopolies and corporations. These have been as yet tolerated by the industrious producers, from their ignorance of the effects such a fraudulent paper circulation has, as a hindrance to their peace, comfort, and happiness, by increasing immensely the great inequality of property, knowledge and power, the nearly equal division of which, is indispensable to freedom. The question of rechartering the bank of the United States has brought into action the omnipotence of universal suffrage; an experiment the conseqnence of which will not be lost on the common sense of the millions, on this side of the Atlantic.

The first ray of freedom which enlightened the darkness and ignorance of modern Europe, in the mercantile republics of Genoa, Venice and Florence, introduced national debts, banks, and other paper representations of property, as the only materials fit for the construction of a monied aristocracy, that could take the place of the physical force formerly maintained to enslave mankind. The same cause produced the same effect in the republic of Holland, a nation that could only arise to any degree of respectability by commerce; their merchants wrought with the same tools as the Italian republics, and transported the Art to England with their king, whence it was transferred to this side of the Atlantic with their colonists. Here territory, almost without limits, gave room for a degree of independence unknown before, increasing the force and intensity of mutual confidence, attached as a drag on freedom, in the ratio of liberty and equality which the wisdom of men have yet been able to bring into practice; so that paper representations of property have kept pace, and gradually increased with that confidence in the security which can only be given by some degree of freedom both of the person and the property.

When the ignorance of the millions enables church and state to keep them in complete subjection, by the physical force of the whip and bayonet, there is no necessity for the cunning machinery of banks or paper money, nor is there the smallest confidence to support them. There are therefore neither banks nor paper representations in Spain, Italy, Turkey, Persia, Indostan or China. Russia and Austria owe their small national debt, to the confidence attached to the mercantile faith of Holland and Britain; the forced circulation of their much depreciated paper money is a proof of the total want of confidence in those despotisms.

France, by her revolution, acquired a greater division of property than ever existed in any civilized country, and must be followed by an equal division of knowledge and power. To counteract this, the elder and younger branches of the Bourbons have quintupled their national debt, and given every encouragement to the establishment of a monied aristocracy, to protect despotism. In place of the old hereditary aristocracy, worn out physically, morally and financially, they have founded banks, monopolies, and corporations, which will inundate France with paper representations of property, in imitation of their rivals on the opposite side of the channel. This will cover the land with paupers, by first accumulating property in the hands of the few and afterwards monopolizing knowledge and power, which is tyranny.

But it is probable the great division of property will have divided knowledge and power, in time to prevent the French people suffering the misery and wretchedness attending the great inequality of property, knowledge and power.

In the small German states, knowledge is perhaps more equally divided, than in any of the other nations of Europe, and may check the growth of a monied aristocracy after their emancipation from physical despotism; but their divided geographical position gives too much advantage to the great powers that surround them, who keep them under a military despotism, which prevents the growth of that confidence, necessary to the support of paper representations of property. So that division into small states, which very much tends to the division of knowledge, is contrary to the division of power; but when by a strict union they conquer their freedom, they will most probably make a good use of it.

BANKS AND PAPER MONEY.

April, 11*th* 1834.

If an equal division of property, knowledge and power are undoubtedly essential to the enjoyment of any degree of freedom, comfort or happiness to the millions, (as I have endeavored to prove in many of my former essays,) it must follow of course that any law, custom, or monopoly, that tends to counteract that natural propensity to equality, must be equally inimical to the happiness of the millions. The greatest obstruction to these properties of men finding their natural level, has been the tyranny of church and state. During the barbarous ignorance of antiquity, the physical force of conquest was sufficient to derange the natural equality, and perpetuate the great inequality of property, knowledge and power, the source and origin of nine tenths of the miseries and poverty of mankind. Since the diffusion of useful knowledge has guaranteed the millions from being frightened by the bloody tragedies of antiquity, the modern farce has been varied by the perpetual change of the actors—taxation, patronage, privileges, monopolies, etc. etc., acting on the great theatre of diplomacy by the most expert slight of hand men, selected from all the civilized nations in close union and strict alliance against the progress of knowledge and freedom. This general and universal union of despotism and oppression has conciliated the petty feuds and national antipathies of the French and British, the Danes and Sweedes, and the Germans, and Italians, which kept them like fighting cocks, to be pitched against one another at the command of their rulers.—This national hatred is now consolidated into the force and cunning of all the civilized governments against the peace, freedom and happiness of the (as yet but half civilized) millions. One of their last farcical representations was begun by protocols instead of prologues on the Dutch and Belgian stage, and now occupies the various German, Spanish, Portuguese and Turkish theatres, protected from the interference of the people by an immense military establishment, maintained by exorbitant taxation, and paper representation of property in the form of national debts, etc. The old state tricks of divine right, public good and patriotism, will not bear the light of reason, that is spread so generally amongst even the conscript soldiers, who begin to reason in place of obeying; so that the chief actors of the holy alliance, are at bay, not being able to conjure up deceptions to dupe the multitude. Formerly the keeping up a rival hatred between two neighboring nations, was sufficient to cool the revolutionary fever by drawing off any quantity of blood, the chief physicians of the people ordained, and kept them always at daggers drawing so as to prevent any union of interest; but this is now absorbed in the universal dispute between the interest of the producers and that of the consumers, of the industrious and the idle, the governors and governed, and only requires the union of action of the many against the few, as has always existed of the few against the interest of the many, to decide who shall rule.

National debts and other fictitious paper representations of property, form a broad foundation on which may be erected every possible abuse, which the ingenuity of either church or state can invent. The British nation has carried that fabrication to a much greater extent, than ever it was before in any part of the globe, and are now reaping the fruits in double the poverty, misery and crime that ever existed in any other country of the same extent on earth. It has been long a government of patronage, poised upon the number of placemen, pensioners, and those who depend on the state either by dividends in the funds or otherwise, so dextrous has been the management that they have hitherto avoided all explosions or violent revolutions, principally by not overloading that safety valve the printing press, which has induced the elder and younger branches of the Bourbons to follow in their footsteps as far as to quintuple their national debt in time of peace, augmenting the other factitious paper representations of property, and, at the same time, increasing the patronage of the crown to such an extent, as to include every one who clothed with the smallest authority, and all their dependants and creatures. But their loading injudiciously that safety valve, the printing press, may be the cause of another revolution, exploding without any warning. The facility with which the British government has accumulated an immense national debt, and an equally exorbitant taxation, has induced all the other governments of Europe, to follow their example, and increase their national debts as far as their credit will permit, and has converted the civilized world into an arena of stock-jobbers, with the emperor Rothschild at their head.

In our Union the universal suffrage has checked the ambition of the few from making war at the expense of the many, which has equally diminished the cause of all national debt. But the ambitious propensity of enjoying power, which is the more easily obtained by establishing a monied aristocracy, has induced the rich and the rulers to form an immense foundation of paper representations of property, as the only possible support to any species of aristocracy in a country whose institutions are founded on liberty and equality. The federal government has granted an exclusive monopolizing charter to a bank, to coin any quantity of representations of property and divide all or any part of them by way of profits, leaving nothing in their vaults to pay their debts, without being authorized by the constitution. The states of the Union have granted 705 monopolizing bank charters, with authority to issue as many representations of property as their interest may dictate, and to divide all or any part of them by way of profits; though such monopolies were expressly prohibited by the constitutions of half the states, and contrary to the spirit of them all, (as I have before endeavored to prove,) facilitating much the rapid promotion of mercantile clerks and associations of persons who passed from behind their desks and counters into a capital by bank discounts, without knowing its value, by working for it, or the proper use to make of it by experience; thereby injuring the regular trade, by raising every kind of produce far above its intrinsic value, and causing every now and then a lamentable crop of bankruptcies. This immense circulation of paper representations of property by banks, added to the mercantile and other anticipations of realities have been rolling on like a snow ball for nearly half a century, like stimulants to the stomach of drunkards requiring a stronger dose to keep up the effect, until the amount is equal to the surplus production of the labor of the industrious millions for at least ten years in the whole Union. This inordinate borrowing from posterity has introduced a corresponding luxury and extravagance with their constant attendants, poverty, misery and crime, unknown to our Union before the exaggerated introduction of paper representations of property. All these accumulating evils suggested the idea of giving some check to the rapidly increasing contradictions and oppositions to our simple, equal and free institutions, by President Jackson putting his veto on the renewal of the United States bank charter, in which he was supported by an immense majority of the people at his re-election.

This was a return to the true principles of the constitution, (which did not authorise the federal government to grant bank charters,) by refusing them a privilege which the federation had no right to grant, and the bank had less right to expect, even if it had been constitutional; the principles of freedom and equality prohibited it being lavished on one set of favorites. Any impartial observer witnessing the rage, malignity, violence and hatred, employed by the bank directors, their friends, favorites and customers would suppose that the government, in place of doing their duty in protecting their constituents from the arbitrary usurpation of a purse proud faction reveling on public property, would suppose that the government by military force were violating all justice and reason, by seizing on the property and incarcerating the persons of all who belonged to that unconstitutional establishment called the United States bank. No despot in Europe ever supported his pretensions to divine right, or any batch of the privileged orders of hereditary nobility, their claims of invested rights, more violently than this upstart monied aristocracy demanded the privilege of monopolizing the circulating medium of a country of liberty and equality. It is a lesson to the common sense of the American people that will not be forgotten: it will teach the power of union even to the insignificant few, and lead them to reflect on the immense power of combination by universal suffrage at the ballot-boxes, where no bayonets dare interfere: and proves the vast advantage over the trades unions of the old world, may thank their good fortune that a check has been put to the forging of chains by means of paper, before it went so far as to swallow up all the independence of the country.

BANKS AND PAPER REPRESENTATIONS OF PROPERTY.

April 23, 1834.

By a statement of the bank of England's accounts in the Times, of the 19th of September, 1831, the bank owed 24,200,000 sterling and had only 23,900,000 to pay with: a deficit of 300,000, owing to their continuing the dividends of ten per cent. on their capital of 14,553,000, which for the time amounted to 6,580,850, whilst their profits, at 900,000 a year for the same time, amounted only to 900,000 a year, or 4,050,000, leaving 2,498,850, paid out of the capital; so that the directors had contrived to get rid of 4,500,000 of the capital of the bank between 1819 and 1831. Further, they had only 3,000,000 of specie in their vaults to pay 18,000,000 of notes in circulation. In 1823 they bought 585,740 annuities which cost 13,089,419 payable in several instalments, the last falling due in July 1828, and in case of war the said annuities would not be worth more that 7,500,000. The bank of England is under more cautious management than any other bank of discount in Europe, excepting the bank of France, which was judiciously organized by Bonaparte. The banks generally in Europe will not discount any wind paper, and the bank of England makes it a rule, when they discover any such paper, to reject all with any of the names that were on said paper for six months, to ascertain whether they trade on false capital or not. Their directors were selected from retired merchants, who had no occasion for discount themselves, and of course better able to be impartial in the distribution of loans by discount to others, which they give only to the security of bills drawn for property sold and delivered, by anticipating the payment of real transactions sixty days, and are strongly opposed to furnishing capital to any kind of merchants to trade on. Their dividends are likewise limited. If notwithstanding so many precautions and guarantees against abuses, the directors of the bank of England have sacrificed the public good to the interest of the stockholders who elect them, by dividing so much of their capital by way of profits, it is a convincing proof that no managers of any establishment, not responsible or interested in the ultimate result of profit or loss, can be depended on for the faithful performance of their duties. Banking in Europe is conducted by those who have money to lend, but with us by those whose circumstances oblige them to borrow. This is a sufficient cause for all the great abuses, which have been, and must continue in all the 600 banks of our Union.

Besides the immense difference in the circumstances of the directors, the rules and regulations are all contrary to what the prudence and experience of our forefathers in Europe, have judged necessary to insure the success of such establishments. Our banks discount all kinds of wind paper, made for the purpose, without the security of any real transaction of property sold and delivered, and they renew the same by replacing the old with new bills, to continue the false capital on which their customers trade. There exists no limitation of dividends. This allows them to divide the capital by way of profits, which must have been the case with the 165 banks already failed. They have no correct register of their notes in circulation, but receive them and pay them away without a check, at the risk of paying forgeries. Nor do they ascertain by a sale the value of property they get for debts, but let it stand for the debt, though it would not sell for the amount; by which irregularity they cannot make allowance for their losses. The facility with which the legislatures grant charters and renew the old, prevents the people from knowing the consequences of winding up the affairs of a bank. The only one yet forced to finish without a bankruptcy was the old bank of the United States, which did not pay much more than the principal to the stockholders in fifteen years. Had the different state legislatures given their constituents the information of the winding up of the 600 banks they had licensed, the people of the Union would have been much better judges of the nature and utility of such banks, and might have avoided part of the injurious consequences that may result from the finish of 600 banks, authorized to trade on such different and contrary regulations to any that have heretofore existed. What may be the result is in the womb of time, but certainly it would have been more advantageous to the public, to have had the practice of the final result of some, before so many had been legitimate.

Banks, like all the contrivances of church and state, and particularly all paper representations and anticipations of property without labor, are all for the benefit of the few, who have the exclusive use of them, and at the expense of the laboring many, who alone can produce the property to realize them, and are therefore the cause of an unnatural and degrading inequality, producing vice and luxury at one end, and misery and crime at the other end of civilization, and as such are the greatest enemies to the freedom, happiness and independence of mankind. When a bank receives the exclusive privilege of stamping on paper, intrinsically worth only a few cents, the value of four or five millions of dollars, which while said paper is made the remuneration of labor to that amount, the bank acquires the force and power of 2000 laborers, without any other trouble or fatigue than signing in a few minutes scraps of paper, and when, by the mismanagement and extravagance of the directors and their customers, they are unable to pay their engagements, the industrious workman, who had received their notes in payment, loses the price of his labor, without at any time deriving any advantage from the bank during its solvency, but adding to the number of the nonproductive classes his labor is forced to maintain. For evidence of this, see the situation of the working classes in Holland and Britain, which were the first contrivers and are still the largest circulators of paper representations.

While the monopoly of property in the hands of the few was restricted to the produce of labor, there was some limits to the oppression of the working classes: but since the ingenious aristocracy of church and state, have extended the bounds of artificial representations of property to infinity, the weight of the burden on the shoulders of the industrious millions, is augmented in proportion by the paper representations, in the form of national debts, bonds and securities of public bodies, great part of which are never realized. Mercantile and bank notes pretending to be the representations and anticipations of the produce of labor, a great deal more of which are never realized, than their advocates, who live by their circulation, are willing to admit, and all profits of trade are blazoned forth in exaggerated terms, to give more credit to those engaged in it, whilst losses and bankruptcies of merchants, banks and other corporations, are buried in oblivion as soon as possible, for fear of exposing the truth of their nature and insufficiency, to the millions, whose labor must pay for all losses, as the only source from which property can be derived.

It is a singular coincidence, which goes far to prove the destructive effects of paper representations, that Switzerland, the only government of the old world that has any claim to representation, should be free from all the burdens and injustice of the national debt; without any banks or circulation of paper representations or anticipations of the produce of labor: and though a country from its elevated situation and the nature of its soil, incapable of feeding its population with its own produce, and consequently one of the dearest countries to live in, yet from its prudence, care and economy, which ought to be the characteristics of all true democracies, the people are governed at an expense of one dollar per head, whilst the rest of the European nations, where they can live for at least one third less for the necessaries of life, the expenses incurred by these governments are from three to thirty dollars per head of man, woman and child. The dearest are those who have the greatest amount of paper representations in national debts, bank notes, and other circulating paper. From all this it would appear that the wretchedness of the working classes, is in the ratio of the quantity of artificial paper representations of property, circulated and supported for the benefit of the few at the expense of the many, and that the oppression of the industrious millions is aggravated by the weight of this factitious property, in proportion to the number of idlers who live on it, increasing the toil and labor of the producers who maintain them as well as every other class of society. Full nine-tenths of the ingenious stratagems of both church and state, have been occupied in mystification, sophistry and deception. To prevent this evident truth being understoood by the millions, which constitutes the arcanum and complicated difficulty of governing nations by the reverse principles of their true interest, which would cease if the interest of the majority ruled with truth and utility for the test of all actions, public and private.

It is natural that a system, founded on hereditary aristocracy, should strive to extend the foundation of their artificial powers and privileges, by increasing the poverty, ignorance and slavery of the millions, on which alone depend their superiority and authority. But that a system based on liberty and equality, guaranteed by universal suffrage should tolerate such usurpations of power and approaches to tyranny, presupposes a state of apathy, indolence and ignorance bordering on madness. It is *fe lo de se*, in the destruction of all the materials of freedom, comfort and happiness. Those who were born and educated under the colonial bondage, may indulge in their ancient prejudices so far as to copy the laws and customs which have till now supported the aristocracy of old mother Britain, but the young *eleves* of our revolution, will most probably adopt some system of politics, laws and commerce more congenial with the knowledge of the day, and not continue to grovel in the ancient abuses of feudalism.

PROGRESS OF CIVILIZATION.

April 30, 1834.

Considering the great portion of the earth's surface yet peopled with ignorance, it is consoling to humanity to observe how many nations are emerging from the simple savage state, to a state of civilization, perfect in proportion to the diffusion of useful knowledge, that has spread through the surrounding nations, and to remark with what rapidity they pass over all the intermediate stages, which nations as well as individuals make when left to themselves, to graft on the simplicity of their primitive state, the perfections which the modern inventions bring to their doors from all quarters of the civilized world. There are two centres of civilization in the southeast of Asia, New Holland and Indostan, from which will emanate the perfection of European improvements. The first has already humanized New Zealand and other islands of the Pacific, for when knowledge is to arrive from abroad, islands acquire it the quickest. Barbarous Africa is innoculated in three or four places, the Cape of Good Hope, Algiers, Egypt, and on the west coast of the steam navigation of the Niger. Civilization will be introduced into the interior. Already has the experiment of the progress of improvement, unfettered by the privileges of hereditary aristocracy, been advantageously exhibited by the unprecedented prosperity of the United States of America, and confirmed by the immense progress made by the free states of South America, in the short time of their emancipation from a foreign despotism.

Much of the disadvantage of a slow improvement in civilization arises from the selfish propensity of mankind to monopolize inventions for the benefit of the few, who may have first stumbled on them, which gives them an interest in preventing the propagation of more perfect principles. This may be proved in the difficulty of introducing all mechanical, physical or moral melioration, with the obstacles that a great number of previous imperfect habits and modes of action attach to every thing new. This is more particularly evident in all mora. changes of church and state, which are perhaps thousands of years behind physics. The accumulation of property in possession of the few, has rolled on like a snow ball with the progress of civilization as far as it has yet gone, producing the immense inequality in the moral and physical state of our species, the cause of most of the misfortune and wretchedness of mankind. It has hitherto urged the whole population into the two extremes of poverty and wealth, starvation and luxury, oppressing the many to feed and maintain the extravagance of the few, dividing society into producers and consumers, the toil, labor and oppression of the first, being in the exact ratio to the indulgence and extravagance of the latter, constituting a contradiction in the two great classes of society, a jar in the social order, which can only be reconciled by a more equal division of property, knowledge and power, which the result of the French revolution, seems to prove must be the consequence of the present changes in church and state.

In the present wide diffusion of useful knowledge, with the quick circulation of it on the wings of steam to the utmost limits of land and sea, distance and time are almost annihilated. The obstructing boundaries of seas and mountain ridges, vanish before the velocity of intercourse. The nations all round the globe benefit by the ingenuity of the more civilized people, in the shortest possible time, and the most savage must be soon brought on a par, in the useful arts and sciences, with the most refined. The senses, through which come all our positive and useful knowledge, are as acute, if not more so, in savages, and their power of imitation is greatly superior to those who have their senses blunted by the luxury and indulgences of civilization, and nothing could root in them in a state of barbarous ignorance, but that the acquired knowledge of each individual dies with him and is lost to his posterity; but placed in the vortex of the circulating knowledge of civilized countries, by the aid of a rapid communication, their progress will far exceed all former calculations founded on analogy.—First, because of their equality of knowledge and approximation to equality, of property, they all start fair, unimpeded by exclusive privileges or hereditary monopolies. Secondly, the field of experiment, though uncultivated, is unincumbered by the blundering inventions and machinery of a half civilization; the introduction of more perfect machinery is not opposed by the interest of those who live by the use of those less perfect; the adoption of simple and well defined laws is not obstructed by a host of lawyers, who live on intricacy and litigation, the growth of centuries of misrule; the means of communication by canals and rail roads are on the most improved principles that have been tested by the experience of the most civilized nations; all their useful arts and sciences, are grafted on the perfection, the civilized world has arrived at, by a thousand years of industry, ingenuity and experience. The principles and practice of their barbarous religion will be obliterated by the smallest ray of reason, which will be sufficient to guard them against the follies of foreign ones. The instruction of their schools will go directly to utility, and the quackery of the dead languages, and equally dead antiquity will not be the model of their rising prosperity, as they will naturally imitate those from whom they have received the most useful examples. It will be a new field sown with foreign seed; a new house furnished with articles of the newest invention and most perfect construction.

Hitherto the printing press has been the advocate of aristocracy, the only class that could pay for its support. Most of its publications were made to please its paymasters, either as history, poetry, romance, etc. Of course their foibles were flattered, their vices extenuated, and their crimes defended under the mask of patriotism and public good. A new light has been thrown lately on the lot of humanity, and the printing press maintains the cause of truth and utility. The Penny Magazine, and half a hundred such cheap publications to the number of 200,000 copies in an edition, are read by many millions, diffusing useful knowledge to all the ramifications of the British empire, through the whole of which they are sold at the same price, the editors paying the expense of carriage; and the Connaisance Utile and many other two *sous* publications distribute 200,000 copies in an edition to the utmost extent of the French empire. These works contain condensed, plain and well defined truths in all kinds of useful and practical knowledge without any mixture or sophistry, declamation, wordy eloquence, party misrepresentation or fulsome flattery, to either the political or religious rulers of the day, and prove that there are many millions of readers capable of estimating the value of such useful information, and that the cheapness of the price by the unprecedented extent of the editions, is sufficient to repay the editors, notwithstanding the shameful tax of £70 sterling on the paper used weekly in the British publications.

Much unoccupied property, in all savage or barbarous nations, tempts the surplus population of civilized and populous countries to emigrate, who will now, from the general diffusion of useful knowledge, carry with them a mass of information, which will make the place of their residence a focus of instruction, they will benefit all the surrounding nations. Formerly the emigrants carried abroad a load of religious, political and local prejudices, which retarded the progress of civilization in the countries where they settled, but now every migrating laborer will be capable of diffusing more useful and practical knowledge than could formerly be communicated by the learned professor.

One of the most correct modes of judging of the future state of our species, would perhaps be to register the progress of the useful arts and sciences in those parts of Africa and Indostan, where civilization has been engrafted on the simplicity of savage life, and calculating the future progress, by the past, on a scale of geometrical progression. Perhaps the improvements introduced into the free states of South America, would be as good a criterion as any, to form a tolerable exact opinion of what change can be made by the intercourse of a high civilization, with a half barbarous people, who had acquired many of the vices with scarcely any of the advantages of civilization. But these ideas are consoling for the millions only; to the few who depend on the ignorance of the many for the abundant supply of their food, clothing, luxuries and indulgencies, such doctrines are destructive to their hopes and are ridiculed as Utopian and as appertaining to the millenium. They assure us that scarcely an European will leave the country with a fortune; and that the barbarous people must be hundreds of years in arriving at any degree of civilization: from which opinions I differ as widely as possible.

PROGRESS OF REVOLUTIONS. THE BANKING SYSTEM AND EFFORTS OF CHURCH AND STATE, WILL NOT SUCCEED IN DESTROYING FREEDOM.

July 14, 1834.

It is a curious coincidence, that in all civilized nations at present, there exists great discontents, and in many places open rebellion against the ancient establishment of church and state. Considering how peaceably the millions have submitted to the arbitrary despotism of the hereditary rule of kings and nobles under the tyranny of church and state, from the most ancient epochs of history, down to the last half century; how the interest of the many was so completely sacrificed to the interest of the few; it seems evident that such a change in public opinion must be founded on an equally universal change in the knowledge and experience, physical and moral, of mankind. It is discovered that the immense inequality of property, knowledge and power, constituted the interest of the few, in direct opposition to the interest of the many, and facilitated the monopoly of all three by the few; an unnatural order of things, which must be reversed by a more equal division of property, knowledge and power.

Most of the improvements in physics preceded the melioration of morals some thousand years, yet the late mechanical inventions, by subjugating brute matter to the aid of the laborer, have elevated the industrious producers, nearer to a par with their former masters, the indolent consumers. That the invention of the steam boat and rail road, which almost annihilating space and time, should remain rooted to the soil like a cabbage, was impossible. That the rapidity and facility of communication would reduce knowledge as well as every thing else, nearer a level, was the natural consequence of the reaction of the physical on the moral world. In both ancient and modern history, the physical inventions were almost limited to the arts of conquest, war and butchery; now that utility is considered, moral and physical improvements will go hand in hand, and reciprocally aid each other.

The first government where the representatives of the people, by universal suffrage, assembled to form a political association, conformable to the common sense and knowledge of the day, was that of the United States of America.— The unprecedented prosperity exhibited by this experiment, astonished the world, and awakened a desire in all people to follow their example. The French revolution was an attempt to copy the freedom, that had been attended with such great benefit, but was partly marred by the coalesced armies of civilized Europe. Enough was left, however, to produce another revolution, which was likewise spoiled by a hereditary executive. Yet the remains of both revolutions, most probably will be sufficient in time, to produce an elective system of universal suffrage. The Spanish revolution was put down by the gold and bayonets of the French Bourbons, but enough of the principles of freedom was left to be hatched, even under the icicles of a despotism into a representative system. All the blood and slaughter of the allied enemies, only tend to spread the spirit of freedom and to lead the millions to know their interest, and the power they have to assert their rights.— So thoroughly are the despots of Europe convinced that physical force cannot coerce moral conviction, that they have not dared to go to war for the last twenty years: but trust to the sophistry of diplomacy, a war of words without meaning, which they endeavor to have all in their favor by destroying the liberty of the press; a childish farce that might have deceived the grand fathers of the present generation, but in the extended diffusion of useful knowledge, all these slight of hand tricks, only expose the weakness of their cause, and that to their great armies, maintained at a vast expense and taxation, they owe the precarious authority they still retain. Those numerous armies exhaust their resources, increase their national debt beyond the ability of their subjects to bear, prepare a bankruptcy, the fraudulent way of equalizing property, while the number of disciplined men facilitates a physical revolution, when the spread of knowledge has trained society for the change.

Britain was one of the European nations, emancipated from the slavery of the feudal system, though their powerful hereditary aristocracy retained their barbarous laws, which secured to them their exclusive privileges. Mercantile confidence, the result of their emancipation and their insular situation laid the foundation of an erroneous moneyed aristocracy, national debts to an unprecedented amount, and other paper representations of property, beyond what had existed before in any other country. The weight of such an enormous load on the laborers, pushed industry into the extreme of production, whilst the unfair indirect taxation ground down the millions into poverty and ignorance. A change in public opinion, to the conviction of the impossibility of supporting such extravagance, produced the reform in parliament, raising the elective nearer on a par with the hereditary power; with the rapid diffusion of knowledge by the great improvement in printing cheap books, carrying instruction to the smallest ramifications of society on the wings of steam; a state of things that must proceed in a geometrical progression. Whether the powerful moneyed and hereditary aristocracy, will give way to the accumulating force of public opinion, and permit a gradual, peaceable and radical reform in the abuses of church and state, or by resistance, cause a physical explosion and violent revolution, time alone must decide. One thing is certain, the industrious producers have the great superiority in physical force, and when joined to the moral improvements of intellect, nothing can withstand them.

A new edition of church and state with additions and amendments, arose out of our revolution, during which our resources were almost exhausted, and the annihilation of the paper money, by which every one lost in proportion to the circulating medium, he possessed, falling principally on the rich, produced an equality of property, unknown to civilization before, so that all classes of society started nearly on a par, after our revolution. The present state of our Union is very far removed from that primitive equality. Some of the causes I have explained in my former essays. The principal cause were the fortuitous circumstances of the neutral trade, aided by the bank monopolizing charters, corporations and exclusive privileges granted to the few, and denied to the many, on which have been created a moneyed aristocracy, which the millions, even with the aid of universal suffrage, find it difficult to check, but which must be put down; being unsupported by either the holy alliance, or any other foreign aristocracy, it must yield to the omnipotent power of the ballot boxes. Notwithstanding that the actual majority, guided by the common sense and reason of the millions, has the legitimate power of regulating all, yet the violent opposition that a small insignificant minority, supported by an upstart moneyed interest, has been able to make against the government, only because an unconstitutional exclusive privilege was not renewed to one of their banks, ought to be a warning to all free people, not in the smallest instance, either for the benefit of commerce, politics, or religion, to grant any thing to the few which is denied to the many.

Every where the millions seem to have acquired a knowledge of their interest. Even in the half savage states of South America, what numberless political and military chiefs, have usurped the arbitrary power of despotism, and have been quickly put down by the force of public opinion, without infringing on their elective system by universal suffrage.— On the contrary, every return of representative government, has been with some change in favor of the millions. If a people only yesterday emancipated from a foreign slavery, have already acquired sufficient knowledge of their interest, to resist all intrigues and conspiracies of church and state, to turn their elective system into a despotism, how is it possible for the hereditary aristocracy of the old world, to retain their arbitrary power and enormous abuses, in the midst of the light of reason, which radiated from the French revolution, and has been since flashing conviction to the utmost corners of civilization.

The theory of the great advantages of freedom, has been generally known from Greece downwards, and frequently exaggerated; it is only the fraction that the millions want, which the stopping the press cannot prevent, even if they would annihilate it. They forget the old Hebrew adage "stolen waters are sweet and bread eaten in secret is pleasant." There are ten who would run all risks to read a prohibited publication, for one who would have any desire to peruse a sheet of legitimate sale. The absolute rulers of France, Germany, etc., seem to think to stop the progress of knowledge by prosecuting the press; it is like damming up a river and leaving the source to flow freely. Besides an immensity of most useful knowledge may be given, as in the Penny Magazine, without touching on politics, leaving the readers to apply it as their necessities require; for in general every thing about church and state are so mystified, disfigured and deviating from truth, by both parties, that little useful information can be expected from such quackery.

INCONGRUITY OF A MIXED POWER IN GOVERNMENT.

June 25th, 1834.

In all governments where the two sources of power, elective and hereditary are mixed, there has been no concord on any essential point, unless one controled the other, by some superiority of property, privilege, combination, or physical or moral force. Even in systems where all is elective, on the equality of universal suffrage, if the power is divided to produce, as is pretended, a balance, it has been constantly attended with disputes, and compromises between right and wrong. Nor has any hereditary executive and elective legislatures agreed, though their authorities have been as judiciously separated as the undefinable nature of language will permit. In spite of all the practical faults and imperfections, owing entirely to the nature and form of the political association, all the people of the old world under an absolute ruler, are endeavoring to obtain a mixed or limited monarchy. And those who have already a limited monarchy, are striving to augment the elective power, whilst the hereditary is fighting as hard to increase their dominion; all tending to bring them nearer to a par, that the conflict may be more destructive and lasting. On this side of the Atlantic, where the hereditary power could not deceive the most ignorant, and has been banished from all the representative democracies, even here the experience of half a century has not taught them, that power must be a unit before it can act, and the more they divide it they greater will be the trouble, delay, and expense of uniting it to fit it for practical purposes. It must always be understood that one legislature, however numerous the majority is a unit, and the same with an executive, and the nearer they are poised in time and salary, the more likely they are to act in concert, and the less time and money will be spent in dispute; like the constitution Franklin gave to Pennsylvania; one house and a committee of seven, yearly elected out of and by that house, for an executive.

Since the diffusion of knowledge has forced the rulers to consult the interest of the millions, in exact proportion as the people have learned the power they have of practising it, many principles of every species of government have been changed, and none is more obvious than that no government hereditary or elective is capable to make laws that will suit the interest of a great extent of territory. What is dictated by the interest of the North, is opposed to the interest of the South, and what suits the interest of the East is contrary to the interest of the West. This has been, and will be every day more and more the cause of disputes between the rulers and ruled. In the present dispute in Britain, the Irish wish to dissolve the union and make their own laws. The tax in France on the importation of cattle, agrees with the interest of Normandy, because a breeding country, but contradicts the interest of Alsace, who import their cattle from Germany. The wine growers in France want free trade and the abolition of the custom houses, but the manufacturers of the north want their monopolies supported by a tariff of taxes and restrictions. The same contradiction of interest between the South and the North in the United States, had nearly caused a civil war, when the elective congress modified the tariff and compromised the dispute for the present, leaving the cause of interfering in the governments of the States, as a nest egg to hatch future quarrels and to promote the evil of long speeches, and declamation of our law legislatures.

In every government where there is a mixture of hereditary and elective power, there is a great difference of interest and of course of opinion. For instance; the house of lords and of commons in Britain. The king and house of representatives in Bavaria. The king and house of representatives in Wirtemburg. The king and the house of representatives in Baden. The elector and house of representatives in Hesse-Cassel. The king and house of representatives in Saxony. The duke and house of representatives in Brunswick. The king and house of representatives in Hanover. The king and house of deputies in France. The king and cortes in Spain. In all the British colonies where the governor represents the hereditary, and the assemblies the elective; as in Nova Scotia, New Brunswick, the two Canadas, and most of their West India islands; governors and assemblies are in constant quarrels, and nothing but the British troops answer the orders of the governors and retain them in subjection, for which the people in Britain pay all the civil and military expenses, only to increase patronage and support the abuses of church and state.

In the representative democracies on this side of the Atlantic, founded on liberty and equality, in place of following the true principles of that liberty and equality, they made a president for four years, subject to be re-elected as long as he lives, with a salary of 25,000 dollars a year; a legislature for two years at six dollars a day, whilst they serve, a senate for six years with eight dollars a day; and, as might have been expected, the senate represents the opinions of their constituents six years ago, before they had opened their eyes to the injury they suffered from the banking system. The legislators only two years distant from public opinion, vote against renewing the charter of the bank, in accordance with a majority of the people: the senators are advocates of the bank and negative what the legislatures do; the legislatures negative the acts of the senate, so that Franklin's prediction of the cart standing still, having one horse before and one behind, is verified. The former Spanish colonies in South America, forced into the theory of liberty and equality by circumstances beyond their control, have been kept in constant agitation by their military usurpers, none of whom have yet succeeded to establish despotism. The Mexican federation adopted our federal constitution, having all its faults and contradictions exaggerated by military despotism, against which the states have ineffectually opposed their divided force, though sufficient to prove that most of their disputes and civil wars originated in the undefined right given to the federation to interfere in the internal governments of the sovereign independent states, along with the procrastinations and contradictions by the adoption of our senate added to their natural indolence, brought into evidence all their imperfections in the federal compact, which they had neither cunning nor dexterity to conceal, and very soon produced their injurious effects, and may be the cause of a reform in the federal constitution.

Considering how very difficult it is to find two individuals who agree in opinion of their interest, even where they are near an equality of property, knowledge, power and consideration, we must perceive how much more difficult, nay impossible, to find two classes of men to agree who are differently brought up and educated, the one in luxury, extravagance, and flattery, like the hereditary privileged orders, the other chosen for their reputation, common sense, conduct and honesty, by the electors. Both theory and practice prove the impossibility of these agreeing in any point either of church or state, on any thing equally speculative, when their interests clash. In an elective government of universal suffrage, where all in theory are equal, but one part of those in power have possession of it for six years, and others only for one or two, it is more than probable their views of their interest will be so different as to make them dispute; even supposing them to be elected for the same period of time, but one elected by the few, and the other by the many, a difference of interest will originate a difference of opinion. As to secure the interest of the many is the only avowed use of governments, the only way to secure that is, that all should be elected in the same manner and for the same period of time, and to receive the same profit or salary. This is the only possible way of perpetuating that equality, without which liberty is a name, that cannot be practiced to the extent which the peace, comfort and happiness of the millions require, but must, by the inequality of property, knowledge, and power, which follow and depend on one another, depreciate into tyranny, as is proven by all history to have been the fate of all ignorant people, which unfortunately, until lately, included all the industrious producers on earth.

It has been the eternal cry of the rich against the poor, that holding no property, they have nothing at stake in the welfare of society, and therefore ought to have no influence in the mode of governing, laws, or taxation. But this is a fallacy, like most of the attempts at reasoning, of the aristocracy in all countries; for the poor have all their peace, comfort, and happiness at stake in the welfare of society, and being limited to one locality, if that fails they have no resource. Whereas the rich have their independence spread over the surface of the country they inhabit, and often have wherewith to secure an independence in foreign countries, so as to have much less of their peace and happiness at stake in the society in which they live, than the poor who have their all at issue on the spot where their poverty fixes them. Their industry produces all that maintains the laws and pays the taxes, and all abuses of both fall on them, as the rich have found means to make use of the laws to enable them to tyrannize over the poor, and by unjust, partial, and unequal taxation, they avoid paying their quota of the public expenses.

To elucidate this—I was in Paris when the allied army took possession of it, and remarked that my two servants felt more for the wretchedness of their fallen country, overrun by foreign troops, than all the merchants and bankers in Paris, who whilst their iron chests and trade were safe, thought little about the honor or glory of their country. The reason is plain, the poor people had as large a share in the honor and glory of their country, as the rich, and it was almost their all; having no compensation in the contents of strong boxes, or prosperous foreign trade, when they lost their pride and flattering gratification of belonging to a country whose renown had spread over the earth, they had lost what nothing within their reach could substitute.

One of the stilts of overbearing aristocracy, on which they greatly depend, is the assertion that the people are so ignorant that if left to themselves, they would run to ruin and destruction. This has never been verified, even in the unrepresented democracies, where all the people assembled in a kind of mob to make the laws, as in the democratic cantons of Switzerland; much less can it be applied to the present diffusion of knowledge, and the well known properties of election, where, if one in a thousand is sufficiently informed to make laws for the rest, it only requires his constituents to make the selection. The little knowledge necessary to make a good choice of representatives was strongly evinced at the beginning of the French revolution. The first time the French exercised the rights of universal suffrage they elected a galaxy of talent, honor and honesty, that has not been equaled since. At that time, law making had not been formed into a profitable trade; bribery, corruption, places and pensions had not been organized, but the people were left to themselves, and their good sense was not warped by the intrigues and deceptions of place hunters or ambitious demagogues. Even the half barbarous people of Mexico, the first time they exercised the right of universal suffrage, elected a more talented, honest, and respectable congress than has been since. The evil is not in the ignorance of the electors in making the selection, but in allowing them after they are elected, to establish their own pay, patronage, privileges and perquisites. After the example of the hereditary rulers of the old world, in place of the sovereign people electing every officer of power or profit, and regulating the pay and profits, they trust both the appointment, pay, perquisites and patronage to be regulated by one of their servants, who uses it to secure his future election.— All the abuses of church and state have been introduced by and for the few, at the expense of the many. The millions are the only class interested in reforms, and no radical reformation can be made until the millions govern by universal suffrage, and not even then until they shall have a knowledge of their true interest.

ARISTOCRATIC DECEPTION. PROGRESS OF REFORM.

May 31, 1834.

Civilized society is divided into two great classes, those who produce property by their labor, and those who consume it. Their interest is as opposite as the two ends of a balance, when one goes up the other goes down; the gain of the one, is the loss of the other. Had this balance been that of justice, equally poised, the majority by their weight and utility would have greatly controled the few or minority. But hitherto our species have been weighed by the Roman steelyard, (like the Roman laws, in favor of the few, and against the many,) in which the accumulating weight of the millions on the short arm was always counteracted by church and state, removing the pea on the long arm a little further from the centre. The millions, ignorant of the properties of the political lever, seeing the beam equally poised, are deceived by this slight of hand, and drag on their chains as the natural consequences of humanity. Not being able to fathom the mystery how the stringing of wordy sophistry by the lawyer or politician, the preaching and praying of the priest, or the signing the name of the banker, which can be done in a few hours, should, in the long arm of the steelyard, outweigh the labor of the thousands of hardworking producers, for many years on the short end. They wonder at the magical effects, without ever analyzing the cause. The lawyer, with his long worded declamatory sophistry, asserts that without his intricate, expensive and undefined laws, all would be confusion, robbery and plunder; though in truth the general result of his interference is to cause disputes and quarrels, to fill his pocket with extravagant fees. The cunning politician boasts of the civilization introduced by his wars, national debts and treaties of commerce, by his expert diplomacy in balancing the power of nations and regulating interest for the public good, but the result of all is a division of spoil, a privation of the means of the diffusion of knowledge, and plunging the millions into poverty and ignorance. The priest preaches that there is no morality but in believing in his doctrines, whilst experience teaches that the more the faith in his dogmas, the more immoral vicious and criminal are his hearers. The banker pretends that the wealth of the nation depends on the circulation of his notes, whilst the whole of his act is to substitute rag money in place of real, and to rob the public by gaining an interest on what intrinsically is worth nothing. Such are the assumed pretensions of most of the nonproductive classes, who live on the labor of the productive, and who have had the art and cunning to combine and unite all their power, privileges and prerogatives, to grind the face of the laborers, and extract as much of the produce of their labor for the maintenance of their luxury and extravagance, as the ignorance and want of union of the millions will permit.

Certainly the industrious producers work for their own interest, like all the rest of our species, but they have the candor and sincerity to avow it. No farmer pretends to plough or sow; no builder of ships or houses, no maker of shoes or clothes ever pretends to work for patriotism: it is only those nonproducers who give nothing physically tangible for their maintenance, who pretend to the disinterested motives of patriotism, philanthropy and charity, which is a veil they mask their selfishness under, and which ought to be torn off, for the general benefit of humanity. The producers are paid for their ingenuity in simplifying, expediting and rendering their work more perfect, commodious and useful to their customers, but the nonproducers have as yet been paid in proportion to the accumulation of difficulties, the multiplication of intricacies, mysterious forms, and incomprehensible doctrines, with which they can surround their mystery. The longer the producers practice their art or calling, the more dexterous they become in all their operations; but the longer all the dependants of church and state practice, the greater and more detrimental to society have been the abuses, corruptions and deceptions they practice on the public. The industrious, hard working producers are paid and acquire esteem and reputation in proportion to the fidelity and accuracy with which they comply with their engagements; but the nonproducers of church and state have been remunerated in proportion to the chicanery, intrigue and dexterous deception, with which they can dupe those who depend on them. The producers are more likely, from the nature of their trade, to be frank, candid, honest and honorable, than the nonproductives, who, striving to appear more than they are, build their fame and fortune on false pretensions. It is to the lawyer, priest, politician, banker and trader, to whom may be added the stock jobber, whose existence depends on one of the greatest abuses of power, the creation of national debts, it is to these worthies who have an interest in complicating, mystifying and rendering obscure and difficult of comprehension every operation that passes through their ministry, it is to these classes who have a retaining fee to defend all abuses, and oppose all reforms, who are united in close combination to maintain their exclusive privileges and usurpations, it is to them that has been entrusted the direction and management of church and state, and from whom the ignorant millions look for reform! To expect all or any of the above classes to act thus contrary to their interest, is to expect the sun to rise in the west. It would appear that the hard working, industrious producers are the only class, who as a class, are interested in a rational reform of either church or state, the only class who pays for all the public abuses, extravagance and plunder, and being the only class who gain by a radical reform, must be the only class who can be reasonably expected to advocate or execute the reform of abuses.

On this side of the Atlantic, elective governments, by universal suffrage, place the power in the hands of the millions, to make all or any reform their knowledge of men and things may dictate to them; but hitherto their ignorance and the want of union, have prevented them benefitting in practice by the complete freedom they have had in theory—the superior cunning and intrigue of the nonproductive classes, have as yet baffled all the attempts that the producers' knowledge has enabled them to make towards a reformation agreeably to their interest. The slavish imitation of the hereditary governments of the old world, and failing to produce that useful economy and judicious laws, have injured the cause of democracy and popular governments. But the millions have lately combined at the ballot boxes and promise in a few years to give an example, which may probably be followed by the whole civilized world.

France got equality by her revolution, in spite of the allied powers, who deprived them of their freedom. Some kind of freedom may exist without equality, but equality cannot continue long without freedom. The last and present hereditary executives, follow blindly the British system of extravagance, and augmenting the national debt and consequent taxation; the elective part of their government is a mere mockery, and whatever melioration the millions gain in France, it must be as it has always been by physical force, which they manage with greater dexterity and success than any nation in Europe, and have been made a military nation by the resistance of the coalesced powers to their revolution, and whoever attempts coercion against public opinion will find them so.

The elective part of the British government having gained much strength by the late reform, is nearer a par with the hereditary, between whom there may be a violent struggle for dominion. It is probable there will not be much tranquility until it is decided who shall rule. All the legislators composed of two bodies of different classes, time elected, on salaries, are at present at variance on both sides of the Atlantic; which must be where there are different interests and different opinions that cannot be reconciled under a regimen of the least portion of freedom, without coercion. The two hereditary executives of France and Britain have made a closer alliance, more to protect each other from the encroachments of their own subjects, than the smallest intention of interfering with other powers. The strongly manifested public opinion, prevents them from taking part with their class the aristocracy, and their ideas of their interest, deter them from assisting the liberals. The elective and hereditary part of the British, Bavarian, Wirtemburg and Baden governments are at variance; the French, United States of America, South America, where there are two houses, have been all less or more in dispute; the British colonies, where the governor represents the hereditary and the legislatures the elective, have been constantly quarreling. How long will the world strive against the grain.

DIFFERENT IDEAS OF CIVILIZATION. ADVANCE OF FREEDOM.

June 12, 1834.

Civilization has advanced so far, and into such a variety of channels, and continued under such different circumstances, that a comparison of the different means adopted, and the deviating paths followed, may perhaps facilitate the arriving at a more correct knowledge of the origin and progress of the different ideas of the word civilization. With the politician civilization depends on the arrangement of power, so as to act on the passions, hopes and fears of the mass, so completely divided as to be easily cowed by the united few. With the lawyers civilization depends on the complication, intricacy and mysterious number of the laws, so as to be out of the reach of all but themselves. With the priest the faith in his dogmas and doctrines; with the merchant, the extent and profit of his trade: but nine times in ten, all these are rather the abuse than the use of civilization.

Let us endeavor to trace the progress of political civilization towards a more equal division of property, knowledge and power. The small nations of the Jews and Spartans are the only ancients who founded their institutions on any thing like liberty and equality, whose equal division of property has been cautiously avoided by all founders of political associations ever since. Of all the small republics of the middle age, the only one which remains is Switzerland, kept up by the poverty of their soil and climate. The first attempt of a division of power to any extent, arose out of the quarrel between the king and barons of England; which by degrees emancipated the millions from personal slavery, and produced all the prosperity and superiority to which the British nation has since attained. The elective power has been slowly and gradually gaining on the hereditary ever since, and must continue to encroach on the hereditary privileges, in exact proportionto the diffusion of knowledge amongst the electors.

By the revolution of the United States of America a gigantic stride was made towards liberty, to which was joined the theory but not the practice of equality. Both legislators and executives, elected by a free and equal representation, based on universal suffrage, secured as far as possible, the interest of the great majority. A divorce between church and state, placing religion on the equitable footing of every thing else, to be paid for only by those who wanted it. The two great principles of freedom, have produced an unprecedented prosperity, population and power, in spite of the great drawback of retaining the monarchical laws and the feudal division of territory, retarding the progress of useful civilization, as well as the comfort and happiness of the millions.

Following the example of the revolution of the United States of North America, freedom crossed the Atlantic and burst the bonds of slavery with violence in France, opposed by a hereditary nobility, and richly endowed church whose organized resistance to the just rights of the people, was supported by the coalition of the whole European aristocracy. This violent opposition urged the revolutionary spirit far beyond what was originally intended. The first time the French people were entrusted with universal suffrage, they elected a galaxy of talent, honor and honesty, that has not been equalled either before or since. But in consequence of the constant wars, waged against their freedom by the combined allies every succeeding constitution was a further deviation from universal suffrage, until at last they were forced under the dominion of a military chief, as the only salvation from a partition amongst the conquerors and annihilation as a nation. The immense and lasting improvements, the remains of the French revolution are, 1st, a more equal division of property by a total change in the laws of inheritance; 2dly, a simple, plain, and well defined code of laws, which guarantees the equality of property and consequently knowledge; 3dly, the total abolition of the ancient political, military and ecclesiastical division of territory by a new and accurately equalizing political division into departments, arondissements, cantons and communes, thereby annihilating all the old abuses of customs, regulations, privileges, monopolies and corruptions, attached to and inherent in the locality; clearing the field of all obstructions to a new and more rational order of things; a fundamental revolution still existing in Belgium, Holland, and on the borders of the Rhine.

In Spain, the Cortes sowed the seeds of freedom, though smothered and repressed by the gold and bayonets of the French Bourbons, yet still keep hold of public opinion which may soon be manifested and practiced by actions. But the great addition to freedom by the Spanish revolution, was the emancipation of their South American colonies. Protected by the tyrannical interference of European despots by the Atlantic ocean, they have been left much to themselves and have occupied a fair field of experiment, which, for rapid changes and great variety, have not been equalled by any former state of political association. Most of the free states of the southern hemisphere have experienced all the vicissitudes of different governments, from a military despotism, through all the gradations to elective representation by universal suffrage. After every change and return to the representative system, it has been always with some improvement, and never the smallest propensity to resist the universal suffrage or limit its general influence; on the contrary, in the short space of time since their emancipation, more political and military usurpers have been punished by death or banishment, than is to be found in the history of any people for thousands of years. They have suppressed the tyranny of priestcraft—abolished tithes, and appropriated their ill-gotten wealth to more useful purposes, such as schools, etc.; they have disbanded their standing armies, and trust to their militia for external or internal protection; they have done more in the short time they have had any pretensions to freedom, to secure their liberty and independence, than any nation of the old world has done since the commencement of their history. It is not yet twenty years since the first ray of freedom broke through the darkness of foreign despotism which yet threatens their independence, the mother country still continuing hostilities. Where must we look for the cause of a people just emerged from foreign slavery, making such rapid progress in arts, sciences and civilization, but in the general diffusion of useful knowledge? They cannot look on a neighboring nation without learning the perfection to which ages of industry, genius and talent have brought the inventions of the useful arts, nor open a port to the free circulation of foreigners without receiving the perfection of centuries of gradual improvements to graft on their young and unsophisticated habits. Is it, that the facility of communication brings nations nearer to one another than individuals used to be, and that governments are like all other arts and sciences, the last experiment is the most perfect?

If the different states of our Union would condescend to benefit by others' experience, and adopt a code of laws, like the Napoleon code, that every man might have in his breeches pocket, it would advance civilization more in one year than it will do in a century of their own dear bought experience. And if they could impartially examine the vast advantages of the power, rights and jurisdiction of the New England townships of six miles square, they would divide all their surface into townships of six miles square, and endow them with all the rights and privileges of doing every thing for themselves, their interest required, without waiting the leisure of distant legislative bodies, no way interested in the locality, but greatly interested in extending their sway over as much of the population as possible, whose power and dominion is augmented by the intricacy and mysterious nature of their laws and regulations. If the old world knew a twentieth part of the advantages this side of the Atlantic derived from universal suffrage they would adopt it.

It is not so much the invention of new systems, as the equalization of old, tested by experience, that is wanted to the improvement and useful progress of civilization, which can only begin by an accurate examination and comparison of the origin, progress and utility of what at present exists, this would at least silence the eternal cry against novelty, on its not being tryed, and the doleful prophecies of its practical faults and terrible consequences, when attempted to be put in execution.

PROGRESS OF CIVILIZATION.

June 19*th*, 1834.

A most interesting enquiry is, relative to the time it will require for a savage people, surrounded by civilization as far as it has yet gone, to arrive at the degree of perfection of their neighbors, compared with the time it required for the civilized people to acquire the degree of civilization they now possess.

All those who, by force, fraud, cunning, or even industry, have accumulated a greater proportion of the advantages of life, the favorite few, who, at the expense of the many, possess a much greater share of the moral and physical advantages than would have fallen to them by a more equitable division, are willing to believe and persuade others that all people emerging from barbarity, must follow the same slow path to improvement, which the first pioneers did. As well might they insist on the navigator continuing to creep along shore without either compass or quadrant; the boat crawling up the Mississippi by the branches of trees; or the traveling by land up to the belly in mire, not advancing as far in a year as they can now in a week, as to expect or suppose that any aggregation of inhabitants on earth, can be so benighted in ignorance, so lost to all sense of their own interest, as to toil over the intricate and fatiguing road of their own discoveries and inventions, when they can receive from their neighbors, through the rapid facilities of communication, the improvements and contrivances of thousands of years of progressive civilization.

To repeat all the aid and assistance mankind have received from a proper application of the different elements through the medium of mechanism, chemistry, etc., would require volumes. All we shall notice at present, are those most conducive to the diffusion of knowledge, and the equalization of all that depends on it. The improvement in morals, by the agency of church and state, has been almost stationary for many centuries; the same superstition and bigotry in support of the incomprehensible dogmas of mysterious religions; much the same political despotism, producing wars, cruelty, and carnage, propagating immorality, slavery, and crime, retarding morals, thousands of years behind the physical improvements, which must in time influence morals, though as yet the effects have been little. The principal improvements in physics that will accelerate the progress and diffusion of knowledge, are, the facility and rapidity of communication, approaching nations within the sphere of daily intercourse, scarcely known formerly between farm houses, by the agency of railroads, transporting every kind of men and matter twenty or thirty miles an hour, merely by the force of dead matter, converted into steam by fire, without the aid of either animal or manual labor, inexhaustible as the elements which give the motion, with the same undiminishing power and force. This immense curtailing of distance by land, annihilates most of the obstructions of space, opposed to the free circulation of knowledge and property, whilst the steamboats moving ten to fifteen miles an hour against wind and tide, approaching continents and islands within habitual and frequent intercourse, so that men, property and knowledge will be wafted with the velocity of steam, from one corner of the globe to the other, and all the essential freedom, knowledge, and happiness be equalized over the surface of the earth, in spite of the obstructions of seas and mountains. Men will not be crowded to suffocation in a small space, nor the arts and sciences limited to the bounds of any country or people.

From the different foci of civilization in Europe, New Holland, Asia, the Cape of Good Hope and Algiers in Africa, will radiate the arts, sciences, freedom, and happiness into the surrounding countries, and through the great rivers of China, Russia, and Indostan, will circulate the useful arts of civilization, long before their information has taught them the utility of railroads. The late discoveries of the river Niger, will introduce into the heart of Africa, steamboats loaded with the wealth of European arts and manufactories, which will enable those savages to begin at the point of perfection, to which the civilized world has arrived by thousands of years of labor and experience, at the same time retaining part of that simplicity which characterises mankind when emerging from the state of nature.

On this side of the Atlantic, freed from the accumulating prejudices, follies, and injustice of hereditary power, and privilege, the improvement of society will advance with an unprecedented rapidity. All the impediments placed in the way of every thing useful, by the great inequality of property, knowledge, and power, being removed, the melioration of the great human family will outstrip any precedent in the annals of mankind. Society will advance without fear or dread of novelties, never having changed either morals or physics, church or state, but for the great benefit of the millions, who rule by universal suffrage. As the United States of America are further advanced in useful civilization than any other part of the globe, their useful arts, sciences, and knowledge will fly on the wings of steam over this whole hemisphere, already in unison as regards the theory of their political institutions. The steamboats will double Cape Horn, and impregnate the coast of the Pacific with all the accumulating improvements of the towns on the Atlantic; whilst those from the banks of the Ohio, Missouri and Mississippi will transport all their useful arts, sciences, and knowledge to the sources of the rivers Magdalena, Oronoco, Amazon and La Plata. Space, for the circulation of knowledge and property, will be almost annihilated, and not the smallest analogy left between the past and future, to build an antiquarian hypothesis on, to deceive the ignorant.

If the foregoing conjectures are correct, and warranted by the events and political revolutions that have taken place in church and state, during the last fifty years, we must change our mode of reasoning or anticipating what is to come in religion, politics, laws, commerce, habits and customs, that must be put in harmony with the foundation of society, bottomed on the more equal division of property, knowledge, and power. The old mode of judging the future by the past, must lead to error and disappointment, and must cease to be adopted by all men of common sense, when they cease to be analogous.

Mankind have hitherto been divided into those who make use of their heads, and those who work with their hands, as the consumers and producers; the first living on the produce of the labor of the last, the burden and oppression of which has been gradually increasing with civilization. That is, the toil and labor of the producers, is in exact proportion to the quantum of their property wasted or expended by the consumers. This excessive burden has been accumulating on the hands of the industrious producers ever since the commencement of civilization, and has got to that exorbitant pitch, that the industrious producers can bear it no longer, and are forced to make use of their heads to direct their hands how to emancipate themselves from the drudgery of maintaining so many rich, idle, and to them, useless classes—as exemplified in our revolution and that of the French.— In the present state of what has been called the civilized world, it is difficult to divine the time required for all these events to mature, as the laws of art, are not so certain and unchangeable as the laws of nature. But, one thing may be predicted without much risk of being mistaken, that the millions are too far on the road to improvement, and useful knowledge is too generally diffused for the present impulse to fail, or the march of mind to retrograde. The opposing physical force to opinion, has in all instances, as well as in the French revolution, only strengthened, and scattered it far and wide, and it is probable, the exertions of the coalesced powers, did much more towards disseminating the principles of freedom, than all the hot-headed jacobins in France. And it is more than probable, that the despotic opposition of the present "holy alliance" to the gradual, reasonable, and constant progression of the knowledge of the day; that the German Diet in endeavoring to annihilate the liberty of the press, are only stopping the safety valve, which will accelerate the explosion that will scatter their hereditary power, authority and privileges into imperceptible fragments, dividing property in the same proportion as the division of knowledge, which might have remained for ages in the hands of the few, had church and state been allowed to descend by the peaceable and natural inclined plane of the equalization of knowledge.— It would appear that the same violence which accumulated property in the hands of the few, is requisite to divide it amongst the many.

ON THE INJUSTICE AND OPPRESSION OF OUR BANK CHARTERS.

June 22, 1834.

It is ascertained that in the United States, five hundred and sixty-eight banks are yet solvent, one hundred and thirteen bankrupt banks, and nine hundred and sixty different description of notes on different banks forged and in circulation. With such a dreadful picture of loss, ruin and crime before their eyes, it must astonish every impartial observer, that there can be found any legislators, so lost to all feeling for the interest of their constituents, as to increase the quantity of evil, by granting more exclusive charters without a limitation of dividend, thereby putting it in the power of shareholders to elect such directors as will divide all capital and money received for the notes they issue under pretence that it is profit, and leave nothing in the vaults to pay the public for the notes they have taken, on the faith and credit given partly to their charter and partly to the stock said to be responsible. In Europe, there was only Law's bank at Paris, and the "South Sea bubble" in London, that was trusted with a charter without a limitation of dividend, such as all the bank charters in the Union. Both those companies divided the capital under pretence of profits, which raised the stocks six or seven hundred per cent., when the knowing ones sold out, the companies failed, and ruined some hundred thousand persons who bought the stock. Whether the same cause will produce the same effect on this side of the Atlantic as on the other, may perhaps be judged of by the great number of these banks already failed. Whilst the banks are solvent, merchants and men of business borrow money by discounts from them, and when they fail, pay them in their depreciated notes; by which they gain just as much as the holder of their shares, and notes lose, which is generally the industrious producers. The statement of the said banks, and the forgeries upon them, towards the people of the United States may stand thus: suppose 568 banks to keep in their vaults on an average $50,000 each of specie, and to keep in circulation seven times more of their notes. This would give them a circulation of 170,500,000, that they could lend to their customers, mostly of the nonproductive consuming classes, at an average in the Union of seven per cent. per annum interest. This would yield them a profit, over and above the seven per cent. on their capital of about 12,000,000; all of which may be considered as a loan from the public, who take their notes as specie. Which profitable trade, the legislatures, by granting exclusive charters, and prohibiting all other citizens from issuing notes to bearer, give the banks a monopoly; a great advantage not granted in England to their only chartered bank, which has only the privilege of preventing more than seven individuals from joining in a banking company; thus establishing in our free country a monopoly more in favor of the moneyed aristocracy, than is to be found in the most aristocratic European nations.

Supposing the 113 bankrupt banks, each owed the public by circulating notes and otherwise, $200,000, their debts would amount to $22,000,000, of which on an average, after many years of collecting and arranging, they might pay one-third; their defalcation would be 15,000,000 of dollars, most of which would be a transfer from the pockets of industrious producers into the pockets of those who were benefited by the banks during their solvency, which generally will be found to be merchants and men of business in the towns, or the nonproductive consuming classes. From all this it would appear, that the invention of all kinds of circulating paper, public loans, mortgages on posterity, etc., substituted for real property produced by labor, have been and will continue to be the most efficacious, quick and certain mode of transferring the property from those whose labor brought it into existence, to the use of those who have assumed the right of consuming it; and that the inequality of property, knowledge and power, have been in the exact ratio of civilization, as far as it has yet gone.

The 960 forged notes of different sums and on different banks, are the reward of crime, a premium to immorality.— Suppose each note, on an average of twenty dollars, and that one hundred of them, some more and some less, were passed for specie; the amount of the fraud would be nearly two millions of dollars, tranferred mostly from the pockets of the industrious producers, into the pockets of the criminal forgers, their aids and abettors in acilitating the circulation. This fraud augments the demoralization of society much more than would at first appear, by tempting those who take a forged note to endeavor to pay it away as a good one, and thus become equally criminal with those who forged it, as they receive a value for what they know to be of no value. The vast number of these fraudulent notes constantly passing from hand to hand, multiplies the fraud ad infinitum, and renders a great part of the population familiar with deception and cheating.

All property is produced by labor, and when represented by any species of bank notes, bonds, public loans, etc., it is forestalling the produce of labor for the benefit of those who receive the value specified on such paper, and who are for the most part the nonproductive consuming classes, it enables them not only to expend the produce of that labor created at the present time, but it mortgages the produce of the labor of future generations, to administer to the luxuries and extravagance of the nonproductive consumers. It not only mortgages posterity to pay the principal, but it receives an annual interest from the producers at the present time, which in cases of public loans, for the most part forms a perpetual annuity from the labor of the industrious producers, paid into the pockets of the idle consumers, and saddles the working classes with the support and maintenance of a vast additional number of idlers, double or triple what could be fed or clothed from the real property: as in Britain at present, whose immense national debt is the original cause of all the misery and wretchedness of their laborers. Those who by favor or fraud constituted themselves the governors of the people, either by divine hereditary or any other right, often having monopolized all real property, such as lands, etc., found it their interest to create a factitious property in paper, more consonant to their views, as being without limits, occupying hardly any space, yet extending the sphere of their power, authority and profits far beyond the restricted influence of real property, which without labor, is worth little, and requires some knowledge and ability to manage. The contriving of a fund like the British national debt, which without any care or trouble, would transfer nearly three hundred millions of dollars yearly, out of the produce of the working people into the pockets of the idle consumers, was an invention mankind owe to civilization, which has oppressed the millions in the ratio of its extent, whose comfort and happiness is curtailed, and their miseries and wretchedness increased in proportion to the amount of such a debt. The quantity of every species of circulating paper, stamped to pass for an unlimited value, without the aid of labor, places the consumer apparently out of dependence on the laborer, by complicating and mystifying the deception, though actually all he receives for his paper is created by the laborer, and without the possibility of such an exchange, the paper would be worth nothing. Such is the complicated and artificial state of civilized society, that the few live at the expense of the many, without the former suspecting their complete dependence on the laborer, or the latter having any knowledge of their positive superiority of independence. The Union will soon be free from a federal debt, and it will be their own faults if they permit the state governments to involve either them or their posterity in the burden of a debt to accomplish any thing beyond their present means, as all the anticipated advantages cannot equal the injury of transferring a perpetual annuity from the working people to the idle.

FICTIONS OF CHURCH AND STATE CONTRIVED TO OPPRESS THE WORKING MEN.

July 26, 1834.

Imagination begins where the senses end, which are the foundation and store room of the imagination. All the variegated materials, natural or unnatural, on which the imagination works, come through the senses. When things are figured in the mind, according to their natural or regular situation, form a texture, perhaps the proper word for such a resuscitation of real ideas is *memory*, and only unnatural combinations of ideas received by the senses, like our dreams, are the fruits of *imagination*. A person deprived of the sense of seeing from his birth, cannot conceive any idea, arising from the sense of seeing; the same of hearing and all the other senses. Imagination therefore does not increase the number of phenomena, or create new, it only arranges, combines, or unites the different parts of objects received by the senses, into an unnatural and fantastical form and structure. Had it been possible for men to invent or contrive some form different from those received by the senses, they would certainly have exercised their ingenuity in the form of their gods, godesses, angles and devils; but most nations have formed their gods after their own image or a compound of its different parts, and have even clothed them with their different virtues, vices, passions and propensities. Imagination seems to change, disfigure and distort nature, not to make her more useful or less injurious to the common operations of life, but to indulge an exorbitant craving for novelty, which will most probably diminish as the estimate of the utility of realities increases. Why such a visionary quality of our minds has been so much valued as to occupy full the half of the field of intellect, may be difficult to explain; but we may enumerate some of the principles which have governed civilization, as far as it has yet gone, the power of which is supported by an imaginary arrangement of objects.

Religious dogmas are often as far out of nature, as they are beyond our comprehension. The mysterious actions of beings, supposed to be endowed with supernatural powers, the result of whose operations are contradicted by all the laws of nature, which our experience has brought us acquainted with, opposite to and unlike any thing we receive through the evidence of our senses, entirely dependent on the fictions of imagination for all the deceptions and representations, those who have invented and contrived them have handed down to us, which includes all that powerful and influential class who live by the delusions of the church, forced to vindicate the fictions of the trade by which they live, and fervently to defend their incomprehensible doctrines against all the evidence of realities. This forms a powerful band who have an interest in maintaining the superiority of the fictions of imagination, over the evidence of our senses.

Politicians and men in power whether by divine, hereditary right or by elective, know well how much their salaries, safety and security is ensured by occupying the minds of those under their authority with the fictions of the imagination, without a particle of common sense or useful information, leading them astray from any investigation of the causes of their oppression, misery or wretchedness. In most countries the millions of productive laborers have been the dupes of such deceptions, and where church and state are closely united to keep up such illusions, the combination is so artfully organized as to baffle all the knowledge, energy and exertion of the governed to free themselves from the oppression of the governors.

Conquerors and all those trained to the destruction of their species, are beholden to the fictions of the imagination for the toleration of their butchering trade. The reality of a field of battle is an arena of bloodshed and butchery, but being disguised under the fictitious high sounding illusions of heroism, glory, honor, loyalty, patriotism and public good, which has been the theme of all histories, it has passed for the *ne plus ultra* of human perfection.

Poetry, or the flight of imagination, has been applauded by those whose occupations could not bear the plain truth. Poets, from Horace to Byron, have spurned all realities as beneath the attention of their divine inspirations. Realities may be warped and distorted by imagination; but can receive no explanation or elucidation from imaginary visions. In no instance can they be useful in common life, and when aiding and assisting superstition and bigotry, are very much against the peace, comfort and happiness of mankind.

Oratory when made use of to misrepresent truth, enters into the regions of fiction and gilds the pill of deception to imitate realities. It has not yet been the interest of the rulers, either of church or state, to draw a distinct line of separation between the real and ideal. The oratory of lawyers, etc., may be represented by tons of falsehood made into pills, gilded with pounds of truth, adapted to the reasoning powers or ignorance of their hearers; fiction and reality are so confounded and mixed up together, as to puzzle the multitude to analyze them, and is the fruitful cause of deception and the propagation of ignorance.

The fine arts, such as painting, sculpture, etc., when not representing realities positively useful, are fictions of the imagination, representing gods and godesses, the mythology of all countries and a chief part of history—the greatest part of painting and statues, only serve to flatter those who have been the most active in causing the misery and destruction of their species.

Our pride, vanity and self-conceit, by denying that self is the motive of our own or our friends' actions, (though willing enough to attribute selfish motives to all the actions of our enemies,) arrogating the lofty motives of patriotism, philanthropy and charity, bring a great part of these motives into the region of fictions of the imagination, and sanction pretensions that have no existence in reality.

Divine right, the infallibility of the pope, and most of the dogmas of all religions, are the extreme of visionary fictions, and owe all the knowledge we can acquire of them to heated imaginations. Perhaps any thing out of the reach of our senses can only be embodied into any conjectural form by the fiction of the imagination. Faith in what we neither understand nor comprehend, is an imaginary fiction.

Is it the natural indolence of mankind, that makes them prefer the dreams of the imagination to the labor of observing the nature and properties of realities? Or is it like most other habits, the effect of education? When we consider the vast time and pains that are spent at our universities and colleges, to teach metaphysics, theology, rhetoric, moral philosophy, and other dexterous use or abuse of words, to the neglect of the exact sciences, and the nature and properties of things, and consider the preferment and commendations that have been bestowed by church and state on the dexterous use of words in preference to the positive knowledge of things we shall be inclined to attribute this rage for fiction to the great encouragement given by the nature of our education.

Giving ideas by the things themselves or exact representations, is a great improvement in the diffusion of useful knowledge. Whilst both real and ideal were described by vague, undefined and undefinable words, it was more difficult to distinguish them, particularly for children, who learned the sound of the words by memory, not only without distinguishing the difference between realities and fiction, but without having any correct idea of what was meant by either. The teaching children by the things themselves or exact representations, will form an epoch in the mode of instruction for many evident reasons. 1st. It would draw a broad line of distinction between what can be represented, and what cannot be figured, from not being cognizable and out of the reach of our senses. 2dly. It would imprint at a glance, the correct idea, by transferring the figure of the thing direct into the mind, and would be retained a great deal longer that any description. 3dly. It would avoid the dry and irksome study of undefined words, which tires the patience and fatigues the attention of children, rendering punishment necessary to secure any progress, whereas things or their representations, would be studied with pleasure, as their utility would be evident to the senses. The great number of representations in the Penny Magazines and the numberless cheap books lately published for the instruction of the millions, prove that the diffusion of knowledge and civilization are taking a direct course towards utility, by facilitating the giving knowledge to that class who are most interested in making the best use of it for the peace, order, comfort and happiness of society.—Could that marked preference of words to things, originate in the influence of those learned professions, the greatest part of whose stock in trade consists of words which gives them an interest in the extension of their power and value?

THE ABUSE OF PAPER MONEY ISSUES IS A CHIEF SUPPORT OF INEQUALITY.

July 31, 1834.

Elective governments by universal suffrage are novelties in the annals of mankind, and have only been partially practiced in the United States. From the number of laws, habits and customs adopted from hereditary aristocracy, opposed and contradictory to every principle of freedom and equality, our experiment can only be called a partial result of the effects of universal suffrage. But if carried to the extent which its benefits to mankind, or the effects on the happiness of the human family, as far as it has yet gone, would warrant, there can be no doubt, of the vast advantages that would accrue to our species, by the extension of the principles of freedom and equality. Of the two great natural parties which divide mankind, (from which most parties take their origin,) producers and consumers, the last is the only one whose interest has been yet advocated, or who have had the means of feeing lawyers or advocates. In all countries these two parties are opposed. Yet the opposition of interest is more perceptible and better defined, under free institutions, relieved from the complicated mysteries of divine and hereditary rights. In governments of universal suffrage, the interest of the millions of industrious producers, must be considered the aim and object of all delegated power, and in reasoning impartially on the perpetual conflict of these two opposing interests, sufficient allowance must be made for the pre-occupying influence of the vast number of ingenious advocates, that the power and riches of the consuming classes, have enabled them to fee for the purpose of pleading their cause with all the ornaments of eloquence.

Paper is a modern invention: the ancients did not know the use of it; and paper money is a still later contrivance, introduced by the hereditary and moneyed aristocracy after they had monopolized all the real property, to extend their power and influence on an artificial base, limited only by the supply of rags, of which their tyranny and abuse of power furnished abundance. Amongst the many other copies of old mother Britain, paper money has been introduced, and as it is almost the chief support of inequality, on which all aristocracy must depend, it has been extended, through the medium of banks, to an unprecedented length, both in amount and principle; as I have endeavored formerly to show.

In Britain, the national debt, the bank, mercantile, and other paper representations of property, have been carried to the most extravagant length, so as to divide the whole population into the extremes of poverty and luxury. Great as is the opulence and dissipation of the ruling few in that country; it can only be equalled by the poverty of the many. But the wretchedness and misery of the working people under the accumulated evils of British aristocracy are too well known to require elucidation. Next to Britain, Holland is the country in which a national debt, mercantile speculations, and paper representations of property, have been extended far beyond the ratio of general happiness, and in spite of the proverbial economy of the Dutch, poverty and misery are the lot of the laborer; who is poor and oppressed in all countries, in proportion to the quantity of artificial representations of property, put in circulation for the benefit of their masters. France, by the revolution, was relieved of two-thirds of her national debt; and having only one bank, whose paper has but a limited circulation, secures to her working people an equality and competency, not to be found in any other European country.

Paper is a cheap representation of property, fabricated with so small a quantity of labor, as to have little or no intrinsic value. Its economy is the principal cause of its adoption in preference to the precious metals, of which the value is the quantity of labor necessary to their production; but the great facility of making and stamping a factitious value on paper, constitutes the great temptation to abuse, which greatly counterbalances the advantages of a cheap circulating medium. But as this is foreign to the present inquiry, it may be admitted as a saving labor machine, without interfering with its political or moral consequences. In an association of men, founded on liberty and equality, whose interest must force them to reject every thing that can endanger or interfere with the enjoyment of either, every thing that tends to derange the equality of property, knowledge or power, by heaping any of these three essentials of freedom on the few, at the expense of the many, naturally endangers both liberty and equality, and curtails in the same proportion, the happiness of the millions. That a representation of property, requiring no labor to make, produces riches to those who do not labor, and wretchedness and misery to the working people in all countries, I have endeavored to prove by the situation of society in such European countries, as have made the greatest use of paper as a representation of property. That the same cause has produced the same effect and will continue to do so, in spite of our free political institutions guaranteed by universal suffrage, may be proved by ascertaining that all the bank and other paper representations of property, are for the use and accommodation of the non-productive and consuming classes, whilst the parties on whose responsibility they circulated are solvent, and when they fail, the industrious producers, as the principal holders of their notes, are the greatest losers. This monopoly of exclusive privileges, to issue as much value of paper as they please, and divide as much under pretence of profits, as their cupidity will prompt them, granted by our legislators to the few at the expense of the many, has already established an inequality of property, knowledge, and power, endangering the existence of that freedom and equality, on which our political institutions are founded. These are a few of the political evils which oppress our industrious producers, by the artificial paper representation of property; and morality is equally injured and depreciated, by the great temptation which the immense isue of notes from 568 banks, offers to counterfeiters, by the facility of passing their forged notes, from the difficulty of detection, as it requires a lifetime to obtain any competent knowledge of them. Thus immense number of forgeries are in circulation. The demoralizing source is not confined to the criminals who make a business of counterfeiting, but it extends to the many thousands, who, having from ignorance received a forged note, are tempted to commit the crime of passing it; all of which crimes are practiced with impunity, proportioned to the vast extent of our territory.

The advocates of the monied interest, capitalists and non-productive consumers, plead the great services which the U. S.

bank has rendered the country, by what they call regulating the currency: without explaining what these words mean. The only thing capable of regulating a paper currency is the confidence of the public, and the law, when it is able to enforce payment of the artificial value in real property. But the bank can scarcely regulate its own issues, much less that of any other. For the directors of all the banks, are forced, by the interest of their stockholders who elect them, to issue as much paper as the public will receive, and too often exceed the quantity necessary to transfer the real property bought and sold; by which they raise the price of both exports and imports, above their value, and, in the same proportion, lower the exchange on countries, in which the circulating medium is specie. This superabundant issue of paper, lavishly given by the banks, to increase the amount of their discounts, creates an artificial competition in the produce market, and raises the articles above the value which can be procured for them, in countries where specie is the circulating medium, and is one of the causes of so many bankruptcies, amongst our merchants, reversing the old principle of buying cheap and selling dear, by buying dear and selling cheap. Another property, supposed by the pleaders in favor of the bank of the United States, is "preventing the States issuing paper money." A poor compliment, this, to the common sense of the States' legislators. They likewise assert that the bank is indispensably necessary to transport the revenue of the Union to where it is disbursed: all of which I may endeavor to show at some future time, is equally fallacious.

GREAT ADVANTAGES OF FREEDOM AND EQUALITY TO THE ARTS, SCIENCES AND HAPPINESS OF MANKIND.

August 10, 1834.

Some credit has been given, by the different literary productions, to every species of religion, to every species of government, to every conqueror or founder of a monarchy or despotism for the supposed good they did to mankind; but few or no authors have been so candid or impartial, as to attribute to freedom the immense advantages it has bestowed on the millions: and none have traced the vast consequences and influence an human affairs, that the junction of equality with freedom has produced on the destinies of mankind. This is for a reason, founded on the selfish principle; the millions have not been able to fee authors or to buy or read their books, therefore the objects of their praise and commendation, have been those who, from force or fraud, have monopolized power and property. In Europe, the British were the first who conquered a little freedom, by throwing off the most slavish part of the tyrannical feudal system. This has been the foundation of all their superiority over their slavish neighbors. Before that, they had neither arts, sciences nor commerce; but were plundered and conquered by Danes, Norwegians and Normans, yet their prosperity has been generally attributed to their commerce, in consequence of their insular situation; though their commerce was only one of the fruits of freedom. The poverty of both soil and climate, in the mountains of Switzerland, was the cause of their equality and independence which produced some freedom; yet the merit is given, both by natives and foreigners, to William Tell. Most of the credit of our emancipation, and all its wonderful effects, have been given to the prudence, conduct and courage of Washington;—though he was dead before the great prosperity, emanating from freedom, began to appear. Bonaparte, though the European aristocracy hated him, yet they preferred giving him credit for all his conquests, rather than to attribute them to the real cause, the spirit of liberty, which was both in him and his armies.

It is not their church or state, privileged orders, army or navy, that have given Britain such a vast superiority amongst nations, but the ingenuity and exertions of the millions of industrious producers, who have covered the globe with the fruits of their arts, sciences and manufactures, in spite of the obstructions of tythes and taxes, and the enormous expenses of civil, military and naval establishments. It is not the aristocratic privileged orders who have made the 500 goat herds on the top of Mount Jura, from the poorest and most ignorant, one of the richest and best people in Europe, forming the republic of Neufchatel,—but entirely owing to the equality from which they all started, producing rational freedom, and the most unlimited tolerance, surrounded by states more or less oppressed.

Our emancipation from British dominion produced the first government in which freedom has had a fair trial, and certainly the only one in which the theory of as perfect political equality, under the guarantee of universal suffrage, as can possibly exist, has been permanently established. It is therefore from the results of our experiments, from the rapid progress of our moral and physical experiments, that fair and impartial conclusions can be drawn, of the immense benefits the whole human family, are to derive from liberty and equality.

Before, during and for a considerable time after our revolution, there was not a pound of cotton exported from the United States. Now there are 800,000 bales produced yearly: nearly equal to what is grown on the whole surface of the globe. Until lately, there was no sugar cultivated in any part of the Union; now from 80,000 to 100,000 hogsheads of sugar, and nearly as many of molasses are annually produced; and from the yearly increase of about 15,000 hogsheads, in four years the whole sugar that is consumed in the Union, will be the growth of the country. While the temporary advantages of the neutral trade, prevented our citizens from looking at home for permanent advantages, the few unsuccessful experiments made in planting vines, were left to foreigners, who searching for heat, as in their own country, neglected to secure water and failed. Since which there have been more experiments made in planting and grafting vines, in every part of our Union, than has been made in all Europe for the last thousand years. In the south of Spain and Italy they have followed the routine of their forefathers, with little or no change since the time of the Romans. And even in France it is only since the revolution, that much improvement has been effected in agriculture. Silk until lately was not thought an article of production fit for our climate; but since the various trials have been made, the climate is found more congenial to the rearing of silk worms, and the silk superior to most of that made in Europe, and a native tree is found, (Maclura Orangia,) the leaves of which are fitter for the feeding of the silk worms than those of the mulberry. By the comparison made and stated in the American Farmer, 11th vol. page 179, the worms fed on the leaves of the Maclura grew faster and made their cocoons ten to fifteen days sooner than those fed on the leaves of the mulberry; besides the Maclura is a tree of a quick growth, from six to eight feet in a year, remarkable for thick set branches, large leaves and sharp prickles, fitting it for hedges; which at the height of five feet, gives a great facility for gathering the leaves, and serves at the same time two useful purposes, enclosing our fields and feeding silk worms. So that it is probable, that in a short time the impulse of freedom will enable us to be exporters of sugar, wine and silk, in a proportion nearly equal to what we now export in cotton.

The useful mechanical arts have made a still greater progress than agriculture, which is evinced by our machinery for making cards, screws, nails and brads, turning gunstocks, shoemakers' lasts, and other irregular figures on a lathe, etc.; our improvements in ship building and navigation, and the anticipation of all other countries in the perfection of steamboats, and our many thousand miles of roads, rail roads and canals, unprecedented in the history of mankind. The preceding observations only tend to prove, that the advantages of freedom and equality have been hitherto suppressed and concealed, by the arts, cunning and intrigues of the aristocracy, and the sunshine of reason and common sense, are only beginning now to penetrate the dense clouds with which arbitrary power has obscured it from the perception of the millions.

A still stronger proof of the elastic force of freedom is to be found in the late French revolution. Though their neighbors only allowed them to enjoy the first a very short time, yet short as it was, neither the military tyranny of Bonaparte nor the civil despotism of the Bourbons, could eradicate the immense benefit the people obtained by a few short years of disturbed liberty. The spirit of freedom oppressed by the weight of European aristocracy, accumulated force, with the assistance of equality, (produced by the just and wise laws of inheritance enacted by the first revolution,) to burst asunder their chains, and claim part of their natural rights. It was entirely the work of the industrious producers. The rich and influential did not join until success had proclaimed what was at first considered as a rebellion. A praiseworthy revolution, a great part of which was due to the equality produced by the abolition of the unjust laws of primogeniture and entails, effected by the first revolution. A striking instance that the millions alone can benefit the millions. Belgium, though having tasted the sweets of representation a very short time, but remaining longer under the Napoleon code, that just and equal divider of property, the millions of industrious producers followed the example of their neighbors, the French, and expelled the hereditary power. The Prussian provinces south of the Rhine and Westphalia, having enjoyed for some time, the benefit of elective government, and the absence of the tyrannical feudal system, restored by their ancient masters, were enabled to make the comparison, and to struggle hard for that freedom, which their essential interest so impeperiously demanded. Even superstitious and bigoted Spain, so long sunk under the mire and misery of king-craft and priest-craft, having enjoyed for a very short period, the mild but disturbed government of their Cortes, comparing it with the despotism of Ferdinand, are at present disposed to throw off the yoke of arbitrary power, and return to that freedom they were so unjustly deprived of, by the artifices and tyranny of the Bourbons. Italy having the advantage of a comparison between some kind of freedom by election, and the despotism of hereditary power, most probably will strive to regain their independence under the elective system, which may make the tour of Europe. No people yet have been so well informed as to judge a priori, nor any so ignorant as not to distinguish their interest by the practical comparison, which the alternation of despotism and freedom has lately furnished them. So that it is probable, that no nation having the practical knowledge of the advantages of elective government, will ever be contented under hereditary power.

SUPERIORITY OF GOOD PARENTAL EDUCATION. INUTILITY OF THE OLD SYSTEM OF EDUCATION. VICE AND CRIME INCREASE IN PROPORTION TO INEQUALITY OF WEALTH AND KNOWLEDGE.

August 17*th*, 1834.

Civilization has taken the education of children out of the hands of the parents, and intrusted it to school masters; and the instruction of men is taken from their own experience, and the evidence of their senses, and confided to the fictitious and interested creeds of church and state. This change might have been beneficial to humanity, had either the schoolmasters, or the civil and religious rulers, the same natural interest in the prosperity, comfort and happiness of their pupils, that their parents had. From the old woman's school, which keeps infants in prison, to keep them out of mischief, to the most learned professors of our universities, they are all paid by time, and have a strong pecuniary interest in prolonging the residence of their scholars or students under their control, not benefiting by the utility, convenience or necessity the pupils might have in life for the exercise of useful knowledge, they only teach them what and in the same manner they were taught themselves. Schoolmasters and professors receive an education to fit them for the profession, not to communicate knowledge to suit the progress of civilization of the present day, but the learning of the schools that was thought necessary for the priests and other learned professions four or five hundred years ago. This has caused the general complaint against classical education, that they learn nothing they are required to practice in the present advanced state of society, but that all, except perhaps divines, must be taught all that is useful through life, by their own industry after they leave school. Why those who are educated in the rights and ceremonies of the church, have in all christian countries been employed as instructors of children, may arise from the strong prejudices and violent attachment, that all ignorant people have to the learned mysteries of religion; their faith in them, being in the exact ratio of their incomprehensible nature, or of the pleasure of the imagination, increased with the distance they are out of the reach of all our senses; all which is added to the various and contradictory suppositions and conjectures of where we shall go, what we shall do, or whether we shall be eternally happy or miserable after death, and this is considered of more utility, and is greatly preferred to the positive knowledge of realities, and to the accurate ideas of men and things which surround us, and without the aid and assistance of which natural production, our existence could not be prolonged. As the old monkish system of the dead languages, taught us little or nothing that we could make any use of, but left us to learn the useful after we left school, the education by savage parents could not do less, but the little they taught would have a reference to utility, to put their children in the right road to benefit by their own experience, and to acquire the knowledge necessary for their existence in the circumstances that surround them. This is the reason why few savages fail in the necessary adroitness and skill, for supplying all things fit for their situation. Whereas not one in a hundred, in civilized life, accomplishes the end he proposes, or passes through the world with any independence or reputation! but loaded with misfortunes, disappointments and misery, he descends, by a premature death, with sorrow to the grave. The old adage that 'a sensible mother makes a sensible child,' shows the esteem in which parental education was generally held, and all those who have had knowledge, justly to appreciate the Pestalozzian system of education, were in hopes that when all fathers and mothers were so instructed, there would be no necessity for schoolmasters; for that all classes of parents could communicate to their children, both what they had learned at school, and all they had learned since they left it. It is therefore probable that civilization, in creating a distinct interest by the profession of teachers, has not benefitted the millions of industrious producers, however it may have favored the monopoly of knowledge in the few, always liable to be used at the expense of the many.

In the infancy of civilization, both the civil and religious authorities were vested in the same chief; and it was not until after the intricate and complicated contrivances of civilization, had extended the sphere of their artificial and multifarious action, that they were separated into different squads, to drive the vehicles of physical force or moral faith, according to the different roads on earth, or towards the heavens above, which their interests induced them to travel. But they remained always closely united, for the mutual support of their arbitrary authorities, and have increased in their luxurious affluence and expenditure nearly one thousand fold in the greater part of the civilized world, within the last four hundred years. For instance, in the year 1421, the revenues for the support of the state in Britain, did not exceed £60,000 sterling, and at the present day they exceed sixty millions; and the church have augmented their fees, perquisites and opulence nearly in the same proportion, during the whole time of this gradual accumulation (though the industrious producers were forced to furnish by their labor, one thousand times more to the public, and still more to the private expenses,) yet neither their numbers, comforts nor happiness have increased. The working people were more comfortably fed, clothed and lodged four hundred years ago than at present, and all this exorbitant increase of one thousand times more, exacted from the industrious millions of producers by the few consumers, has been swallowed up in the bottomless pit of church and state extravagance. The kind of education or deceptive information they could possibly be expected to give their subjects, could only be to keep up the delusion against the evidence of their senses, that all this pomp, parade, luxurious show and extravagance, was positively necessary to their well-being here and hereafter; that without all this expense to govern them, they would be cutting one another's throats on this earth, and be condemned to eternal flames in the next world. They have trusted to this ignorance of their people, that they should not be capable of comparing the increased quantity of robberies, swindling, murders and other crimes of the present time, with what existed four hundred years ago, and of perceiving that all those outrages on morality, have kept pace with the exorbitant expenses, and consequent great inequality of property and knowledge. Setting aside the fine spun theories of refined and elegant civilization, and judging from the practice of the multitude of all descriptions, one would be tempted to doubt of the advantages of civilization, to the millions of industrious producers, as far as it has yet gone.

Let us hope that this iron age in passing away before the sunshine of sciences and the arts; that this transition from the savage state, to a kind of civilization, in which most of the customs in favor of the few are retained, and as many of the practices in favor of the many, abolished; let us hope that a just equality will unite the whole human family in one common interest, taught by experience, that liberty without equality is but a name, and no security against the encroachments of the strong against the weak; that great inequality of property, knowledge and power must originate great abuses, and that vice and crime must be in proportion, as I have endeavored to prove in a former number, by the state of society in most of the nations in the old world.— Statistics are the only criterion to judge of the situation of nations, as accounts are the only possible mode of judging of the solvency of a merchant; they are the only part of history in which the smallest dependence can be placed. If a comparison could be made between the increase of our public expenses, the increased inequality of property and knowledge, the increase of hazardous speculations, the increased luxury and extravagance of living, and the increase of immorality, vice and crime, since the end of our revolution and the present day, I have not a doubt that there would be found nearly an exact proportion, in the gradual progression of all these perpetual attendants, on what has been called civilization, as far as it has yet gone. Figures and drawings may be representations of many of the properties of things, but language is so imperfect, vague and undefined, as to leave great doubts and difficulties, as the innumerable commentators on all our ancient records evidently prove. The ameteurs of history may be flattered by the latitude given to each of affixing his own construction to the historic page, but numbers are invariably the same in all ages and languages and need no commentator, even to the most ignorant of the millions.

MORALLY INTOXICATING EFFECTS OF POWER. MONOPOLY OF POWER LEADS TO A MONOPOLY OF PROPERTY. THE INTEREST OF THE WORKING MEN WILL LEAD THEM TO CHANGE THEIR OFFICERS FREQUENTLY, TO ABOLISH MONOPOLIES AND TO RESTRAIN THE PAPER CURRENCY.

August 20, 1834.

Power is a poison, which intoxicates all mankind. The partial page of history, which flatters the rulers and the great and disguises their misdeeds under the high sounding names of patriotism, heroism, etc., contains little else but illustrations of abuse, usurpation, rapine and plunder, with the various cunning contrivances, by means of which the well combined few, duped and deceived the ignorant;—the numberless ingenious inventions practiced by the consumers to convert to their own use the property of the industrious producers; the different modes of monopolizing power and profit under the specious pretence of general good, but founded entirely on self-aggrandizement and gratification. History sounds aloud the praises of those far famed conquerors, those wholesale butchers of their species, who, more cruel and savage than the tiger or lion, destroying and slaughtering what they cannot consume, are all the same scourges of humanity, from Alexander to Tamerlane, and Kouli Khan. Their eulogium has filled the deceptive pages of history, to the utter exclusion of the merits, interest or convenience of those who labor supported and maintained all; these are only mentioned numerically as the passive destroyer and destroyed. An individual dining at a great general's table, where the famous warriors were fighting their battles over again, tired of their repetitions, exclaimed, "in all your tactics you have forgotten one essential part of a soldier's education, that is to eat all he kills, and then the day of battle would be the day of feasting," and he might have added, it would be some excuse, though a bad one, for the butchery.

Might has always trampled on and tyrannized over right, and the quantum of injustice and despotism, has always been in proportion to the quantum of power, or the great inequality of the condition of men. The same actions performed by an individual, or by the public rulers, have not the same name. Deceiving and overreaching in individuals, is called swindling; but when dextrously managed by the great statesman, is called good policy and praiseworthy wisdom. There is an immense difference between the ideas acquired by looking down and looking up; on looking down objects are confused, and the vision is apt to be deranged so as to create giddiness. The same takes place in all moral elevations to superiority in power, with this difference, that the physical giddiness by looking down from great heights, ceases by habit; whereas the moral derangement by power increases in the ratio of the time possessed; and though the quantum of power which a man can possess without intoxication, is a good criterion of his force of mind, yet there is a dose which no man can withstand. Bonaparte perhaps resisted as strong a portion for as long a time as any one who preceded him; but at last he was overcome, and his marching into Spain, was one of the fist symptoms of it.

In elective governments of universal suffrage, every citizen has frequent opportunities of practically convincing himself of the baneful effects of power by observing the change in opinions and actions, which takes place in his fellow citizens, who happen to be elected or placed in power, by those who have the right of appointment. This change will be greater in those who before professed democracy, than in an aristocrat, who will only become a little more violent in his old opinions; but the democrat will most probably be entirely converted to the aristocratic creed, and though the dose of power be small, and its continuance very uncertain, yet so strong is the poison that it is capable of affecting the conduct of the individual during the rest of his lifetime. With this view of the subject, it would appear great injustice and cruelty to continue, by re-election, any individual so long in office as to make him depend on power for his comforts or happiness; for the longer he is in office, the more attached he will be to artificial superiority and the greater must be his disappointment and chagrin, in being forced to quit it, as a continuance in any elective office, under a system of liberty and equality cannot reasonably be expected; though the ignorance and apathy of the millions, have created a set of office hunters in every part of our Union, whose trade must cease to be profitable when the working people claim their rights. As they will naturally prefer those of their own profession, who have become respectable by their utility and industry, and who from a practical knowledge of their real interest, and a fellow feeling for their wants and necessities, are most likely to legislate in favor of their own professions.

If a certain division of property, knowledge and power is necessary to the enjoyment of liberty and equality, the monopoly of power by any class of citizens must counteract that equality, as it leads to a monopoly of property. Witness our monopolizing bank and other charters which must finish in a monopoly of knowledge, which will at last root out liberty and equality from society. The only cure is wholly in the power of the millions, by universal suffrage to divide power equally by the ballot boxes, in never electing the same individual twice to any place of trust or profit, and all giving their votes to those of the same trade with themselves.— That is, let all the laborers or tradesmen vote for those who work with their hands, and who consequently are in the class of producers, and being only once in office, cannot contract an interest in monopoly, and will therefore legislate for the interest of the producers, from whom and by whom they were elevated to power for a short time, and to whose condition, circumstances and relative situation they must return for the remainder of their lives.

When property and knowledge have been by misrule, monopolized in the hands of the few, they can be justly and fairly equalized, only by the equal division of power, which in all elective governments of universal suffrage, is the right of the millions, and may any time they please, be put legally into practice; when the equality of property and knowledge must follow as the shadow follows the substance. By annulling all bank and other exclusive charters and monopolies, they will restore the practice of liberty and equality, by allowing every citizen to do what cannot hurt others, all having the same and equal rights. To lessen hazardous speculations, exorbitant credits, law litigations and mysterious intricacies, they can withdraw the power of coercing the payment of debts, excepting where property is deposited. But to restrain the paper circulation within a prudent and useful currency, all issues of paper that may be substituted for specie, either payable to order or bearer, on being refused payment, the protest should be a judgment and warrant to sieze on the property of all who ever received any dividend, if a bank note to bearer, or endorser or accepter, if to order. All voluntary contracts of sales or purchases between individuals ought to rest on the honor and honesty of those contracting to pay, without any dependence on the coercion of the law in case of defalcation. The aristocratic tyranny of the Roman laws, in sacrificing the rights, privileges and liberties of the person to property, is the origin of our despotic debtor and creditor laws, introduced in barbarous ages and rigorously maintained by all governments, whether hereditary or elective, that have been as yet swayed and controled by the interest of the rich and aristocratic orders. Now when heads are to be counted at the ballot boxes, the interest of the many, who have been the debtors, must prevail.

VICE AND CRIME ARE IN PROPORTION TO INEQUALITY. IMPROVEMENTS WHICH OUGHT TO BE MADE BY THE WORKING MEN. FEW CHARTERED BANKS IN EUROPE.

August 28th, 1834.

Morality follows equality, as the shadow follows the substance. Immorality is in proportion to the artificial inequality of conditions, the consequences of the various devices, combinations and intrigues of civilization as far as it has yet gone. Temptation to injustice and tyranny, in those who are above character or responsibility, is too great to be restrained by any laws, and the propensity to retaliation, by those reduced below, is equally out of the reach of legal restraint. Where the state of society is reduced to masters and slaves, it is the greatest possible inequality in the condition of mankind, and at the same time it presents the greatest habitual mass of immorality. The master, by the force and combination of laws, deprives the slave of the fruits of his labor, and the slave to regain part of it, uses every artifice, cunning and underhand roguery; so that it is a perpetual war between force and fraud, whether the slaves are of the same white race as their masters, as in Russia, or of a black race, as in the West Indies and our Southern states; the same causes produce the same effects, we are all the children of surrounding circumstances. The habitual seat of immorality and crime, is the two extremes of luxury and poverty, the middle ranks, are where virtue and honesty have taken refuge in all countries. A constant temptation of luxurious abundance in the face of starving poverty, is the cause of crime, whilst the means of supporting that extravagance, produces every species of injustice, tyranny and oppression.

Compare the quantity of crime in France and Britain, the two countries the nearest a par in civilization, excepting that France has had her property and knowledge equalized by a radical revolution, and Britain has been increasing the inequality of both knowledge and property, by heaping it on the rich and starving the poor; in consequence, there is nearly five times the crime in Britain in proportion to the population, that there is in France. In Germany the feudal tenure of landed property, one or at most two days labor in the week for the rent of a farm, though dear enough at the time it was fixed, from the improvement in agriculture and the rise in the value of landed property, is not now more than a fifth of what the land would rent for, which has been gradually equalizing property and consequently knowledge in Germany, and in the same proportion has been diminishing crime. In Spain and Italy, the tyranny of church and state, have pushed the whole population into the two extremes of riches and poverty, though for the want of a free press, one-tenth part of the crimes committed are not known, yet crimes have increased, and will continue to increase, in proportion to the great inequality of conditions. The great equality of property and knowledge in Switzerland, has almost annihilated crime. The accumulation of wickedness is in proportion to the monopolization of power.

Laws are but a weak remedy against perpetual temptation, even if they were fairly, justly and impartially made and administered, which is impossible in a state of great inequality of condition. It is the rich, influential and powerful, who have both the making and the administering the laws; and to expect equal justice to the poor, would be to expect the reversion of all nature's laws, in contradiction to all the known motives of human actions! Where laws are the will of despots, and administered by their minions, justice is sold to the highest bidder in all countries. When a partial representation gives some power to public opinion, it is the partiality of the laws in favor of the rich who made them, and their multifarious complicacy, which places the execution out of the reach of the poor man's pocket, and keeps him subjected to the will of the wealthy, more rigorously than the will and caprice of a despot. For a well informed despot, can have no interest in punishing his slaves with litigious and ill defined laws, having no dependence on the laws which regulate the conduct of one subject towards another, for the support of his authority.

We therefore find the most explicit and well defined code of laws made by despots, as for instance the last and the best, the Napoleon code; but the execution of their laws is always corrupt, being entrusted to the small ramifications of the despotic power, in the hands of judges. Nothing short of the division of power by the equality of a jury of independent citizens, can secure equal or impartial justice; there can be no honest decision, but by a jury of equals, and no upright judges but those kept so by a jury.

Equality is the key-stone of freedom; inequality a mine which saps the foundation of human happiness; a thief that steals on the unwary by slow and imperceptible degrees, always under the pretence of furthering the interest of the people in this or the next world, equally fallacious and hypocritical, whose flattery and adulation all free people ought to be on their guard against. Substitute the word *my* for their word *public*, in all their declamatory orations, and change those of *philanthrophy*, *patriotism*, *benevolence*, *charity*, etc., which issue from the pulpit or the forum, into *self-interest* as the only possible means of not being deceived, and made the dupes of religious or political quacks.

Our working people, by insisting that all the children shall be fed, clothed and educated on an equality, at the expense of the people's purse, will secure equality in the next age, but unless they annihilate the sources of inequality in this, they may find the accumulated strength of a well organized opposition, supported by the monopolized wealth of ages, too strong for all the energy they can command in their present state of knowledge and their unfortunate division of temporary interest, sacrificing future happiness to present ease and indolence. When they shall elect a majority of legislators who have an interest in their welfare, that is, of their own trades and professions, without which they can do nothing, they will find it easy to prove that all bank or other monopolizing charters, are contrary to the letter or spirit of all the constitutions of the Union. The annulling of all such charters may be done in one session; which will deprive the moneyed interest, their opponents, of the use and assistance of all the circulating money of the Union. Substituting direct for indirect taxation on consumption, would relieve the millions from the greatest part of the weight of public expenses, as I have formerly endeavored to prove, by raising the necessary revenue on every species of property, making all persons pay in proportion to their property protected by the state. They ought to give a free circulation to property and knowledge, by relieving them from the clutches of custom house and excise officers, and making every port a free port; reduce the wages of political labor to a par with other useful or necessary labor; elect all officers of trust or profit, and thus take the patronage from the people's servants, thereby taking away all temptation to intrigue, bribery and corruption at elections.

Those who live and trade on bank discounts, will cry out "poverty, destruction, and annihilation of commerce;" but they may be answered by enquiring how do England and France, who have only one chartered discount bank to transact their business; how do Holland, Hamburg, Bremen, etc., who have nothing but a bank of deposite, and no bank of discount; how do the greatest part of Germany, Spain, Portugal and Italy, who have no chartered bank either of deposite or discount; do they not all carry on as much commerce as their surplus produce will permit them? and what addition can the redundance of circulating paper make to the surplus produce of labor? the only materials that can possibly support a profitable commerce. Does not an artificial paper capital tempt and encourage a greater proportion of the population to go into non-productive trades and professions, by facilitating their various contrivances for living on the industry of others, and thereby lessening the sum of surplus produce? The few who complain, may have selfish reason to do so, because it may force them to work harder and spend less; but it would be the height of presumption to pretend that it is the interest of laborers to feed and maintain a greater number of the non-producers, than are necessary. All callings and professions pretend to be productive; that is, by their calling appropriate a certain proportion of the produce of other's labor to their own use; but most of those who have been called nonproductive, would find it difficult to show in what article, substance, or trade, they have increased the production. Most of them only administer to the ideal wants of civilization, which as yet have added little to the happiness of the great bulk of mankind.

PROSTITUTION OF THE PRESS. ALL OFFICERS OUGHT TO BE APPOINTED AT THE POLES.

August 30, 1834.

So many of our newspapers are filled with electioneering squibs, as to give foreigners the idea that the editors of our gazettes, control and dictate to our electors. Ever since the commencement of our federal government the party spirit of foction and rage for places and salaries, have increased so rapidly, as to become a nuisance which occupies the columns of most of our periodicals, to the total subversion of all truth, reason or rationality, incurring an immense waste of the money, time and labor of our industrious producers. The fulsome praise and flattery they bestow on their patrons or payers, can only be equaled for its deviation from truth, by the scurrility, defamation and detraction, which they utter against their adversaries. As no real or useful knowledge can flow but through the channel of truth, it bewilders the electors in a labyrinth of contradictions, preventing them from making use of the little information their limited experience affords them. Such inveterate intriguing is an expenditure of money and morals, both to the office hunters and all concerned; throws obloquy on the elective system, by giving the enemies of freedom some pretence to depreciate its great advantages, and creates a violent ill will and hatred between citizens, whose essential interest imperiously requires union, concert and friendship, as the only solid foundation of the social system.—The pecuniary loss of time and labor to the Union, may be guessed at, but the moral depreciation, by meetings, clubs, political associations, drinking, propagating falsehoods, and false promises on canvassing for votes, etc., etc., are consequences whose demoralizing effects are beyond calculation.—The losses of time and labor to the Union estimated in money, may be stated thus, viz:

Suppose 500 printing presses publishing political falsehoods, each having 1,000 subscribers is 500,000 subscribers, which would require 1,000 reams of paper per day, at 365 in a year, will be 365,000 reams in a year; at an average of $4 per ream, is $1,460,000

Suppose six men at each press on average at $2 per day, is 6,000, a year, say about 2,190,000

500,000 subscribers, and we may safely suppose ten more readers to every subscriber, is 5,000,000 of readers who lose half a day, say 150 days in the year, 750,000,000 of days at an average of half a dollar per day, is 375,000,000

$378,650,000

This enormous sum is not only lost to the Union, but doubly so, as wasting both labor and time that might be occupied in circulating some useful information and knowledge to the advantage of society. Besides all the ill-will, quarrels and disputes, often ending in duels and bloodshed; the time lost in making and hearing stump speeches and tavern orations, with the drinking and rioting attending canvassing, etc.

Were all these detrimental expenses, inconveniences, disputes, demoralizing principles, vices and corruption, inherent in or attached to the elective system, people must grin and bear it, as a set off against the many and great benefits they have and must always derive from the advantages the representative governments give them, of having all laws, rules and regulations, constituted and made for the benefit of the great majority, by universal suffrage; but the contrary is evidently the fact, the instructing one or more individuals, elected into place by the voice of the people, with the power of appointing to offices of trust and profit, is and must always be in opposition to every principle of representation. The people, in a well organized elective government, are the only source of power, and are the best judges of all their agents, as being the sole benefiters by their just, judicious and honest conduct and the only sufferers by their incapacity, negligence or roguery—besides being on the spot where the agents' duty is to be performed, and without any temptation to partiality, constitutes them the fittest and most impartial judges of their agents' conduct. This power of appointment ought not to be delegated by the people to any of their agents or governors, as it is subject to many abuses, besides the before mentioned evils and vices, created by patronage at elections; for the rulers will certainly give the places to their friends who are seldom the friends of the majority of the people, of whom they are quite independent, having only to please and obey their master who made them and can unmake them. This is like all other imitations of hereditary power, whose existence depends on heaping authority on the few, but it is destructive of all free governments founded on liberty and equality, whose safety depends on the power being left in the possession of the many. The fault is not attributable to the representative system, but to the heterogeneous mixture of the complicated and arbitrary principles and practices of hereditary despotism, with the simple and natural rules and practices arising out of the interest of the majority in elective governments, which like fire and water, cannot exist peaceably in the same body politic.

If the opposition to those necessary reforms for the interest of the millions, were limited to those who could possibly enjoy the right of appointing to offices of trust and profit, their numbers would be so few, that their voice would scarcely be heard amongst the majority of the nation. But in a system of freedom and equality, every man who enters on a political career, supposes the possibility of his arriving at the highest stations of power and prerogative, which induces many thousands to advocate their privileges, per-

quisites and profits for one who can benefit by them.—
This accounts for the accumulation of patronage to such an
alarming degree as to threaten the peace and tranquility of
the Union for many years before every election. There cannot possibly be any good reason adduced against the inhabitants
of the locality amongst whom the duties of the office are to be
performed, electing the officer at stated times, to continue him in
place, or reject him according to his merits. In an elective government of universal suffrage, to give the right of every man
after the age of twenty-one years to be a judge of the merits and
capabilities of presidents, senators, governors, legislators, etc.
whose duties are so complicated and distinct from the common understanding of the electors, and their field of operation
so far removed out of the reach of their inspection, and at
the same time to deny them the right of electing an inferior
officer, such as a collector or a postmaster, whose duties are
all performed under their eyes, subject to their daily inspection,
is so contrary to all common sense, reason or rationality, as
only to be accounted for by the strong love of power inherent
in mankind who command, and the ignorant habits of submission contracted by long subjection, in those who obey.

Reduce the wages of political labor to a par with other
useful occupations, and give the millions all the rights and prerogatives attached to the representative system, without any
interference of the principles and practices of arbitrary hereditary power by allowing them to elect every officer of trust
and profit, and there would be no more canvassing, intrigue or
corruption at any of our elections, than there is now at an
election of a governor for the states of Connecticut or Virginia. The elective sheriffs of Virginia and Vermont, and
some other states, collect the state taxes at a small expense,
without any loss or inconvenience, and there can be no good
reason why elective officers might not collect all the revenue.
Postmasters are more immediately servants of the people
where they do their duty, than even collectors, and still less
necessity exists, of their being under the immediate control
of any executive. In a country where violent political parties

run so high, and where a great many nonproductive consumers depend on public salaries for their bread, it is dangerous to intrust the post office to the control and direction of one, who must always be at the head of one of the political parties. Even supposing that he may be above temptation, it cannot be expected that those he appoints will not strive to keep their patron in power, as the only way of being certain of retaining their places. It would be easy to take away the temptation, and at the same time reduce the profits and patronage—the cause of all the wrangling and fighting for public employments.

ARMIES RAISED BY CONSCRIPTION MORE FAVORABLE TO FREEDOM THAN THOSE OF ORDINARY ENLISTMENT.

Sept. 5th, 1834.

Perhaps the only thing, that the millions of industrious producers, in all countries, have to fear, is their ignorance of their own independence, utility and power, producing diffidence in their own exertions, a want of knowledge of their own abilities, when united for the general welfare. Although the force of union is understood by all our four-footed neighbors in their natural state, yet the lords of creation have been kept ignorant of it by the cunning contrivances of priests and kings, the deep-laid plots of church and state. The abolishing of the unjust laws of inheritance, with the effects of physical force, produced in the course of revolutionary enthusiasm, has returned those countries nearer to the natural equality, and divided property, knowledge, and power, more congenial with the comfort, happiness, and freedom of the millions. Of all these concurring circumstances, the revolution in France is the latest fruits, which an unprecedented equality has produced. A military spirit, created by freedom during the first revolution; disciplined by Bonaparte; fomented by the coalition; and which the bigotry and superstition of the Bourbons attempted to suffocate, exploded in the form of a million and a half of national guards, of which there are not perhaps five thousand nonproductive consumers, forms a novelty in the history of mankind, which beggars all former analogy. It exhibited a million and a half of armed men, united to obtain freedom, elevated, by the great division of property, above poverty, and kept below luxury, in that middle state of society, from which all energy, talent and genius spring, having a fellow feeling with the same class scattered over the civilized world. The consequences of such a chronological union of unprecedented events, must be looked for in other registers, than the partial, delusive pages of history, which from the barbarous ages to the present, describe human nature as revolving in a vicious circle of actions. Nothing elucidates better the vast advantages of combination and union, than military evolutions; and though hitherto soldiers have been fighting to accumulate riches, power and honors on the aristocratic few, yet the mode of recruiting by conscription, since the first French revolution, changes the nature of the materials, as well as their views of their interest, by allying the soldier to the citizen, may assimilate their opinions, and approach both to a par with the knowledge of the day, and turn the former instruments of despotism into advocates and supporters of freedom.

It is an anomaly in the history of our species, that people have only yet been trusted with the election of their chief political agents, though the complicated extension of their duties, removes them out of the reach of the inspection of the electors, while all the subordinate offices, are left to the patronage of the political chiefs, though the sphere of duty of the inferior officers is completely within the cognizance of the citizens, amongst whom their duties are performed. The elective system having succeeded so well in the appointment of the superior officers, where the difficulty of choice required so much more experience and knowledge, it was natural to expect the extension of the elective system to all the subordinate officers, of whose capability and conduct the electors were more competent judges. But all the constitutions of representative governments, have been made by the superior political agents, who, though they might neglect the interest of their constituents, did not forget their own. Yet the election of every officer of power or profit by the majority of the people who maintain and pay them, is the only possible mode of reconciling the jarring interest of the governors and governed, and establishing, on a permanent base, that equality so essential to freedom.

In the commencement of the first French revolution, the national guards elected their officers; out of which first choice, Bonaparte was enabled to select the most of his expert generals. The second revolution has followed the example of the first only in this principle, being perhaps as necessary to reconcile the interests of the officers and soldiers in the military, as it is the rulers and ruled in the civil departments. Had the representative and federative governments been a banking, mercantile, or manufacturing scheme, that had so completely succeeded in what it was intended for, the interest and happiness of mankind, its fame and qualities would have been blazoned forth to the four quarters of the globe, and its beneficial principles would have extended to every congregation of human beings, where circumstances required a delegation of power to be used for the interest of the majority, as the only possible means of insuring that the authority so delegated, shall be justly, honestly, and judiciously used, for the benefit of those, who producing all, ought to have the right of distributing all. But the simplicity, economy and tendency to equality, of the representative and federative systems, was too much in favor of the millions of industrious producers, to be encouraged by the ambitious, who delight in arbitrary power, and did not serve the interest of aristocracy, founded on monopoly and exclusive privileges, a class that had accumulated sufficient property, to influence the printing, writing, speaking, and almost all the thinking of the community. At first it was declared impossible that the passions and prejudices of the millions, would permit them to enjoy self-government; as if the hereditary rulers were free from passions and prejudices. After experience proved it not only practicable, but infinitely superior in the production of arts, sciences, wisdom, wealth and happiness, to any other form of government; it was then stated to be a system only fit for a young country, as they were pleased to call the United States, but totally inapplicable to any old thickly inhabited country.

So much are mankind the children of habit, and so little ruled by reason, that although we have thrived under a flood of accumulating prosperity for the last half century, entirely owing to the partial adoption of the election of our superior political chiefs, yet we have not attempted to extend the beneficial principle to subordinate officers, but left the patronage of their appointment in the power of elective rulers; which has become such a bone of contention, increasing with our rapid population, as to threaten the peace, prosperity, and happiness of the Union at every election. Common sense might have whispered, if her modest voice could have been heard in the midst of the contention, tumults and broils of violent political parties, that a principle which selected so judiciously those capable of wielding the destinies of the nation, in the highest offices, could not possibly fail in electing fit and suitable candidates for all the inferior offices of trust and profit, and at the same time retaining the sovereignty in the hands of the majority of the millions, agreeably to the evident principles of elective power by universal suffrage, *never to delegate authority but from the necessity of circumstances, and then only for short and stated periods; to make rotation in office as complete and universally practicable as the suffrage on which it is founded, perpetuating an equal division of property, knowledge, and power, as the only solid basis of freedom.*

Our working people, claiming their rights, so long dormant, of a representation in proportion to their numbers and utility, will be the commencement of a moral revolution, that will most probably extend the sphere of universal suffrage to the smallest ramifications of delegated authority—retaining the full power in the great majority for promoting "the greatest happiness in the greatest number." When the millions of industrious producers, by the power which universal suffrage gives them, shall have learned to prosecute their interest, with as determined a union and combination, as the nonproductive consumers have hitherto done, when equality shall have given every individual in the society, his share of power and consideration, then the interest of the many, neither in peace nor war, will be sacrificed to the ambition of the few; the whole principles and policy of governments will be changed; in place of aggregating vast empires, where corruption, vice and crime are in the ratio of the extent, the political associations will be confined to the smallest possible limits for internal regulations, united in the most extensive federations for external protection. This is as certain a consequence of the more equal division of property, knowledge and power, as the contrary has been by the monopoly of all three in the possession of the few, at the expense of the many.

EVILS OF THE PRESENT SYSTEM OF BANKING. PROPER SYSTEM.

Sept. 10*th*, 1834.

In place of the United States Bank regulating the currency, as is pretended by those who have an interest in being its friends and advocates, it, in conjunction with the other banks, helped to derange the currency, just when it was most necessary, for both public and private affairs, to have a sound and effective circulating medium, at the beginning of the last war. All the banks, excepting those in Boston, having abused the unlimited power granted them by their charters, of issuing as much paper, and paying as large a dividend, as their interest or cupidity required, were unable to take up their notes, which the diminution of commerce or confidence could not keep in circulation, stopped payment and threw the loss on the public; in place of stopping discounting, and throwing the loss on their customers, who had been the principal gainers by the circulation of their notes. At Paris, during the winter that Bonaparte remained at Vienna, the want of confidence caused a run on the Bank of France, etc., though it did not stop payment, there was a crowd at the door, of half a mile long, waiting to get their notes paid, which were at a discount of 12 to 15 per cent. The directors being all bankers or merchants, finding it their interest to support their customers, kept discounting and increasing the amount of notes in circulation, thereby throwing the loss on the public, for the purpose of saving their customers, though, had they acted as justice, and a due consideration for the credit of the bank required, and suspended discounts for 60 days, they would have taken up all their notes without any advance of specie. Bonaparte, on his return, saw through the trick, discharged his treasurer, reorganized the bank, doubled the capital, put a governor and two directors, without whose consent no discounts were to be made, and reduced the interest on discounts from 5 to 4 per cent., under which regulations the bank continued without the smallest inconvenience or complaint the whole time of his reign.

All the banks of the Union stopping payment (excepting those of Boston,) caused a loss to the public of from 5 to 7 per cent, ascertained by the premiums of drafts on Boston, the only place in the Union, that retained their specie circulation.

The consequence of this defalcation of the banks, was to reduce all their notes to a depreciating paper currency. For though no law was passed to make them a legal tender, yet the necessity of taking them, or nothing, was equal to a law. From which it would appear, that banks, in place of regulating the currency, have been the principal means of depreciating and deranging it, so as to render it a fluctuating standard of value. Thus in Britain, when the bank, by stopping payment, caused the public to lose 30 per cent on all the bank notes they had issued; to which there were no limits, while they were freed from the necessity of paying them by an order from government; a necessary preliminary in Britain, which was dispensed with by our banks, who break their contracts without any authority, and so far from preventing the states from issuing paper currency, they forced a paper currency on the states; for which they received an interest of from 6 to 8 per cent according to the legal interest of each state.

The pretension that the bank of the United States is necessary to transfer the revenue from the place of collection to the place of distribution, is an imitation of Britain, without a necessity. The British system is so overwhelmed with debts, tithes, taxes, etc., etc., that nearly 400 millions of dollars, are yearly transfered from the producers to the consumers, which requires all the invention and machinery of the most complicated financial machinery to extract it out of the producers, and a machine equally intricate and mysterious, to give the appearance of impartiality and justice, in the arrangement and distribution of such an enormous revenue, which, if collected and circulated in silver, would require half the horses and waggons in the island to transport it. But our small expenses of thirteen millions of dollars, the most of which is disbursed at or near the place of collection for merely the receiving of which, the United States bank has the use of five millions of dollars at 6 per cent interest, (300,000 a year,) is certainly an enormous exaggeration of even British expenditure, the most expensive government on earth; the aristocracy of which has found the means to make the people pay dearly for the small portion of liberty they permit them to enjoy; and our self-created, monied aristocracy, by following so closely their example, would in time reduce our working people to the same deplorable condition.

There are two kinds of banks: that of deposite, and that of discount with a paper circulation. The former is a simple means of distributing capital for the encouragement of industry and commerce, under such strict rules and regulations as to exclude all favoritism and abuse. The latter depending entirely on personal responsibility, is liable to all the abuse that must arise, from the partiality of those who manage for their friends or favorites, particularly when they are merely directors, without risking any pecuniary loss by the failure of the bank. And should they place themselves as debtors to the bank, in the situation of gaining by its failure, there is still greater temptation to every kind of mismanagement and abuse. The facility given to the transfer of property by the cheap medium of circulating paper, if not counterbalanced by the loss in counterfeits, and the excessive issues of notes, is the principal advantage, the public in general gain by such banks. But there is no good reason why monied institutions should not be organized with all the advantages of both systems and avoiding the defects attached to either. A bank of deposite might be established in the capital of each state, or of the United States, under the superintendence of the elective officers of government, to lend money for stated periods of six, nine, or twelve months, at the lawful interest, under fixed rules and regulations. So that it would require only clerks, and warehousemen to transact the business, agreeably to the list of values, that were to be advanced on each species of property, after its deposite in the bank warehouse. And when it was necessary to renew the term of the loan, it might be arranged by the chief directors, to suit the funds of the bank. And in case of the necessity of a sale or foreclosing the mortgage, all might be settled so as to avoid all recurrence to the law, by a well defined and clear specification of the terms, on which the loan of the money was granted. Said banks of deposite, might issue notes payable to order, after as many days sight, as might suit the convenience of the bank, and the security in case of a fraudulent transfer, on a sheet of paper for the endorsement of those through whose hands they passed. This would make it impossible to counterfeit, as they would only be current on the responsibility of the endorsers, and would save the trouble of all complicated engraving, to increase the difficulty of forging. They might be made of sums from 50 to 1,000 dollars, on thin paper for the saving of postage, and never be issued twice, but be cancelled, as the notes of the bank of England, after having been checked with the check book, out of which they were originally cut. It would be well, for the soundness of the circulation, to have none under fifty dollars, and specie for all the small affairs. This would completely save the immense loss in forged and defaced notes, which perhaps may be calculated at five dollars per year per head, of all the inhabitants of the Union, or nearly sixty millions of dollars. These notes would pass current on the responsibility of the states or of the United States; the endorsement taking away all risk or fear of counterfeits, might be received at all the banks in the Union; by a constant exchange of their notes by the post, as all risk or temptation to rob the mails would be taken away, for no robber could pass one of them without being known as a responsible man to guaranteee his endorsement.

The deposite banks of Amsterdam, Hamburg, etc., are the oldest banks. The bank of England was the first discount bank, and it was forced to have recourse to deposite, in 1826, to relieve the distress of merchants and traders; a proof that where assistance is most necessary, banks of deposite are the safest and most effectual means of relieving the distresses of trade, as it does not increase the capital of the trader, only changes into a circulating form, that part of his capital, which lies dead on his hands for the want of the properties necessary for a circulating medium, at the same time it lessens the risk of the bank, enabling them to lend at a lower interest.

OUR WORKING MEN OUGHT TO PROFIT BY THE EUROPEAN ATTEMPTS AT REFORM AND SECURE THEIR OWN INTEREST HERE, BY REPELLING THE ENCROACHMENT OF THEIR RULERS.

Sept. 17, 1834.

It is natural for all classes of mankind, to think well of the laws, customs, and habits, of the age and country, in which those of their own rank in society have the complete control of their fellow beings. This accounts for the reverence which our modern aristocracy has for the ancients, the Romans, etc., their laws, etc., and makes them look back with regret on the feudal system, composed of cerfs and lords of the manor, slaves and masters. They are so wishfully fixed on the charms and delights of ancient despotism, whilst the whole mass of matter, motion, arts, sciences, and knowledge are advancing rapidly, that it is not astonishing, they should stumble, and blunder, in endeavoring to oppose the current of civilization, and that they should be overwhelmed, and layed much lower by the force of popular opinion, than they would have been by swimming with the stream, and endeavoring to direct it into channels more congenial with their interest. Bonaparte used to advise them to put their political institutions on a par with the knowledge of the day; which he would have helped them to do, had they admitted him as a member of their royal fraternity, and left him to govern the French. This late explosion would not then have taken place in the life time, of any of of the present European rulers; and he would, for his own interest and that of his dynasty, have secured to them as great a share of their power and prerogatives, as the diffusion of knowledge would have permitted. When they sent him to die of chagrin on the barren rock, they deprived themselves of the only one, who, by his power and talents, could teach them how to preserve part of their authority.

Most of the political and religious institutious of the old world, were promulgated in the dark ages of barbarism, when men, like their four footed neighbors, were limited to the knowledge which the experience of their own life afforded them. The millions of industrious producers were deprived of the experience of their ancestors, for want of records; the few manuscript books were so dear, as only to be read by the superior class of consumers. Until lately there was not one in a thousand who could either read or write. Even after the invention of printing, it was long before the working people, in most countries, by learning to read could benefit by it. What possible analogy can there be between the past and present? Now mechanics, as well as most working people, know the useful arts and sciences, which contribute to the comforts and conveniences of mankind, better than a Cæsar or a Cicero. The diffusion of knowledge pervades the smallest ramifications of society. The millions of industrious producers have access to knowledge, which the nobles, kings, emperors, and rulers, were deprived of in former times. The cheap and rapid circulations through the medium of the press, brings the useful knowledge of mechanism and the arts and sciences from the farther corners of the civilized world, to the doors of every peasant. The canals, rail-roads, steamboats, and steam carriages, waft intelligence from one corner of the globe to another, with the celerity of the wind. The former obstructions to social communion and union of interest, such as difference of languages, customs, habits and prejudices, may be removed by the facility of intercourse, which may tend to amalgamate the interest of the millions of industrious producers of all countries, into a combination for their mutual protection and support, like the union of hereditary aristocracy in the holy alliance, for the protection of their tyranny.

Notwithstanding such a vast change in the order of society, by the diffusion of knowledge, the Bourbons, by the assistance of the armed aristocracy of Europe, attempted to re-establish despotism in France and Spain. The coalesced powers joined Holland and Belgium under a hereditary monarch, without the consent of the people, whose laws, customs, habits, religion, previous mode of education and practices, opposed such a a union. The despotic feudal system, whose most obnoxious principles were abolished in all countries where the French authorities prevailed, has been re-established in Westphalia and the Prussian provinces south of the Rhine. The king of Prussia, on the faith of whose promise, to give a liberal constitution to his subjects, was enabled, by the assistance of the militia, to drive the French out of his dominions, now refuses to perform his promise, trusting to the bayonets of his armies recruited by conscription, which assimilates them to militia, with whom he has broken his engagements. Poland is subject to a despotism over a foundation of elective government, established in part of it by Bonaparte. The king of Sardinia has established despotism in Piedmont on the remains of freedom by elective immunities, conferred on them by their last conquerors, the French. The freedom granted to Milan and the Venetian States by the French, has been changed into a foreign despotism by the emperor of Austria, who relies, for the support of his authority, on his troops recruited by conscription. All the sovereigns of the old world, trusting to their divine hereditary rights, have been acting towards their subjects, as if they had the ignorance and barbarism of the thirteenth century to deal with.

Already has the elasticity of freedom, aided by the unprecedented equality of property and knowledge, driven despotism from France. Belgium, following the example of her neighbors the working classes in France, has dissolved that Union, made by the force of foreign bayonets. In both those countries, the troops of the line raised by conscription, refused to fire on the people. The millions of industrious producers, have claimed their rights of representation in Westphalia, Hessecassel, and Saxony, where the troops raised by conscription were in favor of the people. In Berlin, the people claimed the performance of the king's promises, but were dispersed by the royal guards; a corps made up by the sons of nobility, not recruited by conscription. There are popular commotions in Britain, Ireland, Portugal, Spain, Italy, Piedmont, and Poland, which clearly show, that all those monarchies are far behind the knowledge of the day, and that the diffusion of knowledge, even at present cannot tolerate the remains of feudality, that oppresses the industrious producers. As knowledge is advancing in a geometrical progression, the political institutions and laws, which satisfy the present population, may not be equal to the claims which a higher state of civilization may induce them to enforce, when the moral powers shall be joined to the physical. When the many understand their interest, as well as the few have hitherto done, the most useful occupations, will no longer be the most despicable and disgraceful, but the scale of utility will regulate the value of all.

Our working people may obtain knowledge cheap, by the experience of their fellows in Europe, who have been forced by the abuse of power to unite and act against all the laws, civil, military, and ecclesiastic, made and ordained by their rulers to oppress them. Our working people may be thus taught to avoid the imitation or adoption of their laws, customs or habits, contrived to keep the producers in slavish subjection, more particularly the feudal practices, originating in the dark ages of barbarism, and extended through many thousands of volumes of arbitrary precedents under the denomination of the common law of Britain. The producers of the old world were obliged to fight and conquer the hundreds of thousands of bayonets disciplined, paid and organized to keep them subject to the will and caprice of their tyrants. This may teach our producers to pay no regular army, but to trust to their militia in case any despots should dare to invade a free people. The industrious producers in Europe, are so thoroughly convinced of the unjust, partial and oppressive nature of indirect taxation, that they have burned and destroyed all the customhouses, when they had sufficient force; and when for the want of combination they had not physical force, they have claimed a change from indirect to direct taxation; a lesson for our millions of producers not to tolerate any kind of indirect taxes on consumption. The strong remonstrances of the industrious producers in Europe, against the privileged orders, monopolies, exclusive prerogatives, etc., prove the advantage gained by the few at the expense of the many, and ought to warn our working people against tolerating any kind of monopoly, any prerogatives granted to the few by the exclusion of the many, or any thing that can derange the natural equality so essential to freedom, by introducing that artificial inequality which is the promoter of misery, wretchedness, vice and crime. The frequent changes of executive officers, even under fixed hereditary power, show the necessity of division of power by rotation in office, and ought to establish it as a fixed rule in elective governments, not to elect the same man twice. If utility, public good and general welfare, flash conviction (in spite of divine hereditary right, privileged orders, long established monopolies, supported by numerous and well disciplined standing armies,) of the necessity of the foregoing changes and reforms in Europe, how much more easy and constitutional will it be for our working people, authorized by freedom and equality, guaranteed by universal suffrage, to change and reform every thing equally to their interest. It only requires them to will it at the ballot boxes, and all must be orderly and legally executed according to their orders. How much more, both of physical and moral exertion it requires on the other side of the Atlantic, to put things on a rational principal than here, and how much more disgrace the neglecting to do it.

A NATIONAL DEBT AND PAPER CURRENCY ARE OPPRESSIVE TO THE WORKING MEN.

September 20, 1834.

National debts and paper representations of property, are modern inventions of tyrannical aristocracy, to lengthen the lever, which weighs down and oppresses the industrious producers. It not only forestals the produce of the labor of the present age but mortgages that of generations yet unborn, without their consent or participation in any of the advantages purchased by an expenditure, to indulge the ambitious love of power, from which the working people who pay all, can derive no benefit. This may appear by an analysis of the loans made by one class of the nation to another, through the medium of the government, who were merely the artificial agents to transfer the property from those who produce it to those who consume it. Suppose an expedition by sea and land is planned by the rulers of one nation, to wrest from another some territory or property which their ambition or cupidity covets, and that ten millions of dollars are necessary to carry said plan into execution; but the industrious millions are already so taxed, that they cannot be loaded with more; the rulers then apply to the moneyed interest, that is, to those who have accumulated the representation of property, either in specie or paper for a loan, which the latter grant for a premium or bonus. But this specie or paper is only the representation of what is posititely necessary to fit out either a fleet or army. The arms, amunition, clothing, provisions, wood, iron, etc. must come from the labor of the working classes, and cannot be got otherwise, these must likewise furnish all the soldiers and sailors, fully equipped for the service. The labor of the industrious producers is evidently burdened with every material and expense in the first instance; and their production and that of their children are mortgaged for ages to come to pay the principal and interest of this loan of the misrepresentation of property, which would have been worth nothing unless the property necessary for fitting out the expedition, was produced by the working classes. Nor would either the specie or paper have been in existence but for their labor.— So that the loan is a transfer of the property of the millions of producers, and of their posterity, for the use and benefit of the nonproductive consumers and their descendants. All this is accomplished through the medium and by the authority of the governors, who have been as yet in all countries, composed of the nonproductive consumers, who are in fact borrowers of of the labor of industrious producers, though they appear as lenders by the political legerdemain; and as borrowers they ought in justice to pay off all national debts, that were contracted for the protection or augmentation of their power and property, and thus relieve the industrious millions, from a burden imposed upon them unjustly, for purposes foreign to their interest.

If a war or any other public expense be incurred for the procuring or protection of property, national honor or glory, every one ought to contribute by a direct tax on property, according to the amount he possesses and enjoys by said protection. And if the proprietors of land and other fixed property, are unable to furnish their quota of a circulating medium, it is they who ought to borrow from the moneyed interest, and give security on their real property, which they might be enabled to pay by curtailing some of their luxurious expenses, and all the duty of the rulers would be, to see that they performed their engagements, not to squeeze it out of the hard earned pittance of the laborer by indirect taxation or consumption, which urges the whole population into the two extremes of luxury and poverty, vice and crime, by a total derangement of that natural equality, on which alone can be based the peace, comfort and happiness of the human family. This is strongly exemplified at present by the misery and wretchedness of the industrious producers in Britain. Notwithstanding that one man's labor, by the help of labor saving machinery, produces more now than fifty men's labor did fifty years ago, yet the laborers are starving. The greater part of their earnings is absorbed by the nonproductive consumers, in tithes, taxes and excesssive revenues, to pay the interest of such an enormous national debt, and support the extravagance and luxury of such a great number of idle consumers. The oppression and misery of the industrious producers must always be in proportion to the number of idle consumers they have to maintain; which is increased an hundred fold by the yearly interest on an enormous national debt, and the monopoly of all real and fixed property by the few, who exact so much for the use of it, as to leave the laborer not sufficient to feed and clothe him and his family. He must then rather steal and plunder than starve. The risk of property becomes too great for the force of law to protect it. Confidence, on which alone any kind of paper representation can be supported, is withdrawn, a run upon the issuers of notes is made, and they not possessing a sufficiency of coin to retrieve their notes, increase the disorder and confusion. Fear paralyzes the exertions of all but those who have nothing to lose, at least ninety-nine in 100 of all civilized societies, the physical force prevails, and destruction is commensurate with ignorance.

Our working people are secure from being whirled round in so vicious a circle of action, by the immensity of uncultivated and unknown land, a certain resource against poverty, and a safe refuge from tyranny. But our nonproductive consumers, who have been living on speculations in paper, far exceeding the real consumption, must suffer by the general discredit of the article, on the responsibility of which they deal, and our 568 chartered banks with the exclusive privilege of coining paper money, must be more prudent than they have hitherto been, to avoid a serious crisis, from the diminution of specie, owing to the great demand from Europe, and the diminished confidence at home; when our circulation, in place of being a representation of existing property, may become a representation of nothing. This is a risk all people run who anticipate by paper representations, property not in existence. The danger of such a crisis would be avoided by deposite banks in place of those of discount, as president Jackson recommends.

France under the dominion of the Bourbons for the last fifteen years, has been fast following the footsteps of Britain, in trippling their national debt for the purpose of endowing their hereditary aristocracy, and increasing their paper circulation. This will cause some distress among the working classes, in spite of the unprecedented equality, established by the first revolution, which was the principal cause of the last, during which the great division of property and knowledge guaranteed them against anarchy and plunder, and will equally continue to preserve them from poverty and crime, the attributes of the two extremes. There cannot be a better practical proof of the benefit attached to equality, and the great depravity and crime, engendered by the great inequality of property and knowledge, than is presented on the two sides of the channel, which will be still more conspicuous, if any thing like a revolution should take place in Britain. The improvement in the social order of France, by equalization of property and knowledge only (for power is not yet so equally divided, but must be by universal suffrage, before any permanent system can be established,) ought to be a lesson to all people, as it clearly points out the road to peace, comfort and happiness, by proving that inequality of property, knowledge and power are the principal sources of poverty, misery and crime amongst the millions of industrious producers, and contributes equally to the vice and depravation of the few monopolizers of those three essentials of general freedom. It can scarcely be expected that the one and a half millions of national guards, who have made the revolution in France, of whom not perhaps one thousand are privileged to vote by the charter, will be contented to be ruled by the few rich, whose title to power is merely their wealth.—Such a result would be contrary to all the experience of human nature. They may tolerate the hereditary appointment of the chief, to endeavor to please the allied powers, but it is not probable they will permit a hereditary aristocracy in the house of peers, or a moneyed aristocracy in the chamber of deputies. It would be falling too far from the the freedom and equality proclaimed and practiced by the first revolution, when the population were infinitely farther removed from the state of equality of property and knowledge than they are at present, with the additional power of a million and a half of national guards, whose existence as an armed force, can only depend on their political rights of representation. The aristocracy of France or of Europe, building their system on any other foundation, than universal suffrage, will only prepare the materials for farther revolutions, whose extent will be as wide, as the spread of knowlege. In the present state of the diffusion of knowledge, to expect that armed men, as soldiers, are to make use of their arms and legs at the will of their chiefs, is out of the question. They have given sufficient proof that they have heads, and are determined to use them, to forward their own interest and the interest of the class they belong to. The old maxim that soldiers have no right to think has been reversed since the French revolution, and may be considered the class who have the best right to think, having the force.

OPPOSITE INTERESTS OF DIFFERENT SECTIONS OF THE TWO FEDERATIONS. INTERFERENCE OF THE GENERAL GOVERNMENT WITH THE INTERNAL POLICY OF THE STATES. HOLY ALLIANCE.

September 27, 1834.

In the two most extensive federations yet organized, the United States of the north, and Mexico, the geographical, fiscal, mercantile condition and modes of industry, their navigation, outlets for their surplus produce, and their communication with the other parts of the earth, are so distinct and separate, by such a vast continent, that their interest must be equally opposed and contradictory. This calls aloud and imperiously for a simple and economical federal government, where neither the individual states nor the federation shall have the right of interfering with the internal relations of any of the federative states, but the duties, utility and sphere of action shall be confined, as in the federation of Switzerland, to intercourse with foreign nations, settling any disputes that may arise between the federal states, and regulating the proportion of men and money in case of a war. The federation of the north has the separate interests of such a great variety of latitude and longitude, climate, soil, customs, habits and laws to contend with, originating from their different civil organization and localities, as to preclude the possibility of our legislatures giving satisfaction to all. The productions of the free population of the north differ from those of the southern slavery. Their civil, political and social intercourse being equally opposite and contradictory, the freedom and equality of the north, maintained and supported by universal suffrage, cannot have the same feeling or interest as exists in the great inequality of master and slave in the south, where the license of the one annihilates the freedom of the other, where all civil, political, mental and coercive power is monopolized by the consumers, and nothing but toil and labor is left to the producers. All those jarring interests must become more opposite and contradictory, as the working people in the north gain their rights in the representation, and make the laws, rules and regulations agreeably to their interests. The breach between them and the interest of the consumers in the south, must widen, and it will become daily more impossible for any one legislature to give satisfaction to both. The contradiction of interest between the Atlantic states, and those west of the Alleghenies, is equally opposed to peaceable submission to the fiscal, territorial, mercantile, political or manufacturing rules or regulations made by a joint representation of all those states in a federalism, partaking of the military, fiscal and coercive power of a centralism to enforce their laws and decrees, within the jurisdiction of each of the federative states. They tax an article at the sea port, which requires three dollars to pay it fifteen hundred miles inland, so that the inhabitants of the interior, are forced to work three or four days to pay what the citizens of the sea ports pay with one day's labor, and should that tax be doubled or tripled to encourage homespun, all those who neither spin nor weave cry out injustice. The Atlantic states are subject to be invaded and pillaged by foreign fleets, and must fortify their sea ports and keep up a fleet at great expense. The western country only reach to the sea by one bad harbor, inaccessible to ships of war; but are obliged to pay a great portion of that expense of protection, which nature guarantees them against. The eastern states, through the medium of their federation, would make the western states pay for canals and rail-roads, to carry their trade and produce out of the channel of their great rivers, across the Allegheny mountains, to feed and support the Atlantic sea port towns with the profits on the sale and transportation of the produce of the western people's labor. So distinct is the interest of the several states, made so by their natural production and localities, that the federation bordering on centralism, at Washington, cannot lay a tax, enact a law, or execute it by their judiciaries, without encroaching on some one or other of the individual states, by making them contribute to an expense, which can be of no use to them, and which must often be prejudicial to their interest, as is the case of the tariff. Besides the foregoing causes of dispute and disunion, there is a double expense of collecting taxes, judiciary and military, the unnecessary and hurtful effects of which, I have endeavored to elucidate in my former observations on federation.

The Mexican union, founded on the principles of the constitution of the United States of the north, has the same imperfections, unnecessary and extravagant expenses; with this serious additional fault, their expenses are at least double what the industry and civilization of their country can afford. This keeps them constantly in a state approaching to bankruptcy, forces them to break their engagements and resort to all kinds of immoral means of procuring money, to the total annihilation of credit and confidence, which demoralizes the private as well as the public transactions, withdraws all confidence, between the citizens, and raises the interest of money to three and four per cent. per month. During the revolution, the military chiefs acquired an ascendency and power, which they still retain, and by force or fraud, acquire all places of trust or profit. Ambitious and disposed to carry all their plans with military energy, they interfere with elections, taxes, laws and regulations of the individual states, and disregarding the constitutions, give rise to conspiracies, revolts, civil wars and bloodshed; both parties being equally distant from the order required by laws, pretend to have right on their side, and might makes right in all their political struggles. The Mexican states on the east, or the Gulf of Mexico being separated from the west on the Pacific ocean, by the high range of the Corderilas of difficult access, offering great obstructions to any useful communication, creates a separation of interest.— The commercial intercourse of the east is with Europe, that of the west on the Pacific, tends naturally to have their connections with Asia, and the productions of both sides, by the nature of the climate are so similar as not to afford much encouragement for exchange, so that nature and art, moral and physical, forbids any species of union or federation approaching to the sweeping authority of centralism.

The holy alliance in Europe, was a federation of despotic monarchs to defend the arbitrary authority of their divine and hereditary usurpation, against the claims of the millions for their natural and indefeasible rights and prerogatives.— The end and object of that compact was to regulate and interfere with the internal government of any nation, where the people had knowledge to unite for recovering any part of their freedom, which might not be agreeable to the rules and regulations made for the promotion of the interest of the said allied powers. This intention could only be effected by an intererfence in the internal regulations of what has been called independent states. But it would appear not to be either necessary or the interest of free and independent states, enjoying liberty and equality under the guarantee of universal suffrage, to permit a federation so far to approximate their power to centralism, as to extend their control over their fiscal, judiciary or military systems. Because it creates a double expense for state and United States collectors of taxes and revenue officers, of judges, lawyers and armed forces. Because it establishes rivalry and competition, subject to constant collision, between the two sovereign powers in the same body politic. Because it increases the patronage of the federal executive, beyond what ought to be trusted to an elective officer, thereby offering a premium to all kinds of intrigue, bribery and corruption at elections. And it does not appear that the individual states can possibly reap any benefit from the interference of the federal government with their fiscal, judiciary or military, to compensate for the demoralization and derangement, it may occasion. If the inhabitants of each state are sufficiently informed to govern themselves by universal suffrage, it becomes an officious act of supererogation for any authority out of the state, to dictate what taxes they shall pay, what laws they shall obey, or what military force they shall maintain. The utility of federation is confined to foreign intercourse, protection against foreign force, and as a council on arbitration to settle all disputes between the federative states, and to prevent internal or civil wars. When it extends to any interference with the internal laws or regulations of the individual states, it assumes the power of a centralism, with all the misrule, inconvenience and blunders which appertain to both, without the advantages inherent in either. All of this is clearly proven by the disputes, civil wars and bloodshed between the federal standing armies and the inhabitants, during the very short time the Mexican Union has existed. The federal troops facilitate every species of usurpation that the military chiefs can contrive, which would not take place were the federal powers not verging into centralism, though our rulers have had the address to keep the contradiction of *imperium in imperio* out of the sight of the apathetic public, for nearly half a century.

OBSTACLES TO THE IMPROVEMENT AND PERFECTION OF OUR POLITICAL INSTITUTIONS. THE REMEDY IS EASY AND OBVIOUS.

Sept. 30, 1834.

All the consequences that naturally follow divine hereditary right, are opposite and contradictory to what would naturaily arise in an association of men founded on liberty and equality, guaranteed by universal suffrage. Many of these glaring contradictions of the interest of the consuming few, against the vital interest of the producing many, I have endeavored to show in my former observations. The different opinions and views that would naturally occur, as to motives of action in a hereditary legislator, and one who is not certain of his place, above a year by election, would, one might conjecture, be very great. The former being always in power, might safely enact laws in favor of power; whilst a legislator of the latter, uncertain how soon he may be reduced to an obeyer of laws, and payer of taxes, might be supposed to have an interest, if not wholly in favor of his constituents, at least mixed. But the little practice which mankind have yet had of the elective system, seems far from confirming what would naturally be supposed. In all the mixed governments or limited monarchies as they are called, the hereditary power has controlled the elective, except in cases where the physical force has interfered. The governments in which equality is maintained, all power being elective by universal suffrage, are so few, and of so recent a date, have been so calumniated and misrepresented, by the privileged, powerful and rich, who control the press, that none but the few, who have had practical proof of their utility, and sufficient good sense and penetration to distinguish truth from falsehood, are able to form any correct judgement of the immense benefit, mankind may reap from the propagation of freedom. In consequence of the ignorant infatuation of the millions, who have given their votes to the rich and consuming classes, and very often re-elected the same individual, thereby approximating the government to hereditary, in acting for their own interest or that of their class, to the total neglect of the interest of the great majority of their constituents, (which is exemplified in a most striking manner by the history of our Union since the last federal government was made,)—there is no monarchy, or even all the monarchies of the old world together, who have granted so many exclusive privileges to the few at the expense of the many, so many monopolizing bank, mercantile, trading, manufacturing, insurance and other company charters, to enable the few consumers to live at the expense of the millions of industrious producers, as in our country. All this in addition to the speculations in roads, canals, etc., intended to give an exorbitant profit by way of interest to the monied aristocracy; for which, though the people pay, they may get some remuneration, yet it is the means of forestalling the labor of the industrious, by providing an artificial fund, on which the stockholders live, of the same nature as regards equality, as a national debt, though not so injurious, as the producers reap some advantage, but not equal to what they pay, and the national debt, is all pay and no profit to the industrious producers.

Perhaps the imitative faculty is the most natural to all animals, and the apish propensity, the most easy to practice, as we see in the Chinese and Hindoos. But our liberty and equality, being the first that ever existed as a political foundation, we could not, without injury, take example or imitate any thing of the kind which preceded us. We have therefore, in our laws, politics, and religion, followed the example of old mother Britain, and adopted many of her rules, regulations, customs, habits, and fashions, contrived for the maintenence of their great aristocratic inequality, but destructive of their liberty and equality, on which all our institutions ought to be founded. We likewise imbibed a great share of that mercantile spirit, that trickery, trading and manufacturing propensity, which leads people abroad to look for comfort and happiness, which is better and more securely obtained at home. For nearly half a century, has our monied aristocracy been looking up to that complicated system of misrule, for precedents to regulate all our public and private transactions; our division of political power into three; the forms and ceremonies of our executive cabinets, judges, courts of justice, etc.; our cooking, eating, drinking, lodging and clothing, the cuts of our coats, caps, hats, etc., with all the luxurious minutiæ of our tea tables, dining and drawing rooms, livery servants, and all that useless etiquette which keeps up the distinction without a difference, of the inequality of the different ranks. Most of this deviation from simplicity, was begun and fostered by the neutral trade, which commenced with our federal government and was the chief support of its expenses. Whilst our merchants monopolized so great a proportion of the commerce of the civilized world, by our flag being the only neutral on the seas, our farmers were selling their wheat at three dollars the bushel, and other produce in proportion. A few idle mouths, more or less, fed by the labor of the industrious producers was not looked at. But when the neutral trade, like a bird of passage took its departure, and the laborers were forced to work hard and enjoy but little of the fruits of their labor, they began to examine into the management of their affairs, and to endeavor to choose their rulers amongst their own class, who had the same interest and fellow feeling with them. It was then that the office hunters, who had revelled so long on the people's purse, began to cry out anarchy and rebellion, stigmatizing the people with all the epithets they had learned from European aristocracy, which was re-echoed by all the servile presses which their former riches had bribed, and they so intrigued as to divide and confuse the industrious producers, and caused the failure of the first trial. So long had the office hunters, kept the undisturbed possession of all elective places, that intrigue, canvassing, and soliciting for posts of power, honor or profit, became a trade by which they lived. They complicated their official duties, by various mysterious and intricate contrivances, one of their most profitable occupations, so much so that during the presidency of John Adams, it was said, that only one man in congress understood the treasurer's accounts, and he used to take five or six weeks in close investigation at the treasury, to unravel the complex and mysterious folds and turns in which they were involved.

All trades and professions make a mystery of their art, to enhance their pay or perquisites, even where there is a fair competition and a customer can change if he find himself deceived, either in the learned profession of the law, gospel or physic, as well as in any of the commonly useful trades, how much more may such tricks be expected from a public officer, who is always certain that his customers cannot get their business done else where, and at the same time when he is certain of holding his place, there is no end to the difficulties thrown in the way of his official duties, to increase his fees, or magnify the obligation. The only remedy, which is perfectly easy and practicable in an elective government, is for the electors to make it a fixed and unalterable rule, never to put the same man twice in place. Then, however willing he might be to feather his own nest, he most probably would not take great pains to feather the nest of a successor he would not know; particularly, as an obeyer of the laws, and a payer of taxes, the cost of the feathers would fall on himself. The immense advantage of a certain and quick rotation in office, has been very much neglected hitherto, by the very few governments of universal suffrage. How long they will remain ignorant of their most essential interest, time can alone determine.

The million and a half of the French national guards, electing their own officers, (who must always be in unison with the majority,) having learned by practice their force, weight, and utility to society, will form a nucleus, around which will cluster the population of the civilized world. They will be a centre from which will radiate light, life and knowledge, that cannot fail to emancipate surrounding nations.— And though it begins with a physical exertion, it will lead to a moral perfection, which no combination of physical force can withstand. Our working people have long commanded the legitimate physical force of the nation, and only require a knowledge of their interest, and the moral courage to assert it. But morals have remained hitherto so many centuries behind physics—that it will require more exertion and energy than they have yet demonstrated, to keep up with the physical reforms of the old world, for whose benefit we have created beacons and guide-posts to enable them to begin where we have ended, and prosecute, with the vigor of youth, their progressive improvements. Whilst we, from the pride, presumption or vanity, of having been the first, sleep on our laurels, and permit those we have considered far beneath us, as subjects of arbitrary power, to pass us in the race of civilization.

DESPOTISM AND MISRULE IS GENERALLY PROPORTIONED TO EXTENT OF TERRITORY AND POPULATION.

Oct. 5th, 1834.

In all governments of the old world, their misrule, corruption, tyranny, injustice, plunder, and pillage, is nearly in a ratio with the extent of territory and number of inhabitants, who are subject to their control. For instance Russia, possessing the greatest number of square miles, and it is said fifty three millions of subjects or slaves, is the most despotic and corrupt nation of Europe. Austria being the next in point of extent of territory, is the next in despotism and tyranny.—And Spain, when the sun never set on her dominions, may have been ranked next to Austria. The various other intermediate countries, where the rough rider of revolution has broke into a more or less civilized state, being still in a progressive state of improvement, cannot be quoted at present as examples; but the comparatively well regulated governments of the small states, though under the same arbitrary rule of hereditary aristocracy, may serve as a confirmation of the maxim, that all political associations are corrupt and despotic in the ratio of their extent and population, and rational, moderate and useful, in proportion to the limited extent of their territory and number of inhabitants; as Tuscany, 395 square miles; Switzerland, 696 square miles; the small dukedoms of Saxony 384 square miles; Wirtemburg 359 square miles; Baden 276 square miles, etc. Any traveler of observation, passing from the territory of a large empire, into the superior improvements and civilization of a state of small extent and population, cannot help being struck with the vast superiority of their cultivation, useful arts, sciences, and civilization; the great change for the better in their roads, convenience and accommodation in their taverns, and comfort in their houses and clothing. The moral improvement of the inhabitants will be still more conspicuous. The progress of intellect and useful information of a peasant in Switzerland, Tuscany or Saxony, etc., differs from the ignorance of a Russian or Austrian boor, in almost the whole scale of human intellect.

On this side the Atlantic, our Union is composed of inhabitants originally from the same country, in which are the same laws, language, customs and habits. This and the improvements in all kinds of mechanism, give such a vast facility and quickness to the circulation of every kind of knowledge, amalgamating the physical and moral faculties of the population so equally, as to render the distinction between the small and great states more difficult to perceive or desscribe; yet the progress of all the useful arts, science and civilization, in the small states of New England, is superior to that of the great state of New York, their neighbors. The simplicity and economy also, in the management of their public affairs, their habitual rectitude, morality, and freedom from crime, though not so strongly contrasted as in Europe, is evidently in favor of the small political associations. And the vast advantages derived from the power granted to the limited extent and population of the New England townships to regulate their own affairs, is one of the strongest practical proofs, of the immense benefit resulting to society by the division of power, and placing it in the possession of those who are to reap the immediate benefit from it, which can only be effected in small political associations, protected from external aggression or internal injustice by a federation, whose powers are limited to the defence of the Union in case of invasion, and settlement of differences in case of disputes between the federate states. Of the last, there is scarcely a possibility of the occurrence, as no such has taken place for five hundred years in the federal government of Switzerland, nor any disputes for the last half century, between any of our individual states, though frequent quarrels and disputes between our state and the United States, have taken place, in consequence of the constitution of the Union vesting a power in the federation to interfere in the internal governments of the federate states.

Any federative system, having the right of interfering with the internal laws, rules, and regulations, of the federate states, approaches so near to a centralism, as to be liable to many of its defects, and to partake in some measure of the corruption, injustice and tyranny, universally attached to extensive territories of numerous population, under the control of one authority, located and concentrated in one place, at an immense distance from the extreme confines of the nation. Our federation have got the better of the states in all disputes, touching their prerogatives; which proves that in politics as well as physics, great bodies control and regulate the motions of all inferior bodies, when their powers or privileges are permitted to come into collision; and this injurious collision, must be in the ratio of the extent and population of the Union so bound together, and the force of cohesion equal to the means possessed by the superior, to coerce the different inferiors, whose interest not being attacked all at the same time, may by intrigue and management be kept from uniting.

Most contrivances, both of church and state, have been for the purpose of the more easily tranferring the property of the industrious producers, to the use and benefit of the non-productive consumers, whose views in the sense of what has been thought their interest, all their mysterious complicacy and intricacy, are good and indispensibly necessary to the interest of the few—as Canning very laconically observed of the British constitution, "it works well;" but measured by the interest of the laborers, who have the toil and fatigue of producing all, the result is different; for the more the idle consume, the harder must the laborers work. It is therefore in the sense of the interest of the working people, that the present observations are made, with a certainty of being contradicted, perhaps reviled, by the numberless advocates, whom the riches of the consumers have been enabled to fee.

Federalism, arproaching to centralism, by having the power of interfering in the internal government of the federate states, is injurious and destructive of the interest of the millions, in three essential ways; first, by transferring so great a proportion of the fruits of their labor, in the unnecessary double employment of two sets of tax gatherers, for collecting the States' and United States' taxes, when a judicious and economical arrangement would make one set of collectors sufficient; secondly, by the double employment of military for the States and United States, under the frivolous pretence, that a standing army of six thousand soldiers can possibly add any thing to the protection of a frontier of nearly six thousand miles, when during the last war, the only serious attacks, at Plattsburg and New Orleans, were repulsed by the neighboring militia, the only safe defence of any free people. All hereditary despotisms maintain standing armies, more to keep their subjects in subjection than for external defence. Our federal military establishment, is more in imitation of the European aristocracies, than for any use they can be, to the security of our free institutions; thirdly, by the double employment of judges and lawyers, under the ridiculous pretence of a uniformity of decisions, when the States' juries decide all causes by the States' laws; another excuse is in the further protection of the rights of foreigners, who are protected in all the states, by having the right of half the jury being foreigners; which is the body in whom is vested all the power of deciding, and alone capable of keeping the judges faithful to their duties, as is proven by the corruption of all judges where there are no juries. But the real intention of the federalists in establishing the federal courts, was to have a control not only of the states' judiciary, but to support all or any usurpation of the federal government on state rights, by pretending that the federal courts of justice have the right to decide in case of any difference between them and the individual states, that is, the federal courts are the federation that assume the right of being judges in their own cause, which in every instance has been decided in their own favor, as might have been expected by every one that has the least knowledge either of himself or others. This has appeared so glaringly inconsistent and unprecedently contrary to common justice and all the motives that actuate mankind, that a tribunal has been proposed of members from each state, on purpose to judge of the disputes between the states and United States.— How much easier and better would it be to simplify, in place of complicating the federal union, by taking away all right of interference in the internal governments of the federal states.

IMPOSITIONS AND OPPRESSIONS OF CHURCH AND STATE.

October 11, 1834.

There are two things which the ignorance and delusion of the great mass of mankind have never permitted their common sense to examine into, or pass judgment upon, though essential to their peace, comfort and happiness. I mean politics and religion. These have been always secluded in the dark corners of monopoly, masked by the impenetrable curtain of hypocrisy, superstition and mystery. The few who move the wires and play the puppets behind the scenes, are alone informed of the legerdemain and phantasmagoria, which elude the blunted senses of the multitude.

"The world is a farce, and all things show it;
I thought so once, but now I know it."

And the principal actors in this farce are politics and religion, personified by church and state. To this farce the people are admitted, those who labor the most, paying the dearest for a ticket of admision to this graduated theatre, where the expectants of office, such as prompters, scene shifters and candle snuffers, are placed nearest the stage, having an interest in prospective, for concealing the mystery. Whilst the producing millions, whose labor maintain all, are pushed back into a dark corner, whence they can only perceive the various disguises assumed by the actors to dupe them out of their hard earned wages.

The most ignorant and thoughtless of our working people, are far above being deluded by the legerdemain of divine and hereditary rights, assumed by the royal and privileged orders, to sanction the tyranny which oppresses and torments the industrious laborers in the old world. Our conviction of the rights of equality at the ballot boxes, almost every month in the year, prevents the possibility of such a delusion. But they have been silly enough to allow themselves to be fleeced by the pretensions of demagogues and place hunters, who, under the mask of "the public weal and the interest of the people," have sacrificed the peace, happiness and comfort, of the millions of industrious producers, to augment their own profits, and increase their power, perquisites and preeminence. They shift the burdens of public expenses from their own shoulders, to those of the laborers, as in the case of the European aristocracy, by indirect taxation on consumption, thereby rendering necessary a swarm of custom house and other officers, to prevent the smuggling of merchandize, so easily accomplished on such an extensive frontier, which so increases their patronage as to create bribery, corruption, broils and bloodshed at elections. They fix the wages of political labor, their own salaries, so much higher than other useful or necessary labor, as to cause disgraceful intrigues, disputes and scandalous contentions, to obtain the public offices. They double the number and expense of the fiscal, military and judiciary officers of the Union and individual states, for the execution of the same duties, or which might be included in the same service, only creating collision between the United States and the individual state authorities; and at the same time they double the patronage, the bone of contention in all governments, and in none more injurious and destructive of all good principles, than in an elective system, where the people, in order to possess the full benefit of the elective franchise, by universal suffrage, ought to have the appointment of every officer of trust or profit, and not delegate to one elective servant of the millions, the right of appointing under him subordinate servants. These will always consider the one who can make and unmake them as their master, whose orders it becomes their interest to obey, whether for or against the public weal; which I have endeavored to explain in some former observations. They expend so great a sum of the fruits of industry, in fortifying the mouths of rivers and seaports for the benefit of surveyors, engineers and contractors, whilst the probability or even the possibility of the country being subject to a foreign invasion, could not be supposed by any but those who get paid for constructing the forts and batteries. Even in France or Britain there are no forts on the sea-board, but at their marine deposites, though both nations have been sixty years in every hundred at war, for centuries. They expend large sums for building a fleet, which will have time to rot twice over, before it can be of any service. All this increases the non-producers at the expense of the producers, and accustoms a certain proportion of our citizens to live on the toil and labor of their fellow beings.

Their anticipations of resisting force, is more necessary for protecting European despotism, against the retaliation of their oppressed subjects, than against a foreign enemy; but such anticipations are as useless and injurious to our liberty and equality, guaranteed by universal suffrage, as all our other imitations of European despotism. The time is perhaps come, when freedom ought to show that it can rest safely on its own basis without having recourse to the moral, physical, military or marine restraints, policy or fortifications, so necessary for the support of arbitrary power in the old world.— Most of the wars, for the last age, have been more to crush the aspiring freedom of the oppressed subject, than to obtain territory by conquest, which the jealous fears of the despots, of one another, render it difficult to acquire. The last of consequence, was the division of Poland by Russia, Prussia and Austria, which is a bone they may not be allowed peaceably to pick, depending on the union of the millions to assert their rights; which is yet in the womb of futurity.

Fortunately for the inhabitants of the United States, they are removed, geographically, politically and morally, very far from the causes of the present turmoils, wars and bloodshed in the old world. They are freed from the necessity of forcing by violence, a rapid atonement in a few months, for the injustice, oppression and tyranny of many centuries. They can benefit by the dear-bought experience of what has been called the civilized world, by tracing the melancholy and destructive effects of despotism from its first grafting on what has been called the savage state, to its final extinction in useful civilization or the general diffusion of knowledge. They can coolly look on the revolutionary scenes in Europe, learn by the past, and benefit by the future; imitate the good, and avoid the evil; they are thrown into the most enviable situation, if their prudence and foresight enables them to take advantage of such an accumulation of favorable circumstances which now surround them.

Our free and independent citizens are not forced to build churches or to fee priests to preach and fill them.— They are not burdened with tithes and taxes, to maintain luxurious popes, cardinals, bishops, and the numberless tribe of all figures and denominations, that constitute the well combined and firmly united hierarchy of the old world, who aid, by the moral oppression of the church, the physical tyranny of the state, leagued together by a marriage of interest, to enable them to live without labor. Freedom has divorced that matrimony between the church, and state, throughout the whole of our Union, and the Gospel shops, like all other trades, are only paid by those who choose to wear their metaphysical merchandize. Long and inveterate habit, that persevering supporter of both good and evil practices, fills our churches with crowds, who go to see and be seen, and by purchasing their seats, subscription, etc., pay the priest a salary, which though it may be small, is more than they could earn by any profession, in which so little moral or physical labor is necessary; depending on the charity of their customers, they have the spur of necessity to stimulate their industry, by which they chiefly work on the ignorance and gullibility of the women, by means of a variety of sects, whose incomprehensible dogmas are calculated to suit the fancies and whims of all descriptions of people. But these itinerant apostles by their constant interference with education and family affairs, obstruct the dissemination of useful knowledge much more than the indolent priest, full fed on tithes and taxes.

IMPOSSIBILITY OF ARRESTING THE PROGRESS OF FREEDOM.

Oct. 14*th*, 1834.

"Men convinced against their will, are of the same opinion still." There never can be a more complete confirmation of that maxim of Hudibras, than the present state of revolutionary Europe; which has been kept ever since the French revolution, in its present political state of political and geographical division by the force of bayonets and immense standing armies. The vast expense attending the maintenance of such great military forces, has rendered all the governments of Europe, more or less unpopular. The combined aristocracy of Europe, under the firm of the coalesced powers, forced the Bourbons on the French people, who, to convince the world that they were of the same opinion, banished them, and made the late energetic revolution. The coalesced powers forced the junction of Holland and Belgium, which separated as soon as their influence ceased, by the energy of the Belgian revolution. The congress of the allied powers, divided the plunder of the long war against French liberty, as it suited their individual interest, without consulting those they were thus separating from all their customs, habits and prejudices. They gave the provinces south of the Rhine to Russia; restored the feudal system in Brunswick and Westphalia; forced despotic governments on Piedmont, Venice, Milan, Rome, etc.; most of whose people are now giving strong hints, that they are still of the same opinion. One hundred French bayonets, favored by the hereditary executive of Spain, restored the despotism under Ferdinand, that the strong hold which catholic bigotry, and superstition have got of the people, can scarcely maintain. The three despots of Russia, Austria, and Prussia, conquered and divided Poland amongst them; which foreign yoke the Poles seem disposed to throw off; and although the weight of Russian barbarism may again subjugate them, yet it will only be another unsuccessful attempt of force, endeavoring to crush opinion. The right of conquest has always been a very insecure title to the obedience of the conquered, even when the transfer has been made from the grasp of one despot to another. But where the despotism is attempted to be grafted on ever so small a quantum of liberty, it requires the strictest union of savage and barbarous military force with ignorance, and its progeny bigotry and superstition, to keep up the appearance of any kind of union between such heterogeneous materials.

The three great continental powers of Europe, Russia, Austria, and Prussia, consist of a forced junction by conquest of a great many small states, formerly independent, whose customs, habits, interest, and prejudices, have not been united by any stronger tie than that of force, and may in time be left like the jackdaw in the fable—(by every one picking out a feather,) altogether unfledged. In the present state of civilization, any other motive of union but that of interest, cannot be lasting, and the only possible mode of ascertaining that a union of states is agreeable to their interest, is by an equal and impartial federation, for mutual protection from foreign aggression, and the peaceable settlement of internal disputes, without the smallest right of interfering with any of the internal laws, customs, habits or regulations of any of the federal states. There has been no government yet formed, that is not disposed to govern too much, and treat the governed like chilren who are incapable of managing their own affairs. But a federation, permitted to interfere with the laws, taxes, military and civil organization of the federate states, is an order of things necessarily complicated; a double employment of rulers, which must aggravate in a tenfold manner, that propensity to over govern, and stretch their power, hampering the people of the states with two kinds of leading strings, which seldom draw alike or the same way, causing them to have a tottering uncertain march towards their real interest. Nothing can encourage more an officious interference with individual interest, than the double dose of a federative system, having the power to interfere with the laws, customs and regulations of the federate states. It is a complication that must increase the intricacy, in proportion to the number and difference of the civil, religious, political, mercantile and manufacturing interests of the associated states; an opposition of interest that must originate constant disputes and quarrels, as is strongly exemplified in the new states of Mexico, where the contradictions between the federal government and the states have been the cause of constant civil wars and bloodshed. The late attempts at federation, show the foolish aversion all people have against benefitting by the experience of others, by their great deviation from the simplicity and economy of the federation of Switzerland, that has existed for five hundred years, without a difference or dispute, and most probably will still continue unchanged; though the different aristocratic cantons, that form the union, may be revolutionized into elective governments, without in the smallest degree interfering with the simple duties in the federation, which can unite in the same friendly bonds, of mutual protection, every species of government.

Our good natured citizens, content with the theory of liberty and equality, are deprived of the excuse which the Europeans have for the abuse of power, that is forced on them against their will. Our privilege of universal suffrage, bestows on the majority, the right and power of putting immediately into execution, all and every law, rule or regulation that can possibly conduce to their comfort or happiness, and perhaps the having it in their power to do it when they please, is what prevents them from doing it, like the man who having lived seventy years in a town without going out of it, had a pension given him with the provision that he should remain always in town, but he had immediately so strong a desire to see the country, that he went and forfeited his pension. Freedom, like many other things, may be too cheap with us to be valuable, and we certainly are deprived of that long and sharp spur of necessity, which goads on our European brethren, though after having been ridden for nearly half a century, by the demagogues and office hunters, the spur began to prick a little, and they began to feel what Judge Chase, was said to have told them, at the end of our revolutionary war, "that all must either ride or be ridden, and I am determined to ride, for which purpose I have put on my spurs, and taken my whip."

As mankind get wiser, and revolutionary improvements go on, the gullibility of our species in former times, is more striking and astonishing. The late king of France was dethroned, and his ministers tried for their lives for advising measures, that formerly would have been thought meritorious, as protecting the divine hereditary rights of the grand monarch. The king of Holland lost Belgium for exercising one of the least of kingly rights, choosing his ministers. The late British ministry were changed for following all former ministers in opposing a reform in parliament and advocating the interference in continental politics—Pitt's greatest merit.— But "the times change, and we change with them." Who dare venture to predict that the most liberal and patriotic act of either church or state now, may be considered, in fifty years hence, the most despotic infringement on the rights and liberties of mankind? Or that the laws and regulations which appear now the most necessary for the protection of the public weal, may not in fifty years hence, be considered the most arbitrary and unnecessary interference with individual rights and independence? Who can consistently presume that our temporary artificial laws, made for and by the circumstances of the moment, can possibly possess the unchangeableness of the laws of nature, though even they are supposed by the dogmas of all religion, though without any proof, to be liable to a total change? We know but little of the present, still less of the past, and nothing of the future; yet most of civil or religious reasoners go on the analogy of the past through the present to the future, though there is no more resemblance between them than between the actions of our president and the emperor of Morocco, or between a slave and a free citizen.

ON HEREDITARY AND ELECTIVE POWER.

Oct. 18, 1834.

In every thing, from the origin to the end, hereditary power is opposite and contradictory to elective; the salvation of the one, is the destruction of the other; what feeds the one poisons the other. The sources of hereditary power, either as under the patriarchal, or as conquerors, is founded on the superiority of physical force. It is the union of the strong to subject the weak. For which purpose all the laws, taxes customs, habits, fashions, privileges and policy, are contrived to support that assumed superiority, perpetuated by the union of military force, acting on the scattered and unconnected millions.— Fearing lest the power of the sword, the right of might, would not be considered either legitimate or just, or the junction of church and state, they conjured up *divine right*, assimilating it with the mysterious dogmas of religion, that both might be swallowed in one pill by the undistinguishing faith of the multitude. So has church and state mutually administered to each others wants, conveniences and interest, though opposed to the comfort and happiness of the great majority of mankind. All hereditary power originated in the subjection of the moral faculties to physical force, and must vanish before the light of reason, diffusion of knowledge, and improvement of intellect, by the millions learning the use of their senses, and trusting to them alone. Elective power has only recently had any thing like a fair trial. It is the child of reason and rationality, nurtured under the conviction that intellectual qualities are not hereditary, but acquired, and that those who are born to possess power, are the last to obtain useful knowledge, which can only pass by the channel of truth, that seldom comes to the ears of those who are heirs of hereditary power, through the swarm of flatterers who surround them.

Hereditary power, resting on the combination of physical force, must be opposite and contradictory to elective power, the result of reason, and a correct use of the moral faculties, through all their varied organization to their ultimate consequences, and so completely opposed are they by their nature and origin, that like fire and water, they cannot exist peaceably in the same body politic, until one gains the superiority and control of the other, as I have endeavored to prove in a former number, by the history of all governments where they have been attempted to be mixed as checks and ballances; all of which is confirmed by the late revolutions.

Hereditary power is compelled by its interest, to heap property, knowledge and power on the few, and starve both the moral and physical powers of the many. The electors of representation by universal suffrage are still more forcibly impelled, for their own protection, comfort and happiness, to divide property, knowledge and power as equally as circumstances will permit.

Hereditary power is under the necessity of maintaining numerous armies to enforce obedience to their arbitrary commands, and to collect large revenues to pay their extravagant expenses. This acts as a reciprocal necessity; the heavier the taxes, the more force is required to collect them; and the greater the force, the heavier must be the tax to pay them. Elective power being the will of the majority, can change, reform, and correct all abuses without recurring to physical force, or hiring one half to subject the other.

Hereditary power must have a strong and well organized police, to watch over and prevent their subjects from uniting in any serious revolt or conspiracy, the risk and danger of which is in proportion to the diffusion of knowledge. Elective power has each citizen feed and paid as an officer of police, to watch over and secure his freedom from the usurpation of any who might attempt to break through the laws or regulations of society.

A great inequality, and consequent injustice, must be the support of absolute, hereditary power; but some degree of equality must be the origin of elective power by universal suffrage, and the practice of it must equalize property, knowledge and power, more and more every day, as the only mode of perpetuating freedom.

Any reform in favor of the majority, in absolute hereditary power, can only be accomplished by force against force; by war, bloodshed, and slaughter: but in elective power all changes or reforms can be made through the ballot boxes peaceably, without any one having a right to say he is injured. So that the political machine can be made conformable to the knowledge of the day, to suit the convenience and interest of the millions, without any violence or injustice.

Absolute hereditary power has an interest in keeping the millions poor and ignorant, by raising all the revenue by indirect taxes on consumption, whilst the voters to elective power have an interest, that all the revenue should be paid by direct taxes on property; and that each individual should contribute to the public expenses, in proportion to the property that is protected and guaranteed to him by the public force; to maintain which the greatest part of the public expenditure is incurred.

Hereditary power has a strong interest in monopolizing patronage and appointments to office, as well as increasing the number and profit of them; but the voters to elective power, have a still stronger interest in the extension of elections by universal suffrage, to the appointment of every officer of trust and profit by themselves, as the only possible mode of ensuring that their duties will be performed for the public good, and the interest of the great majority.

The interest of those, who by force or fraud, have usurped absolute hereditary power, is so contrary and in direct opposition to the interest of the millions, who by universal suffrage make and unmake elective power, that it would appear to be madness, and a total deviation from common sense and reason for the voters by universal suffrage to permit their representatives to follow or copy any of the laws, habits, or customs, invented or contrived for the support and protection of arbitrary, hereditary power; though it may be the interest of their rulers, (and certainly appears to have been) to imitate the power and profit, assumed in all countries, by the hereditary rulers; particularly if the voters re-elect often the same individual, and clothe him with patronage, so as to approximate him to the situation of a ruler of the people by divine right, they cannot possibly expect any thing but the like consequences from the great similarity of mankind in following the selfish motives of individual interest.

Our working people have made a bold beginning. Whether they will have wisdom to persevere in a firm union of forces, to bring the practice of universal suffrage up to its theory, and the elective system up to a par with the knowledge of the day, must be seen. Certainly the energy and activity of their fellow laborers in Europe, in freeing themselves from their chains, riveted by many centuries of aristocratic intrigue and ingenuity, ought to encourage them to persist until they shall have carried their point.

DELUSIVE EFFECTS OF ORATORY, OPPOSED BY A PROPER USE OF THE SENSES. QUARRELS ABOUT BELIEF, FAITH, ETC., HOW PREVENTED.

October 24, 1834.

Knowledge is power. When knowledge is monopolized by the few, the few have all the power, which is tyranny, under all the forms of political associations; though the hereditary few have an exclusive privilege which does not belong to the elective, where knowledge is less or more divided amongst the many, power is equally so, which is freedom. Knowledge may be either useful or detrimental to society, according to the application of it. The positive knowledge of things, is less liable to be twisted and opposed to the comfort and happiness of mankind, than the dextrous use of words, in sophistry, too often dignified by the name of eloquence, a mode of reasoning or logic, which seizes on the foible of imagination, and turns it astray for their purposes, deceiving the moral faculties in the same way as the conjurer with his legerdemain, cheats the physical senses. Our present orators, in imitation of Demosthenes or Cicero of antiquity, make a grain of truth gild over a pound of falsehood, and arrange the size and component parts of the pills to suit the swallow and digestion of the multitude. So our forums resound with the brawling, thundering oratory of two or three days' speeches, consisting of such wandering circumlocution, so irrelevant to the subject, that the hearers are so bewildered as to forget what was the subject in dispute; as if they expected their ignorant constituents would value their speeches like a piece of Osnaburgs, by the yard. Phantasmagoria, by explaining the nature of optical deceptions, has exposed the tricks on which the supernatural and mysterious deceptions of ghosts, spectres, etc., depend; any contrivance that would expose the artificial delusion of language and mere sound, would very much conduce to the happiness of mankind.

The properties of matter are fixed and cannot be altered by the change of name. A carpenter or blacksmith cannot be deluded by any species of sophistry, in the nature and properties of the work they have finished. This is positive knowledge, of which no one can learn too much, as it is the antidote to deception, delusion, cheating and consequent disappointment; imagination is stopped on the threshhold, by the evidence of the senses: but in dreaming, where volition cannot refer to ideas furnished by the senses, full scope is given to the imagination, and we fancy we see cows horns on the head, hoofs on the feet and wings on the shoulders of men; we can congregate on one object the figures and representations of ten or ten thousands of things, which in nature were never seen together; we can conceive and believe the sun to go back, water to run up, and the whole laws of nature to be reversed in as lively and lucid a figure as any reality of which we could not be undeceived by the evidence of our senses, and for those, who, in matters of belief do not trust to their senses, they must remain in a constant state of delusion, to which there is neither beginning nor end. Mahomet dreamed he rode through seven heavens in one night, and all good and true musselmen must believe it; like the dogmas of most other religions, he that has faith to believe in impossibilities will be saved and he who doubts will be damned.

Men are the children of surrounding circumstances. To account for their great veneration and faith in words, and the small experience of knowledge they have of things, we must recur to the nature of their education, and the impressions stamped on their blank sheets of intellect which nature has bestowed on them; convinced of the non-existence of innate ideas, every figure or idea in the mind must be the representation of some external object, the nature and properties of which are ascertained through the medium of the senses.— When the child is born, it is generally entrusted to an ignorant nurse, who silences its cries by fear, and puts it into a stupifying sleep by soporific doses. When it can walk and articulate sounds, it is sent to what has been called a school to learn to read, where, chained down to a stool in as irksome and unnatural a position for the body, as the constraint on the mind, by being forced mechanically to repeat from horn books and spelling books, without any idea of the sense or utility, through the constraint and fear of punishment, sours the temper, and gives a disgust to mental labor during their lives. They are then forced by the fear of punishment, to read by rote, books filled with complex ideas, the sense or meaning of which they do not understand, and too often containing incomprehensible fictions. To that succeeds the classical learning of Latin and Greek works, and is followed by metaphysics, theology, etc., all words, sounds without sense, *vox et praterea nihil*. On such a foundation, what superstructure can be expected, but fiction, folly and the useless trifling of killing time.

The positive knowledge of the useful arts, and exact sciences, (which fortunately are becoming more in fashion every day as mankind approach the much to be wished for era, when utility will be the seal of value, "the greatest happiness to the greatest nember,") are necessary to the comfort and happiness of all ranks; whilst the vague, voluminous, unfair and partial knowledge of the past through the page of history, (which acquired literary nonsense during the barbarous ages, when the universal darkness made a rush light a luminary,) are unnecessarily retained, though there is no analogy between the civilization of the present and past. The knowledge of the present, is drowned in a flood of literary fictions, poetry, plays and romance, which require more than ordinary patience to wade through, and for your trouble, you have exaggerated fancies of the imagination, but little reality.— The tithes of Christendom are expended in purchasing the suppositions, suggestions and prophecies of the dark and

and impenetrable futurity and legions of priests paid and maintained in luxury, for the purpose of divining, exploring and surveying that *terra incognita* beyond the grave, and erecting beacons and guide posts on the road, to direct the penitent sinner how he is to work out his salvation; though of all the many hundreds of religious sects, no two of them travel the same road, yet all pretend to go on the only true path to everlasting salvation.

The knowledge of the past is worse than useless since the improvements of the present, render all imitation of their tyranny, cruelty and abuses, physical and moral, injurious to the rising generation. The knowledge of the present, will extend and become more rational in proportion to its diffusion, and the millions become instructed in their real interests.— The pretended knowledge of the incomprehensible future, which has caused so much war and bloodshed, is immensely varied and undefined, each sect making every exertion to force all to travel on their road, thus creating more disputes, quarrels and ill will amongst mankind, than all the other differences about the affairs of this world. It may perhaps, be left to every individual to take his own road, provided he does not jostle his neighbor; then the high fees and perquisites of the pretended pilots, will be saved to the community.— For though each may have a right to take a risk of his own salvation on himself, yet in the immense differences, contradictions and uncertainties, it would appear to be too much responsibility, for any one to burden himself with the risk of another. Who can venture to predict that most people will not become in fifty years as wise as the Quakers, and dispense with the services of both priests and lawyers, taking the management of their affairs, both here and hereafter, into their own hands: at least it will not be those who have accurately and impartially observed the progress of civilization for the last fifty years.

PRODUCERS AND NONPRODUCERS.

Oct. 26, 1834.

A broad line of distinction divides the occupations of men, which has not yet been sufficiently noticed, to have its full effect either on public or private opinions. The most immediately and perceptibly productive, or those who labor with their hands, or are some way instrumental in the management of the produce of said labor, all those require a positive capital, an accumulation of the fruits of industry, as the foundation on which they trade and do business, the losing, expending, or wasting of which, reduces them to bankruptcy and ruin, the only way their funds can be misapplied to the injury either of themselves or others. Intellectual labor, the working of the brain, in acquiring some specific information on the nature, rights, and peculiarities in certain professions, differs materially in its cause, origin and consequences, from the evident and tangible fruits of manual labor. Their stock in trade consisting in theoretical ideas, that cannot be wasted or exhausted, but augments and becomes more practicable the more they sell or give away, places them in the certainty of never losing their capital or becoming bankrupt: it induces them to speculate more on the *gullibility* of the public and tempts them to use their abilities to the injury and prejudice of their fellow beings. Their arts being little understood by their customers, too often masked by a veil of incomprehensible mystery, leave full scope to chicane and deception, the temptation to which is in proportion to the ignorance of the multitude with whom they deal, bribing and paying them a large retaining fee to oppose every improvement that can tend to the general diffusion of knowledge and consequent happiness. Once tutored to the profession, it would be as reasonable to find fault with their eating and drinking as to blame them for following the means, in the present state of society, by which they procure a living.

Amongst the occupations which require a positive, visible, and tangible capital, may be reckoned all the useful and mechanic arts, farmers, merchants, and all those employed in the distribution or disposing of the produce of their labor, whose utility varies through the extensive range, from the simple necessaries of life, to the indulgence of the fancies of imagination, in supplying the most superfluous luxuries. The fine arts as executed by the hands, may stand on middle ground, though more depending on the head than muscular exertion, and except the art of designing are very limited in general utility, being confined to the amusement and pleasure of the rich, in a state of society where great and unnatural inequality has been produced, by the abuses of power of both church and state. All teachers and professors of the exact sciences, though not laboring with their hands, yet from their great utility to those who do, ought to be considered as productive.

Those professions which require no visible or tangible capital to enable them to practice their calling, (excepting a few books more for show than necessity,) consist principally of the three learned professions, divinity, law, and physic. The priest trades on the souls of his hearers, who pay him for his ministry. The lawyer's capital is in the purse of his clients. The physician deals on the constitutions of his patients. All receive their fees and perquisites whether they serve or disserve their customers. Their professional abilities are involved in such mysterious uncertainty, as to screen them from all responsibility. The lawyer pleads the "glorious uncertainty of the law," the physician the certainty of death, and no one can know how the job undertaken by the priest is finished. Surgeons, by a manual operation can be certain of relieving the patient, and they as well as engineers, architects, surveyors, etc., work principally with their heads, yet they ought to be considered, from their utility, as producers. In the present state of civilization, when the great inequality of property, knowledge, and power, founded on physical force and conquest, and perpetuated by unjust, partial and monopolizing laws, all these professions have obtained great respect and consideration, which will diminish, as the light of reason increases through the millions; when each pair of hands is guided by a head, sufficiently informed to protect their natural rights, and a just and fair distribution of the produce of their labor, shall take place.

Another powerful, numerous, and well combined class, whose occupation does not require any capital, or accumulation of the produce of labor, but who are fed, clothed, lodged, and often luxuriously maintained by others' labor, are the officers of government; the executive, legislative, civil, military, naval, etc., through all the minute ramifications of church and state power and influence; whose necessary duties and relative authority depend on the nature of the power under which they act, whether hereditary or elective, despotic or conditional, if to protect an absolute, hereditary power, their principal occupation is to intrigue, combine and fortify their usurpation against the natural resentment of an oppressed people; for which purpose numerous and well disciplined standing armies and fleets are necessary, with swarms of police officers, to watch and detect the first embryo of revolts and conspiracies; to pay and maintain these, legions of collectors and revenue officers must be kept in pay, to squeeze out of the industrious producers, by indirect taxation, the money to feed, clothe and maintain such a numerous train of dependents. All of which means of coercion, must be in proportion to the diffusion of knowledge amongst the industrious millions; so that the Russian cerfs are kept in slavish submission with one fourth of the expense and patronage, that could subject the people of any country as far advanced in civilization as France or Britain, where public opinion is a check on tyranny and injustice, in proportion to its legal or permitted means of manifestation. In the commencement of civilization, the few who first acquired the command of moral or physical force, subjected the many to toil and labor for them; but the further progress of civilization, tends to diffuse and equalize both moral acquirements and physical force, and gives a bias to society to return nearer to that state of natural equality, from which the first rude steps of civilization had so far removed them.

The elective system by universal suffrage, has not existed long enough to enable the fortunate people who possess it, to form or mature laws, rules and regulations, to protect their natural and lately acquired rights. The brilliancy of emancipation, so dazzled the multitude, that they were content with the theory of freedom, and left the practice to the will of the few, who during the reign of hereditary monopoly, had acquired both superior wealth and wisdom, and as the best means of retaining the power their property and knowledge gave them, they imitated the laws, customs and habits contrived to perpetuate absolute hereditary power.

In this they have been yet but too successful in all countries, where more by chance than good guiding, they have stumbled on elective governments by universal suffra g How long the voters by universal suffrage (entirely confined to this side of the Atlantic,) will permit a junto of aristocratic combinations to trample on their natural rights and interests, time must determine. No notice is here taken of those occupied in extending their profits or plundering their ancestors, otherwise the distinction of occupations comes very near the division made by Adam Smith and other political economists of productive and nonproductive.

ON THE RIGHT OF SUFFRAGE. ABSURDITY OF A REPRESENTATION OF PROPERTY AND OTHER OBSTACLES TO UNIVERSAL SUFFRAGE.

October 30, 1834.

In the present great national dispute between the exclusive interest of the few, and the just and natural interest of the many, between the monopoly of power by hereditary and divine right, and the natural equality and division by representation, it is perhaps time that the interest of the millions ought to be investigated. Experience, as far as it has yet gone, will perhaps authorize us to admit, that the division of power amongst the many by the representative system, is the most certain means of producing "the greatest happiness to the greatest number," and that the comfort and happiness of the great majority who produce all, should on all principles of reason and justice, be preferred to the mistaken interest of the few, who live on and consume the produce of others' labor. Even in the representative system, there is a claim made by the monopolizers of property, to have land, money, etc., represented, to the exclusion of personal rights when deprived of such a proportion of property. The inherent nature of property is to give power, consideration and consequence to those who possess it, liable to be abused in proportion to its extent. By adding the artificial privilege of representation to the natural advantages of property, you increase the means, and double the temptation of the rich to tyrannize over the poor, increasing the misery of their poverty in proportion as you extend the artificial privileges of the wealthy. Vesting the right of suffrage in property, is an approximation to divine hereditary power, by dividing the population into two distinct classes, the rulers and ruled, the makers and obeyers of laws, with this difference, that the rulers are increased by the addition of all those who by force, fraud or savings, acquire the necessary property, and so augment the number that must be maintained by the labor of the industrious producers, who are mostly political slaves, the rulers having the sole right to make laws, and to enforce them to perpetuate their power and superiority. Britain is the only instance of a nation long under the suffrage of property; and all the working classes who permit themselves to be governed by a representation of property, must expect in time the fate of the British laborers. A laborer being asked on the hustings for his property, stretched out his sinewy arm as an answer; and he might have added, that such were the original titles, as being the producers of all kinds of property, and it would be the extreme of injustice and cruelty to deprive them of the advantage of what they earn, only because they were silly enough to allow themselves to be duped out of it, by the cunning and combination of the artful consumers.

Another absurd and unjust exclusion from the right of suffrage is made by those who have no property test, in the depriving of menial servants of the right of voting. These are a useful and necessary class, to all those who are not able or willing to serve themselves, and much less dependent than revenue officers and other servants, who are made and unmade by the government, a power much more subversive of liberty than any individual can possibly be. All this shows how small a portion of men's reason has been occupied with the doctrines or constitutions either of church or state.

All the arguments of the monopolizers of power, are founded on false principles. They assume rights which nature and justice deny them; they presumptuously demand, "what right have those to a participation in power who have nothing to lose, nothing at stake in the public property?"— They have their all, their every thing at stake: whereas the rich have only part of their property at risk on any event that can possibly happen; for it may easily be conceived, that a working man who has only one means of existence, his wages of labor, risks his all, which is a great deal more to him, than one who by his wealth has a dozen strings to his bow, and can live independently if left with but one of them. When the allied powers took Paris, and subjected France to their despotic will, the servants and working people felt more for the dignity, honor and interest of the nation, than all the bankers, merchants, and men of property, who having secured their iron chest, land marks, etc., lost none of their profits, privileges and prerogatives, in proportion to the quantum of despotism introduced by the change. But the working people, in losing their share of national glory, lost along with their freedom, their part of the respect attached to every individual of the great nation, whose triumphs have reached to the fartherest corners of the earth; and you could see their sorrow in their down castcountenances for a long time afterwards, and the most of them even then, under a judicious combination, would have risked the little that remained, to recover the national reputation, which they have so effectually done since, and will no doubt continue to do, in spite of all the aristocratical intrigue, contrived by the acme of European diplomacy.

Once proven that all property is the produce of labor, it follows of course that the interest of the laborer must be opposed and contrary to the interest of those he feeds, clothes and supplies with all their necessaries and luxuries, who must have a propelling interest to possess as much of the produce of the working people's labor, as they can by hook or by crook, and the laborers have an equally forcible interest in parting with as little as possible, and retaining as much as they can of the produce of their industry for their own use. It must be equally evident, from the poverty and misery of the working people, as well as the luxury, extravagance and dissipation of the consumers in all civilized countries, that the whole civilized improvements and machinery of both church and state, have been for many ages energetically at work to transfer under various pretences, by laws, rules and regulations the earnings of the industrious into the pockets of the idle. And it must be equally evident that the consequences of this moral revolution now in progress on this side of the Atlantic, and the moral and physical revolution which at present agitates the old world, must terminate in a complete change, in all the laws, rules, regulations, habits, customs and fashions, both private and public, political and religious, made and established for the benefit of the few at the expense of the many. Now that the many have acquired wisdom enough to claim their natural rights, and perseverance enough to unite their overpowering force the favorite few must give way, and the natural flood of equality will overflow the civilized, as it has always done the savage state, and mankind at last will enjoy the benefit of what is good and for the interest of the great majority, and be relieved from the errors and abuses of both the civilized and savage states. All this can only be accomplished by every ramification of power being elective by universal suffrage, under the control of a people who know their real interest, and are determined to act accordingly.

All theory and practice, both ancient and modern, favor the few who possess power; every page of history, poetry and romance, are filled with the flattering praises of heroic aristocracy, whilst the merit of the millions, whose power and force achieved all, is passed over in silence. What a reversing of principle, when the interest of the millions is to be advocated! What a Herculean task is the cleansing of the augean stable of all the filth, corruption, depravation and vice, accumulated, during thousands of years of despotism and misrule. At first much obstruction will be opposed by the quantity of the production of labor, monopolized by the arts of the consuming classes; but the producers persevering in stopping up the sources, what has already accumulated will be soon dissipated by the extravagance of the consumers, with their ignorance of the means of production. The moral reform on this side of the Atlantic, will succeed in time to prolong and be grafted on the improvements of the physical revolutions, which at present agitate the civilized world, and the melioration of rational freedom will continue to flow from west to east, still keeping ahead of the civilization of the rest of the globe, as it began, when we gave the first germ of political liberty to our species in the old world, half a century ago, and which seems from the luxuriance and rapidity of its growth, to have been planted in a rich and kindly soil, bidding fair to extend its branches over the whole earth.

SUGAR TAX FOR THE SUPPORT OF SLAVERY. SLAVE LABOR REQUIRES A PREMIUM TO ENABLE IT TO COMPETE WITH FREE LABOR. SLAVE HOLDERS OUGHT TO PREPARE FOR A GRADUAL ABOLITION, WHICH MUST TAKE PLACE.

Nov. 5th, 1834.

Amongst the many inconsistencies in the exercise of representation by universal suffrage, there is one which is peculiarly striking, both from its nature, and the serious consequences attached to it. Although full three fourths of the citizens of the Union, are convinced of the vast injury, and destructive consequences, entailed on a free people by the existence of slavery, yet they allow their federal representation, to levy a heavy tax for the maintenance and support of that slavery, which is so prejudicial to their interest, so derogatory to the reputation, honor and character of their liberal institutions, founded on freedom and equality. It is well known that sugar is almost the only production of the soil that can at present pay the expense of slave labor, and that it is enabled to pay that expense by the great premium of four dollars per hundred pounds, given by the federal government, on all sugar produced in the Union, (excepting that made from the Maple in the north;) that is three dollars on all foreign sugars, and one dollar for freight, insurance, commission, and all other charges of importation, makes the premium amount to four dollars, equal to the expense of cultivation, without which it is probable slaves could not pay for their expense of waste and maintenance, either by that or any other production. It is that great premium that enables the slave holders to work out of the toil and labor of their slaves, a sufficient quantity of sugar to pay the prime cost of the slave in less than three years. It is that immense premium that has raised the price of slaves to six and eight hundred dollars a head, which has induced the slave holders of some of the northern states, where climate will not permit the growing of sugar, to breed slaves for the consumption of the sugar planters, and droves of our species are seen daily chained together, driven from north to south to supply the market like oxen, sheep or hogs; and this shameful and disgraceful blot on the character of our country, has been a trade from the profits it produces, in consequence of the high premium on sugar, which has induced many otherwise respectable individuals to follow it. And who are to blame? The legislators who offer so irresistible a temptation, or the individuals who yield from convenience or necessity to the weight of the bribe? All this only shows the impolicy and inconvenience of trusting the taxation of so extensive a continent to our central power. No one mode of raising revenue can possibly suit the interests, opinions, or prejudices of so widely extended a latitude, longitude, climate or produce, and strongly proves the necessity, for the peace and harmony of our Union, to adopt the simplicity and economy of the federation of Switzerland, which interferes neither with the fiscal nor military laws of the individual states or cantons, which is the principal reason why it has existed nearly five hundred years without a dispute or collision between the states or cantons, and the federal powers. As centralism has proved lately to be only a precarious and weak cement to bind together small states, who formerly enjoyed the advantages of limited powers within the contracted circle of small jurisdictions, should any political convulsion or revolution dissolve the military bonds which alone keep up the appearance of union, we in the progress of civilization may see federalism extended to Italy, Austria, Russia and Prussia.

Now that the federal legislature are at a loss for means to dispose of their surplus revenue, they may perhaps find it useful and beneficial to their constituents, to relieve them from that heavy tax of nearly 100 per cent on sugar, now by habit become a necessary. It would increase the consumption of that healthy and nutritious food, and diminish the indigestible load of fat pork and other gross animal food, crowded on our tables three times a day; one of the great causes of our bilious and yellow fever diseases. It would so reduce the value of slaves, as to withdraw the temptation for that barbarous and unnatural traffic of breeding our fellow beings like black cattle for a market; and would in the end make slave labor of so little value, as to bring the occupation of a slave holder to be unprofitable, when no one would follow it for pleasure, and the general emancipation would be opposed by none. In all instances where slave labor has been brought in competition with free labor, free labor has under wrought it; as in the case of the indigo in India, the tropical productions in South America, etc., and I have not the least doubt, that by the time the division of property and knowledge is left to find its level, by the abolition of all unjust monopolizing charters, laws and regulations, that free labor will produce in abundance, every article that can be grown on the soil, from the equator to the poles. The aristocratic side of the question only, has yet been heard; the working people have just begun, in any country, to claim their rights, and put their shoulders to the political wheel, which must run round agreeably to their will and interest, if once they have the good sense to pull all one way, a strong pull, a long pull, and a pull all together. The greatest part of the evil which torments mankind, when traced to its origin, will be found to arise from the misrule and corruption of church and state, the only two powers, who by their cunning combination, could support injustic, plunder, and pillage.

Freedom and slavery are in morals, what fire and water are in physics, and cannot exist peaceably in the same body of society. Whilst our slave states rested on the West India slavery, and on a more rigorous despotism under the Spanish yoke in South America, there was a comparative despotism, which both physically and morally inclined in their favor, but since the emancipation of South America, since more than twenty millions of free citizens have been thrown into the scale of liberty, it will make slavery and despotism kick the beam in every climate and country on the globe. A new era begins in the annals of mankind; a tropical climate and production, where both slavery and despotism are abolished, and their freedom and equality rest on the broad basis of universal suffrage, whilst all such situations around the globe are paralized and oppressed by the most slavish despotism, the consequences are beyond the reach of analogy. The physical advantages of a vast extent of a fine climate, a rich soil, abounding in all the tropical productions, the variety and surety of which have hitherto supported the expense of slave labor, with the facility of an inland navigation of many thousands of miles; all this added to the moral inducement of freedom and equality guaranteed by universal suffrage, will most probably lower the production of the soil below what can be afforded by slave labor, and render slaves a loss instead of yielding a profit. These and many other considerations, merely in a pecuniary point of view, ought to induce our slave holders to contrive some means of gradual emancipation, and avoid the risk of loss by a violent change.

Let them look at the immense changes, since the French revolution, the great division of property and knowledge, which has thrown all political power into the hands of the millions in France, and has been the cause of the late revolution, and may by the help of a million and a half of national guards, make the tour of Europe. Let them inquire what proportion of the habitable world the unnatural traffic in men is permitted, where one portion of humanity is allowed to sell and enslave the other, they will find it does not exist in the Chinese empire or its environs, nor in Hindostan or the eastern countries. The babarous practice is only to be found in Russia, in the whole extent of Europe, and amongst the barbarous tribes of Africa, who limit the punishment of slavery to their prisoners taken in war, or to their criminals; whilst we sell and trade in our servants and nurses, on whose labor and milk we have been maintained and nourished, and even in the colored children, in whose veins circulate the blood of their masters. In every country, civilization is spreading, and tyranny diminishing, with the extension of equality.

DESIRABLE AND PROBABLE DIMINUTION IN THE COST OF BOOKS, FOR THE MORE GENERAL DIFFUSION OF KNOWLEDGE.

Nov. 10, 1834.

Book making is like gold beating, the greater surface a few grains of gold can be spread over, the more profit to the man with the hammer, and the more pages a few ideas can be made to occupy, the more profit to printers, booksellers and authors, whose interest is the only one consulted, by this enormous quantity of printed quackery, thrown on the voracious public, for the amusement of such an unnatural proportion of society, enabled to live without labor, by the various contrivances of hereditary power, monopolies, corporations, exclusive privileges, and the mysteries of church and state. Ecclesiastical history, theology and metaphysics are fast dissolving in the waters of Lethe; as there is little analogy between the past and present, the utility of all kinds of history is fast diminishing; when the use and benefit of law and gospel shall be transferred from the preachers, professors and practitioners, to the industrious producers who maintain those learned professions, more practical observation will render the speculative study of such an ocean of letter press unnecessary. When people learn, like the Quakers, to manage their own affairs, both in this and the next world, then poetry, plays and romance, the dreams of former times, will cease to amuse the present, and become less entertaining to the future. The great improvements in all the useful arts, render the description of agriculture and mechanism, as they were even thirty years ago, useless, and their study a loss of time to the present and future generations. All elementary works of the arts and sciences, where so many of their pages are filled with the former slow progress made, may flatter our pride and vanity by learning how superior the knowledge of the day is to the errors and blunders of our ancestors, but can add nothing to the state of perfection at which the science has arrived. Aristocracy, tyranny, despotism, hereditary and divine right, are no doubt interested in keeping the attention of the public fixed on the "glorious times of antiquity," when *their* interest was all, and the comforts and happiness of the millions nothing; when the monopoly of knowledge, used to be bound up in the elegant gilt binding, fine paper, hot press and large margin of a few hundreds of copies in an edition, out of the reach of the pockets of the laborer; but things are vastly changed now, when as much real knowledge can be bought for a cent as used to cost a dollar, with as much time lost in looking for it amongst the multiplicity of book making pages. Now small books, from six to thirty pages, are selling from two to six cents, published in editions of hundreds of thousands, in place of hundreds; each page containing as much useful knowledge as used to be found in a volume. This diffusion of knowledge, this equalization of intellect, is only beginning now to have its practical effects on society, by the industrious producers claiming their long dormant political rights, and placing themselves in the position which their number and utility entitle them to.

The change, though radical, will be gradual; depending more on the improvement of the moral than of the physical man. The producers learn to retain more of the produce of their own labor for their own use, the superfluities of the consumers will be curtailed, and the profits of all those trades and professions that used to administer to their luxurious expenditure must decrease, and the nature and value of the articles in which they deal, must change. All perishable articles, not subject to accumulation, and articles of necessity, the consumption of which is constant, may not fall more in value than the rise of the medium of exchange, in consequence of the diminished confidence in the circulating paper money, almost the only currency made use of in civilized countries, the small intrinsic value of which and the facility of manufacturing it, have been the cause of an excess above the necessary quantum for the regular trade of buying and selling. But on all property for show, pomp or parade, indestructible as diamonds, and ornamental precious stones, or from their lasting properties, capable of accumulation, the depreciation must be great and rapid, as the class who used to own them, become unable to retain them; in which depreciation the pictures of what have been called the great masters most likely will participate.

A great change most likely will take place in the book trade, for many reasons. Books being made to suit the customers, like all other fabricks, and those who hitherto could afford to buy them, being of the aristocratic classes, they have been made to flatter their interest and opinions, and even to praise their vices and faults; their elegant and ornamental forms were made to suit their luxurious tastes, and the few copies in an edition, to accommodate the few readers, whilst the prices were such as to retain the exclusive monopoly in the rich and superior orders. When the millions of industrious producers become so elevated in the scale of humanity, as to know, claim and insist on their natural rights, when the more equal division of property produces the more equal division of knowledge and power, it is then that their abilities and numbers will constitute them the chief purchasers and consumers of books, and then the doctrines they preach must be in favor of the producing classes, and their interest, opinions and principles are the only theme that must occupy their pages.

That books must be both printed and bound in the most economical manner; five pages, by condensation, containing as much real and useful knowledge as used to be spread over five hundred; and on cheap paper made of straw or *corn shucks*, printed by steam in hundreds of thousands in an edition, so that the paper and printing will constitute the greatest expense, and bring every kind of information within the reach of the poorest. It only requires a few correct ideas on utility, to know that gilt edges, hot press, large margins, and larger volumes, add nothing to the knowledge contained in the descriptions, and that rounded periods, florid, redundant and what has been called elegant style, very often obscures the senses, so as to render it difficult to bring the focus to bear on the subject. Some cheaper and more abundant material must be got to make paper; for the rags of the wretched must diminish as civilization and knowledge extend with the consumption of paper in those hundreds of thousand editions, as is proven by the enormous quantity of two-penny books sold every Saturday in London and the other large towns in Britain.

By the ancient, aristocratic order of society, upwards of three-fourths of all the produce of labor was expended by church, state and privileged orders, which enabled them to purchase and use all superfluous luxuries. For instance, the three countries forming the British empire, with a population of 17,000,000, have an income of about 426,000,000 of pounds sterling, produced by the industry of about 8,000,000, who only enjoy about 90,000,000 of the produce of their labor. Contrast this with the state of society in France since the revolution, and an astonishing difference is exhibited in favor of the laboring producers of the latter, sufficient, if well understood, to create a similar revolution in all countries. In France property is so divided, that ten and a half millions of the people are interested in land and other real property which pay tax, and only about 3000 of those proprietors of real property pay more annual tax than from 250 to 1000 francs; the remaining upwards of 10,000,000 pay on an average from one to 100 francs yearly, and may be all included in the productive class, and there are only 3000 of the proprietors of real estate who can live without labor.— Supposing one thousand times more of proprietors of money and other movables, who can live without labor, it would reduce the nonproductive classes in France to 3,000,000, taking the population at 30,000,000, that would be 27,000,000 of producers who have to maintain 3,000,000 of nonproducers; whereas in the British dominions there are 7,000,000 of producers who have to maintain 10,000,000 of nonproducers; each expending at least five times more than the nonproductive can in France.

By the just, impartial and equitable laws of inheritance established in France by the revolution and continued by the Napoleon code, property is so divided, that few can afford to buy luxuries, and expensive editions of books have already fallen to one third of their former prices, and most probably would (with pictures, antiquities and other objects of show and parade) have fallen much lower, had they not been kept up by the rich aristocracy of their neighbors, who have not yet been subject to the revolutionary lever. But the same cause will produce the same effects, and the more or less universal suffrage is aimed at, in the representative system over the civilized world, will in time perhaps not far distant, produce, by laws of inheritance and direct taxes on income, that natural equality, so much deranged and infringed on by the artificial contrivances of civilization as far as it has yet gone. Suppose the abolition of tithes and the greatest part of the interest of the national debt, taken up in an income tax in Britain, where would they find customers for the greatest part of the luxurious collections of books, pictures, statues and antiquities as well as lace and finery of dress, when years of labor are wasted on a frill or ruffle, to indulge the momentary caprice and fancy of an indolent, pampered aristocrat.

GREAT SUPERIORITY OF REPRESENTATIONS TO THE EYE OVER VERBAL DESCRIPTIONS IN GIVING IDEAS. UTILITY OF CARICATURES.

Nov. 15, 1834.

Designing accurately figures, and representations of all things, is the only well defined mode of communicating ideas, the only correct language which all have recourse to, when they wish to be understood, by drawing with their finger or any instrument the figure of the object they wish to explain, and the more correct and expeditious they have learned to delineate, the quicker, truer, and more easily they communicate their ideas to others. This general acknowledgement of the superiority of representation over description, marks the road which the evidence of the senses ought to take, in imprinting ideas on the mind. Any figure being truly represented, is alike accurately transported to the mind, and saves the trouble of delineating or composing a figure, from a vague and undefined description partaking of the uncertainty of the various definitions of the relative meaning of the words, of which the description is composed.

In forming a judgement of the relative value of figures or representations, we must be guided entirely by the utility of the ideas they represent, whether for profit or pleasure, whether for the serious and necessary occupations of life, or for the amusement, pastime, or spending our days agreeably to the mistaken selfish consideration, without allowing the comfort and happiness of others to interfere. In the graduated scale of utility, it is more than probable the first rank must be given to mechanism and the arts; formerly called the vulgar arts, because practiced by those, who in the unjust scale of consideration, were reckoned the lowest link, though they put a mind into matter, to make it serviceable to the comfort and happiness of mankind; and the nature and complicacy of the machinery is such that it cannot be correctly explained but by representation. As the most useful ought to be the first learned, let the tyro be first initiated into the accurate designing of all machinery invented to abridge and facilitate labor, as the artificial mode of calling in matter to the assistance of men. Next in the scale of utility are the objects with which nature has surrounded us, of which we are in the daily habit of making use, as far as we know how, according to the correct ideas we have obtained of their nature and properties. To facilitate the acquiring of correct knowledge of all the classes of natural history, accurate designs of plants, animals, etc., are positively necessary, and the art of delineating them equally indispensible. Geography, topography, and landscape have already been further cultivated for the pleasure and accommodation of church or state, than any individual industry can go; it is therefore easier to procure the works of others than to make them, except for those who mean to be professors, the acquiring of the art, might be acquiring what they never would be under the necessity of practising; always excepting the drawing of plans necessary to the representation of the mensuration of superfices or solids, an art useful to all classes.

Accurate representations of every thing beneath the skin of the human figure, either by sculpture or painting, is positively necessary to give a correct idea of such essentially useful knowledge; but of all the modes of exhibiting the selfish egotism of mankind, that propensity to delineate, by sculpture or painting the external human figure, is perhaps the most useless. There is not an atom of knowledge got by the representation of figures, the originals of which are every minute subject to our examination, both in our own and in others, persons. The imaginary flattery of our species, by what has been called the beau ideal, is perhaps as distant from utility as it is from truth. All nations represent their gods after their own image, from the fat Josses of the Chinese, to what has been called the elegant Grecian figures of Apollo and Venus, and the paintings of most of the great masters have been made to adorn the churches of christendom in the representations of angels and saints under the figures of virgins, as in the catholic churches; an ingenious invention to render the workship by genuflection more natural and agreeable. All the world were originally idolaters, from the impossibility of forming an idea of immateriality, and the most refined and spiritual religions have not yet got rid of their hankering after the flesh, like the Israelites and their golden calf. Priests of all nations, climates and religions have taken the most effectual mode of imprinting their dogmas and doctrines on the minds of their followers, by representations through sculpture and painting. Mahommed is perhaps the only inventor of a religion whose precepts have prevented his followers from making use of images—trusting to the power of words and the sword for the propagation of his dogmas. The preachers of religious dogmas, in explaining their doctrines by representations, in aid of their descriptions, however erroneous they might be in their moral or spiritual creeds, understood perfectly the most direct road to conviction, by impressing their doctrines on the mind, by some visible and tangible object within the reach of the senses. Their success in thus teaching their incomprehensible dogmas, ought to have taught all the instructors of youth, how easily they could inculcate the useful knowledge of realities on the minds of their pupils.

Why representations have been so much limited to explanations of the mysteries of church and state, by religious and historic paintings, can only be accounted for on their superior address and cunning in adopting the most direct means of accomplishing their ends, with their dexterous use of monopoly. As the priests of all countries have siezed upon the education of children, to imprint their incomprehensible dogmas on their tender and pliable minds, before reason has had time to act, or guide them in the choice of their opinions, intimately leagued with all absolute civil power, for the mutual support of their arbitrary authorities, enforced by the terrors and thunders of both worlds, they have been too strong for isolated common sense to make any progress against their despotic creeds.

That the teachers of children have preferred their ipse dixit descriptions to representations, in imprinting ideas on the minds of youth, must be owing to their love of verbal authority, as they may thus claim all the merit of placing ideas on the minds, though imperfectly, by oral transmission, but they cannot pretend to the same credit of imprinting ideas on the mind when they are transferred from an accurate representation—the facility as well as accuracy with which the figure is placed before the judgment, with the durability on the memory of the learner, lowers the merit of the teacher, whose credit and reputation are in proportion to the difficulties he has to conquer, as in most other professions. This accounts also for the unnecessary intricacies of law, politics, and religion.

Representations of all fixed objects, such as antiquities and architecture, are as well understood and defined as in the reality. In machines that have motion, or animals that have life, the movement of the reality is what cannot be represented, but may be added by memory or analogy, though the reality does not so far exceed the representation, as the representation does the description. It is therefore a saving of time, toil and temper, to instruct by representations, in all situations where realities cannot be had. Placing the faults, foibles or failings of mankind in a ridiculous point of view, by a well drawn carricature, gives ideas at the first glance that could not be communicated so strikingly by many pages of letter press, nor be retained in the memory the one hundredth part of the time; the impression is as instantaneous as lasting. Why this has not been more practiced, is perhaps that the class of society more exposed by their folly to ridicule, have had the arbitrary power to suppress it. Britain was the first to enjoy any part of their natural freedom, and have put the most wit and satire into their caricatures. France during the freedom gained by their revolution, attempted a clumsy imitation, but the zest was marred by the remains of national suavity and politeness.

CHEAP FOOD AND DRINK ARE THE MOST WHOLESOME. EQUALITY CONDUCIVE TO VIRTUE.

Nov. 20, 2834.

Every thing that is cheap or procured with little labor is most conducive to health, wealth and happiness. The most healthful mode of traveling is on foot; it is the most correct mode of acquiring the positive knowledge of surrounding objects, and it is at the same time the cheapest.— The most wholesome beverage is water, the most conducive to a sound mind, and the cheapest. The plainest food is the most wholesome, and the simplest cookery the easiest of digestion; all mixtures and complications to flatter the artificial appetite, only wear out and debilitate the stomach, in separating component parts and making the analysis. Luxurious soft beds are the most debilitating; hard beds are the cheapest and most healthy. Coarse linen next to the skin is warmest in winter, and absorbs perspiration better in summer, guarantees better against the changes of the weather, creates a salutary friction on the skin, and is obtained with less expense of labor. Most of our luxurious and artificial wants are obtained by much care, anxiety, labor and pain, are the creatures of civilization, and when got only generate disease, pain and disappointment, abridging life and all its comforts.—By acquiring, with some perseverance, a taste for oysters, what a fund of disappointment, longing and craving does a person accumulate, if perchance he removes fifteen hundred miles from the sea? The same of that disgusting poisonous plant tobacco, the taste for which is learned with so much trouble, when deprived of it the feelings are uncomfortable, in the exact ratio of the difficulties of learning to conquer the disgust at the nauseous and unpleasant effects, which every one must experience at the first trial. Almost the whole of our tastes are acquired; amongst the few that are natural, milk and sugar are most conspicuous, and every thing in proportion as it resembles them. All sour, bitter or strong food have an unpleasant effect on the palate, and must be rejected by all whose tastes are not vitiated by habit. All kinds of wines or strong liquors that do not approach to the taste of milk or sugar, would be rejected at first by all children; none of the immense variety of artificial dishes, invented to pamper the artificial appetite, would please the natural tastes of children but in proportion as they approach the taste of milk or sugar. The education of children ought to begin not by learning them new tastes, but by rigorously fortifying, maintaining and nourishing the natural tastes of instinct, and carefully preventing the acquisition of any new tastes, which can only increase their wants, and of course, their troubles and misery through life. Men, like all other carniverous animals, are born with an instinctive courage, which ought to be cherished and supported by education; all their lessons ought to be calculated so as to depend on free will, for children are materially injured in all the necessary accomplishments, by being coerced by fear to do what their inclination or natural disposition revolts at. The lessons ought to be made to suit the nature of the child, not the child constrained and new modeled to suit the lessons. The dogma of original sin, founded on the story of Adam and the apple, has had great influence in forming our systems of education, opposed and contrary to nature; "that man is prone to evil as the sparks fly upwards," authorizes all kinds of fine, restraint and coercion, to change and counteract the natural dispositions; and it substitutes the artificial, in accordance with the prejudices, superstitions, fancies or whims of the teacher, placing art in opposion to nature, instead of aiding and assisting in modifying and reconciling them, so as to render the union more perfect, and the direction of the exertions towards general good, stronger and more efficacious. Men have never yet been found in a state of nature, where instinct has had fair play, free from the vices of education. Even our savages, with whom the inclemency of the seasons render violent struggles necessary for existence, have been taught most of their vices, by contact with civilization, and in all the climates where nature has been bountiful, such as in the West Indies and South Sea islands, were in a state of innocence, free from vice and crime, when first visited by civilization; their property was confined within the limits of necessaries, was almost in common, and they lived almost entirely on the fruits of the earth. The first appropriation of land, and afterwards of other property to individual monopoly, is perhaps the origin of cupidity, vice and crime.

If we compare the simplicity, honesty and hospitality of the inhabitants of mountains, where the nature of the locality scatters and isolates them, and where the poverty of both soil and climate starves tyranny, with the cunning, roguery, vice and crime which fills our large cities, we shall be convinced of how great a proportion of misery, wretchedness and crime is the consequence of art and civilization, and how little reason we have to blame nature for the evils we bring on ourselves, by a total deviation from all her laws. In all physics, improvement is simplification, that is requiring less labor; all our mechanism now, is much less complicated considering the work it does, than it used to be; and even in morals, though it is many centuries behind physics, any little amelioration that has taken place, has been by banishing complicated intricacy and metaphysical mysteries, and placing men's motives on the true basis of self, judging the merits of their actions by the good or bad consequences, and leaving the whole catalogue of imaginary motives out of the dictionary of common sense. Equality is the true simplification of society, and the most extensive and solid foundation of morality, producing "the greatest happiness to the greatest number," the true test of utility. Were property, knowledge and power so equally divided, that each individual would be forced to make all or part of what he consumed, superfluities would disappear from our kitchens, saloons and wardrobes, and each would make an estimation of the labor of producing the superfluities, and finding it far exceed the enjoyment, he would drop the one to be relieved from the other.

The French nation is at present in so enviable a state of equality, that there are not much more than 50,000, exclusive of the learned professions and public officers, in 32,000,000 of inhabitants, who can live without labor; and though that equality of property has scarcely existed long enough under the protection of freedom to produce a corresponding equality of knowledge, yet the late revolution, under the auspices of a million and a half of national guards, is a convincing proof of the foresight and wisdom of the millions, with whom alone the revolution originated, and for whose benefit and that of the world at large it will terminate in firmly consolidating liberty and equality, and in placing their advantages to all classes in so strong a light, as forever afterwards to prevent the sophistry of aristocracy from blinding the industrious producers.

THE PRESENT BRITISH PARLIAMENTARY REFORM CAN BE OF LITTLE UTILITY TO THE MILLIONS.

Nov. 26, 1834.

About twelve or fifteen years ago, I wrote a short essay at the request of the editor of the *Revue Encyclopedique*, intended to be published in that work, but it was rejected by the censors as too democratic. The subject was the incompatibility of the two powers, hereditary and elective to exist peaceably in the same body politic. My reasoning was taken from Britain, France, and Spain, at that time under the apparent control of the two powers. I endeavored to prove that Britain, the only one that had lasted long enough to be any example or proof of the result, was entirely under the government of the House of Peers, and of course ruled by the hereditary aristocracy; that the House of Commons were their servants, the king their puppet, and the minister their broker. This and the immense revenue at the command of their brokers, accounts for the apparent tranquility with which the machine has wrought. For though it appears to have three main springs, which have been called checks and ballances, it is entirely moved by the superior force of one, which has strength to control the other two. On reading the recent plan of parliamentary reform, with which the poor people of Britain seem so elated, I cannot see how it can possibly benefit them, or relieve them from their heavy burdens. One of two things must take place; either it will give the preponderating power to the people, the industrious producers, (which nothing short of universal suffrage can do,) or it will lessen the power of hereditary aristocracy, in the same proportion as it augments that of the elective power, and so increase the friction of the political machine, as to require more of the oil of bribery and corruption, to make it go on. If all the force of hereditary combination of both church and state, can scarcely squeeze out of the laborers as much as to lubricate the present complicated machine, what possible relief can the people expect from their burdensome taxation, by increasing the elective power and consequent opposition to the hereditary, to reconcile which, the only mode yet found out, has been patronage, sinecure places and fat livings in church or state; all of which must come from the labor of the industrious producers. With the present great inequality of property, knowledge and power in Britain, what ages of misrule have urged the whole population into the two extremes of poverty and riches, ignorance and knowledge. Can the extension of the right of voting to a two hundredth part of the population, reform the abuses that have gradually accumulated during the last thousand years? Inquire of the result of our universal suffrage for more than half a century, although it originated in an equality of property and knowledge, one thousand times more divided than they ever were in Britain. See that equality gradually advancing to monied aristocracy, by the acts of legislators elected only for a year by universal suffrage; by litigious, intricate and mysterious laws, out of the reach of the pockets of the laborers, that can only be bought by the rich, and kept as a scourge of oppression over the poor; by the five or six hundred exclusive bank charters, giving the monopoly of the whole circulating paper money of the Union, to a few of the rich and influential; by granting privileges to thousands of incorporations, for trading, manufacturing and other purposes, which are denied to the rest of the population; and last though not least the fixing the wages of their own political labor, so far above all other useful and necessary labor, as to create intrigue, disputes and broils, often terminating in bloodshed at our elections.

All the artificial parties of whigs, tories, etc., are merely transient distinctions, which change with every alteration in surrounding circumstances; but the great and material parties of producers and consumers, those who labor and those who consume the produce of labor, the industrious and idle, have split and divided society in all ages, climes and nations. Civilization, as far as it has yet gone, has rather augmented than diminished this division, in consequence of the contrivances of the consuming classes, who have smothered and drowned, in the mysteries of church and state, the natural rights and just claims of the industrious producers. If any further proof is wanted, let the present conduct of the French chamber of deputies suffice. They are deliberating whether or not they shall fix on two hundred francs tax on real property as a title to vote, in the face of a million and a half of national guards, who had just made a revolution, giving them the right of legislating, but by such a constitution, almost the whole of those national guards would be excluded from the right of voting.

Of this natural division of society, what proportion of the right of voting, by the scale of property proposed by the British reform of parliament, will devolve on the great industrious producing classes? Will it be a hundredth or a thousandth part? And what chance has any one to be elected as a representative, who from similarity of situation or interest can be in favor of the industrious producers? Will not they be all chosen out of the consuming classes, whose interest will force them to exempt their own property from taxation, by continuing the burden on the laborers by indirect taxes, and by supporting the intricate laws, of which their property gives them the monopoly? The floodgates of abuse and corruption have run too long to be stopped by any temporary measure; nothing but a radical cure, by exhausting and drying up the source, can have any permanent effect?

The unprecedented enormity of the national debt, and the payment of the interest by indirect taxation, are the principal roots of all the poverty, misery and crime of the British dominion. Will those who receive the dividends of the national debt or are favored by exemption from taxation on their property, willingly curtail the one or change the other?— Those who expect it must be wholly ignorant of their own or human nature. The expectations of the people have been raised only to produce a corresponding disappointment and increased discontent, which the partial and temporary reform cannot alleviate, or bring the adverse parties nearer a peaceable arrangement, though it may place their forces nearer on a par, and make the contention more serious. Suppose for an instant, that the reform was made radical by universal suffrage, and that the elective part controlled the hereditary.—Still their interest would remain opposite and contradictory, and the hereditary, so long accustomed to power, would resist the orders of the elective, and throw out their laws; when the people would join their representatives and the hereditary power would be abolished. There can be no medium. Either the interest of the few must control the interest of the many by a well combined physical force, or the interest of the many must rule the apparent interest of the few by a better combination of right and reason. This limited monarchy only brings aristocracy half way down stairs, from which they cannot advance without risking their necks, and there is no positive security for either party, but descending the whole staircase to the platform of equality, below which few can fall, and above it few can rise.

Civilization has only yet enabled the moral faculties of the few, to domineer over the physical force of the many. At present a new epoch commences, when the many have learned to combine their physical force for the protection of their natural rights against the usurpations of the few, and the diffusion of knowledge has taught them, that however arbitrary power might have suited the barbarous ignorance of antiquity, it is incompatible with the light and knowledge of the present day, as is proven by the struggles the millions are making on both sides of the Atlantic to claim their unalienable rights; with this difference, however, that in the old world they must wrest their freedom from the divine hereditary powers, by a physical revolution of force and violence, whereas on this side, it is by a moral revolution of right and reason, inducing them only to claim the practice of their freedom and equality, the theory of which they have possessed for the last half century. Which of the two may succeed first in their undertakings may be doubtful, as the physical forces of the millions, when called into combined action, must prevail, but the moral superiority of the many over the few, judging of former experience, may be doubted.

Opulence and its accompanying vices and luxuries paralizes all physical and moral exertions. When the greatest part of the industrious producers shall be favored with an useful education, their physical force, joined to their moral accomplishment, must put down all opposition, and make their interest the standard of public good, their opinions the regulator of all customs and fashions, when economy and utility will be the scale to measure the value of all things. Then the equality established in France since the revolution, with all its consequences, will be the envy and command the imitation of all nations.

MISCONSTRUCTION OF THE MEANING OF POLITICAL ECONOMY.

Nov. 30*th*, 1834.

Political economy has been twisted into an intricate and mysterious science, by the vast number of authors disputing on the meaning of words of their own invention, encouraged by the few who live on every kind of paper representations of property, so that the original intention and nature of the properties included in the word *political economy* (being the application of the frugality, saving and economy of a family to a community or political association) is entirely lost sight of, and drowned in an ocean of verbiage, serving as an excuse and disguise, of the wasteful and ruinous extravagance of church and state, for the gratification of the few, who live on the produce of the labor of the many, who buy their books on which they live. These authors cautiously avoid taking notice of the comfort or happiness of the millions, who produce all by their labor, and are oppressed and wretched in proportion to the number and wasteful extravagance of the consuming classes they maintain. Their principal object seems to be, to find out how the consumers can benefit most by the labor of the producers; how the quantity and quality of their physical toil can be stretched to the verge of their moral patience and forbearance; how their hard labor can be apportioned to their strength; how their wages can be restricted to what is necessary to keep them in existence, that the whole regimen may conduce to keep them poor and ignorant, the willing slaves of church and state.

By king-craft and priest-craft and all their adherents, a nation is considered powerful, wealthy and prosperous, when the rulers have credit to borrow and burthen the millions with the yearly interest of a national debt to the full amount of the surplus produce of the labor of all its inhabitants, the principal of which could not be repaid by double the whole surplus produce, for twenty years, of all the industrious workmen; that is, the government have wastefully expended, in less than half a century, by anticipation in paper representations of property, to the amount which the industry of the millions could produce in forty years, as is the case with the British national debt, called by some of those who benefit by it, "a national blessing." Besides this enormous anticipation of property not yet in existence, by the public rulers, there is in bank notes, mercantile and other individual paper representations of property to an immense amount, part of which are mortgages on the labor of futurity without their consent, which may or may not be realized, according to circumstances in the womb of time. All the monarchies of the old world are less or more approaching to bankruptcy, by mortgaging the produce of the labor of their subjects for ages to come, without any certainty of its ever being realized, as none of the national debts of Europe have yet been paid, but by some subterfuge equal to a bankruptcy, perhaps nothing different may be expected of the present national debts.

The only difference between a wasteful spendthrift, without economy, dissipating and mortgaging his property, and a government squandering the people's property, and mortgaging the produce of their labor for centuries to come, is that the one makes use of what belongs to him, the other makes free with what belongs to others. But the want of frugality and economy is the same in both. And inasmuch as individual economy is the limiting expenses within the bounds of individual revenue, so political economy ought to be the various saving means of economizing the public property; detailing the best and most useful mode of frugality and saving in the public expenditure on every public work or enterprize; comparing the cost with the advantage to be gained; investigating under what circumstances the public would be benefited by the government making improvements, or whether they might not be made cheaper and better by individual enterprize; examining the form of government that is most likely to produce the most economy and utility, with the kind of tax that is most just, and easiest paid, and collected at the smallest expense of money or morals. All these subjects might fill the volumes the ambition of the author required, and at the same time afford much more useful information to a people governing themselves by universal suffrage and might forward civilization more than a minute examination of the nature of capital, rents, wages, etc., or whether the landlord, tenant or consumer pay the tithes.

Where there was a fixed hereditary aristocracy of privileged orders, as in Britain and other monarchies, as soon as any part of the moneyed aristocracy had acquired a certain influence by their riches, they were promoted to the rank of the privileged orders. This is one of the means of recruiting the talent, energy and activity of that depreciating class. But the United States of America was a new field, clear of all the obstructions of hereditary rights and privileges. There the influential few had to build up their moneyed aristocracy from the foundation, without the aid or encouragement of a hereditary nobility, and without the assistance of a powerful and richly endowed hierarchy, a chief support to aristocracies in other christian nations. They had to depend entirely on elective legislators to furnish materials by monopolies, for the construction of their moneyed aristocracy. These privileges given to the few and denied to the many, to the advantage of the few at the expense of the many, was following the mode adopted for the elevation of aristocracies in all countries, savage or civilized. The first materials for the foundation of that inequality of property on which alone a moneyed aristocracy could be built, was the funding system by which 80,000,000 of dollars were divided among the few, in the senate, succeeded by the land speculation, by which all the uncultivated lands in possession of the States were granted to the influential few; followed by the chartering of 705 monopolizing banks, mercantile, manufacturing and other corporations, granting privileges to the few, denied to the many. Nature, when left to herself, being an equalizer of property, has left but a small proportion of the effects of the two first speculations. But the exclusive privileges of the banks and other corporated charters, being a growing evil, has been so combined with all the other aristocracies as to give them strength to brave the public authorities, and arbitrarily to try to govern the Union according to their interest. This usurping moneyed aristocracy, for talent, energy and activity, are superior to the indolent, luxurious hereditai y aristocracy of the old world. In the charters of their banks, insurance companies and other corporations, they were not content with following the European precautions of limiting the dividend, but allowed the directors to pay what dividend they pleased, as the interest of the stockholders required of them; so that one hundred and sixty-five banks have failed already, by dividing the capital in place of profits, to the great loss of the working industrious millions, who are the holders of their notes. Merchants and other rich men keep bank accounts, and pay by checks, never keeping bank notes in the house, but owing the bank large sums for discounts, repay the bankrupt bank with their own notes, bought up at a discount of from twenty to seventy per cent. according to the want of confidence in the public. The precarious situation of all moneyed aristocracies, depending on false capital, stimulates their ingenuity to find every possible means of keeping up their usurped elevation, and by great activity with bank notes, mercantile and other specialities, they have set afloat a circulation of perhaps not much less than seven hundred millions of dollars, equal to ten years surplus produce of the whole Union. That is, they have anticipated, by paper representations of property, the produce of the labor of the working classes for the next ten years, supposing the exports of the surplus produce of the Union do not exceed seventy millions a year. All this robbing from posterity, is according to laws made by the elective legislatures, put into power, mostly for one year, by universal suffrage. The blame of the abuse of power, lies entirely with the majority of the millions, who must deservedly suffer for their conduct and ignorance. It will require a new system of political economy to suit the interest of a free people, ruled by liberty and equality, not the mode of forcing them to work harder to produce the most for the use of church and state, but the means by which the smallest portion of their labor can suffice for the conducting their public affairs.

TEMPTATION AND ABUSE OF POWER.

Dec. 6, 1834.

While the affairs of church and state are entrusted to the consuming classes, what interest can they possibly have in economizing the fruits of the people's labor? Would they gain by reducing the taxes on which they live? If every one enjoyed in proportion to what he produced, what would be the share of those who produce nothing but words? What order of things was necessary to force the many in possession of most of the physical force to toil and labor to maintain the physically weak and luxurious few? How came that unnatural and artificial division of classes into those who produce and those who consume the produce of their labor? Now that the unequal division has been made, how is it possible to conceive that those who enjoy the monopoly of property, knowledge and power, can possibly have the smallest inclination to change the state of things which maintains them in a luxurious opulence, at the expense of the labor of others by relieving the millions from any part of their exorbitant taxes, and thereby diminishing the oppression of poverty, and in the same proportion reducing the quantum of ignorance. There are some strong temptations which few men can resist, and almost none who remain long in power: 1st, the collecting exorbitant taxes to support them and their friends and relations in their extravagant expenses. 2d, The levying all by indirect taxation as an excuse for the patronage of a multitude of officers, and tempting the breaking of the laws by smuggling, fitting the people for slavery, as all criminals are humble and subservient to those in power. 3, As property and knowledge are the chief implements of power, the keeping the millions poor and ignorant, is, in all countries, the principal means of facilitating the monopoly of power in the possession of the few, by all their laws, rules and regulations, being made for the interest of the governors, though most of them opposed to the peace, comfort, and happiness of the governed. 4th, Arbitrary discipline, supposed to be necessary in armies by land, and ships of war by sea, makes wars of aggression the means, by conquest, of increasing the wealth and power of the rich and the poverty of the poor, under pretence of protection from external robbery, subject them to more certain and lasting plunder by their internal task masters. 5th, The shifting the burdens off their own shoulders, on those of laborious posterity, contrived the mortgaging posterity by a national debt, which means, "the visiting the iniquities of the fathers upon the children to the third and fourth generation." 6th, The public property bestowed on the church as an extension of patronage in the gift of the powerful is one of the burdens of society that has increased with civilization. All these radical abuses and their attending accessories are the means of originating, and augmenting the great artificial inequality of property, knowledge and power, one of the consequences of civilization as far as it has yet gone.

In all civilized societies there is at least twenty producers for one rich enough to be a consumer; so that in all elective systems by universal suffrage they ought to rule and make all laws, rules and regulations according to the dictates of their own interests, there are perhaps one hundred debtors for one that is rich enough to be a creditor; and yet under our government of representation by universal suffrage, the legislatures have given the despotic authority to that one creditor to incarcerate all his debtors because they are poor; and thereby rendering them useless both to themselves and others, exaggerating on the cruelty of the old Roman laws (from which most of our laws are taken,) where the creditor had a right of selling his debtor—placing him in a situation to be useful and to enjoy more of the comforts of life than starving immured in prison; making poverty a greater crime than robbing or thieving, to the imprisonment for which there is some limits.

Under no government but the elective by universal suffrage, can the interest of the majority prevail. Where the few rule, their interest must dictate all laws, rules and regulations at the expense of the many. Every page of both ancient and modern history (though partial to the rule of the few) proves the truth of the sacrifice of the interest of the many to the few. Popular elective governments by universal suffrage have only yet existed on this side of the Atlantic; have been recently formed under the weight of a great many strong prejudices, opposed and villified by the united combination of the aristocracies of the old world aided by the upstart aristocracies of the new. The people have had scarcely time to know by experience its great advantages. Domineered and deluded by the false pretensions of patriotism, public good, etc., they have not yet learned to distinguish between the candidate for power, who, from his education, property, habits, passions, and propensities, must have an interest opposed to them, and the candidate whose circumstances, trade, and mode of living, assimilates his interest to theirs. The millions have not yet learned to govern themselves; they have only substituted a monied aristocracy in place of the divine right and hereditary aristocracies of their mother country; which is sufficiently proven by this dispute between the bank and the government, where the bankites insist on an arbitrary right to privileges which perhaps no elective governments have authority to grant, and which is against the equality declared by the independence on which alone permanent freedom can be based. This granting of monopolies by bank and other charters, with exclusive privileges, is an *abuse* and *usurpation* by the legislatures; the federal and most of the state constitutions, *prohibiting*, and the *spirit of the whole* of them against granting such exclusive privileges.

NATIONS BEHIND INDIVIDUALS IN THE KNOWLEDGE OF THEIR INTEREST, AND IN CHANGING FROM ERRONEOUS OPINIONS.

Dec. 10, 1834.

Nations and all societies are composed of individuals, and the aggregate of the knowledge, habits, customs, passions and propensities of the individuals, forms the national character; yet an individual can be taught a more perfect knowledge of his interest in one year, than a nation can be, or rather has been, in many centuries. The absurd, irrational or foolish errors and prejudices of an individual can be changed more in one month, than the ignorance, bigotry, superstition, and unreasonable opinions of a nation have been in thousands of years. The other animals are instructed in their mode of preservation, defence, etc., in proportion to their numbers, aggregated together, as the beavers, bees, ants, etc., which when found singly and isolated are not half so ingenious, either in providing the necessaries for their existence or defence. Why the one has so great an advantage over the many, in the human species, and the aggregated many so superior to the one in all other animals, is a question that has been little inquired into. Perhaps the rulers of church and state, perceiving that their intrigues, stratagems, and deceptions against the diffusion of useful knowledge would be found the principal cause of so marked a difference, have not only stopped the dissemination of knowledge, but have had the cunning and address to monopolize it. The attributing it to the supposed great superiority of reason over unerring instinct, is no explanation of the how or the wherefore, for it is probable that the natural equality between the animals of the same species, would in man be productive of a greater sum of peace, comfort and happiness than ever has been enjoyed by that artificial division into classes, where the many are oppressed by the toil, exertion and labor of maintaining the few. Civilization, as far as it has yet gone, has organized this unnatural, great inequality; and the chief occupation of church and state seems to have been the protecting and augmenting by every law, rule and regulation, that degrading inequality. Man by nature is as near equality as any of the other animals. Force, intrigue, cunning, and artifice have alone deranged that equilibrium on which depends that progress towards the civilization and happiness he is capable of enjoying.

The only governments that have been yet rationally and deliberately formed by the voice and concurrence of the great majority, are the representative democracies on this side of the Atlantic; and the only one of them that has had a fair trial is the United States of America, who are at present at the top of the civilization, prosperity and power of all the nations on earth, and where property, knowledge and power are more equally divided; from which it would appear that equality is the principal ingredient of freedom, and not incompatible with the highest state of civilization. The Grecian republics were at the top of the civilization of antiquity and had more freedom and equality than any of the other ancients. Switzerland in modern times was the first to acquire a kind of rational freedom, founded on a proportionate equality of property, knowledge and power, on which alone freedom can be permanent, as is proven by their representative system lasting five hundred years without any great change. It is probable that without a certain equality of property, knowledge, and power, liberty cannot long exist.

The first deviation from natural equality, was most probably the superiority of the old over the young, originating the patriarchal government, which soon changed into an oligarchy, or hereditary aristocracy; and from the necessity of power being a unit before it could act, became a monarchy, and finished by a despotism. The monopoly of power securing the monopoly of property and knowledge, continued and increased exclusive privileges and the privileged orders, until the invention of the printing press, and the great improvements in arts and sciences facilitated the dissemination of useful knowledge among the great majority, who claimed election, as a right, at first restricted and joined to hereditary power in the form of limited monarchies; but gathering strength with the diffusion of useful knowledge, they threw off the burdensome and uncertain abilities of hereditary succession, and by that equality that must always be the consequence of representation by universal suffrage, harmonized church and state with the interest of the great majority, taking that jar in the social order occasioned by the monopolies, exclusive privileges, etc., usurped by the few, contrary to the interest of the many.

One of the causes why nations are so far behind individuals in the knowledge of their interest, is the obstruction of church and state to the diffusion of instruction amongst the millions, knowing both by precept and experience that knowledge is power, the dissemination of knowledge must be the more equal division of power, or a curtailing of theirs. Most appetites have limits, but the desire for power has none; the more they have the greater the craving for more. It is the nature of man to cling to power, and never to give up any part of it, but to the force of circumstances; so that the people who expect any participation in the government of themselves, must be disappointed. The people of the United States of

America, in forcing their legislators, by the power of universal suffrage, to equalize knowledge, in giving food, clothing, and equal universal instruction gratis, to all the children of the Union, at the expense of the peoples' purse, take the most direct, and perhaps the only means to insure freedom, independence and happiness to them and their posterity. For many nations have begun by conquering a part of their liberty, but by neglecting such fundamental precautions, have lost it, through the intrigues, superior knowledge and instruction of their rulers.

There is a gradation in the abuse of power and the exercise of despotism, increasing in proportion to the extent of territory and number of inhabitants; such as Russia, Austria, China, the former Turkish empire, etc.; and the smaller the extent and population of the political association, the better, more rationally and mildly they are governed, and the more widely useful knowledge and civilization is disseminated: witness the Saxon and other small states of Germany, Tuscany, in Italy, etc.; though their arbitrary rulers possess the same absolute hereditary power as the rulers of the great empires. It would therefore appear, that for the interest of the governed, the territory and population cannot be too small, and for the pleasure and despotism of the governors it cannot be too extensive; so in that as in every thing else their interest is at variance. To the great misfortune of humanity the governors have too often the aggregating, by conquest, of many small states into one large empire; the origin of the Roman and all other great empires both before and since: this was a natural consequence before the great utility of federation was found out; since which the small states have the means of retaining their independence and securing protection. All the advantages of federation being in favor of the freedom and independence of the people, will not be adopted by their rulers; and until the people are capable of governing themselves, the superiority of federalism over all other forms of government will not be practically known; for federation, judiciously limited to external intercourse, and a council of arbitration to settle amicably any dispute that may arise between the federative states, as in Switzerland, is cabable of uniting in the bonds of union and protection any number of states, of all the different forms of government, from the smallest to the greatest extent of territory and population, without interfering in the smallest manner with their internal government, leaving the smallest as well as the largest under the complete control of their own sovereignty and independence; putting all on a par as respects protection; facilitating and securing the junction of the smallest possible number of individuals as an independent state or corporation, subject to no laws, rules or regulations but those of their own making. Governments at present are in the savage state of the most primitive barbarism, the strong plundering, oppressing and enslaving the weak with impunity. Federation is a compact between nations, like civilized political associations between individuals, for mutual aid and protection against the injustice of might, and would, when judiciously organized, act like courts of justice, to prevent every one avenging his own cause, fighting and butchering one another, and would, if sufficiently extensive, realise what has been so long considered utopian fiction, perpetual peace.

Federation, by insuring the safety and protection of the smallest communities and aggregations of men, brings their public affairs within the reach of each member of the society and the actions of those in power within the limits of a strict and rigorous responsibility, which is weakened and almost lost in extensive kingdoms: it was for these and many more reasons given in a former essay, that I ventured to recommend the division of all the States in the Union into townships of six miles square, with independent powers to do every thing for themselves,—raise their own taxes, and expend them in the way that best suited the interest of the majority; this would confine the operations of church and state within very narrow limits; all internal laws, rules and regulations made and executed under the inspection of those who were to benefit by the good, or suffer for the bad. Foreign relations being different and under another and distinct authority, would afford less excuse for the abuse of power than when mixed and confused together:—but this, like most others in favor of the many, would curtail and diminish the pay, power, perquisites and consequence of the few influential rulers,—and cannot be expected to take place, nor other radical reforms until the many have common sense enough to govern themselves by universal suffrage; when that much to be wished for period will come depends on the patience and forbearance of the millions. The speculating on the "march of mind" that has lately taken the right road, accelerated by steam boats, railroads, etc., may be of some use, and cannot do harm.

ELECTIVE AND HEREDITARY POWER.

Dec. 16, 1834.

It is perhaps worth observing how the two great sources of power, elective and hereditary, have an interest so completely opposed both in principal and practice, as I have endeavored to show in a former essay, and how the hereditary and moneyed aristocracy, from weilding so long the physical and moral power, have become such dextrous adepts in the combination and union of all their individual and national force and influence, to subvert, vilify, and coerce the elective system, which, being yet in its infancy, has not acquired the sanction of experience to oppose such a powerful combination of physical force and moral acuteness, the accumulation of thousands of years in the best and most efficacious modes of subjecting the many to the will and service of the few; and how lately the industrious many have been slowly but gradually emancipating themselves from the tyranny of the idle few, by the substitution of elective in place of the divine right of hereditary power.

While ignorance and barbarism pervaded the world, despotism reigned triumphant, and the empires of the Medes, Persians, Macedonians, Romans, and latterly the Russians,

Austrians, etc., were established by the right of conquest and the sword, where the millions were transferred from one despot to another, as the caprice, convenience or interest of their masters dictated: the laboring producers were then known and noticed only by the numbers led to slaughter by their ambitious tyrants; and wars were begun for plunder and pillage, and ended in the transfer of the living and dead property from the conquered to the conqueror; the interest, convenience, comforts or happiness of the people were no more considered than that of their four-footed neighbors; even the mask of diplomacy was not thought necessary to disguise the injustice of their rapine and murder; and all those wars were for the extension of their dominion and powers at the expense of their own people and loss of their neighbors.

The first bold experiment of elective government by universal suffrage, or the first attempt of a people to govern themselves, was made on this side of the Atlantic, by the revolution of the United States of America, and imitated by France and other revolutions in Europe, all which were suppressed and rendered abortive by the combined armies of the moneyed and hereditary aristocracy of the civilized world; yet in the great struggle for freedom its principles were so widely spread as to awaken all nations to a sense of their interest, and a knowledge of their power to obtain possession of their just rights and immunities, which has been ever since, and is still acting with such spirit and energy, as to force the European monarchies to change from wars of aggression, to raising and maintaining great armies, to protect their usurped power, perquisites and privileges from the encroachments of their subjects, who, taught by the unprecedented prosperity of freedom in the United States, are struggling for elective governments, and have got so far on the straight road towards liberty and equality as to have acquired much practical and useful knowledge, and will still more easily and expeditiously increase that knowledge by the quickness, cheapness, and rapidity of communication by rail-roads, steamboats, etc., bringing both nations and individuals nearer an equality, by

the more equal division of property, knowledge and power.—
This great change by elevating the millions to that rank their
utility entitles them to, has altered and generalized diplomacy.
In place of wars to conquer, the last twenty years have been
occupied in making expensive preparations to resist the claims
of their subjects, and fight against public opinion, an universal
war of opinion between the governed and governors, every
day aggravated by the expense of preparation, and carried on
as yet by congresses, protocols and diplomatic logic; a war of
words in place of swords, where each government, not satisfied with its own means of self-defence, has entered into a
league with all having the same interest called the holy alliance, as yet consisting of Prussia, Austria and Russia, and
their object is to prevent the spreading of freedom by elective
governments; this forces them to interfere with the government and independence of other nations; at first by diplomatic
intrigue, threatening and bribery, they endeavor to stop the
progress of the elective system in France, Spain, Italy, etc.,
and by an armed force to deprive the small states, as Bavaria,
Wirtemberg, Baden, etc., of the advantage they had gained
by a partial representation, during the French revolution; but
after the last revolution and election of a king in France; the
return in Spain to the Cortes after the death of the tyrant
Ferdinand; the adoption of the first constitution that has yet
been in Europe, in Portugal; the revolutionary spirit manifested more and more in Germany, Italy, and even in Britain,
all their consultations in congresses, where the most refined
diplomacy has been congregated to prescribe for the growing
contagion, having failed to annihilate the apish propensity of
mankind to imitation, provided any of the surrounding nations
enjoyed any of the great benefits of elective government.
They seem now to consider a strict union of all the monarchs
in league against the liberties of their subjects as the only
remaining manœuver to accomplish the end of retrograding
knowledge and civilization some six centuries; convinced that
all governments have an equal interest in the implicit obedience and subjection of the subjects, they want the assistance of

most of them, particularly the Bourbon who now rules the destinies of France; whether they can effect such a coalition, or if they do, whether it will answer their expectations, time must show. The theatre on which are acted all these farces is much the same as it was a hundred years ago; the stage lighted up with the same effect at deception; the actors much the same, and even the orchestra sends forth the same delusive sounds of sympathy; but the audience are totally changed; the pitt and gallaries are brilliantly illuminated, not a dark corner where the church or state conjuror can disguise his slight of hand hocus pocus tricks; the twilight of the setting sun of the privileged orders, in the side boxes, is the only place sufficiently obscure to mask the artificial deceptions of the quacks in politics or religion; the managers turning their backs and a deaf ear to the knowledge of the day, follow the example and take their precedents from barbarous antiquity.

On the political theatre on this side of the Atlantic the managers and actors are changed at short periods, by elections of universal suffrage; the rights of man are substituted for hereditary divine right, by the sovereign power of the ballot boxes; yet both managers and actors clothed with a little brief authority, have imitated the abuses of the old world in forming a moneyed aristocracy, in granting monopolizing charters, corporations and exclusive privileges to the influential few, which though contrary to the constitutions has continued so long as now to be claimed as a right by the banks and corporations of the United States of America, and the church and military of the free states of Mexico. The presumption and impudence with which they attempt to support their unjust usurpation on the property and equal rights of the millions, can only be equalled by the inauspicious time they have chosen for such acts of tyranny, when despotism is vanishing before the light of knowledge even in the old world, where it has so long tyrannized over the destinies of mankind. It is only a further proof, if wanted after it has been attested in every page of history that aristocracy, whether moneyed or hereditary, will abuse their power and influence as far as the ignorance, patience or forbearance of the people will permit them. In the United States of America, the aristocratic part of the legislature, the senate, consisting mostly of lawyers, advocated the bank usurpation and were joined by the merchants, lawyers and rich, the moneyed aristocracy, who had opposed, vilified and calumniated president Jackson in all their hired newspapers, thereby confirming his opposition to all their encroachments, on the liberties of the people. The congress, by being newly elected, represented the present state of public opinion, (whereas the senate, only represented what was public opinion six years before) and opposed the chartering of the bank. The Mexican federation was opposed by the church and all the moneyed aristocracy, who favored the military usurpation of the rights of the people; even few of the state congresses made any energetic opposition to the military usurpation. One remark may with justice be made on this new and free field of political experiment, where all is young and unpracticed in old political vices—that all the attempts at military usurpation have been put down immediately—whereas in the old world military usurpation and conquest have lasted for centuries under the fictitious pretence of divine hereditary right, through a swarm of tyrants for many ages, and every monarchy or empire that has existed in the page of history from the Jews to the Russians, Austrians, etc., has been founded on the right of the sword or of conquest, a striking difference between the origin of the free states on this side of the Atlantic, and the governments which preceded them.

BANK AND OTHER MONOPOLIES.

Dec. 20, 1834.

A new trade, stock jobbing, the invention of refined civilization, threatens to inundate what has been called the civilized world with every species of speculation, gambling, cheating and lying; beginning first by national debts in the Italian republics, of Venice, Genoa, etc., and passing by Holland to Britain, enabling governments to mortgage posterity to facilitate their spending more than the generation they rule could afford to give them; pledging posterity for more than they are worth, to maintain the extravagance of the present generation; loading industry to the third and fourth generation with an immense paper representation of property, to the advantage of the rich at the expense of the laboring poor; increasing the already too great inequality of property, which includes a like inequality of knowledge and power. Since the French revolution, crafty politicians have found more support from a great national debt than they at first contemplated; by being debtors to so many of their subjects, who depend on them for their dividends, they have enlisted a vast swarm of police officers to protect their abuses against the millions. The increasing the indirect aristocratic taxation, to pay the interest, keeps the people so poor, and consequently ignorant, as to fit them for slaves, which is the reason that all the monarchies of the old world are exerting every means to increase their national debts, as their best security; seeing that those who have the largest national debts have been, as yet, the farthest removed from revolution in favor of the people. Added to this immense public paper representations of property, is the acumulating individual paper, such as bank notes, bank shares, insurance shares, canal and road shares, all species of corporation shares, mercantile or manufacturing, spread over and fill all the stock exchanges not only of the country to which they belong, but the paper representation of all nations, forming an immense stock exchange, which, working on the fears and the hopes of the many thousand stock jobbers, falls or raises the price, on which imaginary alternation of low or high, they live, at the expense of the dupes, who, ignorant of the secret means of propagating falsehoods, become the prey of jobbers, and brokers, who exist by such a digraceful trade, tolerated because it is necessary to the existence of monied aristocracy. This gambling on public and private securities is already the principal trade of most of the rich in all the great towns, and if it goes on increasing as it has lately done, will *pervade* the whole society, which will only draw the line of separation broader, and the distance greater between the laborer and the idle, the poor and the rich, the producer and the consumer, and thereby increase the opposition of interest, the cause of most of the disputes, quarrels and bloodshed.— The divine hereditary aristocracy have many bribes to induce them to encourage the augmentation of national debts. 1st, It raises up a monied aristocracy against which they can lean for support in their falling state. 2d, By throwing the burden of the aristocratic indirect taxation on the shoulders of the industrious laborers, it increases his poverty and ignorance, fitting him for slavery. 3, The dividends on the debt binds so many of the influential to maintain the existing state, on which depends their living; enlisting them as secret police officers to defend the system which pays them, besides the swarm of jobbers and other subordinate supporters of tyranny and despotism.

All these contrivances have been accumulating for thousands of years, invented for the purpose of subjugating the many to the will of the few; to maintain, support and perpetuate the arbitrary power of the few over the many. All free people, whose governments are bottomed on liberty and equality, for the interest of themselves and their posterity, ought to avoid the smallest approximation to any of these monopolies or exclusive privileges, in favor of the few at the expense of the many; they ought to be alarmed at the first advantage granted to the one or the few, and denied to the whole, and crush it in the bud, certain that it will grow stronger and spread further until it finishes in absolute despotism. Let us try to trace the progress of the lavish expenditures, craving after the artificial inequality of the old world, (though opposed by all political and national institutions) the natural oposition of interest between the producers and consumers, increasing in violence and hostility by the artificial laws, monopolies, etc., widening the breach between them.

An elective government of universal suffrage must be opposed to wars, and all extravagant expenditures of the produce of the industrious millions; a great check to the contracting of national debts, and an equal inducement to paying off what may have been borrowed, manifested by the payment of our federal debt; though the aristocracy of our State legislatures seem inclined to furnish materials for the foundation of a monied aristocracy, by establishing state debts under various pretensions, (in which the large states New York and Pennsylvania, as the most corrupt, take the lead); and they have made greater progress during the half century that we have been free and independent, than other people, even under despotisms, have made in many ages; by granting exclusive privileges to seven hundred monopolizing banks with a license to issue as many paper representations of property, and to divide the money given them for it, at the will of the stockholders, through their agents the bank directors; granting charters to as many insurance companies on the same nefarious terms: granting an immense number of mercantile, manufacturing, and other corporations on the same unlimited conditions of contracting debts to any amount, while the means of paying is limited to the capital they choose to pay in, enabling them to divide all the capital as profits, and cheat their creditors, while the original shareholders and directors escape with their unjust gains. Add to all this derangement of that equality so essentially necessary to the freedom and happiness of mankind, the immense temptation to forgery which has filled all corners of the Union with forged notes, each of which has bribed perhaps a hundred to the criminal practice of passing it, after knowing it was forged; the demoralizing principles of stock jobbing, propagating falsehoods of a bank corporation, etc., having failed, to purchase their notes and engagements far below par, and not unfrequently the directors themselves pretending bankruptcy, to buy up their notes at an enormous discount, and begin anew; such is their course. The various destructive effects of false capital tempting many to cheat and swindle by spending the property of others to the loss of the commuty and ruin of themselves; the crowding an unnatural population into our large towns, those sinks of vice, debauchery, crime and corruption, by the facility afforded too often of spending other people's money by bank discounts; all these and many more evils are entirely owing to legislators, with limited authority, both as to time and space, usurping the arbitrary power of favoring the few at the expense of the many, by granting monopolies contrary to the letter of most of the constitutions, and opposed by the spirit of the whole of them, as I have endeavored to show in a former essay: but it is not astonishing that these young people on this side of the Atlantic should mistake their powers and be ignorant of the just line of separation of authority, when the old limited monarchies of Europe have granted to the executive (as Britain, France and the others,) the right of making peace and war when neither a law nor a tax of any kind can pass, without the elective part of the system; placing the elective and hereditary power in opposition without any mediator to reconcile them. The same seeds of dissension is sown between the two divisions of our legislatures, proving how little wisdom or rationality has been exercised in the formation of governments, and how much is left to chance and hazard. While the divine hereditary, and other executives could, by force or fraud, rule the other, all went smoothly; but since the elective claims the rights which its number, utility and force entitles it to, there must be a constant opposition of interest, until reform makes power a unit, most probably in the possession of the elective.

This quarrel between two members of the government and the bank, which seems to brave the constitutional authorities and to be supported by the third power, the senate, exposes one of the great errors in the forming of our elective government, that is, dividing the legislature into two bodies, elected for different periods, and with different powers, pay and perquisites, and may lead to a reform making power, a unit in the majority of one house, and teaching the bad consequences of granting monopolies to the few at the expense of the many; by enriching the favorite few, enables them to claim as a right, and produce confusion, anarchy and bloodshed, in that struggle to maintain their arbitrary usurpations. If it open the eyes of the millions to the selfish motives of their legislators, and force them to elect representatives of their own class, it will be some reparation for the evils the banks and paper money have entailed on the industrious producers.

TRADES' UNIONS, ETC.

Dec. 22, 1834.

A great noise is making on both sides of the Atlantic about trades' unions, principally by those who have no trade, or whose stock in trade is words, which never diminish, as they can give away their whole stock as often as their hearers will pay for it, rather increasing than diminishing their funds by practice, though occupying time and not unfrequently wasting it; yet it occupies little or no space, having some of the properties given to immaterialism by metaphysicians, and some portions of these sounds are given to the winds under pretence of describing immaterialism. The cry of these nonproducers is against the injustice, iniquity and crime of the industrious producers, (who feed clothe and lodge them,) because they have lately acquired the good sense to combine to retain a little more of the fruits of their toil and labor for their own purposes. The trades' unions lately combined are the industrious, hard working men, called producers, because the agricultural laborers bring property into existence which did not exist before, and the mechanics and manufacturers of all kinds work various substances pre-existing, into different forms more valuable and better adapted to the conveniences, luxuries and necesities of mankind: this class of men in most civilized societies has been kept toiling from morning to night, exhausting all the vital powers in muscular fatigue, leaving neither time nor vital force for the improvement of their minds by acquiring useful knowledge, but depreciated so far as to become the ignorant dupes of those who have usurped the superiority, which is solely owing to the superior education and freedom from manual labor, which the monopoly of the fruits of the labor of the working classes enables them to obtain. The vast improvements in mechanism, particularly in every thing belonging to the printing press, have given such facility to the universal diffusion of general knowledge, that the class of industrious producers begin to know their interest and the power they have to obtain their natural rights, copying those who have so long maintained their usurped superiority by combination and union, they had information enough to perceive that the only possible mode by which they could regain the free use of part of their time and property, was by union; and being separate and divided, deprived by the laws, habits, customs, etc., of the means of communication, they were forced to adopt physical aggregation at which the non-producers took the alarm and endeavored to prevent it.

The nonproducers from the infancy of politics and religion, from the beginning of governments and priest-craft, have had their well combined unions to enforce all laws, rules and regulations that could possibly favor their interest. All governments, elective or hereditary, consisting of executives or legislatures, with all their attendants, army, navy, police and revenue officers, with every other officer appointed and paid by them, have had the uncontroled power of establishing their own salaries, fees, perquisites and powers, which have always been according to their interest, with little regard to the value or utility of the services performed, neither limited nor restricted by the value of other labor—the reason why political labor in all countries, (free from competition) is so much higher than any other. The close union and combination of lawyers, have given them the fixing of their own fees, perquisites and profits, not limited by their real value or utility, often charging for a few hours labor as much as an industrious working man could gain by a few years toil and fatigue. The wages of the priest are equally unlimited by either their value or utility, but kept up at the highest price the people can bear by injurious combination and strict union. The bankers, brokers, merchants and all who transport property from one land or place to another, without making it better or adding any thing to it, have all the fixing their own commission and profits, and are in constant correspondence to unite their efforts for their mutual interest. From which it would appear that all the rich and nonproducers are firmly bound by their interest to obtain what they live on from the industrious producers, at as cheap a rate as possible, and all the practice of civilization hitherto proves that they had settled it as an axiom, that the harder and longer they can work them, the poorer and more ignorant they can make them; the more submissive and better slaves they will be, even if they should push misery into crime; for by the laws and regulations of civilization, as far as it has yet gone, one would be tempted to conjecture, that civil governors thought it their interest to rule over rogues and priests, to tyrannize over sinners, and that they considered honest and upright subjects too independent to submit to their arbitrary control.

The same line that divides producers from nonproducers divides the trades' unions from those who oppose them, having on one side those who furnish society with real material property, created or made by their toil and labor, of which they themselves are allowed to enjoy but a small share; on the other side all those dealers in words, sounds without sense, and those occupied with shifting, transporting or circulating after it is brought into existence, but neither producing nor adding to the quantity or quality; though by the arts and inventions of civilization they have contrived to consume a great proportion of the real property produced by the sweat and labor of the most useful classes. This was an unnatural state of things commensurate with the degraded state of poverty and ignorance to which the working classes have been reduced by artificial monopolies, restrictions, laws, habits and customs, introduced for the support of the great inequality of property, knowledge and power, the attendants on civilization as far as it has yet gone; but cannot long contend against the general diffusion of useful knowledge, by the geometrical progress of improvement, first of the physical arts and mechanism which must be followed by the mental melioration; so that it is probable civilization, by its extension on the road it has lately taken, may tend towards the natural equality of mankind; not by depressing the usurped superiority of the privileged orders, as the aristocracy has endeavored to make us believe is the only mode of reestablishing equality, but by the elevation of the most useful classes to that grade and consideration their utility and numbers entitle them to.

On this side of the Atlantic the incubus of the privileged orders of church and state having been taken off and their copartnership dissolved, both trading on their own bottom, has allowed the millions by universal suffrage to claim their natural and unalienable rights. The working producing classes in the United States of America being at leat 100 to one of the nonproducers, are united at the ballot boxes by universal suffrage to put into power a majority of all elective officers of their own class, who will act from interest, sympathy and habit, agreeably to their orders and interest, and as soon as they obtain a majority in the legislatures, they will make a radical reform in all the civil, fiscal, general and particular laws, rules and regulations. The great economy, justice and impartiality that will be introduced into every department of government, will give a practical example of the little benefit not to say injury, of making laws to collect a man's debts, branding the debtor as a criminal by incarcerating him in prison during his life because he is poor; bribing a manufacturer by premiums to make one species of fabric in place of another that would repay him without any premium; laying heavy duties on imports or exports, encouraging smuggling, and all other laws that cannot be executed, tempting to break through them and demoralizing the people. Two-thirds of the legislative enactments interfering with the management of individual affairs, favoring one class at the expense of another, are hurtful and unjust, and show that elective as well as hereditary legislatures make many laws to support their own interest and consequence, irrelevant and injurious to their constituents. Those who have the direction of the state machine rather gain than lose by its pressing and grinding the face of the poor multitude; the millions are interested in lightening and simplifying the mechanism of power; and the only possible mode of bringing their interest into action is by election under universal suffrage; which was imitated by the French and Spanish revolutions, and some little approximation by the last British reform; but when once the vast advantage of the full practice is proven it will be adopted by all people who have the common sense to govern themselves; for church and state have been yet far behind the knowledge of the day, and never will have approached to it unless drove by the superior information and force of the millions who must help themselves.

NATURAL EQUALITY OF MAN. MONOPOLIES. THE VETO. REFORM OF CHURCH AND STATE. ADVANCEMENT OF CIVILIZATION FACILITATED BY STEAM.

Dec. 28, 1834.

That all men are born equally weak and helpless (provided they possess all their senses) has lately been denied by the usurpers of superiority over their fellow men. By a kind of sophistry they resuscitate the old exploded doctrine of innate ideas, under the name of genius, which they argue is a gifit, though they are forced to acknowledge is not given to one in ten or a hundred thousand, yet bring it in as a reason against the possibility of equality, and instance a Shakspeare, an Arkright, a Watt, etc., as the proof of native genius sufficient to exclude equality from the natural attributes of our species, forgetting that even granting that assumption of the gift of genius, it is seldom or ever given to one of their class, but always to the inferior or middle ranks of society; so that in place of supporting them in their pretensions of ruling and arbitrarily governing mankind, it would exclude them from all power as being deprived of the gifts they pretend necessary to the exercise of it. If all men, who from surrounding circumstances were enabled to act a great part on the theatre of the world had written their lives with the same candor and impartiality as Franklin and Rousseau, such deceptions could not succeed. Aristocracy is entirely artificial, and at war with every principle of nature. Since the delusion of divine right has become too absurd to impose on the most brutal ignorance of subjects or slaves, they have been ransacking all the arguments of mechanical logic to endeavor to prove that equality is incompatible with the nature of man; and because perfection is a point not perhaps possible to attain, all approach towards it is impossible. Equality is a scare-crow which frightens all ambitious demagogues or usurpers aiming at power or superiority, and was only once mentioned in our declaration of independence, and cautiously avoided in all constitutions and public documents ever since; for equality during and for some time after our revolution, was more complete than it has ever been since. The aim and object of a majority of our legislators would appear to an impartial observer, to be the increasing the already too great inequality of property, knowledge and power. The great inequality of property has been begun in all countries by the combination of physical armed force, wresting it by conquest from the hands who produced it, and generally preceded the loss of their natural liberty and rights, as is proven by the history of all conquerors. The means taken since our revolution to create and augment the moneyed aristocracy are, 1st, the continuing and multiplying a collection of litigious and undefined laws, the spawn of feudal tyranny. 2d, the paying the public expenses by indirect taxation favoring the rich and oppressing the poor. 3d, granting an unprecedented number of monopolies, corporations, exclusive privileges, etc., in favor of the few at the expense of the many. The nearly equal division of property, knowledge and power, is the only permanent and solid foundation of rational freedom, and the great inequality of these three essentials of happiness, the only support of tyranny and despotism. At the commencement of most governments, when the millions emerge from the savage state, power and property are monopolized by the combination of armed physical force, and continued by the monopoly of knowledge, the consequence of the great inequality of the other two; but in elective governments of universal suffrage, power is as completely and radically divided as it can possibly be, and too strongly entrenched in the public interest and opinion to be attacked in front with the least hope of success; but the monopoly of property by the various ingenious schemes and speculations, as the funding, land banks, corporations, exclusive privileges, etc., imperceptibly saps the foundation of the division of power and progresses slowly but surely towards the tyranny of the few over the many. The banking system and paper money alone, if allowed to progress with the rapidity it has done, is capable of bribing the legislators to obstruct all attempts at instructing the millions; to multiply the monopolies in favor of the few at the expense of the many; to burden the circulation of property and knowledge by laws, taxes and custom-houses, to bribe, as in Europe, one part of the millions to enslave the rest; to carry on all abuses of power by money, which the arbitrary governments of Europe do by armed physical force. Where gold is the god of a money making nation it is difficult to set bounds to its influence; where each individual, avariciously grasping for himself, loses sight of public interest or of the share, he as a member has in public good; but one single veto by the courage and perseverence of an individual has checked the headlong progress downwards, threatening to retrograde all the advantages of our revolution, and has given the common sense of the community time to rally and to analize the consequences before they go any further. It is not only the great injustice of robbing the industrious producers of so great proportion of the fruits of their toil and labor, but the saddling posterity with a swarm of idlers, united and combined under the banner of a moneyed aristocracy, to oppose every thing that can tend to the peace, happiness and interest of the millions, sowing the seeds of a perpetual warfare between the industrious labors who produce and the idle who consume, violent and inveterate in proportion to the theory of liberty and equality that has prevailed and been heretofore supposed to be the basis on which politics and religion, church and state were bottomed, on this side of the Atlantic.

The growing prosperity of so great a number of free independent states, acting on a free field of experiment on this side of the Atlantic, will change church and state, politics and religion, from being an aggregation of passions, prejudices, chance and hazard, to a science of calculation and certainty, where a combination of certain proportions of the moral and physical properties of men, will produce as certain results, as the compounds in a chemist's laboratory, and all that mystification, sophistry and vast variety of the nature and properties of our species, will be exploded, and that all men, whether European, American, Asiatic or African, possesing the same senses, the same natural appetites, and surrounded by the same circumstances will produce the same effects may be reduced to an axiom, on which all may act with certainty of reaping the consequences of truth when freed from fallacies. In this extended forest every new settler who wanders into the wide woods is a new edition of society, with additions and amendments, a sociable machine, moving on new and improved pivots, grafting all the improvements of civilization on the natural equality and simplicity of a virgin soil, unadulterated by the tricks, deceptions, corruption and crimes of a vitiated civilization; every step they advance in the wilderness they are further removed from the vices of their forefathers, and from that apish propensity of imitating their predecessors, and will form laws, rules, regulations, habits and customs adapted to, and arising out of their situation.

The immense and unprecedented prosperity of the United States of America, merely from a part of the abuses of church and state being reformed, from the very small change in the theories of politics and religion, and still less in the practice, owing to the apish principle in mankind, following examples of old habits and customs, often in proportion to their hurtful and injurious consequences; notwithstanding the immense drag on their progress by the servile imitation of the laws, habits and customs, of their old mother Britain, yet the consequences of a small quantum of common sense and reason being first introduced into the formation of a political association, must astonish the impartial observer, and hold up a beacon to show posterity the shortest road to freedom, comfort and happiness, which will fly on the wings of steam, through the medium of rail-roads and steam-boats, to the farther corners of the earth. Every advantage our working classes obtain, over our masters, the nonproducers; every step towards independence and emancipation from the slavery, toil and labor of maintaining such a swarm of idlers, will spread useful practical knowledge over the face of the earth, and will be as well understood and more quickly imitated by nations emerging from the savage state than by people who have been for centuries following the badly paved and crooked road of civilization as far as it has yet gone. This must gratify every one who takes the smallest interest in the freedom and happiness of his species; and considering the great proportion of our globe yet covered with barbarous people, the idea of their rapid and more perfect civilization must be consoling to all the friends of humanity, and interest all mankind in the success of our present moral revolution for elevating the millions to that rank and consideration their numbers and utlity entitle them to.

PROGRESS OF CIVILIZATION; THE DIFFUSION OF USEFUL
KNOWLEDGE AND THE CONSEQUENT DIVISION
OF POWER AND PROPERTY.

Dec. 30, 1834.

All things artificial must change with the diffusion of useful knowledge and civilization; nothing but nature and her laws will remain fixed; the inventions, arts, sciences and contrivances, which suit an ignorant and half savage population, cannot suit a well informed people; and the improvement, change, or revolution, in politics, religion, laws, etc., must be in proportion to the quantum of useful knowledge disseminated amongst the millions. While knowledge was monopolized by the few, property and power became their hereditary birthright. Now that knowledge is diffusing among the many, property and power must be equally divided; and by the certainty and rapidity of communication by rail roads, steam boats, etc., not only the individuals of the same nation, but all the nations on earth must be brought nearer on a par as to property, knowledge, and power, the nearly equal division of these three essentials constitute rational freedom. The velocity of communication liquifies all things so as to find their level, and perhaps in morals as well as in physics, to fill the lowest levels first. As yet the millions in all countries have been so depressed by poverty and hardships as to render an acute use of their senses necessary to their existence; they are therefore trained and exercised in receiving their ideas pure and unadulterated, direct through the senses, without being flattered with the tempting and delusive tints of the imagination; not being accustomed to indulge in ambitious fictions, nor at any time to view the sunny side of fortune, they take their ideas simply as they come through their senses and apply them to the practical purposes their necessities require; they do not lose their time or confuse their understanding with metaphysical or theological logic; they test the idea by experimenting on the arts they know. The numberless old books of history, poetry, metaphysics, etc., give no useful ideas to the millions of productive laborers, even if they had wherewith to buy them; even the elementary works on science are more calculated to display the knowledge of the author than to give useful information to the multitude; but the cheap penny publications in Britain and two sous publications in France, with 2 or 300,000 at an edition, will convey such knowledge as the laborers can understand and use, immediately to further their interest. The wings of steam will transport to the door of every laborer as much real useful knowledge for twelve cents, as the rich could obtain from their expensive libraries, and none of it will remain idle like the contents of the luxurious shelves of the rich consumers, but each of the periodical numbers will be read by hundreds and spread the knowledge they contain through thirty millions. Then the pyramid of society will be placed on the broad base of universal knowledge, in place of tottering on its apex as it has for so many thousand years.

May not we transport the above reasoning to the intercourse between nations, and the great and rapid benefit ignorant and savage nations may reap from the general diffusion of knowledge, and the facility of communication without being condemned as an Utopian. It is not long since the slow and uncertain progress of the sail and the oar took as many months to navigate up and down large rivers as the steam boats now take days; and that all the rivers in the civilized part of the world are being covered with steam boats. Is it absurd to conjecture that all the large rivers in America, Asia or Africa, such as the Amazon, Ganges, etc., will be navigated by steam boats, and carry the utmost improvement of knowledge and civilization into the heart of those as yet barbarous continents? Would it be foolish to suppose that a locomotive conveyance or a rail road through Europe to India, would diffuse more useful knowledge in one year than all the commerce by sea has done in centuries? And suppose all change of communication from sea to land to have the same effect on the diffusion of knowledge through the countries the rail road traverses, what an immense acceleration of civilization over the whole globe; all the great improvement in morals or physics, politics, religion or mechanism, have been of so recent a date, that there has not been time to ascertain much of their influence on the different states of civilization, we must therefore conjecture from the elements of society found in the savage state, how far they will contribute as a foundation to civilization, and the rapid and kindly reception of this flood of instruction, which the multiplied inventions and contrivances of the already civilized part of the world are prepared to pour on them; and then examine if the very few nations lately emerging from the savage state will confirm this hypothesis. Perhaps the most easy and certain criterion as a scale of comparison would be to judge how far the savage state favored the nearly equal division of these three essentials of happiness, property, knowledge, and power. Most savages, before they acquire artificial wants, are satisfied with necessaries which are afforded them by the spontaneous production of the soil and wild animals; the quantum of property of any kind on hand is exceedingly small, and the surplus after maintaining the population, still less—leaving little or nothing for the accumulation in the possession of the few, and establishing an equality, only deranged by the approach towards civilization, the cause and origin of all inequality. They receive their knowledge through the medium of their senses without any artificial assistance, which is on a par of equality with the means by which they obtain it; no classification of instruction, no records to add the knowledge of the past to the present, they remain almost all equally ignorant without the delusions of the imagination to warp them from realities. Accustomed by all former habits to trust the evidence of their senses, they are not predisposed to believe in dogmas beyond their reach, as the experience of all the christian missionaries sufficiently proves. The superiority of power in the savage state depends principally on physical force, which vacillates and changes with the property which produced it. Even the old have little authority over the young, or the parents over the children. Freedom is the birthright of the savage, and slavery of the millions the consequence of civilization as far as it has yet gone. But there is at present some symptoms of the advanced progress of useful knowledge and civilization turning towards the freedom and equality of the savage life; which would render the simplicity, freedom and equality of the state nearest to nature, a better and more secure foundation to build the present more perfect civilization on than any half approaches towards it, by the destruction of men's natural rights, and the classification of mankind into masters and slaves, tyrants and subjects, rich and poor, etc.,—from which it would appear that a nation emerging from the savage state in the present diffusion of knowledge, and the rapid means of communication, is nearer a greater degree of perfection in civilization, than those nations who have been toiling for centuries against all the obstructions which church and state could oppose to the well-being of humanity.

The present advanced state of improvement has been of so short duration, (considering that nations do not advance further in ages than individuals do in years,) has left little time for the experience of practice. Russia, though the state of slavery almost annihilates improvement, yet in all the arts and sciences she has adopted from a higher state of civilization, such as her spinning mills, steam engine manufactories, hospitals, universities, schools, etc., are upon the most perfect principles to be found in any country, and nothing remains in a state of barbarity but such arts as were begun during their savage state; a proof that it is much easier to introduce new than to mend old. The civilization of Egypt, which perhaps took its rise from the short period the French men of science remained there, and the changes taking place in the greatest part of the Turkish empire, may be instanced as a proof how quickly barbarism gives way to the light of reason in the present advanced state of the diffusion of knowledge and civilization. Hindoostan, though under the government of a jealous mercantile monopoly, whose interest it was to seclude them from intercourse with the rest of the world, yet has adopted the most perfect of the arts and sciences from civilization, and the only remains of barbarism are the old arts, habits and customs. Going west, the great continent of S. America, for three hundred years under the oppression of a foreign yoke, and a foreign priesthood, even the few years they have been partly emancipated, have made as astonishing progress in the adoption of all the arts and sciences at the highest perfection to be found any where, as the usurpation of military chiefs and the tyranny of Catholic priest-craft would permit them. But the islands of the great Pacific, more accessible to the knowledge of the day, from their insular situation, are the best proof of the hypothesis—which have been converted in a few years, from the most savage barbarous state to a scale of the most astonishing civilization, adopting not only the arts, sciences, habits and customs of a higher state of civilization, but the languages of the civilized people they imitate in their schools, where all are taught to read and write. New Zealand, formerly a hoard of cannibals, has progressed in the useful arts so as to have arsenals, to build ships, converting their flax into cordage, canvass, etc., and bids fair, in a very short time, to be on a par with the most civilized countries, and have already disproved the fallacies of the christian dogmas, which the missionaries are endeavoring to instil into them by taking their children, finding it in vain to attempt to convince adults in opposition to the evidence of their senses. In Asia there are two foci from which will radiate the light of reason and civilization, New Holland and Hindoostan. In Africa, there are three, the Cape of Good Hope, Algiers and Egypt, besides the colonies on the west coast all running with the velocity of steam to fill the vacuum of common sense and civilization.

SELFISHNESS THE MOTIVE TO ACTION.

Jan. 1, 1835.

The first trial of any thing approaching to political equality was the election by universal suffrage by the ballot boxes in the U. States of America, and the unprecedented prosperity resulting from it, has influenced more or less every political change since, on both sides of the Atlantic. From their servile imitation of the old world, from whence the first settlers on this side descended, they have been yet deprived of most of the advantages of self government, by permitting themselves to be ruled by cunning lawyers and place hunters, brought up and instructed to make dupes of them; so that the theory of liberty and equality without the practice is all that they have yet enjoyed. Within the last few years the facility of acquiring useful knowledge has diffused it through the smallest ramifications of society, and enabled the millions of industrious producers to claim their unalienable rights, for which the working classes of our Union have been striving for the last six or eight years to conquer the difficulties and obstructions opposed to their interest by the strict union and corrupt combination of the few, who have enjoyed the monopoly of property, knowledge, and power, that they think they have prescriptive right by inheritance, in imitation of the despotism of the old world. This combination of nonproducers joined to the exclusive privileged banks and other corporations, whose monopolies are threatened by the reforms proposed, and having the command of the circulating medium, forms a powerful monied interest in opposition to the public good.— But in a country where every pair of hands has a head to direct them, and every head has as much power in the ballot boxes as the greatest, richest, wisest, or most powerful in the country, their numbers must legally bear down all opposition and their interest, when they know it, must dictate all laws, rules and regulations. Where there is equality there must be liberty; tyranny and oppression are in exact proportion to the greatness of inequality between the classes; for no one will submit to the despotism of his equals in property, knowledge and power. The working classes of our Union by their system of reform propose to lay the axe to the root of all abuses. First: to secure equality of knowledge, that all the children of the Union shall be fed, clothed and instructed, at the expense of the people's purse, formerly called the public purse on the treasury of the government. 2dly: to secure the equality of property, the abolition of all exclusive privileges and licensed monopolies; the abolition of all indirect taxes, and an equal taxation on all kinds of property; an effective lien law for laborers; reform in the present complicated and expensive laws, by a condensed code, that all may understand and regulate their conduct accordingly. 3dly: to secure the equality of power, abolishment of capital punishment and imprisonment for debt: an equitable, fair and impartial militia law: no legislation on religion: a district system of election: and they further hint at no law process for the collection of debts; a total prohibition against all legislatures mortgaging posterity by contracting debts; and they might perhaps add, for the prevention of disputes, abolishing the double legislature by senators; and the reform in the federal constitution preventing the federal government from interfering in the fiscal, military, or judiciary of the individual states. When by union and perseverance at the ballot boxes they obtain a majority to carry effectually the practice of all the reforms, liberty and equallity will not only be secured to themselves, but to their posterity to the latest generations; and the example of such a flood of prosperity, power, comfort, and universal happiness, that must flow from such sources, will cause a moral revolution, in time, over the surface of the earth.

Amongst the many evils which the pride, vanity self-conceit and presumption of man have entailed on our species, is the believing that they are more perfect than either nature or art has made them. As a necessary qualification of the rulers both of church and state for making dupes and deceiving the ruled, it was necessary that they should have the pretensions to act on disinterested, charitable, patriotic, philanthropic, etc., motives; and to cloak their selfishness, they preach and propagate that it is one of the distinguishing and meritorious attributes of humanity to be guided in their actions by some one of those ideal motives, for which they cannot be too richly rewarded by those for whose interest they sacrifice their own. Let public opinion be once enlightened with the great natural and unalterable truth, that all men are actuated by some one of the many thousand selfish motives, and from their depending on food, clothing, lodging, etc., they cannot be otherwise, these pretensions would vanish like falsehood before truth; and in the same proportion all those cunning deceptions practiced on ignorance to support an artificial superiority, would cease to enslave the millions and save them from bartering their hard earned property for a mouthful of unmeaning words. Were all classes of society allowed an equal right of reclaiming this superior and dignified motive of action, it would not derange so much the natural equality; but unfortunately these ideal motives of munificence, philanthropy, charity, etc., are monopolized by the rich and privileged orders, only to enhance their artificial superiority, dominion and power over the millions, adding a moral and mysterious force to the too many physical tyrannies of that great inequality, the principal cause of the miseries and wretchedness of mankind; it augments that natural selfish propensity of supercilious pride, vanity, and self-conceit so injurious to the well being of humanity. The pretence that placing motives on their real foundation, self, would detract from real merit, is mere sophistry, for it is the effect of the action, understood by all that the actor obtains his merited reward. The excusing a bad action under pretence that the motive was disinterested, is a fallacy that may cover all crimes, and excuse the old principle of church and state, "the end justifies the means," often pleaded for the most unjust, despotic, and cruel actions. The massacres, burnings, assassinations, tortures, etc., practiced by good christians for religion's sake, were all motived on the great good of doing the will and wish of the Lord, and the effects of the murder and cruel death of more millions than perished in all the wars of ambition. The Spaniards slaughtered many millions of innocent Indians in South America, under the pretended religious motive of converting them to the true faith, and driving them on the direct road to paradise.— Mahomet propagated his doctrines by the sword, and there is no action, however horrible, cruel and unjust, that may not be palliated and excused by ideal and imaginary motives. All malicious, unjust, and calumnious persecutions for religious opinions are sanctioned by holy motives of doing good to those they slander and destroy. Self seems the centre on which all things turn, *in medio tutissimus ebis*, between good and bad motives, and the error from truth is equal, which ever side we deviate to. One has a rival, enemy, or opponent, in any of the thousand ways men come in collision with one another, and he attributes the bad, malevolent motives to all his opponents actions: it is not that those forms that selfishness choses to give his action, does really exist; it is only following what he supposes is his interest, to lower his enemy in the opinion of others; thinking, as is too often the consequence of ignorance, that one raises himself by pulling down another; a common fallacy which originates most kinds of envy, malice, detraction and calumny; all of which would vanish before a well understood selfishness, that is, every one knowing his real interest, and having foresight enough of consequences to act up to it. The more equal division of property, knowledge, and power, can alone reconcile these jarring materials of civilization as far as it has has yet gone.

Were all the human species to remain as ignorant as they came into the world, or to receive exactly the same instruction, we have no good reason to doubt that they would be all equal in knowledge. All the experience of the civilized or savage state has taught us that the nearer a state of nature, the greater the equality. But man has never yet been found in a state of nature; the nearest to it is the Bosjesmen at the Cape of Good Hope. All the arts of civilization, as far as it has yet gone, tends to divide men into the two extremes of poverty with its consequence ignorance, and riches with knowledge; and until the experiment is fairly tried, it is all conjecture concerning the result in which the knowing few have been allowed to form and propagate theories according to the dictates of their own interest without allowing the ignorant many to influence the decision, as they have done in all theories on speculative objects.

PROGRESS AND ADVANTAGE OF FREEDOM, ETC.

Jan. 13, 1835.

Over all the old civilized world the existing contest is between elective and divine hereditary power; for the new world, on this side of the Atlantic, the contest is finished in favor of elective power by universal suffrage, and all our millions have now to do, is to put in practice the theories they have been long in possession of. In this great and general war between the people and their rulers; between the idle few and industrious many; between freedom and slavery; between liberty and despotism, it does not require the spirit of prophecy to foresee the result, though the time it may require to accomplish it may be more difficult to predict. When the light of reason shall have penetrated into the dark recesses of Russian despotism, when their millions of bayonets shall be unable to support their absolute authority, but shall partly join in the emancipation of their fellow slaves, what may not be expected from the rest of Europe, where the experience of a small portion of freedom has taught them its immense advantages. It is more than probable that the Polish nobility emancipating their serfs, and investing them with small portions of land, may spread the contagion of liberty to the Russian provinces, and that the fifty states of which the Russian empire consists, may in remembrance of their former condition, claim their independence, which will be easily effected provided the Russian nobility, following their true interest, by giving liberty to their serfs, put themselves at the head of the revolution, in place of opposing it at the risk of both their property and lives. For it must be very evident that where there are more than one hundred slaves to one master, of the same class and color of the soldiers, who are used to coerce them, when they shall be influenced by an invading enemy just emancipated, the masters must succumb and retaliatory destruction will be their fate. The situation is similar as if the slave islands in the West Indies were protected by negro soldiers and attacked by free negroes at St. Domingo.

If Austria is deprived of her ill-gotten share of that unjust and scandalous partition of Poland, it may rouse the small, formerly independent states, of which the empire is composed, to claim their rights—all of them under different laws, customs and habits, and some of them governed by a kind of representation, not united by any common interest, or even by the ties of a similar language, but bound together by the force of military despotism. Prussia is in a similar situation—an aggregation of little states, conquered by the well disciplined armies of Frederic the Great, and left by him to his successors, as the most certain and expeditious means of accumulating power and possessions at that epoch. So that three of the great continental powers, are composed of an assemblage of small states, held together by the right of conquest, and united by no stronger tie than military force. It may be doubted in the present division of knowledge if any thing short of a common interest can firmly unite states, long accustomed to different laws, regulations, practices, prejudices and language, and the means of manifesting the union of interest of the great majority, can only be accomplished peaceably by a federation, which shall have no power or right to interfere with the internal government of the federative states.

Suppose by way of speculation on futurity, that the present revolutions and commotions in Europe should settle down in four federal governments, of Italy, Austria, Prussia and Russia, and that each small state should regulate their own affairs by an elective system, as similar to their ancient laws, customs and habits, as the knowledge of the day will permit, they would of course form different constitutions, more or less free, according as the influence of the few or the many, the aristocracy or the democracy prevailed---nor would it be of great consequence which prevailed in the beginning, provided after the example of the free states on this side of the Atlantic, they permitted a reform to keep them on a par with the knowledge of the day. What change in the morals, peace, comfort and happiness of society would such a renovation of both church and state make? What alteration in the intercourse, commerce and trade, both foreign and domestic would most probably take place by such a radical revolution? The change would most probably be in favor of the peace and happiness of the millions, as I have endeavored to prove in a former essay, that political despotism, corruption, pillage, vice and crime, were in proportion to the extent of territory under one government—and knowledge, freedom, honesty and industry, were in the ratio of the smallness and confined limits of the political association.

On a comparison between the surplus produce exported from Russia and the United States, I made the labor of one free man equal to ten slaves. As the small federative states under the elective system, would enjoy some degree of liberty, and might increase their surplus produce in proportion to the quantum of freedom they would enjoy—where would they find barbarous ignorant nations unable to supply themselves, for a market for such a quantity of surplus produce created by the exertions of freedom? will the consequent energy and industry arising from a little freedom in Britain, where they have glutted the markets on the globe with their manufactures, be an answer, or must we resort to the United States, who, in a few years, have produced cotton enough to lower the price below what it can be grown for, and will in a few years more fill all markets with her produce and manufactures? Look to France, who, since the revolution, is a large exporter of all kinds of produce and manufactures, for which under their arbitrary government, they were depending on foreigners; the Netherlands the same; even Spain, since the short experience of her revolution, has become so far independent of foreign supplies of breadstuffs as to export wheat.— The immense benefits of freedom have never been calculated, but have always been kept in the back ground, by the arbitrary combinations of aristocracy, and only mentioned as the propagator of anarchy, confusion, strife and misrule.

In proportion as the freedom and consequent industry of all countries render them independent of foreign supplies, in the same proportion foreign trade must diminish, for it acts doubly; if one nation gets independent of supplies from another, that other nation must, from the want of wherewith to pay, cease to take supplies from her, and the ultimate consequence would be that each nation must supply itself with what they require, either by raising the article themselves or substituting something they can make in place of it, like the beet sugar in France, or the United States, when they had glutted the markets with cotton, corn, bread stuffs, etc., turned their industry to raising sugar, silk, wine and dried fruits, all of which they used to import from foreign conntries; but in a few years, like the cotton, they will most probably be large exporters of all these articles. Release the millions from a part of the innumerable impediments and constraints imposed on them, in all countries, by church and state, (for in no country, as yet, has more than a part of the tyrannical restrictions been removed,) and their progress towards their own comfort and happiness would be incalculable.

ADVANTAGE OF SMALL POLITICAL ASSOCIATIONS. DIVISION OF POLITICAL LABOR.

Jan. 19, 1835.

I have often dwelt on the vast superiority of small political associations for internal government and of federation for external defence, separating politics into two departments, which require different kinds of knowledge and experience to manage judiciously. In the regulation of the internal affairs of (suppose) a township of six miles square, every man in the township would be capable of directing the limited operations within the reach and cognizance of every one, whose interest would induce him to watch over the expenditure of money coming so directly out of his own pocket as to leave no doubt who would gain by the economical disbursement of it, or lose by waste, negligence or pillage. The representatives of the federal council would be those who join to a local knowledge of the interest of their own districts, some knowledge of political economy and foreign intercourse: this mode of dividing political, would like all other labor, simplify and perfect the result of both; and in elective governments save the electors much trouble and research in choosing, for, except in time of war or disputes between the federation, the federal council would have little or nothing to do and might be managed by any one of ordinary abilities, and the internal government of the townships, so confined and simple as to require still less talent or intellect. The present mixture of internal regulations with external relations forces the electors to attempt to find all the representatives capable of both, perhaps one of the causes why so great a disproportion of speechifying lawyers are put into the legislature. From the mystery and quackery in which diplomacy has yet been involved, t^h millions suppose those cunning men of the law are fitter to manage the intricate chicanery with which all public offices have yet been conducted. This division of political labor, producing a more perfect and cheaper article; would invalidate all objections against the impartial collection of a direct tax on property as in the New England townships; each individual would be a check on his neighbor in detecting any fraud in the valuation of his property, being from his vicinity a competent judge, and from his paying for the defalcation of any, forced by his immediate pecuniary interest to detect any fraud or smuggling. The townships would be a check on one another, for the same reason, and the whole necessary revenue would be collected and disbursed at little or no expense except in time of war, when the townships would have to pay their quota into the federal treasury, and would have an interest to watch over the faithful disbursement of it, and might aid in the economical expenditure of every thing within the reach of their locality. It would bring the public expenditure so immediately flowing from the individual pocket, that the most stupid would see what he lost by public extravagance or gained by public economy. It would abolish all custom houses excise with the swarms of officers obstructing the circulation of property and knowledge at the command of their masters. It would make a free port of every port in the Union, and save so much time and money as to give all foreign articles for about one half, and very considerably raises the prices of internal produce. It would destroy patronage, that corrupter of both the ruled and the rulers; annihilate bribery, vice, lying and deception at elections, and allow the electors freely to choose the representative best suited to the interest of the majority. It would reduce all nearer to equality by the authorities acting in a more confined circle, subject to be checked from injustice, by the interest of all around them. It would equalize power by a constant rotation in office, by abolishing mystery and complicacy in public affairs, reducing them to the abilities of all ranks and professions. It would place the burden of public expenditure on those for whose benefit political associations were made, and make every one pay in proportion to his property protected.

In the federal council for external intercourse they ought not to have the right of making war; that would be giving them the right of fixing their own pay, perquisites and power. The right of making war ought to remain in the majority of the townships, who have to produce all the property necessary to carry it on, as well as all the property that will necessarily be wasted, destroyed and pillaged during that unnatural strife of trying 'who can do each other the most harm. This would establish the long wished for principle or desideratum, that the same powers who make wars should fight them and pay for them. One class making war and pocketing the spoils while another class pays for it with their blood and treasure, may be one reason why the earth has been so long deluged with blood. Favoritism might be lessened by all the officers under the generals being elected by the men, and not eligible to be reelected until they served in the ranks. But it may be considered an act of supererogation to provide for an attack by land on so powerful a federation of freedom, where every citizen is a soldier and every soldier a citizen, after the attack made by the most powerful maritime nation in the world, on the two extremes of the republic, Plattsburgh and New Orleans, so easily defeated by the local militia. If it can be rationally supposed that the piratical robbery of marine warfare can subsist after the diffusion of knowledge has the interest of the many in place of the ambition, power and interest of the few; it might be more difficult to fit out a powerful fleet under the management of the townships, and perhaps might require the united operations of the federal council to build, man and equip a large naval force. Both law and religion, the cause of much of the misery, vice and injustice in the former order of things, might be simplified and rendered more rational by the township system; a well defined code of laws, like the code of Napoleon, and the adoption in every township of the quaker system, to manage their earthly and heavenly affairs without brokers, dispensing with the interference of priests and lawyers in business, in the arrangement of which they can have no other than pecuniary interest, to fill their pockets and live on the labor of others. The New England townships that have existed for nearly two centuries as the most perfect political association that has yet been contrived even in the barbarous ignorance of past ages, goes far to prove that there can be no difficulty in the present enlightened times, (when the diffusion of useful science pervades the smallest ramifications of society,) to greatly improve the township system, by extending their authority to every thing requisite to the freedom, comfort and happiness of society. And for the advantageous working of the federal council limited to external intercourse the five hundred years successful experience of the Swiss federation ought to be convincing proof that it fully served every purpose, in situations much more difficult and dangerous from the envious and jealous interference of the surrounding despots, than any obstructions aristocracy can raise against the mode the free people of America may choose to perfect their political system; in all of which they may be encouraged by recollecting they have never made any change either in church or state, but for the better; and it is perhaps impossible in the present state of civilization for the free will of any people to make any change but for the better: to obtain which free will in an elective government of universal suffrage the subject must have the greatest publicity, the pro and con must be debated in all the periodicals and become the subject of universal conversation, and reasoned on according as it may effect the interest of the majority, that it may be carried by them.

That some of the many thousand forms, self-interest puts on to delude the self-love and vanity of our species, actuates and must be the motives of all such dependant beings on food, clothing, etc., is the pivot on which turns all these opinions as well as many preceding, which is confirmed by the history of all nations and individuals, and at no period has it been more strongly exemplified than at the present, when all the European monarchies keep up large armies to subjugate their people to their arbitrary will, while the fear of their own subjects paralyzes the ambition of foreign conquests. Can any one who has been an impartial observer of the immense changes in the situations of church and state during the last fifty years, set any bounds to the probable changes that may take place the next fifty years. The dividing the whole Union into townships, and making a division in political labor, like all others, to have more perfect results, cannot astonish the short sighted more than many of the events of the last half century.

KNOWLEDGE HOSTILE TO THE GOVERNMENT OF THE FEW.

Jan. 19, 1835.

Of all the States of the Union, it was in New York where church and state ruled with the most arbitrary sway. There the hierarchy was organized nearer the principles of the Old World. There the number of churches, the influence and wealth of religious establishments, were nearly on a par with the junction of church and state in Europe. There the hereditary aristocracy of families prevailed; even political parties took the name of their chief, such as Livingstonians, Clintonians, etc. There the habits, customs, opinions, and fashions of Europe predominated, and coerced public opinion. To that mercantile emporium was attracted many Europeans who found there a state of society nearly similar to what they had left at home. In every town of the Union, speculation is carried beyond all profitable or prudential bounds, but in N. York it is pushed to the utmost pitch of extravagance. There a man's feet cannot keep pace with commercial changes, but a vast number of hacks are constantly driving from street to street in search of the object of speculation. There the quantity of paper securities is multiplied ad infinitum, and a whole street to the very garrets is peopled by money brokers. It is irrelevant to the present purpose to enquire, whether the fact of its being the quarters of the British army during the revolution, may be the ultimate, or its local situation the proximate cause of the turmoil and bustle, so exceeding the operations either of church or state in their neighbors. It is sufficient to ascertain, that the political, religious and mercantile influence, and dominion, was better combined, and more artificially united, to put into successful operation, all or any of their aristocratic plans, than in any other part of the Union; and notwithstanding this powerful combination against freedom and equality, New York is the first place where the working people have had any success in asserting their claims to rights and privileges, given them by all their political institutions; but which have lain so long dormant, as to have become obsolete.

In our southern states, slavery has annihilated equality and monopolized all freedom to the master, who is of the nonproductive and consuming class. The life, persons, and property of the producers, are possessed as a lawful inheritance by their owners, and the broad line of distinction of color, seems to place an insurmountable bar to general emancipation. The aristocratic monopoly of political rights, wealth, and power in the hands of the white descendants of Europeans, destroys all means of a gradual and peaceable improvement in the state of society, removing this unnatural and unjust state of the population, out of the reach of all moderate, or temperate means of a change, towards the equalization of property, knowledge and power, the *sine qua non* of rational freedom. This great difference of the rights and immunities of the population, widely separating their relative interest, may perhaps be the cause of a reform in our federation. By removing the cause of collision and dispute, through the right of interference in the affairs of the individual State governments given by our present federal constitution, which might be done without weakening the federal tie, as the great interest which the States have in union would be augmented by the great saving and economy of a federation similar to Switzerland.

Our northern States the nursery of population, long habituated to the equalization of knowledge, through the means of their township schools, which has produced a corresponding equality of property and power, and given them great influence over the other States to which they emigrate, have been gradually ameliorating their political institutions, so as to acquire the denomination of the country of steady habits, thinking themselves further advanced in civilization than their neighbors, they may be longer in making any great change, though the working people begin to claim the remainder of their rights even in New England, and must make every thing bend to their interest, by their numbers in the ballot boxes.

While the federation was ruled by the interest of the same class of society from both the north and south, the acts of congress were considered partial and unjust towards the ministry by the mode of taxation. How much more reason will the southern ministry have to complain, when the congress are controlled by the interest of the great class of producers, who will most probably charge the rich consuming classes* with their full share of public burdens by direct taxation.- The producers in the southern states, being slaves without any political rights, property, knowledge, or power, must be governed by the interest of the consuming class, whilst the north will most probably be ruled by the interest of the great class of producers. These two interests being in all countries opposite, and irreconcilable, will be the cause of a constant augmenting collision between the interest of the north and of the south, which can only be remedied, by preventing all interference of the general government either in the judicial, military or fiscal departments, of the individual states, leaving each state to be regulated by its own laws, defended by its own militia, and to lay its own taxes, according to the will and interest of the majority, as in Switzerland.

It must certainly be false logic, to reason that the Union will be weakened by making the compact more agreeable to the interest of the contractors, by giving them a constitution that leaves them more independent, at far less expense, and with equal protection, as has been fully proven by the five hundred years experience in the federal constitution in Switzerland. To assert that making the federation more conformable to the interests of the individual states is a dissolution of the Union, would be equally absurd as to insist that all the reforms made in the State's governments are their annihilation. The framers of the constitution aware that it would require reforms to fit it to the knowledge of the day, only stipulated that it should have an undisturbed trial for ten years, before any change. That all those who now benefit or expect to reap any advantage by the patronage and expenditure of the federal government should advocate its extension of power and privileges, is perfectly agreeable to the nature of our species; but that the millions who pay and obey, who must work harder and live more sparingly in consequence of the extra expense of the federation, should be in its favor, requires more apathy and ignorance, than one would expect to find in a country where there are so many facilities of instruction.

Formerly it was thought that a political association, so cunningly organized in favor of the consumers as was New York, was much more secure and lasting, than one in which the influence of democracy was greater, and the interest of the producers more respected. But with the diffusion of knowledge, most things must change; the greater the power of the few, the greater the abuse, the sooner it will exhaust the patience and forbearance of the millions; who in governments of universal suffrage, have only to will it and it must be done. Even in despotic tyrannies, when the forbearance of the people is exhausted, a revolution must succeed; from which it would appear that in the present state of civilization the propensity to the equalization of property, knowledge, and power, is in exact proportion to the spread of useful information, and as that is extending wider every day, so will the improvement and amelioration of mankind. It was the privileged orders of church and state, having the power, and abusing it, that was the cause of the French, and all other revolutions. The more information and useful knowledge is diffused amongst the people, the less injustice and oppression they will tolerate. As the influence of the moral increases, the power of mere physical force must diminish; and the moral revolution must be substituted for the physical, which has too often forced an equalization of power, before the equalization of property and knowledge was fit to support it.

The increasing power and influence of the millions, even in Europe, is evinced every day by the stand of the people, through their representatives, make in France against the hereditary power, though sometimes by a charter, at first acknowledged under the military coercion of the combined aristocracy of Europe. The late triumph of representation over the divine right of kings in Holland, and the symptoms that even the tyrant of Spain cannot govern his kingdom without the aid of representation, from the reports of his calling together the Cortes to settle and adjust the affairs of the country, that are in complete anarchy and confusion at present; all these circumstances evidently prove, that any kind of equal representation, never can submit peaceably to divine right or hereditary power.

DIVISION OF SOCIETY. EFFECTS OF CLIMATE ON THE FORMS OF GOVERNMENT. INEQUALITY OF PROPERTY AND KNOWLEDGE HAS BEEN IN PROPORTION TO CIVILIZATION.

Jan. 20, 1835.

As all political associations must be divided into two natural classes of producers and consumers, the industrious laborers, and those who live on the fruits of their labor, all analysis of society must have reference to those first principles; for though it is easy to conceive a state of equality, where all could be producers, it is impossible even to imagine the existence of a state of society where all would be consumers; of course the industrious are the only base and foundation, on which can be founded any aggregation of our species; and their interest, comfort and happiness, ought to be the object, end and aim of all civil, religious and political associations, maintained and supported by their labor. How it came that the world has been governed as yet, in direct contradiction to such self-evident premises, must perhaps remain like most causes, a problem difficult to be solved. But many of the artificial means of counteracting the natural bias to equality, is the theme of all our histories, both civil and religious; constitutes the subject of most of our poetical dreams and romances, and has exercised the acumen of the few who have tyrannized over the many in all ages. Most of our complicated legislations, our political rules, regulations and maxims, seem contrived to facilitate the subjugation of the ignorant many to the will of the knowing few.

Men, like all other animals, at first, made use of their physical force to procure the necessaries of life; and all in a savage state, the nearest to nature, wrought for themselves, and were all producers. The first attempt at civilization, was the creation of civil and religious rulers, founded in the beginning on a small moral superiority, which augmented by being maintained and supported by the labor of the many; left in ease and idleness to contrive the best means of combination to preserve and increase their artificial superiority: this, (as I have endeavored to prove in essay number II, on the effect of climate on the forms of government,) was easy or difficult, in proportion to the facility or difficulty of obtaining the surplus produce to feed the rulers; and the natural birth place of despotism was in climates of perpetual spring; as in Spain, Italy, and large empires that extend into climates of perpetual production, which enables them to keep in subjection their northern subjects, where the difficulty of raising a surplus would tend towards freedom. Civilization has certainly increased property and knowledge, but as far as it has yet gone, it has made an unfair and unjust division of both, depriving the many of what would add to their happiness, and burdening the few with what only increases their cares, anxiety and trouble; placed so high in the scale of humanity, the fear of, and guarding against a fall, gives them much uneasiness and vexation, whilst the facility of indulging to excess in all physical appetites, accumulates disease and torment towards the close of their lives, which finish by a premature death just when they have learned how to live. Inequality of property and knowledge has been in proportion to civilization, (except where the force of a physical revolution has swept all nearer to a level;) for instance, Britain is at the top of European civilization, and is in a state of the greatest inequality of both property and knowledge; her insular situation guaranteed her against the influence of the French revolution, and the wars that spread equality over the continent of Europe, increased in a most astonishing degree the inequality in Britain; for the immense national debt created during the war equally increased the number of idlers to be maintained by the labor of the industrious producers; until at last they cannot both maintain themselves and the vast numbers political misrule has saddled them with, and must either throw off the excessive burden of taxation or starve.

HEREDITARY AND ELECTIVE POWERS. SUPERIORITY OF ELECTIVE GOVERNMENTS OF UNIVERSAL SUFFRAGE.

In nations where the ignorance of the producers has permitted the consumers to rule with an absolute sway; where the combination of divine hereditary rights have annihilated and crushed public opinion into the silence of death and despotism, there the machine of power rolls down by main force, all opposition, and every muscle and fibre of the community si compressed into apparent tranquility: this is what the aristocracy of all countries denominate regular and orderly government, until the elasticity of knowledge bursts asunder the chains, and the violence of the explosion scatters abroad all the incumbent materials. Between this extreme of despotism and the opposite of freedom by universal suffrage, there is an intermediate state, where the force and numbers of the producers have more or less checked the power and presumption of the consumers, which has passed under different denominations by both Greeks and Romans, but at present has taken the name of limited monarchy: a mechanical idea of weighing the interests, rights and pretensions of the two opposing classes, as dead matter in a balance, so as to keep the constant equilibrium by makeweights thrown into either scale; forgetting how impossible it would be to find a just and disinterested holder of the balance or distributer of the makeweights; and however plausible the theory founded on the analogy of matter, the practice has always failed when applied to mankind; and the junction of elective and hereditary power has been a perpetual contention, until one acquired force to domineer and control the other; and the violence of the disputes is greater the nearer to equilibrium of power and force the contending parties have obtained; so that there is no peace until one has subdued the othrer. Britain is the only attempt at an apparent mixture of the powers that has lasted long enough to be an example of the consequences, and the hereditary power has always domineered except during the usurpation of Cromwell, when the elective power drove off the hereditary.

In France and Spain the hereditary, by the assistance of foreign force, subdued the elective, since which, in France, the elective has driven off the hereditary; and in other countries where the mixture of power exists it has been of so short duration as not to be a precedent by which to judge; though it is more than probable the two sources of power, hereditary and elective, are composed of so different and contradictory materials as not to exist peaceably in the same body politic. From which it would appear, that there is little security for the hereditary despot who trembles on the top of the stairs, always afraid of being thrown over the banisters, and as little peace and permanent stability for the limited monarchies, that come half way down the stairs of state; so that the only solid foundation is to be found at the bottom, on the platform of equality, where all are equally interested in the prosperity of all; which can only exist in elective governments of universal suffrage, where the practice of freedom and equality has existed long enough to equalize property and knowledge, as the only means of securing to each individual his natural rights and share of comfort and happiness.

If our working people persevere with that union and energy which a due regard to their most essential interest requires, they will be an example to their fellow laborers in every country and climate, by showing the immense advantages of universal suffrage, which has been reprobated and calumniated by the aristocratic factions in all countries, and made synonymous with riot, anarchy, confusion and misrule, though the only secure foundation for the perpetuation of freedom.— Give power to property and you make slaves of all not possessed of that property—nine-tenths of the human species are at present in that predicament.

SPEECH MAKING. NATIONAL DEBTS. STANDING ARMIES POLITICAL ECONOMY.

Jan. 22, 1835.

Book making, pamphlet making, waste much time, patience and money; witness the corn laws of Britain, that have filled so many thousand pages, fatigued the tongues of so many thousand orators, only to explain, that the prohibitions on the corn trade, keep the staff of life from fifty to a hundred per centum above the prices it can be purchased for in other parts of Europe; which is a tax on the millions in favor of the land owners; adds so much to the price of manufactures, and enables other nations to undersell them in foreign markets, which they have already done, and must continue to do, until the expense of living at home excludes them from all markets of which they have not a forced monopoly. National debts, and millions of calculations made on the best mode of squeezing money out of the labor of the industrious, without their knowing it, and keeping up the delusive hopes of repayment by sinking funds, which only add to the burdensome amount; but not a whisper on its real nature, of mortgaging the labor of posterity to feed and maintain the ambition, luxury, whim, caprice and extravagance of the few consuming idle, at the expense of the industrious; nor of the inseparable consequence of reducing the millions to poverty, ignorance, misery and crime, exhausting all their faculties by excessive toil and labor, and fitting them for slavery and degradation, which is argued by the sophistry of these oppressors, as a reason for retaining them in bondage. Not a word about the demoraliszing principles of war, the pretence and excuse for contracting national debts, all for the benefit of the few powerful and ambitious, at the expense of the blood and treasure of the many; nor of the realities of plunder, pillage, robbery, cruelty, slaughter, etc., concealed and disguised under the high sounding and fallacious titles of honor, glory, national dignity, etc., producing the consequences of one swarm of ignorant dupes to slavery, another crowd equally irrational, only to perpetuate their own bondage by increasing the number of cut-throats, under the appellation of a standing army, to keep the conqueror and conquered under the yoke of military despotism. All history is full of the pompous account of what the powerful and consuming few gained by the rapine and destruction of war, but no notice is taken of the time, money and lives it cost the many.

Political economy, which, as the late writers have treated it, may rather be called an excuse for political extravagance, consisting of ingenious contrivances to enable the rulers of the people to extract from their subjects or slaves, with the most ease, expedition and safety, the greatest quantity of surplus produce for their own use, under pretence of public good; to facilitate the contracting of national debts with the best mode of redeeming, paying the interest, and keeping up the delusion; the dividing and subdividing property into capital, wages, etc., seemingly to annul the great truth, that property is the produce of labor. Rent is the difference of value between rich and poor soils, in place of the plain and simple statement, that rent of land is the surplus after paying the cost of seed, labor and capital. The long dispute of who pays the tithes, contradicting Adam Smith, who, without considering the deranging effect of British monopolizing corn laws, made the general statement to suit all countries—that it was the land owner; which would be true were the trade in produce free; but legislative restrictions warp and disfigure that, as well as every thing else of individual concern, it meddles with. Adam Smith wrote on the means of increasing the wealth of nations, (the reverse of the "greatest happiness to the greatest number.") Under a monopoly the consumer must pay the greatest part of the tithe. All their metaphysical minutiæ serves to conceal and disguise the real and original meaning of political economy; which is, like the individual economy of a family, the cheapest and best way of administering a political association; which ought to be an inquiry whether an elective or hereditary system is likely to be the best and cheapest for the great majority; whether the dominion of one is cheaper and better than the rule of many; whether the union of church and state is likely to augment or diminish public burdens; whether a direct tax on property is the most just, the fairest and best tax, or an indirect tax on consumption, and which of them can be collected at the least expense of money and morals; whether the expense of a standing army is necessary or useful in a popular government, either for internal tranquility or external defence; and whether a well regulated militia, where every citizen is a soldier, is not the cheapest and surest defence of freedom; whether small states united by federation is not the cheapest and best protection for liberty and equality; whether it is cheaper and better for a people to make improvements of roads, canals and public buildings for themselves, or allow their government to make them for them; whether any species of legislation can make laws to suit the convenience or interest of an extensive empire of different climates, products, habits, customs and interests; all these queries might be brought under the head of political economy, and solved agreeably to the interest of the great majority, to the great advancement of useful knowledge and civilization.

Public speech making is mostly confined to politics, law and religion; these three great nonproductive consuming classes, and dealers in words, have wielded the arms and power of rhetoric in all countries, where a portion have been able to paralyze or suspend part or the tyranny of absolute power and despotsim. Where the physical force ceases to be able to enslave mankind, the moral influence of words by rhetoric and eloquence, is substituted to keep the ignorant in subjection to the knowing; and the sphere of speech making is extended with representation, and commensurate with liberty. Britain was the first place in Europe where public speaking was tolerated. Where armed force could coerce ignorance, the despots never descended to moral influence; and even the courts of law carried on their processes in suits by written pleading, so much was tyranny afraid of publicity.

Oratory is the weapon to assert superiority where physical force has lost its power. Public speaking is in proportion to the quantum of liberty and equality; and there is perhaps four times more of it in our Union, than in any other part of the earth, of an equal population; and the time, patience and money lost to the public, by our popular debates, are in the same proportion: they drown the matter in dispute under such an ocean of words, that it is lost sight of, both by themselves and hearers. A wordy lawyer will obstruct the operations of congress for three days, by beating a few ideas so thin and watery, while all the common sense or utility in the declamatory oration might be said in an hour, and ignorance will give him credit as they do their linen draper, by the yard; and this will continue, like most other political quackery, until the general diffusion of knowledge teaches the millions it is not their interest to waste the produce of their labor on sounds—*vox et praeterea nihil.*

Lawyers are hired to plead on both the right and wrong side of a cause, and from the habit of always considering the side from which they receive the fee, as the right side, after practicing for ten or fifteen years, on such a scale of equity, they lose the distinction of right and wrong. When the evidence either written or oral, is before the judge or jury, the whole truth that can be produced, is exposed, the pleading or speeches of the hired lawyers on both sides, do not clear up or elucidate the evidence—on the contrary, the whole intention and aim of the lawyers on both sides, are to warp, disfigure and disguise the truth, so that the side they receive the fee from, may appear the side of justice, law and equity.— The principal art of forensic eloquence is to deceive by sophistry and ingenuity, distorting the truth so as to make the worst appear the better cause; and on this view of the character of lawyers' speeches, they are often not only the loss of time, patience and money, but encourage crime by being the cause of its going unpunished, and sacrificing honor and honesty to deception, swindling and roguery; it likewise much augments the superiority of the rich over the poor, by warping justice to favor the wealthy. The Athenians provided an antidote for that partiality of lawyers' eloquence in favor of the rich and against the poor, by appointing some of the first orators of the republic to plead the cause of the poor gratis; and even that would not place them on an equality, unless the state paid as high as the rich.

In preaching and speech making, or attempting to reason on religious dogmas, the priest has an advantage over the statesman or lawyer, in having no opposition; all is passion, obedience and non-resistance to their dictates; which perhaps enables the church to be such a firm support of all kinds of despotism. Attempting to reason about dogmas beyond the comprehension of all, what no one can either affirm or deny, and which must remain so until the nature of man and most other things are changed, is at best the loss of time, patience and money, and adding to the trouble pain and anxiety of the present, the fear and terror of the torments, pain and punishment of the future, concerning which we know nothing. Words are so undefined and undefinable, being mostly relative or comparative, not positive, that it holds out too great a temptation to all classes who deal in words to twist, stretch and apply their meaning to their own purpose, which ought to teach the unsuspicious how cautious they ought to be in placing confidence in their ears, the most deceitful of all the senses, through which come the most of the fallacies, quackery, tricks and deceptions which leads them astray from their real interest on which are founded their faith and misplaced confidence in the rulers of church and state.

ADVANTAGES OF SMALL POLITICAL ASSOCIATIONS.

Jan. 24th, 1835.

There is a remarkable coincidence between the relative situation of the inhabitants and even the animals, whose lot is cast in extensive societies, whether great political empires or kingdoms, large plantations wrought by slaves, or farms upon a large scale—all of them have been considered in favor of the power, perquisites and profits of the rulers, owners and proprietors; though much against the comforts and happiness of all the beings who, by their labor produce and maintain all. I have (in a former number,) endeavored to prove that the despotism, oppression and misery of political associations, are in proportion to the extent of territory and number of inhabitants over whom they rule, and equal misfortune attends the slaves, who are yoked in great numbers to extensive plantations, under the lash of overseers, who, like the subordinate officers who wield the authority of the chiefs of large empires, are only interested in the quantum of produce and profit they can force from the miserable slaves subjected to their will, whose comfort or happiness, by being properly fed and clothed, seldom enters as an item in the calculation of master or agent. When the small planters with ten or fifteen negroes, happened to be placed in the vicinity of extensive planters of many hundreds, used to complain that the pilfering of these negroes cost them a certain per centage annually, they excused it, knowing that the slaves on large estates are not half fed or clothed; while in small numbers, under the eye of the master they are treated well, just as the master expects they will treat him and all that belongs to him: even the animals on large plantations, left to the care of slaves, are but indifferently treated, as the slaves retaliate on them their own harsh usage.

Where the working people enjoy some kind of freedom, and are not bought and sold like oxen or sheep, their situation on large farms, is much more uncomfortable than on small ones;

the happiness of twenty or thirty small farmers and their families is sacrificed to the profit of the owner in turning his land into a large farm, wrought by unmarried men; it being the interest of the proprietor not to burden himself with families. So that in every situation, country or climate, the interest of the slave is contrary to the interest of the master. The interest of the many industrious producers is contrary to the interest of the idle consumers. The interest of the governed is contrary to the interest of the governors. It is in vain to attempt the changing or remedying the contradiction of interests, without abolishing or amalgamating the circumstances, which are the cause of the opposition. There is no cure for slavery but the emancipation of the slaves by making all more equally free and independent. The only possible way of reconciling the interest of the producers and consumers, is by that equality that shall force every consumer to be at some time a producer, and the putting the governed and governors on such a footing as to neutralize their interests, can only be done by the division of power, alternating and reciprocating authority, so as to make the governed of this day, month or year, the governors of the following day, month or year. Where the society consists of masters and slaves there is a perpetual war between force and fraud, an eternal strife and dispute between the consumers seizing and purloining as much of the property of the industrious producers as their ignorance will permit, or the producers contending to retain as much as possible for their own use. Governors of all descriptions are interested in squeezing out of the governed as much property as the intrigues and contrivances of church and state can accomplish; and the governed are equally interested to counteract their plans by every means of evasion; by which it is evident that the seeds of contention, broils and bloodshed, are abundantly sown, in the interior of all political associations, principally owing to the great inequality of property, knowledge, and power, introduced by civilization as far as it has yet gone.

For the exterior wars and bloodshed between states and nations, they are equally frequent in all the situations in which humanity has yet been placed, as often occurring in the savage, as in the civilized state, with this difference: each individual, in the savage state, participates in the toil, labor and expenditure of life and loss of the expedition, and has an equal share of plunder and profit; but in the present state of civilization, the toil, labor, waste of life, as well as all other expenses, is borne exclusively by the millions; and by a late invention of a national debt, they and their property are bound to pay an annual revenue to the influential and hereditary few, for the expense of acquiring power and possessions, exclusively divided amongst the supposed possessions of divine hereditary rights, to augment their means of tyrannizing and oppressing their subjects, and riveting the chains of slavery.

It is natural and agreeable to all the motives which actuate our species, that those who have by force, intrigue or stratagem, acquired the divine hereditary right of absolute power, should increase and fortify that authority by conquering all the small states or nations within their reach, and uniting them in one solid mass of despotism. Such has been the conduct of the rulers and founders of all empires, history gives us an account of, from the African, Persian, Grecian, Roman, etc., down to the Prussian, Austrian and Russian empires of the present day, which consist of a great number of small states formerly independent, conquered and subjected by the superior force of the despotic empire. That all this injustice and exercise of arbitrary force should arise out of the interest of those clothed with divine hereditary rights, to gratify theirselfish ambition and unlimited avarice, is in the nature of both men and things, and when once the cause exists, the effect may as certainly be expected as the accomplishment of any of nature's laws.

But the cause being totally changed, the effects ought likewise, when the few who supposed they inherited this divine right, are entirely deprived of it, and all their power and prerogatives transferred by the elective system founded on universal suffrage, to the majority of the millions of industrious producers. All laws, customs, habits, and practices, founded on the interest of the hereditary few, ought to cease and be annulled, and replaced by forms, regulations and practices, conformable to the interest, comfort, and happiness of the industrious many. The interest of the consuming few has been always (as I have before endeavored to prove,) contrary to the interest of the producing many; and as those invested with hereditary power, in following their interest have accumulated power and possessions by conquest, it most probably would be the interest of the millions to divide by vesting every small district with the right of governing themselves agreeably to their own interest. Now as the successful practice of federation, as a complete protection against all foreign aggression, has been sufficiently proven by experience, the only objection that has been made against such an equalization of property, knowledge and power, has been completely done away. The New England townships of six miles square, that have been in successful experiment for more than a century, might be taken as the extent of territory and any one of the states of the Union might invest said division of territory with full power to regulate their own affairs, with a federation in place of a state legislature, elected by the townships as a court of arbitration in case of any disputes between the townships, and to manage all intercourse with exterior relations, without any right or authority to interfere with the internal government of any of the townships. The tax might be raised as the expenses of the New England townships are now collected, by a direct tax on property, which would interfere with no one and be collected at little or no expense. If this succeeded with one state, the rest might adopt it, thus putting in practice one of the advantages belonging solely to federative governments. The inhabitants of any of the townships must be great fools if they could not manage their own affairs better than either the states or United States governments will now manage for them: for having all the advantages of small communities, of a perfect knowledge of their situation and circumstances, an intimate acquaintance with the necessity and nature of all their improvements, joined to a strict and well conducted inspection of all public works, they must have an immense superiority over any wholesale direction of a body politic at hundreds of miles from the local, and perhaps much farther from having any interest in the well being of the inhabitants. They might at first make blunders, but none of them having an interest in the perpetuation of abuses, (as is the case in all large political associations,) they would soon be forced by their interest to correct them. Experience has sufficiently proven the incompatibility of large empires with the happiness of the millions. It is high time to try small communites.

EXECUTIVE PATRONAGE; TO PREVENT WHICH EVERY OFFICER SHOULD BE ELECTED BY THE PEOPLE.

Jan. 28, 1835.

Money is the bone of contention in all civilized societies; but when put in the form of patronage, at the disposal of an elective officer, occasions more disputes, broils, and too often bloodshed, than when held out as a bribe to any other enormity, vice or crime; because to all other corruptions there are limits both of territory and population, but in our theory of equality, and the division of power, by all being eligible to office, there are no limits to either; and the deception, intrigue and stratagem demoralize all through the smallest ramification of society—organize and marshal one party against another, with all the violence and enmity attending avarice, under the mask of patriotism and public good; it interrupts all sociability, impairs confidence and buries truth under such a mass of flattery and falsehoood, as not to be perceived by all the acuteness that can be expected from the mass of mankind in any country; it amalgamates and confuses all character, and reduces the choice of representatives to the turn of a die.— One reads with astonishment, our newspapers, on immense sheets, in imitation of the British, without the reason of evading part of the tax, half of them filled with political deceptions in favor of their patrons or against their antagonists, both equally far from the truth, the receptacles of scandal, calumny and falsehood; which shows a great depravity in public opinion, as an unbiassed neutral paper would scarcely be tolerated; all must take a side, to live.

Before the patronage of the federal executive was so extensive and lucrative, the attention and industry of place hunters were divided between the offices in the gift of the State and the United States; a division which lessened the force of competition, intrigue, and stratagem; but lately all is swallowed up in the great vortex of federal patronage, and the pitiful state perquisites seem only a stepping stone to federal preferment; the merit of a state's governor or legislator depending on whether he is in favor of the federal administration, that is, the re-election of the present president, or joined to a coalition to put in a new president. The whole weight of corruption turns on one pivot, and is a further proof, if wanted, that the patronage is too heavy to be borne steadily by any elective officer; and as, where putrefaction exists, there will be a collection of maggots, the only cure is to cleanse the Augean stable, by entrusting the election of every officer to the people, under whose eyes his duty is to be performed; who gain by his fidelity, and lose by his defalcation; when the only bribe that could be administered to so great a number would be the faithful discharge of his duty.

Money is the god of the country, and the high priests, who serve at his altars and divide the spoil, are the bank directors, who, not content with the exclusive right of distributing public wealth, begin to claim a share of the legislature in enacting laws that shall confirm and extend their exclusive privileges. In imitation of their political competitors they are purchasing the services of newspaper editors, to influence the public through the only channel at present open. The U. S. Bank, by its branches, spread over every State of the Union, has become chief proprietor of most of the towns, by lending money through the discounting of speculators' notes with which they build houses, and failing to pay, the bank takes the houses at the value the owners owed them, often three or four times more than they would sell for: this and other manoeuvres create an interest that warrants an original in asserting, "make me a director of the United States branch bank, and I will make the governor."

In a late number I have endeavored to show that corruption, vice and crime, were in proportion to the extent of territory, and number of the inhabitants of the political associciations. The same takes place in all aggregations of mankind, that their moral and physical defects are in proportion to the number collected on one spot, as is evidently the case in all towns that are corrupt and immoral in proportion to their size. When I first traveled in Spain it was a geological expedition, which forced me out of the great roads into the mountains, where I found the inhabitants the most hospitable, kind people I ever was amongst; they were mostly men, for the priests kept their wives in the neighboring villages, and only allowed them to visit their wives on Sunday; but that Sunday schools had not spoiled or corrupted the men, though those who were constantly under the tuition of the priests were corrupt, vicious and immoral; while those isolated on the solitary farms in the mountains, were honest, faithful and hospitable; which I found the case in all mountainous countries, separated from the contagion of fashionable civilization: this contradicts the doctrine of original sin, and proves that men are disposed to be good when not vitiated by the restraints, dogmas, and doctrines of church and state. One would be tempted to suppose, that our religious and political tutors, finding mankind vicious after receiving their education, invented the dogma of original sin to shift the blame off their own shoulders on nature; "that men were prone to do evil as the sparks fly upwards," as a mask and excuse for the vicious and bad instruction their false principles, both religious and civil instilled into them. Men are just what surrounding circumstances make them; surrounding circumstances are under the control of church and state; ergo, it is church and state that make man the vicious, ignorant, unhappy being we find him.

Why men are more vicious, unhappy and miserable in large associations than in small, must have a cause inherent in the nature of numerous societies. In all congregations of men there is a humiliating inequality of condition, squalid poverty and misery in close contact with superfluous luxury, dissipation and extravagance, affording a constant temptation to crime, which no laws, however sanguinary, can correct. The rich and opulent have hitherto made all laws, regulations and restrictions; have taken the lead in all customs, habits and fashions; all of which are in favor of their class. All collections of men crowded on the top of one another, in the same spot, attract every species of idlers: those who cannot work with their hands, must exercise their wits to live, that is by cheating, swindling and every kind of deception. In the towns of our Union there is an additional bribe to extravagance, dissipation and vice, by the vast number of banks giving money on easy terms to all who by hook or by crook, can pretend to live without labor, while the laborers who produce all and pay the losses in case of bank failures, do not participate in any of the discounts. This creates an immense artificial inequality between the nonproducers who benefits, by putting his name on a slip of paper by a loan of from $20,000 to $100,000, from the banks according to the scale of trade or commerce he may have the reputation of carrying on, or in proportion to his influence with the back directors; while the man who labors with his hands and produces all, can scarcely accumulate the value of a month's wages to enable him to purchase the necessary tools and materials for his trade. All these and many more are the premiums and bribes held out in large cities to encourage the accumulation of extravagance, vice and crime, little or none of which is to be found in the scattered populalion of farmers and mechanics, where industry is equally necessary in all to gain a living, and fewer situations capable of supporting the idle and nonproductive. All states of society where the monopolization of property, knowledge and power throws the population into the two extremes of poverty and riches, the one below in character and the other above it, must produce corruption, vice and crime.

FREE TRADE AND DIRECT TAXATION FAVORABLE TO THE GREAT MAJORITIY OF THE PEOPLE.

Jan. 20, 1835.

In changing taxation from indirect on consumption, to direct on all kinds of property, there is only two descriptions of the population of any country, who are losers by it, while all the other classes are vast gainers in freedom, wealth and happiness. One of those who lose a part of their arbitrary power, are governors, whether elective or hereditary; first by the influence of patronage from appointment of such a vast swarm of officers to good salaries, and easy places, as is necessary to watch and detect smuggling, the temptation to which is in proportion to the highness of the tax: and secondly the necessity of clothing all these officers with arbitrary and undefined power, to coerce the guilty, though too often falling on the innocent, at the will and pleasure of the superior, who has the making and unmaking of them; this loss to the rulers is an evident gain to the people, both of money and freedom. The other description of the community who lose part of their surplus money by direct taxation, are the rich and opulent, who have, by inheritance, monopoly or some other fortuitous advantage, accumulated a superfluous quantity of wealth, a greater part of which they would be obliged to pay for their and their property's protection, by direct, than indirect taxes, though not more than the amount of the security they receive from the government, which protection must be always in proportion to the amount protected.

All merchants and traders would gain both time and money, by being released from the inquisitorial search and inspection of officers who are interested in finding them in fault; and under pretence of their duty, are often litigious and capricious; they would increase their business, by the reduction in the value of the articles they deal in, which would very often double the consumption, and by finding a market for more of the production of other nations, would enable them to take more of ours; increasing their profits both on exports and imports; not to mention the moral satisfaction of being relieved from all temptation to prevarication of measure, weight, value or quality of the merchandize they deal in; which being smuggled by a rival, forces them to do the same, or sacrifices the greatest part of their profit, and perhaps even the capital, which must end in bankruptcy. The gratification of independence; every one standing on a footing without the favor or affection of men in power, ought to be of value in a free country of liberty and equality.

All owners, captains, seamen, or others concerned in ships or navigation, would be great gainers, both in time and money, by the facility of expediting their ships free from the let or hindrance of a multiplicity of arbitrary laws, rules and regulations, preventing them from touching or calling at a variety of markets, when their interest might induce them to discharge a part or the whole of their cargoes. All ports being free ports, they would have the choice of as many markets, as the prices would remunerate them for their trouble and expenses.

All the farmers and mechanics would benefit much by having all the articles they consume at much less labor and money while the facility of transporting would give them a more extended market for their produce, and permit them to receive at every landing on our large rivers, the articles they required from any country on the globe, without the intervention of the custom house officers or laws, and to export their produce with equal facility, to all countries where they might be required.

The laborers, tradesmen of all descriptions, would not only be relieved from the exorbitant tax, they pay by indirect taxation, (which I have formerly endeavored to prove was four times more than their proportion, and at least twice as much as went into the public treasury,) but would reap an immense benefit by the general amelioration of the condition of the whole population, enabling them to be greater consumers of the produce of their labor, and would be further morally gratified by the equalization of property, knowledge and power, which would elevate the laborer by making his occupation, honorable in proportion to its utility.

The learned professions would have the advantage of living cheaper, and might reduce the price of their labor, by diminishing their fees, and increase their utility by augmenting the number of their customers, adding much to their respectability by the spread of knowledge rendering quackery useless.

All manufacturers who use raw materials of foreign production, would obtain them so much cheaper, than in countries where the inhabitants were burdened with custom-houses, excise, etc., that they would be able to rival them in every market; and those who manufactured the gross produce of the soil, could not possibly suffer by the competition of foreign manufacturers, who, to all the burdens of excessive taxation, must add also the expenses of freight, insurance, commission, interest of money and loss of time in transporting the raw material to them, and the same in returning the manufactured articles to the place of consumption; which, compared with the facility of each district supplying itself, is an independent situation, which the tyranny of both church and state have hitherto prevented the people of all countries from enjoying.

Besides all the pecuniary advantages accruing to the before mentioned classes, there is the spirit of industry, information and ingenuity inseparable from liberty and equality, which has produced prosperity on the barren mountains of Switzerland and Neufchatel; and a small quantity of it has raised the British islands to a mercantile and political consideration, equal to four times their population on the continent, where the feudal tyranny prevailed hundreds of years after it was partly abolished in Britain.

The separation of the privilege of granting lucrative appointments from those in power, will abolish the trade of place hunters, whose only object is the pelf, perquisites and patronage attached to the place, who in future in place of constant agitation of intrigues, stratagems and deceptions to obtain votes, will be usefully occupied in some productive art or business; there will be an end to the bribery of editors of newspapers to publish scandal, calumny and detraction against the antagonist of their patron, as well as the fulsome flattery of their employers and payers; they must, therefore, to live, occupy their printed sheets with some useful information, on a par with the knowledge of the day, to suit their customers.

At elections, that turmoil and scramble for votes, will be succeeded by that calm and deliberate choice of persons, fit to represent the people, who will serve for the honor attached to the place, by public opinion, not for the pecuniary advantages, which reputation and consideration not being insured by a continuance in office, will induce them willingly to cede the place to another, (the salary being the object, the longer they continue to live to the extent of it, the more necessary it becomes to their comfort and happiness, and the greater exertions for retaining it,) which will cause a constant division of power by a rotation in office, one of the greatest advantages of the elective system.

Even the rulers will be relieved from the tormenting solicitations of hundreds of place hunters, claiming rewards for services done them in canvassing for votes at their elections; and be gratified with the certainty of being put into office by the free and unsolicited votes of their fellow citizens, without being indebted to the intrigues, deceptions and stratagems of those who make a trade of buying and selling preferment; having the wielding of less power, the distribution of less patronage, and living at less expense, the time they are in office, will not form so great a contrast, with their private situation when out of place, and tend much to the future happiness of themselves and families; for however agreeable it may be to augment the show, parade and expense of living, the curtailing and diminishing is always attended with pain, and regret, in proportion to the reduction made necessary by the change of circumstances.

Jan. 30, 1835.

Man being made by surrounding circumstances, what he is, good or bad, accounts for many of the inveterate vices, errors and corruptions of society, as well as for the failure of many of the temporary, ineffectual means resorted to, both by individuals and the rulers of church and state, to correct the evil, while leaving the surrounding circumstances, the original temptation to the abuse, in full vigor, like a farmer whose fields were overrun with noxious weeds, cutting off the leaves and tops, which only strengthens the roots to push out more luxuriously; the only cure in both such cases must be radical.

We complain of the fanaticism, bigotry, and superstition of the enthusiastic sects in favor of religious dogmas, and the intolerant persecution, physical and moral, which flows from them as a certain consequence of the circumstances with which the social order is surrounded: enact laws and ordinances to check the enthusiasm of religious sects, while we encourage and protect a priesthood, whose daily bread and existence depends on the spreading, by what is called conversion, such doctrines, by seizing on the credulity and affections of every child, woman and man, they industriously try to associate with; establish schools, seminaries, and colleges to instruct those religious wranglers in the theological and metaphysical arts, of supporting their incomprehensible dogmas; filling the society with a learned class, whose sole existence depends on their convincing the less learned millions, of their knowledge and influence in the mysterious world to come; legalizing and encouraging all their acts, by the junction of church and state. While the sources of delusion are not dried up by a free, general, and useful instruction, the pernicious abuse of power must continue to act on the ignorance and gullibility of the millions.

We complain of the litigation, multiplicity, and mysterious intricacy of our laws, while we continue to fill our legislatures with lawyers, whose daily bread and existence depends on the incomprehensible nature of the laws; whose interest forces them to make them such, as none but themselves can pretend to understand, and at the same time so vague and undefined, that each party may think they are right and warranted to commence a law suit. Much time, study and reading are necessary to qualify professors of the law, for this sophistical quibbling, twisting and stretching of words and phrases: thus educated, they must exercise their calling by living on the loss and disputes of their fellow citizens; and all temporary reforms by the aid of those who live by the present abuses, only adds to the confusion. The only radical cure is for the electors by universal suffrage to put into the legislatures, as their representation, such men as are interested in making justice cheap, by adopting a simple, plain and well defined code of laws, which every citizen might possess, read, and understand, capable to teach him when he is right and when wrong.

One of the most useful and well informed religious sects that has yet existed, the Quakers, laid the axe to the root of the evils of both laws and religion, by abolishing the trades of both lawyer and priest, taking the management of their own affairs, both in this and the other world into their own hands; thereby removing the surrounding circumstances, the cause and origin of all the evils, and principal source of all the abuses of church and state. Though the successful experiment has now been going on for more than a century, respected and supported in all countries, where the freedom of toleration has permitted them to live, yet so completely has the tricks and stratagems of church and state blinded the millions, that no nation, state or society, has been allowed to imitate them; though it is more than probable the present extensive and universal revolutions may tend towards an order of things that may in some measure resemble the utility and simplicity of their doctrines.

All attempts to reconcile the interest of the states and United States, or to prevent their disputes and quarrels, will be in vain, while the ideal and metaphysical power of federation, has a right to control and interfere with the fiscal, laws, and military of the real and substantial power of the states.— All temporary expedients, while the cause or surrounding circumstances remain the same, (that is the claim of the sovereignty of federalism over the sovereign independent states) must be abortive. The patronage of the federal executive may be extended so as to produce partial dissentions, and to interfere with the elections of each state, as the present electioneering intrigues seem to point at; but the citizens have a common interest in protecting the independence of the states against the encroachments of federalism, and when it comes to a contest, federation must yield; for it is evidently the interest of both the northern and southern states to have the independent management of their own affairs; the apparent difference on the tariff is an accidental thing, which only shows the impolicy of the contradicting powers vested in federalism.

Our working people must be contented to maintain swarms of customhouse officers, place hunters, bank stock holders, and directors, brokers, agents and the whole tribe attached to monied aristocracy, if they continue to elect such representatives, as gain their living by the support of such trades; who are interested in granting bank and other exclusive privileged charters; who are forced by their interest to burden the industrious producers to support the greatest part of the public expenses by indirect taxation, to save their real property, bank, insurance, and other shares, notes, bonds, and the contents of their iron chests, from paying for the support of government which protects them. There is no other cure for these abuses than by changing the surrounding circumstances, which originated all these abuses, by electing legislators from amongst their own class of producers, who have gained their living by labor, and who will be bound by a similar interest to enact laws for their protection against the corruption and combination of the idle consumers, by abolishing every species of monopoly, and making every one pay for the support of government in proportion to his property by a direct tax, thus restoring that natural equality, so necessary to the existence and continuance of freedom, which has been so much deranged by an unjust and iniquitous legislation, oppressing the poor and favoring the rich, feeding the luxury and extravgance of the wealthy at the expense of the industrious laborers. Fortunately for our happy country, the industrious producers have only to will it by universal suffrage at the ballot boxes and it must be done.

Old mother Britain by ages of hereditary misrule, shifting the burden on posterity by an enormous national debt, has now so many idle consumers to maintain, that the whole labor of the industrious, assisted by steam engines, canals, rail roads, etc., cannot keep up the extravagances of church and state; and the oppression on the industrious laborers, has so accumulated, (and always must in proportion to the number and extravagance of the consumers,) that it cannot be longer borne. The British people expect relief from the reform of parliament; but unless they remove and change surrounding circumstances, the cause of the people's distress, all other temporary expedients will be abortive. The only radical cure is the change of taxation from indirect to direct, on every species of property, making every one pay in proportion to what he holds in the public and all other funds, laying the burden on those that levy and expend the taxes, reducing the enormous inequality of property and knowledge within the sphere of a just morality.

In the whole civilized world, there is a contention between the governors and the governed, between hereditary and elective power; but in France the millions are surrounded by such complete equality of property and knowledge, that the contest will soon be settled; nor can such equalization of the essentials of freedom, rest satisfied with any thing less than elective government; something approaching to universal suffrage.

All the surrounding circumstances, invented by the church and sanctioned by the state, in Catholic countries, reduce the population to ignorance and poverty, depriving them, by fasts and holidays, of half their time; all expedients to render them free, independent and happy, must fail, unless they begin by changing the surrounding circumstances, the cause and origin of the evil.

Men are therefore fashioned, formed and made by external surrounding circumstances, constituting a mould in which they are cast, either good, industrious, sober and rational, or vicious, corrupt, idle, depraved, cruel and criminal beings.

Feb. 3, 1835.

Men being fashioned, formed and made what they are by surrounding circumstances, it may be useful to inquire, what class, association or combination, have acquired by usurpation or otherwise, this influence, authority or control, to regulate, propagate or command the circumstances which model society. There are but two aggregations of mankind who have arrogated sufficient power to enforce their precepts, as general rules and regulations for the conduct of the community; that is church and state. By church is meant here every thing connected with, or under the control of religion; and by state every species of legislation, general or particular, that can be brought under the denomination of government. Both of them have been in the habit of pretending that all they do is for the good of others, attributing to themselves the disinterested motive of public good.

Religious rulers of all the numberless sects and persuasions, that have yet acquired consequence on earth, set out by asserting that their doctrines are the only true; that a compliance with their precepts, rules and dogmas, is the only road to happiness, both here and hereafter, which they enforce with all the moral and physical coercion, ages of experience have enabled them to contrive. Most of the ancients were what we call idolators, because their priests surrounded them with such circumstances, as forced them to believe in such chimeras. A man born in Hindostan is surrounded by the Brahmins with such circumstances as compel him to believe and reverence all the absurdities, and cruel penances of their religion. One born in Constantinople reverences and worships all the follies of the Koran; and becomes a faithful Mussulman by believing the pretended inspirations of Mahomet. One brought up a Catholic is assiduously surrounded with such circumstances by his priests as to induce him to believe in the infallibility of the pope, as God's vicegerent, and all the other tenets of their religion which the priests have found it their interest to inculcate. The various sects of protestants are industriously taught from childhood to believe in the mysteries belonging to the dogmas of their sect, surrounding them from the earliest age with such a mass of circumstances as future and more mature reflection can scarcely shake off. The dogmas of all of them are incomprehensible, as far out of the reach of our senses as of reason, and contrary to the laws of nature. The only thing evident, tangible or sensible, is that the priests of all religions live by the propagation of faith in their dogmas, on the labor of others, increasing the physical toil and fatigue of the industrious producers; while they torment the moral with the phantoms of hereafter; adding to the miseries of the present the imaginary evils of the next world: all of which is completely beyond the comprehension of beings constituted like men. The disputes concerning the truth of their inexplicable dogmas have deluged the earth with more blood and slaughter, than all the political, civil and military wars, originating in the inordinate ambition, and usurpation of self-created tyrants and conquerors. The Hindoos prevent the exercise of common sense and reason, in rejecting all religions but their own; the Mussulmen the same; the Catholics the same; and the protestants likewise. If common sense and reason be the rule by which to measure the truth and merit of any, it must be the same for all; each excluding the use of this test in judging of his religion, is a proof that all their dogmas are equally contradictory to both common sense and reason. Morality, on which they have all attempted to hang their dogmas, is useful and good in all religions, and conducive to the interest and happiness of mankind, but unfortunately practiced by none.

In states, there is a much greater variety than in church, for the same dogmas, such as the Mahometan or the Catholic, are believed by a great many different people, but the government of all nations differ in their mode of ruling their subjects. The despotism of Russia would not suit Austria, nor would either tyrannize over the state of information in Prussia; nor any of them work smoothly with the progress of intellect in France, Britain, Sweden, Switzerland, etc. Each government, whether by divine, hereditary right of despotism, or by the mixed form of limited monarchy, has surrounded their people with an accumulation of circumstances, as suitable to the diffusion of information in the millions, as the knowledge of their own interest will permit. Hereditary power can only be changed, improved or ameliorated by physical force. All reasoning against the phantom of divine right is labor lost; and we must wait patiently for the result of the present contest between hereditary and elective; between force and reason, people and king.

Where the millions of industrious producers have obtained all the power through elections by universal suffrage, as on this side of the Atlantic, it only requires the diffusion of useful knowledge through a free press, to reform all the abuses of both church and state, and to put all laws, rules and regulations, in unison with the interest of the majority; which is as great perfection as any association of men can arrive at.— Perhaps during the present generation, the thick crust of ignorance and prejudices with which society has been surrounded by an order of things emanating from divine hereditary right, may conceal and bury the truth under a load of sophistry, declamation and deception; but truth is unchangeable, and must in the end prevail. All those who, from fortuitous circumstances, govern society, and live on the produce of the labor of the industrious millions, oppose all improvement, and cry out changes are dangerous, "we may go further and fare worse," which is perfectly true as respects all those who live on the industry of others; but it is equally true that any change that would lessen the labor and increase the comforts of the working people would not be attended with any danger to them. Few either think or act according to the interest of others; and when any one declared such a thing to be good or bad, it may be taken for granted that he thinks it is good or bad for himself; though it may be the contrary to the interest of the great majority who surround him. This is tho origin and principal support of deception; the presumption of men arrogating their individual interest to be the interest of the whole society: where a civilization is so constituted that the interest of the poor opposes the interest of the rich; the interest of the producer is contrary to the interest of the consumer; the interest of the governors is opposed to the interest of the governed; and nothing but equality of property, knowledge and power, can reconcile, or in any way remedy those jarring interests. Whatever is to the advantage of the lawyer, priest or physician is almost as certainly to be injurious to the client, hearer or patient; for those trades being paid for rectifying something supposed to be disordered or wrong, the greater the evil the more pay. When a man in power accustomed to wield patronage, or his surrounding friends who benefit by it, objects to the reduction of that patronage, by diminishing the number of places, or giving the election of all officers to the people, they act strictly agreeably to their own interest, regardless of the interest of the millions whose labor maintains them; and who can blame them when the millions possessing all the power by universal suffrage permit them. When the rich proprietors shift the public burdens off their own shoulders on to the backs of the millions of industrious producers, by indirect taxation, who has any right to find fault with them; while the millions who have the power by universal suffrage, allow them. When the bank stock holders, directors, and all those to whom they furnish capital to carry on their business, intrigue and make it the interest of legislators to grant them exclusive charters, who can blame them, while the millions who produce all, and pay for all, hold the absolute power by universal suffrage, consent to it, by putting at the ballot boxes, such legislators in place.

Who can prevent shoemakers or any other tradesmen from charging a great price for an inferior article but their customers who employ and pay them, even where there is competition; but public officers, when once elected, are interested in preventing competition; having a common interest separate from their constituents. For one nation that is enslaved by foreign force, there are twenty that lose their freedom by the intrigues and stratagems of their rulers. If tyranny, oppression and despotism had not been the nature of man when unchecked by the slaves or subjects who suffer under it, we would not find such abuse of power, fill every page of history, containing little else but conquest, rapine, blooodshed and slaughter of the weak, by the strong, without the excuse of the beasts of prey, they are forced to kill others, that they may live themselves. It therefore ought to be the principal care of all those people who have escaped from tyranny, by the adoption of the elective system by universal suffrage, not to imitate any of the laws, rules and regulations invented to support divine hereditary right; but to sacrifice all other objects to the perpetueting of freedom; and one of the most effectual is the division of power by the rotation in office, which can only be accomplished by never putting the same man twice in place, thereby producing equality, without which liberty is but a name.

ARMIES RAISED BY CONSCRIPTION FAVORABLE TO FREEDOM. THE MILITARY ARE THE SUPPORTERS OF FREEDOM; THEIR INFLUENCE. DIFFUSION OF USEFUL KNOWLEDGE. FORCE OF PUBLIC OPINION. EFFORTS OF THE WORKING PEOPLE.

Feb. 7, 1835.

In the present rapid transition from despotism to some kind of freedom, it is rather singular that the same force which created and supported the tyranny of the few over the many, should so powerfully aid and assist the millions to relieve themselves from the oppression of church and state. When the exigencies of the French revolution required large armies to defend their liberties, without the means of buying or paying them, forced them to raise soldiers by conscription, and register all the youth in the military service of their country, (a measure imperiously demanded in all nations who have liberty to defend,) the despotic allied powers, coalesced against French freedom, seeing the facility with which the enthusiasm attached even to the semblance of freedom, recruited immense armies, adopted the raising their forces by conscription— forgetting that freedom and despotism are so opposite and contrary that what secures the one, annihilates the other; that in all associations of free men, all are interested in maintaining their freedom at all risks, and that the more they are armed and disciplined, the more secure are their liberties, and all the comfort and happiness inseparable from them; but in all absolute and despotic governments, there are only the despot, and the few whom his money can purchase, who are the friends of despotism; all the rest of the population who suffer, can only be kept under the yoke, by the force of mercenary soldiers. When conscription is substituted and a youth taken from every family, who is not a professed soldier, nor follows it as a trade, but expects to return to his family when his time of service is finished; and in the mean time by frequent intercourse is kept on a par with public opinion, which in the present diffusion of knowledge, is in favor of general freedom, what has happened might have been expected, that all the conscripts, when ordered to tyrannize over the people, by the command of their superior officers, should refuse and join their countrymen, thereby carrying the will and the wishes of the milllions into immediate execution, without any blood being shed. The only exceptions, are the Austrians in Italy, the Russians in Poland, and the Dutch in Belgium; all of whom are fighting against the liberties of foreign nations, against whom it was easy for their rulers to revive ancient prejudices and hatreds; but it still remains to be seen whether any of those troops would have fought against the liberties of their own country.

The military, who formerly were the tools made use of to reduce nations to slavery, have become, by civilization and the diffusion of knowledge, the friends and supporters of freedom. Even civil or foreign wars, which used to be the scourge of the human race, legalizing rapine, murder, plunder, and every species of cruelty and injustice, have become, by the diffusion of useful knowledge, the means of spreading useful information to the millions, both of the nation that invades, and the nation invaded. The mass of mankind are getting above the considering or treating a people as enemies, merely because their chiefs declare war against them. The interchange of useful knowledge is freely kept up between the invading army and the invaded people, by which both are benefited. Perhaps the French armies, in overrunning Europe, diffused more practical information, than all their political or diplomatic authors, consuming the advantages of arts, sciences, freedom, etc., and when they returned home they brought the fruits of their travels; so much so that when traveling in France, from the servant or hostler who took hold of the horses, one could know by his activity and dexterity, whether he had served or not in the armies.

A soldier in his relative situation, like all other classes, is entirely changed by the diffusion of useful knowledge; he is no longer that unthinking machine, moved by the command, and solely for the interest of his superiors; but has shown in most instances where he has been employed to suppress the rising of his countrymen against the tyranny of their rulers, both during and since the conscription of the French revolution, that he both thinks and acts for his own and the interest of the class to which he belongs. Force, like faith, ends where reason begins. In a barrack at the foot of the street where my house was, at Paris, the soldiers, some months before Bonaparte came from the island of Elba, drinking their wine, gave a toast to the health of Verte Violette, (the name the Emperor went by, indicating that he would return in the spring with the Violettes,) one of the officers passing demanded what they meant, and was answered, we see you are not in the secret: that changing of rulers, like the shifting of scenes in a theatre, shows how little dependence can be placed in force against public opinion which the late revolution has confirmed. Jews and gambling stock jobbers, are powerful aids to the aristocracy of the old world; and materially help the rising monied interest of the new. They live in extravagant luxury on the industry of the laborer, by the dividends on national debts, and are interested to crush all attempts at change in favor of the working millions, that would tend to diminish the ration of the idle consumers. National debts are their freehold estates, which fall in value on the commencement of all wars, more particularly revolutionary struggles. Their exertions are united to the existing governments to oppress the people and paralyze the enthusiasm of the late revolution, through the means of the hereditary executive the French have been so imprudent as to establish; which will be a constant drawback on their freedom, accounting for the seeming indifference of the French at the Austrians crushing freedom in Italy, and the Russians attempting to do the same in Poland: but the equality from which emanated the last revolution, supported by a million and a half of national guards, is still in existence to support freedom; and though the present executive may do all he can to disarm and change surrounding circumstances, yet public opinion will be too strong for him, and the force and discipline in favor of liberty will most probably regulate the political affairs of Europe.

In the free states on the southern part of our hemisphere, the military have been struggling against liberty and equality, ever since it had any existence under the theory of representation by universal suffrage: and though every attempt at military despotism has failed, yet there are frequent conspiracies in favor of some military chiefs, which end in teaching the soldiers, who are all of the laboring classes, their strength and influence, as well as the efficient force of their class, which will produce one of these days, a moral revolution, when the millions will claim their rights, as the election by universal suffrage, the theory of which is yet a dead letter in their constitutions, as it remained long in ours; but when once our working people succeed, in their claims of the practice of freedom and equality, it will not be long before it will travel south.

Knowledge, like most things of any value, is acquired by industry and application, the facilities afforded in the present state of civilization, to the millions of industrious producers, to obtain the useful knowledge of their own utility and real consequence to society, have already produced equality in France, and a great change in public opinion in Belgium, Poland, Britain, and a great part of Germany. The diffusion of useful knowledge will lessen the influence of the quackery of church and state, and leave public opinion free from their intrigues and stratagems, to follow the will and interest of the great majority; for public opinion is the only check and regulator of all governments, and the only difference is the facility, or danger of expressing it. Where freedom is guaranteed by a free press, and still freer election by universal suffrage, public opinion has the legitimate control of both church and state. Where all opinions are stifled, except the despot and his friends, public opinion is enchained in a dungeon, until it accumulates force to burst asunder its fetters, when the explosion destroys some good amongst the great mass of evil, and gives some appearance of reality to the great mass of fiction and falsehood so industriously propagated by the enemies of freedom. If the first ray of light that has been permitted to enter into the mysterious darkness of church and state, has already produced such astonishing effects, what may not be expected when the light of common sense and reason, shall by the wish and consent of the millions be reverberated through the darkest corners of the earth. If the experiment now making by our working people succeed, it will teach all who adopt our free institutions, not to lose half a century, as we have done, in disputing about mere theories; but to proceed immediately to practice all the advantages inherent in representation by universal suffrage; so that besides our own happiness, the destinies of nations depend on the result of our struggle between the aristocracy of the few, and the democracy of the many. A people governed by the few, educated in all the tricks and stratagems of power, cannot possess the advantages of self government any more than those ruled by hereditary right. Self government can only exist where the millions by universal suffrage elect those of their own class to rule over them.

STATISTICS OF CHURCH AND STATE.

Feb. 10, 1835.

In most of the political, or political economy discussions and calculations the richness of a public treasury seems to be taken for a criterion of the richness and wealth of the nation, whereas it can only be a proof of the proportion of the production of the industrious laborers, the government have found means to collect for the use of themselves and supporters. It is a criterion, which shows how much of the property of the industrious, the rulers of any people have been enabled to wrest from the hands of the laborers for the maintenance of the nonproducers and consumers; is a proof of the property they exact from the contributors, too often as an exaggerated pay for their services; but no criterion of national wealth, unless you suppose the impossibility of a nation of consumers. On the contrary, the poverty of the industrious millions ought to be in exact proportion to the quantity of the fruits of their labor they are forced to sacrifice for the support of the idle consumers. A society of masters and slaves, where slaves are fed with a few pecks of corn a week, and clothed with a suit of coarse cloth once a year, ought to afford a greater proportion of the produce of their labor to their masters; and all associations of men will approach to the situation of slaves in proportion to the quantity of the fruits of their labor consumed by the idle nonproducers. Let us examine how far the above theories are supported by the actual state of the different nations whose statistics are sufficiently detailed to throw light on the subject; premising that all statistics are arithmetical epitomes of the actual situation of public affairs, it has not been the interest of rulers who are afraid of the truth to make use of them; there is therefore few published, and still fewer that can be depended on.

We shall begin with Britain, long at the top of civilization in the old world, and where the art of taxation has been enabled to squeeze out of the producers the greatest possible quantity for the maintenance of the consumers. The British islands have been supposed to have a population of 17,000,000, and a revenue of 430,000,000 sterling, of which about eight millions of producers expend about 90,000,000, the remaining 340,000,000 are spent by the 9,000,000 of nonproducers, of whom, according to John Gray's statistics, 5,500,000 are useless members of society, spending 218,000,000 sterling; by which it would appear that the 8,000,000 of producers of the whole revenue are left only about one-fifth of their production for their own use. Church and state's share of the consumption of this immense revenue, produced by the labor of 8,000,000 of industrious people may be stated as follows, viz:

Taxation which passes by the general state's treasury yearly, may reckoned at 60,000,000 sterling
do. of the counties, districts, sea ports and inland towns, cannot be called less than 15 do.
Established church in England, Scotland and Ireland may be about 15 do.
Dissenters do. in do. do. 5

95
245 do.

340 do.

The remainder of the 340,000,000 sterling, 245,000,000, is spent by the rich and privileged orders, accumulated by ages of abuse of power, in every species of monopoly, litigious and expensive laws, by which the poor are sacrificed to the rich, etc.

By which it would appear that church and state cost every individual man, woman and child in the British islands twenty-five dollars, and if divided only amongst the millions of producers, would cost each of them fifty-five or sixty dollars; and if we divide the whole revenue expended by the classes of nonproducers and consumers, every one of the class of producers must labor to produce property to the amount of 210 dollars over and above what is necessary to support himself, for the support of such a great number of consumers, a great part of which is owing to the immense inequality of property, principally arising from an enormous national debt, the interest on which is paid by an indirect tax on consumption.

The statistics of no other country enables us to make a comparison of the different classes of society as in Britain.— The revenue of the French empire under Bonaparte, was 1,000,000,000 of francs, divided between 50,000,000 he then commanded, gives about four dollars per head. Under the Bourbons the revenue was augmented to about 1,200,000,000 of francs, which, divided amongst the population of 30,000,000 they govern, gives about eight dollars a head. The only information concerning the equality of property in France, may be taken from the list of contributors to the direct tax on real property, by which it appears there were 8,000,000 under twenty-one francs, 2,000,000 from 21 to 100 francs, half a million from 100 to 1,000 francs, and about 17,745 above 1000 francs; the tax on real property being about 25 per cent on the revenue, equality of property which never existed before in any civilized country; a different foundation for society, which must change the whole superstructure, civil, religious, military, political, commercial, and the relative situation of all classes; the laborers having so few consumers to maintain must relieve them from much toil and fatigue, and at the same time allow them more time to improve both their moral and physical faculties, rendering their situation more comfortable and happy than in those countries where the great number of consumers press so hard on the ease, convenience and enjoyment of the laboring producers.

Our own statistics are perhaps better authority than any other, because made under the control of an elective government of universal suffrage; though that attention is not paid to them which their facility of giving correct information of public affairs merit.

The revenue collected by indirect taxes on consumption
by the federation, amounts yearly to about ... $25,000,000
For the maintenance of the states, counties, townships,
sea ports and inland towns, etc. ... 25,000,000
For the expense of every sect of religion, Bible, missionaries societies and all belonging to the church, ... 20,000,000

$70,000,000

So that church and state costs the 12,000,000 of free people of our union nearly six dollars a head, man, woman and child; much of which expense is owing to the double employ of fiscal, judiciary and military officers in the United States, and the individual states which a rational, conciliating and economical federalism would save nearly half the expense to the Union, besides annihilating every cause of dispute or quarrel.

From the great inaccuracy of the statistics of most European nations, by the interest most rulers have in exaggerating the resources of their country, they can only be considered as an approximation, and none where more exaggeration is practiced than in Russia, who have found it a cheap mode of frightening the rest of Europe with their millions of revenue, inhabitants and soldiers. In 1816 the revenue of Russia has been stated at 132,000,000 of rubles; if in paper money it would scarce be worth, any time since, 50,000,000 of dollars; divided amongst the population, which has been stated at more than 50,000,000, the cost of the state would be one dollar a head; and suppose the church to be one half both church and state would only cost the slaves of Russia one dollar and a half a head, much cheaper than any other of the European nations; which can only be accounted for by the whole population being masters and slaves. The masters being all nobles, paying all the taxes, make use of their control over the autocrat to prevent the augmentation of taxes, and force the government to issue paper money for all internal expenditure, and to borrow money from foreign nations for external disbursements. This ought to be a lesson for all free people under representative systems by universal suffrage, to put all the burdens on the rich by direct taxes on property; that they might be interested in watching over the expenditure; for while the industrious producers pay all by indirect taxes on consumption, the wealthy are interested in augmenting the public expenses, as the more they spend the greater their share of the spoil.

Austria has been stated to have a revenue of $60,000,000; if you add $15,000,000 for the expense of all that belongs to religion, it will make $75,000,000, divided amongst 30,000,000 of inhabitants, church and state cost the inhabitants of the Austrian empire two dollars and a half per head.

Prussia has been stated to have 40,000,000 of dollars revenue; if you add $10,000,000 for the expense of all which belongs to the different sects of religion, makes $50,000,000 divided amongst 11,000,000 of a population, is about four dollars and a half a head, which church and state cost the people of Prussia.

Spain has been stated to have a revenue of $30,000,000; if you double it for all the legitimate and contraband expenses of the church, it and state cannot cost the people of Spain less than $60,000,000; divided amongst a population of 11,000,000, is five dollars and a half a head, the people in Spain pay for the benefits of civil and religious coercion.— The rest of Europe pay from three to five dollars a head for church and state. The late political changes make their statistics, never correct, still more uncertain.

Political economy has been so turned, twisted, drawn and beat, only to cover all defects and administer to the foibles, whims and caprices, and interest, both of governments and individuals who purchase such books, that it is difficult to find the original meaning; but perhaps it was only meant to extend the economy of a well regulated family to political associations; if so, to prevent waste and unnecessary expenditure, to provide the greatest quantity of comfort and happiness to all, with the least expenditure of toil and labor, and that all should furnish to the expense in proportion to their abilities, would appear to be some of the essentials in the economy of a well regulated family; but when we see such wasteful extravagance of the people's money, squeezed out of the fatiguing toil and labor of the millions, by indirect taxes on consumption, collected at a great expense both of money and patronage, demoralizing the people by a temptation to smuggle and break the laws. It may be called policy, but cannot be called economy; as it would be like a father burdening his young offspring with the expense of the household, without giving them time to improve their senses or cultivate their moral faculties.

BRITISH REFORMS.

Feb. 18, 1835.

Now that the British reform bill has passed into a law, it may be a fair object of speculation to endeavor to foresee what changes or reforms may most probably take place in the abuses of church and state, and the relative time and order in which they may probably occur, being one of the principal advantages individuals can gain by foresight, enabling them to avoid the injuries and losses, attending all changes. This reform strengthens the elective power, by bringing it about half a million of voters nearer to universal suffrage, and removing as much further from the interest and dominion of the hereditary, it is natural to conjecture that this addition to the elective power, and consequent diminution of hereditary will equally affect their interest, and cause a corresponding reform both in church and state; but which shall have the precedence, may not be so easily foreseen. The tithes, and other physical church abuses, bear hardest on the rich consuming classes, and if their interest prevails, these may be the first corrected. The taxes and other state abuses weigh principally on the class of industrious producers, and if their interest is consulted the reform will begin by equalizing taxation in proportion to property, that is, collecting the whole revenue by a direct tax on every species of income. In favor of this last, there is the imperious necessity of immediately relieving the enormous and insupportable burdens, that oppress the laboring classes, which most probably will give it the preference, as by a single law, changing indirect to direct taxation on every species of property, they would relieve the laborers; save nine-tenths of the expense of collecting, and, at the same time, put the burden on those who can bear it; and from the advantages they derive from government, being in proportion to their property protected, ought, by right and justice, to contribute to the maintenance of all authority, civil, religious and military, in exact ratio of the benefit, they receive from the exercise of these powers, without whose interference their property would avail them nothing.

In curtailing the amount of property expended in extravagant luxuries and useless pomp and show by the few rich and influential consumers, and in the same proportion increasing the comfort, convenience and happiness of the industrious many, there will be a great falling off in the demand for fine houses, furniture, clothes, equipages, jewelry, paintings, sculpture, etc., and all those who live by dealing in such articles, must suffer by their fall in value, as they do now in France, in consequence of the more equal division of property; but all this will be compensated by the additional quantity of the useful, that will be required to accommodate the millions, who will rise above poverty, misery and starvation, increasing the security for life and property, by decreasing the temptation to crime, with all the complicated systems of judges, lawyers, prisons, punishments, penitentiaries, etc., unnecessary, serving too often by their expensive corruption to increase the evil which they pretend to remedy.

As the basis of elective governments extends towards universal suffrage, and the interest of the millions of industrious producers prevails, reason, interest, and the instinct inherent in all animals, for self-preservation, will force them to adopt laws for their rule of conduct, which they can understand, and not be longer the dupes of a class of men, whose bread depends on the complicacy, intricacy, and chicanery of the laws, but to choose a plain, simple, and well defined code, which every one can read, understand, and carry about him, in his smallest pocket, such as the code of Napoleon, which has introduced into France a social order of equal justice, property and knowledge, equalizing the means of happiness over the whole population, and no doubt will produce the same happy effects in Holland, Belgium, and all other countries, that have the good sense to adopt it, and will be introduced into all countries where the diffusion of useful knowledge will enable them to follow their own interest, and judge of the true merits of such a code of laws, in spite of the sophistry of those, whose trade and profession has surrounded them with such circumstances as to oppose it, and attribute to it the very evils which it has in part reformed, because it has not had time to correct the whole. Ages are necessary to test all public improvements.

In judging of futurity, great caution is necessary to prevent our opinions of right and wrong from biassing our judgment, for these opinions are formed from circumstances, that may have no influence on the mass, we are forced to judge of. Our judgment of the future ought to be directed by the analogy of the present and the past, and the nearer the occurrences are to our own period, the more likely they are to be analogous and a truer representation of facts; freed from the fictions of ignorant antiquity; for instance, in judging of the consequences of revolutions, it would be safer to take the first French revolution than ours, and still better to take the second French revolution, or that of Belgium, as an example of what may be expected from future revolutions.

I endeavored to prove in a preceding essay, that the two powers, elective and hereditary, could not exist peaceably in the same political body, until the one had the complete control and direction of the other, and that the British government by the hereditary king and house of peers influencing the election of a majority of the Commons, made it a hereditary aristocracy, under the mask of a limited monarchy. Half a million of voters added to the elective power may make it independent of the hereditary; when a constant struggle for dominion will show the hocus pocus delusion of the famous checks and ballances, stripped of all its oratorical ornaments, that is, like all other ballances, the heavier scale makes the other kick the beam. The elective, legislating for the interest of their constituents, will encroach on the exclusive privileges of the hereditary, and the contest for superior power and pre-eminence will begin, the people will side with their representatives, that is, take their own side, when the consequences may be easily foreseen. The intrigues and stratagems of the exclusive framers of government have hitherto prevented this; practice making perfect, as in all the other useful arts, but the general diffusion of useful knowledge has thrown light into the dark caucuses of cunning politicians and exposed all their optical and mental deceptions.

For instance, the last and the greatest improvement that has yet been made in political associations may be divided into three kinds: first, what may be denominated simple, a league of nations for temporary defence or offence, as the Greek states, etc.: second, the federation by excellence, for defensive and arbitrative purposes, as the union of the Cantons of Switzerland, where the federative power is limited to foreign relations and arbitrating the disputes between the federative states; the total exclusion of all interference with the internal, fiscal, judiciary or military concerns of any of the cantons renders it cheap and economical, avoids every possible cause of dispute, (the Swiss federation having existed 500 years without any disagreement or quarrel) while at the same time it has united in the bonds of friendship and amity every species of government from simple unrepresented democracies to all kinds of hereditary aristocracies: third, what may be called compound or complex federations, because gubernative, having the power of interfering in the fiscal, judiciary and military operation of the federative states, as our federal constitution, and the Mexican which copied ours, exceedingly expensive, having the double charge of all fiscal, law, and military officers, liable to constant quarrels, and only capable of imperfectly uniting states of the same form of government. When our states gave their consent to our federal constitution, it was by a total ignorance of how it would work in practice, and no small deficiency in the knowledge of men and their ambitious love of power, prompting them to grasp it at all risks. The framers of the Mexican constitution mistaking the prosperity of our country to depend on the form when it was in spite of it, willingly adopted what would clothe their officers with arbitrary authority over tl e states, and lay the foundation of arbitrary control, approaching to centralism, in imitation of their former masters, (which has been more or less the end and aim of all the usurpers in the southern republics,) imposed still harder conditions which the states from ignorance consented to, but which has caused constant quarrels ever since.

In the federal union of central America the states have been more attentive to their interest, substituted a council of revision in place of a senate without the power of a veto, and have introduced more checks in favor of their own independence and that of their people, and it is more than probable that the federation of Buenos Ayres, Columbia, etc., will be still more perfect, limiting the federal powers so as to exclude extravagant expenses, cases of disputes, and facilitating the union of every species of government, one of the most valuable properties of federal governments, which may favor its adoption by the civilized world, and in time produce all the much to be wished for consequences of perpetual peace. As none of the industrious producers can possibly benefit by war even when they conquer, so soon as the diffusion of knowledge enables them to take the management of their own affairs, wars must cease.

INEQUALITY OF TAXATION.

Feb. 22, 1835.

Every species of indirect taxation only encourages smuggling, offers a bribe to the breach of the laws, increases deceit, fraud and perjury, tending to the utter demoralization of society, by enabling one part of the society to cheat and live at the expense of the rest. When our working classes obtain the majority in the councils of the nation, their numbers and utility entitle them to; to ease the laborers of the burdens of the greatest part of the public expenses, and equalize taxation, they must collect the revenue by direct tax on all kinds of property; and in that case, even by the old complicated federal compact, each state will have the option of collecting its own direct tax and paying it into the federal treasury in proportion to their population.— This the legislators would certainly do, if they acted for the millions of industrious producers, because it would be much easier for the states than for the United States to apportion the quantum of tax to the situation and circumstances of each individual, and the collection would be made by the same officers that collect the state tax, without any further expense or patronage, while it would relieve the people from the double expense of United States' officers to collect the revenue, and take from the federation that enormous patronage, the cause of all the disputes, broils, intrigues, vice and corruption at our elections of the federal executive.— Perhaps the fiscal interference with the states being taken away may render the double employ of the judiciary and military worse than unnecessary, and ease the people of that useless expense, by simplifying federation within the limits of utility.

In such an immense continent it is impossible to equalize taxation, either by direct or indirect taxes, through the medium of money. Those at 1000 miles from a market must always give three or four times more of the produce of their labor than those near to seaports, where the market is found. For instance, an article of common consumption pays a tax of $100 at New York or any of our seaports; before it can be transported to any of our western states, for example, Indiana, the expenses make it come to $120. To pay the $120, a farmer or a mechanic must labor for and produce 300 bushels of wheat at 33⅓ cents the bushel in Indiana, whereas the farmer, etc., near the seaport pays his tax of $100 with 100 bushels of wheat; that is, the farmer, etc., in the interior must sacrifice three or four times more of his time and labor to pay the tax than the farmer near the seaport, which is by paying in money he pays nearly four times more of his property than the citizen near to the market; a proposition so simple and plain that it only requires the knowledge of two and two make four to be convinced of it. Yet our political conjurers have so mixed up the value of the article with the tax as to confuse the intellect of ignorance, by making the shopkeeper the tax-gatherer; to make them believe they pay no tax; though they pay the tax with the merchant's and shopkeeper's profits added, which amounts at least to fifty per cent.

If the states collected their direct tax and paid in proportion to their population into the federal treasury in money, the same inequality would exist between the Atlantic and western states. Suppose the population of Maryland to be 400,000, and the proportion of federal expenses to be half a dollar per head, $200,000, and the population of Indiana to be nearly the same, and at half a dollar per head, $200,000; the farmers and working people of Indiana would be obliged to contribute towards the expense of the federal government with 600,000 bushels of wheat, the produce of their labor; but the farmers and working people of Maryland would pay the same with 200,000 bushels of wheat, that is, the farmers, etc., of Indiana would be taxed six dollars per head, while those of Maryland would only pay two dollars per head.—The same injustice and inequality by direct or indirect taxation, when exacted in money, takes place in all countries in proportion to their extent and distance from market; but the limited territory belonging to any of the European nations, whose example we have followed, makes it not so perceptible, and the greatest part of their indirect taxes falling on the industrious producers, to the benefit of the rich and influential, who are the governors, makes them indifferent about the equalization or justice of the taxation, for so small a portion falling on them in proportion to their wealth and abilities.

For a long time, perhaps ever since Adam Smith wrote his Wealth of Nations, labor has been supposed the most invariable scale to measure the value of all things by; but as that might be difficult to ascertain, a bushel of wheat, as one of the principal and most universal productions of labor might be taken, when each state might be taxed for the support of the federal government at so many thousand bushels of wheat in proportion to their population, said wheat to be valued at the average price of the state who paid it, and paid into the treasury in money. This would be the only fair, just and equal mode of taxation, but which could not be adopted under any species of indirect taxes. If any people possessing freedom mean to perpetuate liberty and equality, they must pay all the government expenses by direct taxation on every species of property and regulate the amount by the value of labor or its production, not by money which is liable to fluctuate and generally throws the heaviest burden on those least able to bear it; but by labor or the productions of labor which would save all the trouble of imperfectly adjusting the pay of political labor which is deranged at every fluctuation of the produce of labor either too much or too little. For instance, the salaries of the public officers were augmented, when wheat was three dollars per bushel, and have not been diminished now that wheat is at or under one dollar per bushel. If instead of dollars each had his pay in bushels of wheat, there would not have been the necessity of any change, as their salaries would fall or rise with the price of the productions of labor and consequently as the expense of living fluctuated.

If the power and prerogatives of the federal government were limited to the utility of protection from internal disputes or foreign aggression, as in Switzerland, their expenses would not exceed the expenditure of the smallest state in the Union. All the patronage and profitable salaries, the cause of all the bribery and corruption of federal elections would cease (except in case of war, an event almost impossible in the present state of general freedom and immense force of the union) no dispute by the collision of fiscal, judiciary or military could possibly take place; all temptation to smuggling, fraud or perjury would cease on the adoption of direct taxation, and what the people paid would go into the treasury without the deduction of merchants' and shop-keepers' profits.— The present system is a mongrel between federation and centralism, partaking of all the complicacy, faults and imperfections of both, without any of the advantages of either; as is evident by our own extravagance, disputes and broils, and still more by the quarrels of the southern states of this hemisphere, that have adopted our federal constitution.

All our institutions, fiscal, judiciary, political, naval and military, are copies of the tyrannical feudal practices, the origin of slavery in the old world, and at variance with, and contradictory to the simplicity and rationality of our elective system of universal suffrage, where the whole power is invested in the majority of the people, excluding every possibility of the millions obtaining more by any rising or revolution; of course all those civil, military, naval, political or religious places, pensions, power and perquisites (combinations necessary to the very existence of arbitrary power) are not only useless to the support of our liberty and equality, but injurious and destructive to our freedom, as the same means which have originated and perpetuated slavery in the old world may encourage and foster abject dependence and slavery in the new. The only elective systems by universal suffrage on the globe are on this side of the Atlantic; it is high time that we abandon the foundations of feudality and frame our institutions on the broad, solid and permanent basis of liberty and equality.

SYSTEMS OF RICARDO AND MALTHUS, ETC.

Feb. 26, 1835.

Political economy, as it is now reduced to a science, should rather be called the production and destruction of wealth.

The system advocated by Ricardo, Malthus, McCulloch, and others, is in favor of the interest of the land proprietors, priests and governors, that rents do not enter into the value of agricultural production; of course, the tithes, the rents of the church, and the taxes, the rent of the state, do not augment the price of agricultural produce, let them be ever so high; for according to these political economists, the wages of labor and profits of capital are the sole regulators of the value of agricultural produce; if so, what can be the cause why the price of agricultural produce is so much lower in the United States of America than in Europe, and though the wages of labor and the profits of capital, are so much higher; for the produce pays for the transporting across the Atlantic, while the wages of labor and profits of capital are, at least, double; but this is the difference between practice and theory.

Though politics have a great share in the consumption, not to say the waste of property, yet in all their treatises on political economy, there is not one hint at the most economical mode of managing or arranging public affairs entrusted to any kind of political association. They are all discussions on the relative value of profits, capital, supply, demand, etc., with which neither governments nor politicians have any necessary relation; and fortunate would it be for the people of all countries, if they had the good sense to prevent their rulers from interfering in the production or distribution of individual riches; but confining their duties to removing natural obstructions, and totally refraining from putting any artificial impediments in the way of the industrious producers, by the military, custom house officers, etc. No legislatures ever interfered with individual enterprise without doing mischief and counteracting the interest of the people, who, profiting or losing by the result of their affairs are the best judges of the means of success.

All the calculations of political economists are made on the supposition that the relative situations of the different classes of society will remain the same, but when the foundation of society is changed, as in the effects of the French revolution, and most probably must take place in every other, made by the industrious producers; when great part of the wealth which used to be expended by the luxurious few in pomp, splendor and pageantry, comes to be more equally divided among the millions who produced it, the practice of economy if not the theory, will be materially altered. The demand for articles of mere show and ornament will cease and the price diminish without being regulated by the cost of production.

There is not one of the present French population, who can afford to wear hundreds of thousands worth of diamonds or jewels for five hundred, who could afford it before the revolution, for one who can now afford to furnish his house with elegant, expensive furniture, and a library of highly ornamented books, there were perhaps one thousand before the revolution; there is not now one who can afford to buy costly paintings and statues, for five hundred before the revolution. The stock of all those articles that do not easily wear out or perish, hangs on the demand and depreciates the value without any reference to the cost of production. Articles that are subject to wear out or perish when the demand will not pay the cost of production, will cease to be made, and the manufactories must produce something to suit the market.— Not so with articles that wear long or do not perish; their accumulation weighs on the demand, and unless the great inequality of property interferes in some of the neighboring nations, as was the case after the French revolution, those articles must fall to little or no value to the ruin and loss of all those who deal in them.

Suppose the more universal diffusion of knowledge should produce a more equal division of property and power over the civilized world, and the accumulated wealth, which used to be spent by the luxurious few, was divided amongst the industrious many; all the theories of speculative subjects, made to suit the despotism of church and state, most probably must be changed and many of them scoured to be in unison with the practice of liberty and equality. The extravagant aristocratic wars, carried on at the expense, risk and oppression of the industrious millions, leaving them a legacy of immense national debts to perpetuate their distress and misery.— Should they, following their interest like those who contracted it, cancel this debt, as a burden imposed on them without their consent by their unauthorized predecessors, or even tax all kinds of property to pay the interest of it and other public expenses; it would make a great change in the relative situation of the different classes of society in most countries, more particularly in Britain, as it would bring into collision the monied aristocracy, who live on the dividends of the debt and the hereditary aristocracy, who draw their support from their lands and other sources, the result of which contest might be in favor of the millions, and liberty and equality, putting an end to all future borrowing, as ruinous to nations as to individuals.

Theories, in all associations of men, whether political, religious or commercial, have, as yet, been contradicted by their practice; for it is very easy to express disinterested, philanthropic, patriotic, etc., principles of action, but very difficult to perform, and impossible, when they come in collision with the selfish principle or the views we take of our own interest, all of which are less under the control of public opinion, in an aggregation of counsellors, legislators, commissioners, bank directors, etc., than exercised by an individual, or the division of responsibility leaves a very small share to each, one of the principal reasons why representatives ought to be directly responsible to their constituents for their conduct, and therefore, that the states should be divided into legislative and congressional districts, that each might know by whom he was represented, and not clubbed together in general, tickets, confusing the representation so that no one knows by whom he is represented, and rendering conventions and caucuses, unnecessary to form the ticket. Aristocracies seem always disposed to assemble in large bodies and to hunt in packs; while they take great pains to separate and isolate the millions they command. It may therefore be the interest of the people to combine and unite, separating and dividing power into small portions, that too much may not fall too heavy on any place or person.

Except the little which nature furnishes to agriculture, fisheries or mines, labor produces all other wealth or property, by the acknowledgement of all political economists, however they may differ in the meaning of the words to express the how and the when; yet the interest of the laborer is taken no more notice of, in any of their complicated discussions, than the interest of the horse, the ox, or the ass; all are considered on a par with machinery, how to make the most of them for the benefit of the consuming few, and the rulers of church and state; for whose interest, convenience and the new system, by which Ricardo and others have gained so much reputation, has been contrived; and according to which, neither rents, nor tithes, nor taxes, which are only the rents of church and state, as not being either the wages of labor or the profits of capital, do not enter into the value of agricultural produce, or increase its price; so that by these gentleman, land owners, priests or politicians may revel in luxuries without injuring or curtailing the ration of the laborer. Suppose five men cultivate a field, the produce of which pays their wages of labor and profits of capital; but there come other five men in the form of land proprietors, priests or government collectors, and by force, take from the five cultivators, wherewith to maintain themselves: it seems evident that either the produce of the field must increase or the wages of labor and profits of capital diminish; and suppose the produce of the field only sufficient, at the old price, to pay the labor and profits of five men, it must rise to be able to maintain ten.

Suppose two loaves of bread are produced on poor land and the other on rich, cost ten cents per loaf, paying wages of labor and profits of capital, and that the exaction of rent, tithes and taxes, makes the cost of each loaf increase to fifteen cents: it would appear that the loaves would not be produced unless they sold for five cents each, more, in consequence of the addition of rent, tithes, and taxes.

NATIONAL DEBTS.

March 5, 1835.

It is perhaps a sign of the times, that national debts have been pushed as far in Europe as the knowledge of the day will permit, when both monarchs and stock jobbers are afraid to increase them by going to war with one another, and can only afford the expense of hostilities against freedom, such as Austria against the freedom of Italy, Russia against the independence of Poland, and the Dutch agaist the freedom of Belgium; which is a game, they may most probably lose at, and cannot gain in the present diffusion of knowledge, when not only their subjects begin to claim their rights, but even their troops, on whom alone they can have any dependence, are reasoning on the justice and propriety of cutting the throats of their fellow citizens, merely because they wish to enjoy more of the fruits of their labor, by a little more freedom and independence. The lessons given by the two French, the Belgian, Saxon, Brunswick, etc., revolutions, where the changes were made solely by the union, valor and energy of the laboring millions, and where the troops sided with the people, are forgotten by the councils of diplomates with their protocols, conventions and treaties, etc. Even the experience of the congresses of the holy alliance, arbitrarily cutting up and dividing Europe, contrary to the will, disposition or the interest of the people; the greatest part of which unauthorized arrangements are already overturned, will, it is to be feared, be lost to the politicians, who direct the remaining absolute monarchies of the old world.

When our revolution equalized power by the elective system, bottomed on universal suffrage, more than half a century ago, which has ever since been equalizing property, and knowledge, it was evidently the commencement of a new era in the destinies of both church and state. When the contagion of freedom passed into France, though violently opposed by all the European aristocracies, the military movements during the vehement struggle spread the advantages and utility of freedom, over the surface of the civilized world, whilst the revolutionary circumstances, with the just, equal and impartial laws, which they enacted, established an equality of property in France such as never before existed in any civilized country; from which came the inseparable consequence, the equalization of knowledge, and which must be followed by the equalization of power: from all which fermenting materials sprung the late revolution, originating in, and maintained by the sole energy, courage and union of the millions of industrious producers, and which will, no doubt, be carried to its full accomplishment by the millions of national guards, who, though deprived of their political rights, and disfranchised by the late as well as the former charter, retain both the moral and physical power to do them justice in the adoption of some thing like elective government by universal suffrage, less than which will most probably not satisfy the French nation nor perhaps any of the political associations of Europe.

So great a change in the relative situation of the different classes of society must produce a total revolution in the social order; neither the diplomatic sophistry of cunning politicians, nor the deceptive and wiredrawn theories of artificial monopolies of property, knowledge and power, being necessary to the comfort and happiness of mankind, they must fail to have their wanted effects; they can not now find a theatre sufficiently obscure to disguise their farces, nor an audience so stupidly ignorant as to be imposed upon by their political creeds, or religious dogmas; quackery is exposed and unmasking; the millions have got a peep behind the scenes, and discovered who plays the puppets, which support the deceptions of both church and state.

Hereditary monarchs, and privileged nobility with all the stock jobbers, monied interest and rich have a dread of power being vested in the great majority for fear of their abolishing all monopolies, privileges, national debts, etc.; from which they reap no benefit, but are forced to pay all the profits and dividends, the immediate causes of the greatest part of their distresses and oppression. Judging by themselves, the rich expect the retaliation of the laborers by following their interest in economizing the produce of their toils, and curtailing all unnecessary expenditures of the people's money; and though no people have abused power as they have been abused by it, yet the aristocracy constantly accuse them of the intention of dividing property, agrarian laws, etc., a dangerous accusation, which may tempt the millions, when in power, to realize.— But the aristocracy of no country have been famous for foresight, and the present rulers of Europe are as far from foreseeing the consequences of their actions as any of their predecessors.

Exorbitant taxes, and the derangement of the government finances, have been the precursors of most revolutions. The European monarchs keep up large armies at an expense beyond their means, to support which they must exact heavier taxes, and to keep their subjects from rising against such heavy oppression, they must augment their military establishments, which requires an increase of taxation, and so alternately acting as cause and effect *ad infinitum;* leaving no resource to their subjects, in the present general diffusion of useful knowledge and information, but physical revolution, whereas, had they followed the march of intellect, and put their governments on a par with the knowledge of the day, the moral revolution would have been gentle, gradual, and peaceable, keeping pace with the universal spread of useful information, without either bloodshed or destruction, which in all physical revolutions must be in exact proportion to the strength of the opposing forces; the reason why the first revolution in France was so much more bloody and destructive than the last. Perhaps the present diplomatic intrigues to paralyze and circumscribe the effects of the enthusiasm in favor of liberty may only be the accumulation of human misery, by forcing every nation to resist hereditary and arbitrary power, with all their supporters, singly to the great destruction of life and property, instead of permitting the revolution to pervade all the nations that are prepared for it, by an overwhelming foreign force, which would nullify all opposition.

The millions in all countries are getting awake to their real interests as well as to the conviction of their moral and physical force, to put in practice whatever that interest may dictate for their ultimate advantage. They constitute the military of all nations, and when recruited by conscription, deeply imbued by the popular opinions; being a true representation of every family in the nation, more particularly in every family of the working classes; the rich and influential being exempt from military services under all governments but that of Bonaparte's; which impartiality was the chief cause of so much obloquy and opprobium that was thrown upon it. Armies recruited by conscription are not soldiers by profession, but look forward, after their time of service is finished, to a settlement amongst their relations, friends and neighbors, with whom they are in constant relation and corespondence; not like the former vagrants and vagabonds kidnapped, and collected into mercenary armies, who fought for their pay, having no hopes beyond it, no family to retire to, when they happened to be discharged, no resource but robbing and crime. Being at Lisbon when the soldiers were discharged, after the siege of Gibralter was broken up, the town and neighborhood were overrun with disbanded soldiers, and nothing but robberies, murders and assassinations every night for three weeks, until the government of the Queen encircled the country a few leagues from the town with troops, who progressed gradually to the centre of Lisbon, taking up all who could not give an account of themselves. About four or five hundred, who were all sent to the wooden fort at the mouth of the Tagus.— Notice was given that those who knew any of them might reclaim them. The rest, about three hundred, were banished to the coast of Africa; for the queen never put any criminal to death. Of the many hundred thousand conscript soldiers that were discharged in France under Napoleon, neither vice nor crime were augmented. So great a difference in the nature and attributes of soldiers, recruited by purchase or conscription, must make an immense difference in their mode of acting a theory which practice has fully confirmed by the most of the conscript soldiers refusing to obey their officers when ordered to fire on the people, and joining them; while the mercenaries have been in the habit of obeying their officers in butchering their fellow citizens. The rulers of absolute power, collecting and disciplining numerous armies of such thinking and reasoning materials, is no proof of their wisdom and prudence; for of all professions, the military, if once they begin to think, when congregated into great masses, have the most time, position and communion for reflection, while their constant change of place and traveling furnish them with materials for mental improvement.

KNOWLEDGE WILL SOON BE UNIVERSAL.

March 10, 1835.

Scholastic education has been hitherto considered to include useful knowledge, and perhaps when mankind were emerging from ignorant barbarism, the study of words might be of some use in counteracting the ferocity of actions; but now, since the general diffusion of knowledge and advance of civilization have put all classes nearer a par of correct information respecting their real interest, the sophistry of literature and the vague and undefined meaning of words must yield to the positive properties, utility and qualities of things and practice founded on a correct use of the senses. While knowledge was confined to the mysterious jargon of the learned professions, and all out of the bounds of their convents, colleges, etc., was darkness and isolated, brutal ignorance, the industrious millions, chained as slaves to the soil, bought and sold like the other domestic animals, it was only in colleges and schools, where men dared to make use of their senses, and even then it was only the sense of hearing to listen to their learned doctrines and metaphysical disquisitions. By the total want of roads or any mode of safe conveyance, mankind vegetate like a cabbage without the power of locomotion; in those barbarous days there were few books, and as few who could make use of them; property, knowledge and power were monopolized by the luxurious few and labor, toil and misery the fate of the industrious many; in those ancient days, so much regretted by modern tyrants, the little knowledge which might pervade the mass of ignorance, had no means of circulation, and the improvements of one age were lost to the next, each individual in a manner, beginning his own instruction by his experience which died with him as it does among our four footed neighbors. No wonder that such a great reverence for scholastic learning should be kept up as the only source of knowledge, by the influential interest of the learned profesions, whose pay and perquisites were in proportion to the crop of ignorance they could cultivate: one of the principal reasons why our schools, colleges, etc., under their special care and control have been until lately, copies of the dark ages of monkish superstition and bigotry, whipping into the memories of our youth a heterogeneous mass of Latin, Greek, etc., words, a great many of which have no prototype either on earth, or sea, or air, leaving the unpracticed judgment at a loss to distinguish between the real and ideal or imaginary. It is such a mass of ignorance, tyranny and folly that the present aristocratic politicians, priests and rulers look back for precedents to guide them in the difficult part, the present general diffusion of useful knowledge forces them to act.

It was our revolution which gave the first lesson to church and state, which taught the people to dispense with the divine right of kings, the hereditary privileges of nobility or the expensive protection of state religion. It was on this side of the Atlantic, where mankind dared first to proclaim their natural rights, and form a just and rational government on the broad basis of universal suffrage bottomed on liberty and equality. It was the people of the United States who first gave to the world the theory of self-government, and are now following it up with the practice; it was by their unprecedented and astonishingly rapid progress of population, prosperity and happiness that the world were first informed of the immense advantages attached to, and inseparable from a political association, framed by reason and bottomed on liberty and equality, where the interest and happiness of all were equally consulted and all possibility of a return to tyranny, oppression and injustice were annihilated by the guarantee of equality in universal suffrage.

A spark of liberty crossed the Atlantic and electrified the French nation, whose enthusiasm, stimulated by the opposition to priests and privileged orders, far exceeded any thing hitherto known, roused the rage and resentment of the coalesced aristocracy of Europe, and by repeated and combined attacks forced the revolutionary armies to spread their fame and heroism to the farthest corner of civilization. The sons of liberty scattered the flame of freedom, wherever they marched, to which the extinguisher of the holy alliance and the Bourbons only added fuel, until it exploded in France, Belgium, Poland, etc., and bids fair to neutralize the absolute monarchies of Europe with a small share of representation in spite of the Russian slaves and Austrian horders.

By the more general diffusion of knowledge and the greater equalization of property and power, one of its inseparable attendants the field of intellect is entirely changed and extended over the industrious millions, by the help of good roads, rail-roads, steam-boats, steam-carriages, etc., space and time are brought within the reach of every one's span, and there are now thousands who have the faculty facility and liberty of traveling for one that had either the power, property or permission to travel under the feudal despotism when men were bought and sold with the clod on which they were dropped. The physical and moral improvements are so disseminated through the population that a man cannot go twenty leagues from home without collecting as much useful information of agriculture and the useful arts and sciences as he could have gathered in traversing in the dark and barbarous ages, the most civilized quarter of the globe. The ingenuity of men has put mind into matter and taught inert substances to perform the operations of life, enlisting both nature and art to aid them in the accomplishment of their purposes, in the extension of their freedom and its inseparable attendants, peace, comfort and happiness.

Knowledge is not now confined within the prison walls of convents, colleges or schools, it circulates as freely as the elements under the canopy of heaven, follows every plough-share, and gives movement to every mechanical machine.—No longer shall the most precious time of our youth be wasted in pronouncing the antic sounds of dead languages, through which not an atom of information that can possibly be useful to the present era of civilization flows; the dark, intricate and incomprehensible labyrinth of theology and metaphysics will cease to torment mankind and poison the enjoyment of the present by the inexplicable, superstitious priestcraft of the future, which is as far beyond the utmost stretch of any of our faculties, as it is beyond the grasp of any of our senses.

When mankind shall no longer sacrifice the gratification, pleasure and enjoyment of the present to the phantoms of the future; when the real, solid and useful knowledge of things and the exact sciences are substituted for the vague and undefined meaning of words and their literary arrangement; every production of nature and art will be the never failing source of instruction, and the limits of the school only be bounded by the geographical extent of the globe; with the education of the five senses, as the only medium through which ideas can come, and the culture of the visible and tangible faculties, under whose guidance he that travels farthest will learn most. Practice will consolidate and smooth the road of rational theory, in place of the old school theories of imagination, mounting into the clouds of fancy as far beyond practice as beyond reality.

The physical pleasure will be elevated nearer to the moral enjoyments, and morals, now dragged into the mysterious clouds of religious hypocrisy by their incomprehensible dogmas and selfish doctrines, will descend into the sphere of utility and common sense. The immense change that has taken place in the state of society in France by the unprecedented equality, effected by the revolutionary circumstances and laws during the short period of its existence, may, perhaps, warrant an expectation that instruction will not require any formal schools or schoolmasters, or any of their coercive trammels, which deaden exertion and subjugate natural independence, fitting men for parasites and slaves, but that the parents will train their children in the correct use of their senses, teaching them to read and write; the practical knowledge of men and things they will acquire (as all were forced to learn after coming from school) as their wants require them, by mixing in the social circle, rendered instructive by the interest of all. The equalization of property, knowledge and power, annihilating that artificial state of one class living at the expense of another, tempting to every species of vice and injustice. Those murderers of the most precious gift, time, cards, dice and every kind of gambling will be banished from society, and useful and instructive information take their place; when every one will have credit, consideration and respect in proportion to the merit and utility of his conversation. Our halls and rooms, in place of their walls being uselessly occupied with insignificant pictures and artificial ornaments, whose monotony does not resuscitate one idea, might be covered with exact representations of every thing useful to mankind, from which correct figures might be transferred into the minds of the observers without the trouble of figuring vague descriptions; and all this would be less wonderful than predicting steamboats and carriages fifty years ago.

EDUCATION IN PRUSSIA AND FRANCE.

March 14, 1835.

Scholastic education, as it has been and is still practiced, is by no means the criterion of common sense or useful knowledge; it is too metaphysically theoretical to descend from the stilts of absolute learning into the region of practical utility; and all nations that have been taught elementary instruction for nearly the last century, remain in a state of barbarous military despotism, while their neighbors, two thirds of whom can neither read nor write, by their energy and exertion in their practical struggles, have obtained freedom.

Compare the scholastic learning and feudal despotism of Prussia, with the deficiency of elementary instruction and with the state of freedom in France: it forms an anomaly difficult to be accounted for otherwise than by admitting that the discipline of the schools, teaches people to suffer despotism patiently. In the twelve millions of inhabitants in Prussia, in 1826 there were four and a half millions of children below fourteen years at school, being 366 children to every 1000 inhabitants, or 11–30 of the whole population. In the Prussian dominions, there are 20,887 elementary schools, and 736 schools for more advanced scholars, employing 22,362 schoolmasters, and 704 school mistresses and 2054 assistants; yet during the violent struggles for freedom, and notwithstanding the light that was spread by the two French revolutions, not one exertion was made towards emancipation from that worst of feudal tyranny by the Prussian people, nor by any other of the German nations, though nearly equal in regard to scholastic learning.

In France, of 283,822 conscripts enrolled in 1827, 157,510 could neither read nor write; 13,791 could not write; leaving only 100,000, or only one third who could read and write. By estimations made in France, two thirds of the population were destitute of elementary instruction. Of the thirty-two millions of inhabitants, of whom ten and a half millions are children, from six to fifteen years of age, of which five and a fourth millions are boys, only one and a fourth millions receive any scholastic learning: yet, though deprived of the theories of this scholastic learning the practice of good sense and useful knowledge has burst out in two revolutions, which have emancipated them from the despotism of feudal tyranny, established such laws, and originated such equality, as completely to secure their future freedom. Even those fag-ends of civilization, Spain and Italy, have made several struggles for freedom, the last of which was crushed by the learned German soldiers. A nation that has not the good practical sense of emancipating themselves from slavery, must be considered as ignorant, let their theoretical learning be ever so great.

It is more than probable that the discipline of the old school whipped out of the youth all their natural independence and both physical and moral courage, eight or ten years of tame submission to the dictates of a master, the reason or utility of which they were never taught, transferred from him to the arbitrary order of magistrates and police officers, docile and timid, accustomed to coercion; having acted so long on the motive of fear, they were unable to resuscitate any other, and nothing but long practice of danger can re-establish part of that instinctive courage, which men, as well as all other animals receive from nature for the purpose of self-preservation, and of which they are in a great measure deprived by the tyranny of civilization. Fear is first introduced by the nurse, reiterated by the parents, augmented by schoolmasters, enforced by the magistrate, and mischievously propagated through all the stages of life, by the priest, by his horror of hell, and the torments of the devil, so that from the cradle to the grave, fear is the principal motive of action. Fear is the lever of despotism, the food and support on which the existence of tyranny and oppression depends, is carefully cultivated and propagated by both church and state as one of the most efficient means of submitting their subjects to their extortions and oppression. For that purpose they preach up the contagion of the yellow fever, the cholera morbus, etc., well convinced by the experience of all countries, that if they can saturate any people with the debilitating effect of fear, they can bind them with a straw. Examine all the tricks, schemes and intrigues of civil and religious rulers, you will find fear to be the foundation on which their power and dominion depend.

Fear being one of the principal materials of subjection, those who live by subjugating others to their will and pleasure, by being nourished and supported on the produce of others' labor, and direct interest in increasing their ration of the good things they consume, must be expected, on the selfish principle to sow their seed on the richest and most productive soil, that the harvest may be in proportion. They can scarcely be blamed for seizing, in conjunction with the priest, upon the plastic mind of youth, before reason or rationality has had time to form the intellect, and imprinting on it their dogmas and doctrines, which essential part of the organization of slavery, the state, in most countries, has intrusted to the church, who have made the most of it, to support their usurped authority over christendom, from the well disciplined Jesuits, to the latest and most insignificant protestant sectarians, nor can they be blamed for working at the manufactory, they have been taught to live by, but only those who purchase and encourage their fabrications. The universal prevalence of priestcraft is one of the greatest drawbacks on all scholastic learning and almost counterballances the small quantity of utility gained by it. Fear, which so powerfully favors priestcraft and kingcraft, is very often the child of ignorance, which has induced both church and state to propagate, extend and diffuse their noxious, enfeebling and slavish effects on the mass of mankind, increasing the misery, wretchedness, and crime, that so long desolated the earth.

All these miseries, murders, and countless other mischiefs, which torment humanity, are principally owing to the machinations of the cunning few, combining, ruling, legislating, etc., to the dictates of their interest, which is contrary to the interest of the ignorant many, who are their dupes by not trusting to the evidence of their own senses, but believing in the fables and historic deceptions, fabricated for the purpose of physical and moral slavery. The education of the senses ought to be the foundation of instruction, as the only channel, through which truth can penetrate, and the only one left to judge of the value, utility or necessity of surrounding objects.

All who live by delusions and deceptions dread the evidence of their senses, and the conjuror, who, with his hocus pocus, professes to cheat the senses, is the least dangerous of the gang. The physical deceptions, practiced by most trades and manufactures are more hurtful to society. But the moral frauds and deceits, by the abuse of words, are far more injurious to the peace, comfort and happiness of the species, than any cheats on the accuracy of any of our five senses, because the most of their sophistry begins by pretending they draw their proofs from a higher tribunal, out of the reach of our senses, supernatural, incomprehensible, shifting, varying, and changing with the caprice, fancy and interest of the propagators, confined principally to the wordy wisdom of the learned professions.

Our working people are gaining strength at the ballot boxes slowly but surely, and must finish by a majority that will carry every thing in the state legislatures and federal congress, agreeably to the dictates of their interest. The next is to find out what changes in the old aristocratic arrangements their real interest requires. Of all reforms, the most essential is a reform in the system of education; but if the framing and modelling of the system of public instruction is left with the wordywise, whose whole stock in trade is sounds, modified into words, the greatest part of which are vague, undefined and undefinable, the millions will be dreadfully disappointed, and find, after all their exertions, the very foundation of their well being has no greater consistency or solidity than air.— To avoid this, they must teach by things and their representations. After the education of the senses, practice all of them on mechanism, as the mechanic arts will instil mind into matter for the use of men, followed up with natural history, chemistry applied to the arts, arithmetic and mathematics, where every sound can be fixed to its substance, and every idea imprinted permanently on the mind. Morals, on the general interest, is best taught by familiar intercourse with a state of society as near equality as possible; and religion, concerning which we are all equally ignorant, (fortunately it only interests the individual) may be left to his own reason and reflection, when time and experience have matured his intellect so as to guide him in the dark path, into which no other can throw any light.

The comparison of the learning of most of the German nations with that of our states of Pennsylvania, New Jersey, etc., where there are many men who can neither read nor write, would make a still greater contrast, with the religious and political freedom and liberality of our country, and show how little scholastic learning has to do with the essentials of the freedom, comfort and happiness of the millions. It only requires the answer to a simple question: What interest can a priest, lawyer, or any other of the consumers, of the produce of the industrious producers have in the diffusion of useful knowledge? They who live on the crop of ignorance cannot be expected to diminish their ration, by enabling the producers to retain a greater proportion of the results of their labor; yet it has always been to such classes of society that the improvident millions have entrusted the sacred right of instruction of themselves and children. The consequence, in no country, has belied, what must generally be expected, that they are taught ignorance, prejudices, superstition and bigotry in place of useful knowledge in all countries, where the millions have not the common sense to manage their own affairs, which, it is to be hoped, the result of our working people's exertions will fully prove. When any one intrusts an agent with his affairs, it is positively necessary to have the guarantee of some kind of interest personal, respect of character, reputation or pecuniary advantages, to be gained by a faithful discharge of his trust; but trusting representatives or agents, who in faithfully executing their duty, curtail their authority, patronage, portion, pay or perquisites, would be like expecting those who live and trade on bank discounts, to abolish bank monopolies.

CENTRALISM.

March 19, 1835.

Centralism is the form of government which excites and stimulates the exorbitant love of power and ambition of the hero and the few; federalism is the form which equally divides and diffuses comfort and happiness to the many. Centralism converges power to a focus, which, like the thunderbolt, scorches and hurls to destruction all opposition to its despotic and ambitious designs; like the sun, impartially vivifying and fructifying with its mild and moderate light and heat all nature and her works; centralism is a foaming and raging torrent, breaking through all bounds, and carrying devastation in its rapid course to all the works both of nature and of art; federalism is a gentle and benign shower which scatters its refreshing influence, equalizing its benefits to all human industry and every region of nature: centralism is the high road to despotism; federalism the guarantee of freedom.

There is a mongrel between federalism and centralism with many of the defects of both and few of the advantages of either, which the politicians on this side of the Atlantic are very much in favor of, perhaps as being as near an approach to hereditary power as the knowledge of the millions would tolerate. It is the cause of a rivalry between the real power and prerogatives of the federative states and the ideal dominion of federation, bottomed by sufferance on said substantial territorial foundation of the individual states. It bribes to complicacy, intricacy, etc., in the fiscal judiciary and military only to increase the patronage which feeds and maintains the troops that fight the battles of party at the ballot boxes; and if suffered to go on increasing with our population, must certainly end in broils and bloodshed at every election.

The only country where federalism and centralism have been in competition is the southern end of this hemisphere, where they have been in collision less or more in all the free states of South America, ever since their emancipation from their Spanish masters gave them the theory of a freedom, few of them were prepared to practice; who have been blundering on more by chance than by good guiding between the ambitious usurpations of their military chiefs and the influence of surrounding circumstances. These civil wars and more uncivil political disputes have thrown more light on the different characteristics of the two political systems of federalism and centralism than could properly be expected from such awkward and inexperienced political pupils, where all classes are equally ignorant of the rights and duties of freedom, having from the long habits of slavery nothing better to copy than the despotism of foreign tyrants, into whose vicious tracks all the military usurpers have been well disposed to follow, supported by the physical force of armed mercenaries, as is clearly evinced by centralism being always maintained and enforced by the bayonets of the military chiefs in Buenos Ayres, Columbia, central America, Mexico, etc., as the most direct road to the despotism of the one or the few; while federalism only arose out of the force of circumstances which divided the colonies into provinces enjoying small portions of power, which they were unwilling to relinquish, (the same as originated our federation,) by which it would appear that federalism in all countries originated in the junction of fortuitous circumstances, previously organized for contrary purposes, and adopted by the rulers of the people without foreseeing its effects. Centralism unites power into an active mass, to be hurled like a thunderbolt on all who resist their despotism, while it affords the means of completely separating and dividing the objects of their tyranny, and prevents all communication of opinions, by obstructing the circulation of useful knowledge; while federalism unites the people in one common interest, and separates, divides and scatters power so as totally to prevent its combining against the interest of the great mass of producers, reducing all the operations of government to simple utility, within the limits of the complete inspection and understanding of the whole people who have an interest in preventing inequality and usurpation of power, opposing a strong barrier to all innovation, except in favor of the millions.

Our federation approaching to centralism, by allowing an interference with the federative states; doubles the fiscal, judiciary and military expenses, raises a competition between the two sovereigns, which shall grasp the greatest share of power, complicates the political machine, while it weakens all its energies by the force lost in contention for pre-eminence, occasions a jar as in mechanism, deranges the uniformity of action, which paralyzes great part of the force and utility of union.

By the Mexican union and other governments of South America adopting our federal constitution, its faults and imperfections are exhibited in a strong point of view by the constant disputes and quarrels between the states and United States. The *imperium in imperio*, or two main-springs to the watch, have acted with more energy and less caution than our cunning politician shave allowed in the trial with us.

The states of Mexico bore with some patience the fiscal interference, while the tax on foreign importations satisfied the extravagance of the federation; but when they came to exact more, they resisted, and their judicial and political interference with their elections was tolerated, until they attempted to enforce their constructive explanations of the vague and undefined constitution by the armed mercenaries, when general resistance has been the consequence, and a change or dissolution of the federation may be the probable effects; though the influence of the rulers and ignorance of the ruled may defer the improvement a little longer; for who can expect the half barbarous inhabitants of the south to rectify faults which have been hidden from our enlightened citizens for the last half century.

Federation is an ideal authority, founded solely on the consent and interest of the federative states, without any property, territory or material existence beyond the good will of those who made it, which must depend on the utility derived from the union. The oldest and first were the cantons of Switzerland, which is as yet the most perfect, constituting a council of arbitration, to prevent wars and bloodshed between the cantons, by settling amicably their disputes and holding out to foreign nations a consolidated political body, in which confidence can be placed. So far the utility and economy of a federation in saving expenditure and answering every purpose, is fully proved in the existence of the union of Switzerland without any dispute for the last 500 years. But when the federal power assumes the right of interfering in the internal regulations of the states by fiscal, judicial or military associations, they arrogate the rights which only belong to the proprietors of the soil, and for which their distance and ignorance of the nature of the locality render them unfit, subjecting them to the faults and imperfections of centralism by attempting to regulate the fiscal or judiciary concerns of an extensive territory, which, however suitable it may be for some part of the union, is almost certain to contradict the interest of others under a different climate, productions and circumstances; such infringement on the rights and independence of any sovereign states, without in the smallest degree facilitating intercourse with foreign nations, and rather increasing than diminishing the risk of quarrels and disputes between the states, overlaying them with an extra dose of coercion at a double expense, complicating the political machine so as to increase the friction, render an additional quantity of the oil of influence and patronage necessary to keep it in motion, are so many drawbacks on the freedom and independence of the millions, without an atom of advantage except to those who are well paid for keeping in order so complicated and undefined a system, which is liable to be deranged in proportion to the quantum of useful knowledge diffused amongst the millions.

All kinds of despotism, tyrannies, monarchies, aristocracies, etc. have had their advocates and their pages re-echoed through the false and flattering pages of history, where the heroic deeds of physical force shine forth with a brilliancy which throws into the shade both utility and morality; even democracy has had its share of commendation and obloquy; but federalism, the friend of the millions, is but a child of yesterday, and the people, for whose comfort and happiness all its energies are constantly exercised, have not yet been rich enough to fee either authors or orators to explain or even to take notice of its extraordinary merits: whilst the politicians of the old school, who live by the complicated abuse and wasteful extravagance and corruption of arbitrary systems, have treated it, as they do every improvement that infringes on their absolute power, with contemptuous silence and scorn, agreeably to the selfish nature of man, and inherent in all animals, self-preservation, dictated by both instinct and reason as far as it has yet gone, though disguised under a thousand forms; while the millions either from indolence, ignorance or any other cause, are unable to do any thing for themselves. To expect those who benefit by their incapacity, to sacrifice their perquisites pelf or plunder to the public good, is to expect a reversion of all the laws of nature, the sun to rise in the West, or water to run up hill.

EXPERIMENTS IN GOVERNMENTS.

March 23, 1835.

No sufficient reason can be given, why the framing and mending of governments and all political associations, should not be subject to the old adage, "practice makes perfect," as well as all other works or inventions of mankind, and why the hitherto mysterious arts and contrivances, on which depend the authority and influence of church and state should not change, improve and be put on a par with the knowledge of the day; yet in spite of the field of experiment being monopolized by the few well born, who have an interest in retaining abuses, and fortifying their hereditary or usurped power by all the combinations, and stratagems, their physical or moral superiority can afford them, notwithstanding all those obstructions and bars to the march of mind, the advance of freedom, in favor of the millions has been uniform though slow, and the checks and limits opposed to the arbitrary power of the rulers has been commensurate (as it must always be) to the diffusion of useful knowledge amongst the ruled, by the adoption of representation, federation, written constitutions, etc., which by degrees instructs the people of their interest, and renders them capable of managing their own affairs.

In the old world, the first check to despotism was the undefined British constitution, which, though granting a small portion of liberty, induced a spirit of enterprise, energy, and individual exertion, which placed them in the scale of nations far above what either their population or territory entitled them to; since which freedom, refined and filtered through the United States of America, generated federalism, one of the greatest improvements in political associations, reverberating to Europe, resuscitated the French revolution, which commenced on the broad basis of representation by universal suffrage, by the simple unity of one legislative power (which has not been yet improved upon) but adopted by the limited monarchy of Spain in the Cortes, and deteriorated through a great number of changes by the different constitutions under the elective system, approaching nearer the hereditary power, until it was swallowed up by the gigantic strides of an extensive empire, when acres and the brute matter of the soil were represented in place of men. During this retrograde deterioration of the representative system, the principal actor had influence to establish limited monarchies in Bavaria, Wurtemburg, Baden, Westphalia, the north of Italy, etc., and sowed the seeds of freedom, that will fructify and produce comfort and happiness to the millions in proportion as they are prepared to receive the benefits of liberty by the diffusion of useful knowledge. After this commencement of the amelioration of the condition of humanity, a sweeping gust of kingcraft and priestcraft attempted to re-establish despotism by parcelling out Europe to such as they thought capable of producing slavery which brought on the second French revolution, followed by that of Belgium, Poland, Dresden, Brunswick, etc.; nor can it be expected from the great equality of property and knowledge in France that the people can be satisfied with any thing less than what they began with in 1789, that is an elective government by universal suffrage, in spite of the intrigues, plots and stratagems, of their newly elected hereditary king, aided by all his brother sovereigns to confine the right of suffrage of thirty two millions of people to about 100,000. The parliamentary reform of Britain is perhaps a still greater sign of the improvement of the age by bringing the suffrage half a million nearer to universal, the goal to which all representation tends, the consequence of such an addition to representative power in such a high state of civilization is difficult to foresee. All the above mentioned radical changes and revolutions in favor of the equality, morality, justice, honesty, comfort and happiness of the millions have taken place in the last forty years, and who will be hardy enough to deny that the like beneficial changes may take place, and perhaps, still greater ones, during the next forty years? Which is a convincing proof that even in the old world, where the accumulating evils of many centuries by divine hereditary rights and consequent despotic power, have degraded and enslaved the population; but even there, "practice makes perfect," in the institutions of church and state as in all the other operations of humanity, and that the last political association formed, like the last steam engine or spinning mill, will be the most perfect.

When we cross the American side of the Atlantic, we come on a new field of experiment far from the obstruction of the ancient rubbish of divine hereditary right, privileged orders, etc., where the union of church and state has been, in some measure dissolved, and each trades on his own capital. Before and during the revolution of the United States of America, only one of the states had universal suffrage; all the others were a representation of dollars and cents in place of men; Vermont was the first state formed after the revolution, on an improved constitution, and only one legislature, avoiding all risk of collision, since which all the new western states have adopted universal suffrage, and even the "ancient dominion," where slavery roots the animal to the soil, and reduces the rights of men to fifty acres of land, even they have thrown off some of their ancient prejudices and reformed their colonial constitution. The states of New York, Connecticut, and some others have changed the feudal custom of attaching power to property, and have adopted universal suffrage; so far, "practice makes perfect" in politics as in mechanics, and he would be a bold presumer, who would assert that the operations of church and state are to continue in the mire of barbarism many centuries behind all the other arts and sciences.

A most extensive field was opened to political experiment on the emancipation of the Spanish colonies in South America, including a greater surface and population than ever before were favored with liberty and independence, and where the gradual from vague theories of liberty towards real practice can be traced and accurately delineated by the graduated improvement in the proportion to the diffusion of useful knowledge.—

Emerging from the most degrading physical and moral slavery, with the ignorance inseparable from the state of bondage, they so far improved on the principles of their northern neighbors as to annihilate personal slavery. With only a glimpse of the theory of liberty they spent all their rage on the forgers of their chains, the Spaniards, in place of freeing themselves from the shackles, which the military instruments of their emancipation dexterously contrived to keep on them, subjecting them to nearly the same military tyranny, they had in theory thrown off with the foreign yoke. During the first periods of their prolonged revolution, they passed from under the tyranny of a military usurper to be under the despotism of another stronger and more fortunate. Satisfied with the exaggerated and pompous sounds of liberty, vociferated in the declamatory speeches of their demagogues they remained ignorant of any of the advantages of practical freedom.

The first approach towards order and stability was by the adoption of our federal constitution by the Mexican states and followed by Central America, who united the Spanish colonial provinces of that quarter into a federal union, which still continues in spite of the violent intrigues and ambitious rebellions of the military chieftains, to establish centralism as the stepping stone to despotism. Columbia, Peru, Buenos Ayres and Chili, under the dominion of centralism, maintained and supported by the military force of mercenary armies against the propensity of the different states to establish federalism, remained in a state of anarchy, confusion and civil war which at last seem to have exhausted the patience, stimulated the indolence and apathy, while it diminished the gross ignorance of the population, and paved the way to a more rational and a better order of things. Columbia and Buenos Ayres seem disposed to settle down under a federalism, and though political freedom has not advanced much in these southern states, yet moral emancipation from the tyrannic superstition of priestcraft seems to progress in the ratio of the distance from Mexico, that sink of corruption and principal seat of

Spanish political and religious prejudices, which may, perhaps, be the last part of the country, where civilization and toleration are allowed to take root.

But the greatest proof of "practice making perfect," is in the last constitution proposed for Brazil, wherein a limited monarchy is to be changed into what they call a federative monarchy, by powers given to the legislators by their constituents, to change the present constitution under the following restrictions and regulations. Each of the ten provinces to have a legislature and executive, to make their own laws and govern themselves, united under a federation, having a legislature elected every two years, the executive of which only have moderative powers to cause any law to be re-examined, and if it passes by a majority the second time, to become a law without his consent.— The council of state suppressed, each municipality to have an intendant invested with the same powers as the president of the provinces; taxes for the expenses of the general government to be fixed by the general assembly, those for each province by the legislature; during the minority of the emperor, the realm to be governed by a regent or viceregent, elected by the provincial assemblies, and verified by the national assembly. This is perhaps the greatest peaceable change that has ever taken place in any political association. May not the restrictions on the executive arise from the framers having no chance of wielding the hereditary power? It marks the present progress of improvement and guaranties the future.

HEREDITARY LEGISLATION.

March 27, 1835.

Legislation may be divided into two kinds: positive legislation, where there is a necessity for the protection of the persons and properties of individuals against violence or injustice, and speculative legislation, which may include every interference with the individual management, "which injures no one," either by encouraging what the legislators may think useful or prohibiting what they may think prejudicial to what has been called public good, which, if it mean any thing, ought to be the good of the individuals who constitute the society, who are better judges of their own affairs than any species of legislators can possibly be; though as yet rulers and legislators have been the public for whose benefit the laws have been made. For the last kind of legislation utility has been the general plea, but useful to whom? has been a question that has not been yet satisfactorily solved.

Law makers cannot be expected to make laws contrary to their own interest; whether they have been equally careful of the interest of others let the history of the world explain. There has been a violent rage of legislation, from the barbarous and contradictory ukases of the Russian autocrat through all the grades of civilization up to the elective legislators of the United States, and the number and variety seem to increase with the civilization and freedom, the people have conquered, as a counterbalancing weight thrown into the scale against liberty, to prevent the millions being too independent and happy; so that they have only broken the chains of despotism to have the shackles of complicated and intricate laws riveted on them, which requires a lifetime to understand, and they leave the world before they learn how to steer their course legally through it.

Hereditary legislators by divine right are entirely beyond the comprehension of those who have only their five senses to guide and direct them; ("for we can only reason from what we know.") Acquiring their rights and privileges from such a mysterious and omnipotent source, most of them act as if the lives and properties of their subjects did belong to them and that all within their reach was fore-ordained for their sole use and benefit. Leaving all these mysterious incomprehensibilities to those who suppose they understand them, we shall confine speculative observations to such legislators as those on this side of the Atlantic, where liberty and equality is the measure of all power inherent in the whole population, and only delegated for one or two years to certain individuals to be exercised for the benefit of and agreeably to the interest of the majority of those who by universal suffrage entrusted them with the temporary agency, and invested them with a moderative power over the property of their constituents for a limited time, beyond which they have no right to legislate without encroaching on the rights of their successors, which ought to be left entire without any diminution of the legitimate inheritance of the whole population and their heirs forever.

A legislature so constituted for the limited period of one or two years, having no property, can have nothing to sell, (perhaps our unappropriated lands may be thought an exception, but even these belong to the people and ought to be administered for their benefit, by giving a certain proportion to every one who will engage to cultivate them, as the British government does,) and if possible, still less to give away, all being the property of all, no sectional part have the right of alienating any, much less the right of granting to the few what is denied to the many. The principles and foundation of our free government, liberty and equality, prohibit all exclusive privileges, such as bank and all other charters, all corporations for trade or otherwise, limiting the responsibility, whilst no bounds are set to the contraction of debts, an advantage denied to simple co-partnerships, all distinction of property, making one siezable for debt and the other not, all advantages granted to a part, which is denied to the rest;

besides all the foregoing partialities to favorites being prohibited by the nature and fundamental principles of our free institutions, it is certainly an assumption of power for one temporary legislature to bind their successors by granting favors to their friends beyond the period of their existence in power; for if they have a right to legislate beyond the period of their brief authority one year, they have the same right for 100 or 1000 years, and if they have a right to grant the exclusive privilege to banks to stamp paper money or bank notes, they have the same right to grant exclusive privileges or monopolies to shoe-makers, hatters, or any other manufactories; so that the first legislature elected for one year would forestall all the authority granted by the people to their representatives for an indefinite time, and render representation a mere mockery.

National debts are a late contrivance, (unknown to the ancients,) which give governments a facility of appropriating the produce of the labor of the industrious, without their perceiving it. It may be a query whether any generation under any form of government have a right to mortgage the labor of posterity for expenses incurred, of which the present reap the whole benefit; but is certainly more doubtful whether legislatures elected for one or two years have the right of burdening the labor of posterity with the payment of what they choose to expend in forwarding what they may suppose their interest. It is a profligacy both in an individual and a nation to exceed their income, which ought not to be encouraged at the expense of the toil and labor of the industrious producers. Certainly posterity has seldom complied with the contract made for them by their ancestors without their consent, but it is a fund by the payment of the interest which enables the consumers to live at the expense of the producers, and gives property without labor, deranging that equality without which freedom is but a name, and ought not to be permitted in a political association bottomed on liberty and equality.

The vague and undefined public good is the excuse for all speculative legislation and expenditure without specifying what classes of the population go under the appellation of public. Wars are the common origin of national debts, and who benefit by them? Certainly not those who toil and fight, whose situation is made more miserable, from the beggarly clientele, who grace the train of a Roman conqueror and partician, through all the gradation of ages, down to the poverty-struck laborer and manufacturer of Britain, whose misery and wretchedness is commensurate with the extent of their conquest. The pillage and plunder of the conquered is divided and shared by the few, which enables them by the assistance of standing armies to enslave the many, bribing a part to subject the whole. This state of things is the nourishment, life and vigor of arbitrary power which can only exist on the poverty and ignorance of their subjects, but ought to be avoided by all free people like the plague or despotism to which it is the direct road.

There are some adages or sayings, both political and religious, propagated for the support of church and state, which by dint of repetition have got the value of axioms, though contradicted by the experience of the world in both ancient and modern history. One of the most common and most fallacious is, "to secure peace you must be prepared for war;" that is, to enjoy health, you must collect the materials for disease. What nation on earth was better prepared for war than the Romans? Yet from the beginning of Rome to Augustus, more than 700 years, the token of peace, the temple of Janus was only twice shut. Britain has acted on that principle, and has been engaged in wars sixty or seventy years during the last one hundred. Switzerland, the only representative government of the old world, and the only one that has no standing army, of course not prepared for war, has had peace almost five hundred years, it has enjoyed the elective system. To be prepared for war is to be burdened with the greatest part of the evils and expenses of it, and never to have complete peace. Our rulers, following the path of old mother Britain, without the necessity, have been building a fleet to transport us to the seat of war; as it is not probable that ever the seat of war will be transported to our continent. We have been at great expense fortifying our sea ports, as if there was any risk of their ever being attacked; but there is great risk of their mouldering down and of the fleet rotting before they can be of any use. During the last war, the only two places seriously attacked, were both without fortifications and defended principally by the militia who repulsed the enemy. Freedom does not require fortifications to defend it against the attacks of arbitrary power, and no free people who value their freedom will fight with another. A speculative legislation, to encourage one thing and prohibit another, does more harm than good in all political systems, but is most injurious in all political associations founded on liberty and equality, where too much cannot be left to the good sense of the citizens.

THE INTEREST OF THE PRODUCERS AND CONSUMERS OPPOSITE AND CONTRARY.

March 30, 1835.

Selfishness, as it effects the conduct of men in power, as the rulers of church and state, above all responsibility or retaliation, is greatly different from that of individuals, whose conduct, besides being responsible to the laws, are liable to the loss of character, as well as retaliation for actions out of the reach of the laws. Those privileged by power, can, with impunity indulge in vices, which fear of loss of character, reputation and pecuniary interest, would restrain private individuals from committing. I have endeavored to prove in a former essay, that the apparent interest of the governed and governors, slaves and their owners, servants and masters, producers and consumers, poor and rich, buyers and sellers, are opposite and contrary; and that hitherto the governors, slave owners, masters, consumers, rich and buyers, have had all histories, book makers, lawyers, etc., as their advocates, and the governed, slaves, servants, producers, poor, etc., have been disabled from taking their own parts, or feeing the learned to plead their cause; in consequence, all the sophistry, declamation, rhetoric, eloquence and twisting of words, have been practiced to endeavor to prove that all the actions of the rulers of church and state, were bottomed on patriotism, philanthropy, charity, and the pure love of others; that their education and superior rank gave them honor, glory, etc., as motives of all their actions; though being elevated above responsibility or retaliation, (the principal check to inordinate selfishness) they are tempted to exercise the most unjust, violent and cruel passions towards those who happen to offend them; to sacrifice the life, liberty, property and happiness of their fellow men, to their exorbitant caprice and ambition, as is proven by the partial page of history, though written to excuse their vices and crimes, under the mask of public good.—Those who could not extend their selfishness so far, endeavored to prove that their interest was the interest of all; that the interest of the many who toil and labor, paid and produced all the taxes, was the same as the few who received and consumed all; that the interest of a lawyer who lived by the fees for disputes, quarrels, and too often for fomenting them, was the same as his client, who suffered and paid them. Even books on the exact sciences, are made full of technical complicacy, and so profound as to be out of the reach of common education, and frighten the most useful classes from attempting to study them. The pedagogues of schoolmasters chaining down a child on a stool five or six years to learn the mechanical part of reading, [for that is all the old school teaches,] which might be taught in as many weeks. All has been arranged to keep knowledge out of the reach of the millions, pinched for time and money, and to facilitate the monopoly of property, knowledge and power, in possession of the few influential rich.

The experience of all ages and countries oppose and contradict the claims of the few hereditary rich and powerful, either to utility or superior merit; almost all the improvements, physical or moral, of civilization, have sprung from the middling or poorer classes of society. The most of the ingenious contrivances, that have forwarded the arts and sciences to the perfection they have arrived at, have been the fruit of the labor and industry of the millions. Had the improvements of mankind been left to the interest, genius, and talent of the rulers of church and state, the world would still have been in a state of barbarism and brutal ignorance, occupied with wars, bloodshed, and slaughter, and peopled with tyrants and slaves. Every thing, as yet, has been made for the benefit of the makers, from revolutions, laws, creeds and catechisms, down to a pair of shoes, the soles of which are so narrow as not to cover above half of the tread of the foot, and grinds out the upper leather on the soil, so as to require three pairs of shoes, when one, properly made for the interest of the wearer, would suffice.

The propensity to arbitrary rule is evinced in the conduct of almost all the executive officers, who are in any degree united in power, and under the control of the representatives of the people, as in the instance of king Philip, making and ratifying a treaty with the United States, without the consent of the deputies of the people, whose confirmation, by a law, was necessary to pay the stipulated money, which they refused, and if not passed, must annul the treaty. The like had almost have happened to President Washington, with the British treaty of commerce, which he signed and ratified, by and with the advice of the senate, and when a law was proposed to Congress to put it in execution, there was a majority against it, and had not two of the opposition walked out of the House before the question was taken, the treaty would have been thrown out in the face of Washington. The same may happen in all the governments where the people, by representation, have a portion of the power; and only proves that representation is so new a privilege given to the people, that its power and control is not yet understood, and that the executives of most countries, act as if absolute, and if we declare war, it cannot be because the treaty is not fulfilled, but on the justness of our claims for retribution.

Nothing can so completely prove that the interest of the producers and consumers, the governed and the governors, the poor and the rich, are opposite and contrary, than the present state of all the civilized governments of the world; that the artificial intrigues, sophistry, and deception of the few rulers of church and state, have yet subjected and enslaved the brutal ignorance of the many: and that even the hereditary part of the French government, in spite of the severe punishment the last of their kings have received for their despotism, seems to trust to the Holy Alliance, with Russia at their head, to maintain their despotic rule, in which it is more than possible the British king joins in obedience to his German relations. Aristocracy seems so far behind the knowledge of the day, as "to have learned nothing nor forgot nothing:" stuck fast in the mire of their ancient and Gothic feudality; they are blind to the immense progress, physical and moral, made by the millions during the last half century. Public opinion is rapidly forming agreeably to the interest of the millions, and the velocity of communication by steam boats and rail roads almost annihilates space and time, and brings all classes of every nation into union and combination, to support their mutual interest, an advantage formerly belonging exclusively to the rulers of church and state. This state of things has brought on a crisis between the few, who have yet governed, and the many, who are subject to their usurpations; a quarrel which threatens to produce civil war and bloodshed, which the ignorance of the millions of their interest, and the cunning of the few rulers of church and state, have only prevented for past centuries by keeping them divided, and preventing all union and combination, so long as the intrigues, artifices and cunning of the rulers could monopolize property, knowledge, and power; the present state of mankind must remain as a consequence of discord from the nature of our species.

A man has only impartially to analyze the motives of his own actions and observe those of others, to be convinced that all mankind must be actuated by some one of the thousand motives self-interest puts on, and the smallest candid investigation of the conduct of the rulers of church and state, either by his own observation or the page of history, that their construction of their own interest was opposed and contradictory to the interest of those they ruled, to be convinced of the reason and cause of all injustice, wars, cruelty, tyranny and despotism inflicted on humanity, and that while the cause remains, no temporary change can remedy the effects; for instance, while our federation has a right, by the constitution, to interfere with the fiscal, military and judiciary of the federative states, ten thousand laws and regulations cannot prevent collision: and while the taxes are raised by indirect taxation on consumption, as many tariffs would not prevent the burden of all wars; extravagance, speculation and plunder falling on the industrious producing millions. No regulation can prevent every species of monopoly from producing and augmenting the unnatural inequality of property, knowledge and power. The most refined fiscal laws cannot hinder all commercial restrictions and every obstruction placed to the free circulation of property and knowedge from being injurious to the millions, and an unjust encroachment on their comfort, happiness and freedom. No pretensions for aggressive wars can indemnify the millions for the loss of their blood and treasure. It would seem as yet that the few rulers and consumers were on one end of the balance, and the industrious millions on the other; as the one went down the other went up; and that the cunning privileged orders have had the address to adopt the Roman balance, like the Roman laws, with the long arm in their favor. Every artifice which deranges equality, equally injures freedom and happiness.— The freedom which men have yet been permited to enjoy in the old world, has produced a humiliating and insufferable inequality; witness Holland and Britain. But all proportions of equality must produce a corresponding degree of freedom.

It would appear that a government, such as ours, of representation by universal suffrage, could easily and expeditiously remedy any or all of the foregoing evils, by the power of the millions at the ballot boxes; but long habit and custom have so leagued a certain proportion of the middle classes in the benefits arising from the servility of the poorer, that the opposition to radical reform is both strong and conducted with all that energy and acumen which distinguishes the class, but must in the end submit to the general diffusion of useful knowledge and the force of numbers; when the plans proposed by the working classes of universal instruction, etc., must produce that equality of property, knowledge and power, which will bestow on our species the comfort, happiness and freedom they are at present capable of enjoying. In hereditary governments of privileged or ders, the line of distinction between them and all other classes is so broad and strongly marked that it leaves the most of the talent and genius of the middle classes on the side of the millions, giving mental abilities to the direction of physical force, and must have quickly succeeded but for the interference of foreign despotism, the only hindrance to the success of the French, Spanish and Italian revolutions, and the tyranny which now keeps down the revolutions of the German states.

MARCH OF UNIVERSAL FREEDOM.

April, 5, 1835.

It may appear rather surprising that the whole civilized world has lately, as by mutual agreement, burst out into violent attempts to reform the abuses of church and state; and yet, if we coolly consider the immense improvements in all the arts, sciences and occupations of mankind, while the clumsy machinery of politics and religion has been in some countries getting worse, more absurd and contrary to the interest of the millions, and in all stationary for at least three thousand years, one is astonished that in the midst of such melioration of all other materials of civilizations, those two essentials of human comfort and happiness should be permitted to remain in a state of savage barbarity, and that beings, by a proper use of their senses capable of such vast progress in all the other useful and necessary occupations of life, should have left the ancient rubbish of church and state, the accumulation of many thousand years, to obstruct and oppose all the attempts of reason and rationality, to equalize and diffuse property, knowledge and power for the well-being of the whole; stopping from the rich the care, anxiety and disease engendered by superfluities, to furnish health and happiness in the positive necessaries to the poor. How too such essentials to human happiness, compared to which all others are of secondary consideration, should have so long escaped the penetrating eye of interest, is most astonishing, and does more credit to the hocus pocus legerdemain of priests and politicians than to the boasted wisdom of our species; and when the equality of property, knowledge and power shall have taught the millions to trust only to their senses, all the histories of many hundred thousand beings cutting one another's throats to please the pampered fancy of a luxurious fool, will be considered as works of pure imagination, like the Arabian Nights' Entertainments.

After the example of what freedom and independence, guarantied by representation, elected by universal suffrage, has done for the United States of America in the short period of half a century, a few colonies scattered over an extensive surface, subject to the laws, commerce and interest of the mother country, with a population of about three millions, has risen by the fascinating charm of freedom to an unprecedented pitch of power, prosperity, wealth and independence, with a population of fifteen millions of active and independent citizens, whose surplus produce for exportation is nearly three times as much as that of the Russian empire, with a population of fifty-three millions; whose inventions in navigation and the arts waft them with the celerity of steam over the surface of the globe; whose improvements in the arts, sciences and mechanism place them at the top of civilization; where there are more rail-roads and canals constructed and constructing than on all the surface of the old world, with their hundred millions of population; where the church is divorced from the state, each trading on its own capital, and where no one is obliged to pay for any religion, but pays his priest as he does his grocer for what he requires. Is it astonishing that so great an improvement in social order, such an accumulation of power and prosperity in so short a time should attract the attention, stimulate the hopes and excite the wishes of the millions of all other nations to make the experiment; is it surprising, when the weakness and wickedness of slavery is contrasted with the force and energy of freedom, when the pusilanimity, ignorance and baseness of slavery is compared with the courage, wisdom and dignity of freedom, when the snail paced movement of a slave, coerced to work for his master, is compared with the free-will exertion of a freeman, who reaps the fruits of his labor, whose utility puts him on a par with those around him in a state of society bottomed on freedom and equality, that not only the industrious producers should strain every nerve, make every possible exertion, every sacrifice to obtain freedom, but even the wealthy consumers, if they knew their own interest, ought to wish for as much equality as would neutralize the temptation to crime and violence, as would restore peace, satisfaction and good will amongst mankind; which is turned into constant quarrels and disputes between the rich and poor, between the abundance of superfluous luxuries and starvation, between the humiliating dependence of weakness and the arrogance of power, and the only rational cure for these evils which equally torment both producers and consumers is a moderate degree of equality, by abolishing all privileges, rendering justice easy, cheap and impartial by a simple and well defined code that all could read and understand, and every one carry in his or her smallest pocket as a rule of conduct. The Greeks, the only nation of antiquity who had the smallest pretensions to liberty, though stained and depreciated by domestic slavery, had a temporary custom of making some of the first orators plead for the poor gratis; against which avarice and influence were constantly pleading for the rich; but with all their faults, their laws were infinitely more in favor of the poor than the barbarous Roman laws, so much extolled and imitated by our modern aristocracy.

Universal freedom, which can only be maintained by universal suffrage, is a new plant only introduced yesterday, and though watered with blood from the violent opposition of the privileged orders, has not had a fair trial from those entrusted with its culture, having an interest directly opposed to the public good. The force of circumstances that during our revolution had reduced the society nearly on a par of property and knowledge, naturally led to the like division of power, the origin of universal suffrage.

It may perhaps be a query, if it had not been adopted during the enthusiasm of the revolution, if the world would yet know the immense advantages of universal suffrage, so much opposition has it since met from the different aristocratic parties that have been since hatched amongst us.

No equality of property, knowledge or power, that has ye existed has rendered rights of property more insecure; nothing but the absolute will and despotism of the few has left the property of the many without protection, yet the thousand tongues and pens of the many thousand hirelings are ready at the smallest appearance of liberty and equality, to vociferate anarchy, disorder, plunder, agrarianism, violence and injustice, stigmatizing every step towards freedom with the most opprobrious terms that the imps of tyranny and despotism could invent through a long chain of history from the earliest ages, during which, freedom has not had a place to put her foot, and they have almost finished by convincing humanity that despotism and slavery are the natural and unavoidable state of mankind.

Under such a mass of misrepresentation and obloquy, thrown on freedom by the minions of both church and state it is not surprising that all the fruits of freedom should be considered forbidden fruit by all classes, and that the dogmas of the church should prevail, that misery and slavery here should be necessary to secure freedom and happiness hereafter; from all such gross misrepresentations and deceptions of those who have enjoyed their own share of freedom, as well as those who have unfortunately been subjected to their arbitrary will, it was to be expected that freedom and equality are less known than any other circumstances attending humanity, and that even now the world is ignorant of ninety-nine hundredths of the immense advantages that mankind may derive from the improved and improving practice of liberty and equality, as yet confined to speculative theories.

By a just, universal and impartial law of inheritance, the French are placed in that dignified and commanding attitude, which nothing but universal equality can bestow; from which mass, of accumulated experience prudence and force will radiate the principles of liberty and equality, which will in time pervade the civilized world; though at present the violent opposition of the privileged orders has sown such a confusion of contradiction, such a thick fog of mysterious delusion, as may require another revolution to clear away; but as that positive equality of property and knowledge, on which base was bottomed the last revolution, is by the operation of laws, habits and customs daily increasing, the power of enforcing any change the interest of the millions may dictate to them, is constantly increasing, while the opposition is daily diminishing by the deaths of the old, so that the last may not be the only by many, and each succeeding one will be more mild and moderate in proportion to the weakness of opposition.

The holy alliance, by uniting all the sovereigns, who have no better title to absolute power than divine hereditary right, may in the end teach their subjects, serfs or slaves to claim the same mysterious, incomprehensible authority for uniting to defend their natural and inalienable rights of person and property. This occult, inconceivable pretension, on which has been founded the power and privileges of both church and state, is a mere assumption without the likeness of any visible or tangible title, entirely ideal and imaginary, having no resemblance or connection with any thing in air, seas or earth, to the gift of which all classes of society have an equal right to claim for the protection of their persons and property. Can any man have a right to dispose of the person of another without his consent? And suppose a thing almost impossible, this age is willing to become slaves, have they the smallest right to sell the liberties of the next? All hereditary power over the person must be usurpation, supported alone by the combination of physical force.

Property of all kinds may naturally be supposed to have no right inherent in itself, though the chicane of legislators to favor lawyers, has endeavored to complicate justice by artificial privileges granted to certain property possessed by the ruling few. Property is now generally considered the produce of labor, and must originally be in possession of those who work; as it is still, where men approach nearest to the state of nature; but, civilization, as far as it has yet gone, has found out many innovations to transfer said property from the industrious producers into the hands of the consuming and unproductive classes, amongst whom the greatest monopolizers of the produce of labor are church and state, both of whom have been in the habit of exacting an arbitrary share, without justifying their claims, or satisfactorily proving that they give value received or full compensation to the producers. Their pay and perquisites have been fixed by themselves by laws and regulations made for their own interest, who alone have had the valuing of their services. Let the page of history and the present poverty, misery and wretchedness of the producers in all civilized countries testify to the inadequate returns made by the consuming to the producing classes. The church, through their agents, the priests, pretend to give you an inheritance in that imaginary, unknown country beyond the grave, of which they know nothing but by the tradition of priests, who live by the craft like themselves; make you pay for being your pilots on a road one step of which neither they nor any one else have ever traveled. Priestcraft endeavors to attach its incomprehensible dogmas in union with morals, on purpose to have a claim on the consideration of mankind for the benefits which morality bestows on man, established for the interest of society and no ways dependent on the imaginary dogmas of any religion; though the priests of all religions have siezed on morals to give currency and the appearance of utility to their dogmas.

The morality of all religions is good, and as conducive to the happiness of mankind as the mysterious incomprehensible dogmas are the cause of wars, bloodshed, cruelty and crime. The persecutions and cruelties of one christian sect against another have caused the slaughter and destruction of more millions than all other wars waged since Christianity began; although diametrically opposed to all the principles and doctrines of that morality which priestcraft has so long and so industriously endeavored to graft and make common cause in copartnership with their incomprehensible dogmas. All sects and systems of religion both ancient and modern acknowledge the great necessity and utility of morals, but differ, dispute, fight and persecute one another in defence of the exclusive truth of their dogmas. What an immense dexterity of art, intrigue and stratagem must have been employed to make mankind believe that there was the smallest connection between two things so opposite in their practical effects as morals and dogmas, for the support and conviction of which producers in all christian countries are heavily taxed to keep up universities, colleges, etc., and to teach theological sophistry to keep up the deception and delusion.

The state have some grounds for their pretensions to utility, as the good or bad they do are cognizable and might be within the reach of the evidence of the senses of all; but crafty politicians have had the address so to disguise the truth as to make private profit appear as public good, and the exertions of the millions subservient to their individual interest. That the art and mystery of government has been so improved as to be in favor of the superior orders by maintaining them in luxury and extravagance at the expense of the laborers, may be easily proven by the impartial analysis of all political associations as yet formed, but it may be queried, whether the extra labor necessary to maintain the expenses of the increased quantity of consumers does not counterbalance any small proportion of comfort and happiness the dextrous management of church and state has permitted the millions to enjoy. This account has not been accurately kept, from its not being the interest of the one nor the capacity of the other to register correctly the facts.

The arts of civilization have enabled those who labor least to consume most; that is, the class who by their labor produce all, enjoy but a small proportion of the property they furnish; those who work only with their heads pretend that they contrive the means of producing, though the greatest part of useful inventions has been made by those accustomed to labor. Let all the wise men of the east and west study to eternity, unless they put their hand to work, they will produce nothing or change a single atom of matter into a more useful or agreeable form. The monopolizers of church and state have had the address to make the laborers pay for the endowment of universities, colleges, etc., to enable their children by their superior knowledge to rule and keep in subjection the industrious millions. Knowledge is power, which has induced both church and state to prevent the diffusion of it amongst their subjects or the millions of producers; who are by the enormity of taxes, tithes, etc., kept expending all their vital powers in manipular action for the bare necessaries of life, leaving no time for mental improvement or intellectual culture, kept poor and ignorant by the moral superiority of the few at the expense of the many, through the means of colleges, etc.

Trace the origin of hereditary power or the inequality of property and it will be found bottomed on conquest, plunder and pillage, for did every one enjoy peaceably the fruits of his labor, equality and independence must be the consequences. Wealth accumulated by the industry, abilities and economy of the father is dissipated by the extravagance, ignorance and indolence of the children, if not secured to them at the expense of the public, by unjust laws of entail, etc. By which it would appear that injustice, violence and combination of physical force are the only means that can perpetuate great inequality of property, knowledge and power. The siezing by force of the property of the weakest is the origin of the wealth and power of nineteen-twentieths of the kings, emperors, etc., which the christian potentates in imitation of the Jews have called divine right. What but the divine right of the sword forced the millions to unite and form the Russian, Austrian, Prussian, etc., powers? And what but the division of the plunder amongst the favorites of the hereditary chiefs formed and endowed the privileged orders in Europe principally given as rewards for flattering the foibles, appetites and vices of their hereditary rulers.

The ignorance consequent on the poverty of the millions disabling them from governing themselves has been the excuse given for all absolute power and despotism; but since the United States of America by their unprecedented prosperity (though but indifferently governed by lawyers and other burdensome consumers,) have lighted up a beacon that will direct all nations to the haven of happiness: such sophistical reasoning must cease to have any influence.

OSTENTATION OF LEARNING.

April 10, 1835.

In former times, whilst hereditary divine right ruled the world with despotic sway, whilst the despot, or a few privileged orders usurped all property, knowledge and power, leaving nothing to the industrious many but poverty, misery, ignorance, and wretchedness in those barbarous ages of despotism, the consequence of ignorance, the conduct of both church and state was regulated and controlled by whim, caprice, passion, etc., always contrary to the interest of the millions, and not unfrequently opposed to the interest of the whole society. When all power is concentrated in one hereditary despot, who, by the nature of his vicious education, encrusted with flattery and adulation, never hearing truth or making a correct use of his senses to acquire useful knowledge, must inherit weakness of body and imbecility of mind, subject to be governed by the vicious minions, who administrate to his passions, appetites and vices, the destinies of a nation, the comfort and happiness of the millions depend on the whims, caprices, and appetites or passions of a depraved kept mistress. When the usurpation of power is in the hands of the few privileged orders, the tyranny of the many is often more cruel and insupportable, acting as a body with the united abilities of the whole, their conduct is more comformable to their own interest and more regardless of that of others; their individual passions and prejudices are moderated by a sense of the general interest.

In all such governments, by divine right there is a mysterious uncertainty in their conduct as well as in the origin of their power. Under the control of individual ambition, whim, caprice and passion, it is almost impossible to foresee how they will act in any given circumstances, and the operations of both church and state are enveloped in impenetrable darkness; not being actuated by any fixed principles, but by the passions of the moment, it is difficult to conjecture what they will do in any emergency, or to foresee the crooked path their folly may force them into.

Since the more general adoption of the elective system has brought the interest of the millions more or less to be followed by both church and state as a rule of conduct, the whole foundation of the social order has changed and is changing every day more and more; bottomed on the fixed and invariable principles of the universal interest of mankind once ascertained, there is a rule to form a tolerable prediction of the consequences. The real and positive interest of the majority of our species being much the same, it only requires a knowledge of the means, by which they can enjoy the greatest quantum of peace, comfort and happiness, with the sacrifice of the smallest share of toil, labor and privations.

Britain, by possessing a small proportion of representation, has acquired a superiority over the other nations of Europe equal to at least double her population. The United States of America, by improving on the elective principle, and establishing all power to emanate from free, equal and independent rights, by universal suffrage, have got an increase of population, prosperity, riches and power, unprecedented in the annals of mankind. France, though deprived of most of the benefits of a free representation, by the despotic tyranny of their neighbors, has yet, by her attempt to establish a free and equal representation by universal suffrage, elevated herself in the scale of nations, and been enabled to conquer and temporarily to subjugate a great part of her enemies, spreading the principles and doctrines of freedom and independence over Europe. During the violent opposition of the combined allies to the principles of the French revolution, and in spite of a strong coalesced military force for the support of absolute governments, Bavaria, Wurtemberg, Baden, Spain, part of Italy and Germany adopted limited monarchies, with elective legislatures, and though some of them, on the subjection of France to the arbitrary rule of the Bourbons, have been reduced to their former slavery, yet the strong and violent efforts made by all nations to enjoy the incalculable benefit of the elective system, particularly those who had before experienced any of its advantages, are a convincing proof that mankind are beginning to appreciate their freedom and independence, as well as learning how successfully to claim their inalienable and natural rights, and if we are to calculate their future progress by the last half century, we must conclude that before another half revolves, all the political associations of the civilized world will be more or less elective, and the natural rights of mankind confirmed and secured by the equalization of property, knowledge, and power.

Foresight is the most useful and valuable of all sights to all classes, particularly to those who have no agency in the invention or formation of causes which produce and control events; but are subject to all the inconvenience, trouble and losses arising from the sudden changes in the state of society. The immense change in the social order that has taken place since the revolution of the United States of America, and is still proceeding in a geometrical progression to place the pyramid of the social order on its base in place of tottering on its apex, as it has done from all antiquity, will be the cause of a vast change in the relative situation of both men and things, the reducing all to a par of natural equality, by abolishing all the exclusive prerogatives, which alone support and maintain the power and superiority of all the privileged orders, must occasion a relative change in the demand and consequently in the value of all the articles of luxury, pomp and ostentation, their former enormous share of the produce of the industrious laborer enabled them to waste and consume. This must effectually interfere with the trade of all those who make or deal in such articles, which is so extensive as almost to include all foreign commerce. The hitherto poor and oppressed consume only homespun articles, the produce of their soil and climate, which by the diffusion of knowledge (the certain consequences of every approach to equality) must be much more varied and rendered more commodious and useful to the millions; as is fully evinced by the great change that has taken place in the foreign commerce of France since the equality produced by their revolution.

Every article imagined or contrived for the purpose of pomp, show, parade or ostentation, to make the distinction of great inequality between the grades or classes, must fall in value in proportion to its deficiency in real utility, amongst which will be all the luxury and extensive ornaments of book making, most of the poetry, romances, works of imagination, etc., contrived to kill time for those whose artificial advantages afford them no other occupation, as has already taken place in France, where most of the expensive editions of folios with an ocean of margin enclosing a score of letter press can be bought now for one fourth what they sold for six or eight years ago. In revenge there will be a great demand for the immense great editions of cheap and useful books to instruct and amuse the industrious laborers, who, by the great diffusion of useful knowledge, will have substituted moral pleasures in place of the excess and abuse of the physical appetites, which their brutal ignorance under oppression plunged them into.

All the extravagant ostentation in dress, furniture, equipages, etc., which only serve to mark the superiority of rank and riches, must diminish in value, by the progress of equality obliterating that humiliating distinction which injures those it elevates above character, as well as those it depresses below. As the equality of nature will equally prevent the unhealthy and uncomfortable custom of crowding twenty or thirty individuals into a small house, or permitting an individual the ostentatious superiority of occupying some hundred times the same space. The palaces, castles, and expensive houses both in town and country will be reduced to the value of the materials with which they were constructed, for want of individuals rich enough to hire and keep them in repair, as was the case during the French revolution, when associations were formed to purchase and demolish the chateaux of the rich to make a profit by the sale of the materials. It is the interest of all to place themselves as far out of the risk of loss by such changes as surrounding circumstances will permit.

DIFFICULTIES OF ACQUIRING CORRECT IDEAS.

April 14, 1835.

As all our ideas which constitute useful knowledge come to us through the medium of our five senses, the more accurately we are taught the exercise of our senses, the more correct and true will be the ideas we receive through them; which is only to be learned by practice, as is sufficiently evinced by the manner in which we acquire perfection in the useful arts and mechanism, as well as in all other arts, trades, professions and occupations; by the astonishing accuracy blind people attain in feeling, hearing, etc.; deaf people in seeing and the other senses, by the necessity they are under of exercising accurately the senses they possess, to make up for the one they are deprived of. It would, therefore, appear that the education and discipline of the senses is as necessary to the acquiring of just and correct ideas, as a good road is for the facilitating of the transportation of heavy materials. Why it has not been resorted to in the education of children, is perhaps owing to its ease and simplicity, giving knowledge too cheap, and thereby encroaching on the authority and *ipse dixit* of the schoolmaster. Teaching people to make a proper use of their senses diminishes their confidence and faith in the dogmas, doctrines and theories of others, and renders them less liable to become the dupes of either church or state: a sufficient reason, why it is not encouraged by the learned professions and others who live on the ignorance of the millions. All the difference between knowledge and ignorance, between a wise man and a fool, is the accuracy with which he observes the properties of men and matter, and the adaptation of both to further his interest.

What an immense proportion of mankind with good eyes cannot acquire a just idea of the length, breadth, thickness, or height of the object they look at; or with well proportioned hands cannot acquire a correct idea of the hardness, smoothness, fineness, weight or volume of any thing they handle; or with well organized ears, mouth or nose, cannot distinguish the diference of sounds, tastes or smells; but remain through life deprived not only of the utility of such correct ideas, but likewise of the pleasure and enjoyment of such refined sensations as is propagated by the harmony of sounds in music, etc. An idea is a figure in the mind. No one can figure any substance, matter or motion, the knowledge of which has not come through the senses; he cannot even imagine any thing, the idea of which has not come first through the senses.— Metaphysicians aggregate sounds in the form of words, and flatter themselves that they create ideas; but words are insignificant, unless they have reference to some phenomena, transmitted to us by some one or more of our five senses. We have the faculty of mixing, joining, separating or arranging in a thousand different ways, by memory or induction, ideas received by the senses, which some mistake for innate ideas, proceeding from what they call the inward man; but had they the patience or impartial rationality to analyze these dreams or fancies of the imagination, they would find that not the smallest atom of these imaginary figures existed, but what originated in something seen, heard, felt, tasted or smelled. It therefore appears that the education or discipline of the senses must very much facilitate the acquiring of every kind of useful knowledge, as well as all the practical occupations necessary for the comfort and happiness of our species; and that placing our hopes, opinions or wishes on the baseless fabric of fancy or imagination is like building our house on the unstable foundation of a quick sand, liable at every moment to overwhelm all our hopes and expectations and bury them in its ruins. That civilization, as far as it has yet gone, has neglected the cultivation of our senses may arise from its not favoring the mysteries of either church or state, for whose exclusive benefit the whole social order has yet been organized. All mankind have much the same senses and the natural right of using them for their own benefit and advantage: and attempts of improving them would reduce the old and the young, the rich and the poor, the king and the beggar, nearer to a par of equality; to prevent which the utmost ingenuity of church and state in all nations, ages and climates has been exercised. While the sources of knowledge were disguised and enveloped in the mysterious, scholastic nomenclature, as far beyond nature as out of the reach of our senses, the most useful part of mankind were kept at a distance by the halo and prestiges with which the conjurors of both church and state surrounded themselves; but had the millions been taught a correct use of the senses, as the only channel through which real and useful knowledge could come, it would have given them confidence in themselves, and preserved them from the deceptions and delusions practiced by both religious and political quacks, accelerating the visible and tangible instruction of the nature and properties both of men and things, which is now progressing, and will most probably continue in geometrical ratio. Towards such a natural and rational system of education, the Pestalozzian method was approaching and is fast gaining on the old metaphysical system of teaching sounds by memory without interesting the judgment.

If all correct ideas come through our senses, the only way of obtaining them is by an attentive examination of all things, the properties, nature and value of which are imprinted on our minds directly from the objects; and it must follow of course, that when the things we wish to be acquainted with, are at a distance, out of the reach of our senses, a correct representation or delineation of them is the next best way of obtaining a knowledge of them; and description by the use of words should be the last, as being the most difficult and uncertain mode of arriving at a correct idea of any thing, from the imperfection of language, as being only significant, as far as it has a reference to phenomena which comes to our senses. The acquiring of knowledge from the things or correct representations of them is the easiest, most certain and durable mode of obtaining exact ideas and ought to be preferred in the instruction of children.

It is perhaps owing to the small quantum of utility, that has yet been represented in either painting or sculpture, with the high value put on them, that has prevented their being made use of to instruct children. As yet the principal objects represented are the naked gods and goddesses of the ancients, the follies, vices and vanity of the rulers and rich, the slaughter, cruelties and crimes of the conquerors; and all of them delineate nothing but the different classes, attitudes and actions of men, which the flattery, the little were forced to pay the great, deprived of most of the truth, and even, when true, are useless; as the representation of human figures, which we see daily by thousands, can communicate nothing either new or useful, nor add one iota to our stock of information. One of the most useful applications of designing I ever saw, was 4000 sketches of the manners, trades, manufactories, commerce, politics, religion, etc., of the Chinese, representing things that could not be seen without traveling 5 or 6000 miles, and even then could not be accurately examined, evinced the great utility of drawing; but to delineate the figure of our bodies, which we may examine in nature every minute, is a waste of time, talent and property, for no other purpose than increasing the vanity of the man or woman, who sit for their portrait. The utility of designing, like many things else, has been sacrificed to the vanity, luxury, extravagance and pampered imaginations of the rich, influential, privileged orders, etc.; even our paper hangings, printed calicoes, etc., which might adorn our rooms and persons with the representations of realities both of nature and art, and increase our knowledge of things useful, are with additional toil and labor, covered with imaginary fancy figures that do not communicate a single idea that can be of the smallest use to any class of society, serving only to feed the vicious appetite of fashion with an immense variety of fantastical figures, invented to please the inordinate taste of a depraved and injurious luxury.

DECEPTIONS OF HISTORY.

April, 18, 1835.

Have the people of any country been yet governed in a way agreeable to, in union with, or tending to promote their own interest? Has not the interest of the many been sacrificed to the interest of the few in all countries? Has civilization, as far as it has yet gone, contributed to the increase or diminution of that great inequality of property, knowledge and power, the fruitful cause and origin of most of the poverty, ignorance, and consequently misery, wretchedness, crime, etc., which afflict and brutalize mankind? These are questions which imperiously demand impartial investigation. If no nation has yet been governed according to the interest of the great majority, the world is as yet totally ignorant of the practical effects of such a government and consequently liable to become the dupe of the sophistical deceptions of church and state, whose interest prompts them to increase their power and consequence by mysteriously complicating all their operations and cautiously preventing the diffusion of knowledge which would simplify and facilitate the administration of all laws and regulations for the public security, in lessening the temptation to immorality and crime.

If the interest of the many has been sacrificed to the interest or rather to the caprice and vices of the few, rendering standing armies, fleets, etc., necessary to coerce the will of the millions, and make them subservient to arbitrary commands, which impair, and in many instances annihilates their comfort and happiness, mankind remain ignorant of the great advantages of free will over coercion and punishment, and if civilization, as far as it has yet gone, has rather increased than diminished those evils which afflict humanity, it is high time to change its principles and mode of action by making it progress towards equality, and dividing the comforts and happiness more equally amongst the millions in place of loading the few with superfluities (by exclusive privileges) with the produce of the labor of the many.

It is only from the deceptive pages of history that we can collect our knowledge of the past. During the barbarous ages of antiquity, history is filled with the actions, vices and cruelties of the tyrants, chiefs and conquerors, to whose ambitious views every thing within their reach was subservient, and the millions were never noticed but when enrolled, disciplined and taught the trade of a soldier in the best and most expeditious mode of cutting one another's throats. When successful, they only riveted their own chains, and when conquered, they changed masters, and became the slaves of a foreign tyrant, so that, conquerors or conquered, their comfort and happiness were sacrificed to the ambition of the few, who divided all the plunder and pillage amongst themselves, leaving the millions in their forlorn state of poverty and ignorance, which increased with the small portion of civilization which then existed, as the comfort and happiness of the Roman people (whose history seems best authenticated,) diminished, as the wealth and the power of the patricians increased, which has been less or more the case with all nations, who have run round the vicious circle of action, so common previous to the invention of printing. By which it would appear that the ancients were governed contrary to the interest of the millions, whose comfort, security and happiness were sacrificed to the ambition, luxury, pomp, and extravagance of the rulers and privileged orders.

What change has modern civilization wrought in the condition of the industrious producers? Do they enjoy more or work less? Has not the great increase in the number of unproductive consumers, in the same proportion augmented the toil and labor of those who maintain them? Have modern legislators, monarchs or despots ameliorated the lot of the great family of industrious producers, or rendered their privations less, or their gratifications more? On the contrary, have they not improved, by various inventions and contrivances, on the coercion of the oppressive tyranny of the ancients? Have not the misery and wretchedness of the poor kept pace with the luxury and extravagance of the rich, and the toil, privations and trouble of the producers been in exact ratio of the wasteful extravagance of the nonproductive consuming classes, as is proven by the working classes in Britain?

After the Romans had subjected the different nations which composed their empire, they became corrupt, luxurious and indolent, lost the hardy habits of their ancestors, and in their turn, were overrun by the barbarous activity of the Goths, Vandals, Huns, etc., who reduced to vassalage the inhabitants and established the feudal system, which they brought with them from their forests. The taxes on their vassals were raised by personal services, before the currency of money facilitated the accumulation of wealth in the possession of the few. The feudal baron lived with his vassals, on the mutual ties of protection, gratitude and affection. The feudal lord who could neither read nor write, was on a par of individual improvement with his ignorant vassals; their pleasures and pastimes were the same in hunting and field sports; his vassals were his companions and enjoyed the pleasure of the chase equally with his feudal chief. In the gratification of the physical appetites, civilization had not drawn the broad line of distinction, their food and clothing were nearer on a par than when the refinement of society had placed an immense distance between them, by elevating the master to waste, luxury, and extravagance, whilst it depressed the vassal with the necessity of the additional toil and labor to support the additional consumption. So far the physical condition of the industrious producers was rendered more painfully laborious; whilst the superiority in moral acquirements by schools and colleges was still more in favor of the chiefs and degrading to the vassals, who were left in their original ignorance, augmented by their not having time from their constant labor to cultivate their minds by the use of their senses, as was afforded them while attending their feudal chiefs.

By the progress of modern conquest and civilization, the Moscovites changed the feudal vassals into serfs, bought and sold with the soil, as the foundation of the Russian empire.— The improvement in civilization, as far as it has yet gone, turned a great many of the feudal vassals in Britain into the humiliating slavery of pauperism; the effects of the adoption of the representations of property, in place of real property, by paper money, extending the length and power of the lever of oppression *ad infinitum.*

Until the last century, the industrious producers every where were considered as beasts of burden, who had no other rights than laboring for the benefit of their superiors; (the small exception of the few fortunate inhabitants of the little democratic cantons of Switzerland is scarce worth the notice) their interest, ease, comfort and happiness did not enter into the consideration of priests or politicians, in the formation of plans, pleasures or pastimes of church and state, entirely occupied with intrigues, stratagems and deceptions, how to purloin the greatest quantum of the produce of the industrious laborers, to perpetuate their usurped superiority.

The first successful claim to the natural and inalienable rights of men was made by the United States of America, and secured to them by an elective government of universal suffrage. The first trial of liberty and equality produced such unprecedented prosperity, power, property, population, etc., as to awaken the dormant energies of the millions in the old world, and resuscitate the French revolution, whose principles and advantageous properties to the millions have been beat over the civilized world by the united aristocracy of Europe, in the vain attempt of annihilating moral improvement by the coalition of physical force, consisting of the class of society who were to reap all the benefits of the reform.— Ignorant as the millions have been, this was assuming too much on their passive obedience to the prejudices, customs and habits of barbarous times, which is completely evinced by the second revolution, which bids fair to extend over the greatest part of the old world.

If all nations were governed according to the interest of the millions, all the difficulties which render diplomacy, deception, disguise, intrigue and hypocricy necessary to subjugate the will of the many to the capricious authority of the few, would disappear, as being not only useless but prejudicial. Elective governments by universal suffrage come nearest to that just, honest and happy state of things, but must be administered by an enlightened people, well informed of their real interest, and strong in the mutual confidence in one another to unite in the conviction that the interest of one is the interest of all. We are the only people permitted by the theories of church and state to practice such a system; but we are yet far from that general instruction necessary for the accomplishing of it, as is unfortunately proven by the unsuccessful attempts made by the rational part of the millions, who, though 100 to one, cannot obtain a majority in the legislatures by the deficiency of useful knowledge and the want of that necessary union, which their opponents have to perfection.

HOW TO RESTORE EQUALITY. ADVANTAGES OF SMALL POLITICAL ASSOCIATIONS.

April 23, 1835.

Having in some of my former essays endeavored to prove that an equal division of property, knowledge and power, is essential to the existence, freedom, comfort and happiness of the millions; that equality is the only solid and sure foundation of freedom, and inequality the origin, source and support of tyranny and despotism, with all their inseparable attendants of poverty, ignorance, misery, wretchedness, vice and crime. In the present state of artificial civilization, where property, knowledge and power has been by force or fraud monopolized by the few at the expense of the many, it may be of some practical use to inquire how the natural equilibrium can be restored with the greatest ease, expedition and peace, without suffering the oppression of church and state to exhaust the patience and forbearance of the millions, and render a physical explosion necessary to their relief from misery. In elective systems of universal suffrage, power is as equally divided as the present nature of man will permit. Where power is monopolized in possession of the few, knowledge and property become their inheritance. Useful knowledge originates in and is derived from the senses, of which the whole human species are nearly equally capable of attaining; the artificial accumulation of it by any individual cannot be left as an inheritance to his successors. The useful knowledge acquired by any individual depends greatly on the surrounding circumstances, which, when the diffusion of it is not obstructed by the inequality of power, or engrossed by the monopolizing spirit of church and state, is nearly equally attainable by all; the tyranny and oppression of church and state has as yet been the greatest bar to the general diffusion of useful knowledge. Elective governments by universal suffrage commenced with our revolution, and have not yet been long enough in existence to equalize the property and knowledge accumulated in the possession of the few by the approach of arbitrary power under the colonial system. The almost complete equalization of power and rapid approaches towards the equalization of useful knowledge, would in time equalize property; but could not the millions of industrious producers who by their labor originate property, accelerate the happy completion of their freedom and independence, by the adoption of greater economy and saving in the expenses of gratifying the physical appetites, is the query? In all countries where the ignorance of the producers has heaped to accumulation, the monopoly of property, knowledge and power on the few, the trades' unions or any other associations cannot contend with the few, but by physical force and violence. Once in possession of the product of their labor for centuries, which has been descending from father to son, they are independent for a time of the working producers, whereas the poverty of the working classes makes them dependent for food on their rich employers, and it is either work or starve. Of all the nations, the working classes in France are more on a par with the few rich, by the great division of property, the consequence of their laws and regulations during their first revolution; and are abler to contend with the few opulent than in England or any other European nation. In our union the division of power will facilitate the division of knowledge, and will in time divide property, but for the present, the accumulation of property in possession of the few by bank corporations and other monopolies, will disable the poor many to contend with the rich few, and necessitate the millions by economy and saving to acquire some degree of pecuniary independence.

While the working classes spend all on their backs and their bellies, which the convenience of their rich employers pay them, in imitating the fashions, habits and customs of the opulent, they must be dependent on their employers for bread; but in place of combining in trades' unions and other associations to carry on the unequal contention for a rise in their wages, they would combine in masses of all trades and professions to supply one another with all they required, at fixed prices: the farmers, millers and graziers might supply food; the butchers might furnish hides to the tanners and curriers, and they provide leather fcr the shoe-makers; so with the spinners, weavers, tailors, and all other trades, schools and schoolmasters; each paying or receiving for what he received or delivered by the individuals who bought, to those who sold, at fixed prices; they would have a great number of the same trade in the union, which would afford both choice and competition, and they might dispense with both priests and lawyers, like the quakers, settle all disputes by arbitration; the only restriction or fixed principle in the contract would be the agreement to deal with one another, every thing else would be left to the will and pleasure of each individual.— They might all agree to establish a general custom, calculated for economy, health and utility, saving the expense, trouble, ambition, rivalship and anxiety of following the caprices, changeable whims, and not unfrequently, unhealthiness of the tyrant fashion; they might regulate their tables, furniture and domestic concerns, so as to avoid all competition in useless luxury, the origin of much envy and hatred. This would not be like Owen's community system, where the idle might be maintained by the industrious; every one would enjoy the fruits of his labor and be paid according to the utility of his work, with this advantage of being insured a ready market for at least a part of the produce of his industry; in the society such unions might be made a second edition of the New England townships, by their agreeing to make all improvements of roads, bridges, schools, etc., for their own use, and raising a property tax to defray the expenditure.— This would teach the industrious producers the immense advantages of small associations, where every public operation is performed within the reach and under the cognizance of those who produced all by their labor, and who are only really interestested in the economical disbursement and faithful execution of all public works—different and opposite to largeextensive political associations, where the consuming classes are rulers of church and state, have the disposal and distribution of the wealth produced by the labor of others, and are strongly tempted to appropriate as much to their own use as the extent of dominion, the distance from any check, or ignorance of the producing classes will permit. The aristocratic cant or bug-bear is, that these small associations would quarrel and fight; but all the experience of civilization contradicts it. The small states of Europe have scarce ever been at war; it is the extensive empires of Russia, Austria, Britain, France, etc., that have originated all the wars of ambition for many centuries. The federative cantons of Switzerland have not quarrelled during the 500 years they have been united.— The states of America have not had a dispute since the formation of their federal government. So that their nature and interest secure them from internal strife, and federalism in proportion to their numbers, protects them against external aggression. These bold and daring assertions, like most of the sophistry of the aristocracy, is completely contradicted by the experience of civilization, and they are forced to recur to ancient barbarity and the savage life for examples, always maintaining the doctrines of original sin, and men "are prone to evil as the sparks fly upwards," to which they make themselves exceptions. All history is solely occupied with the interest of conquerors, and the dignity and magnificence of the aggregation of men into extensive empires; the state or lot of the millions is never mentioned except as soldiers to be slaughtered; every page of history may be quoted in favor of the interest of the few and against the interest of the many; from which it would appear that all that has been yet done by church and state either in theory or practice, has been in favor of the few and against the many; in favor of the cunning rich and against the ignorant poor, the only useful lesson to be learned from history.

What a herculean task the working classes of our union have undertaken by this radical reform; besides being new, never was so great a change attempted in any part of the world. It has working hard against it all who enjoy, in the present order of things, more power, property, ease, luxury, comfort and good things than they can expect to get by such a reform, that is, the greatest part of lawyers, priests, politicians, including all place hunters and officers in the pay either of state of federal governments, governors, secretaries and representatives, those now in power or expect to be chose into power, for all having an equal right the expectants are twenty to one of those in possession, the judges, justices of peace, municipal officers, and the greatest part of the consuming classes who live without labor and benefit by bank corporations, etc., united by interest into a moneyed aristocracy; the producers have the greatest part of them fighting against them with the pecuniary weapons their labor has put into their hands. Nothing can be done by the working classes until they obtain by combination and strict union at the ballot boxes, a majority in the legislatures; and even then they only get the theory of reform; the practice will be opposed by all the old sub-executive officers who are attached to the feudal division of the surface into counties, etc., such as sheriffs, constables, mayors, aldermen, common councilmen, surveyors, inspectors, managers of roads, swarms of collectors, and other officers appointed to increase the patronage of executives, when patronage was foolishly thought necessary to the support of power. All must be changed and brought into unison with the simplicity of democracy, before any radical reform can succeed. The division of France into departments, arondisements, cantons and communes, was perhaps the most permanent of all the reforms of the French revolution, and the greatest obstruction to a return to absolute monarchy and feudality. I have hinted in a former essay that perhaps the dividing all the states into townships of six miles square, with an enlarged authority suitable to the knowledge of the day, might be the best foundation for, and secure the faithful execution of those great radical and necessary reforms.

UNIVERSAL SUFFRAGE.

April 30, 1835.

Fortuitous circumstances formed the governments on this side of the Atlantic, nearer the natural equality of property, knowledge and power, than a long and corrupt civilization had permitted the old world to enjoy; and are the only places on earth that possess free and equal representation by universal suffrage. The trial of this new political association has been of so short duration, that few of its immense advantages to humanity have yet been experienced; though the great success of the short practice of the United States of North America, and their unprecedented prosperity have astonished the world, yet the benefit the millions have yet enjoyed has been only in proportion to their knowledge of their own interest, and their general ignorance of their rights, and power to assert them at the ballot boxes, has permitted the few whom chance threw uppermost, to rule them in imitation of the aristocratic usurpations of the old world; though the millions were too well informed to suffer themselves to be enslaved by hereditary aristocracy, hereditary power and a standing army that could control the states' militia, yet by financial, mercantile and political speculations, and monopolies of funding, land and banking, there was nearly four hundred millions of dollars distributed amongst the favorite few, which, with the profits of a long and lucrative neutral trade, laid the foundation of a moneyed aristocracy, which totally deranges the equality of property, producing a great inequality of knowledge, and infringing on the equality of power; so that a rapid increase of luxury, extravagance, vice and crime, the inseparable attendants on the great inequality of these three essentials of freedom, by making the rich richer and the poor poorer; diminishing in the same proportion, the relative peace and happiness of the millions.

In the southern part of this hemisphere, lately emancipated from three hundred years of foreign bondage, the extreme ignorance of all classes of their real interests, from the slavish habits of so long a subjection to foreign tyranny, where the Catholic religion joined their masters in enslaving the moral along with the physical, has tolerated and encouraged an implement of despotism, a large standing army, which, with the wealth and influence of the church, has kept up a constant succession of civil wars, broils, mobs and rebellions, a perpetual usurpation of military tyranny, and though as often put down by the growing public opinion, yet from the general ignorance, has been renewed by the armies, which put down and punished the last usurper. They have copied the constitutions and many of the institutions of their northern neighbors, and have the free election by universal suffrage; all the theories of freedom, yet the practice limited by ignorance, has not yet emancipated the many from the oppression of the few, and although they are freed from hereditary despotism and power, and only burdened with the church and standing army, yet those two imps of despotism by constituting themselves privileged orders, have been able as yet to keep the many under subjection to their will and interest. That the gradation of freedom should so exactly correspond with the gradation of knowledge on this side of the Atlantic, where there are fewer artificial obstructions to knowledge, as well as every thing else, finding its level, is worthy of being remarked. That the millions of our Union have had sufficient useful knowledge not to be tyrannized over by the brutal force of armies, but not sufficient wisdom to prevent becoming the dupes of superior cunning, artifice, intrigue and deception.— That the natives of the southern end of this hemisphere are so lamentably ignorant, with the same theories of freedom as to be hired one portion to enslave the other, and to suffer the humiliating despotism of their chiefs; for the vicious pleasure of tyrannizing over others, the chief bribe and reward of man-slayers, under the uniform of soldiers, may sanction the idea that knowledge is the greatest good, and ignorance the greatest evil that ever was on earth.

The few, who rule either as despots, limited monarchs, or are chosen as yet by ignorance in elective systems, are much nearer a par of knowledge than the many they domineer over. It is amongst the millions where the quantum of freedom and happiness is commensurate with the useful knowledge diffused through the smallest ramifications of industrious laborers, and our working classes will lay the axe to the root of all evil, by insisting on a free, equal and gratis, food, clothing and instruction to all the children of our Union; that they may all start fair like the Jews after the jubilee year, one of their best, most just and humane laws, but almost the only one that has not been copied by the Christians, whose commandments are almost all to protect priests and property. The nearest thing in our time to the agrarian law of the Jews, is the British distribution of uncultivated lands, by granting 200 acres to each settler; but we have been too great Christians to follow that example, and have preferred selling them by wholesale to the moneyed aristocracy, that they might exact an exorbitant price from the poor laborer, who had the justest claim to them.